DATE DUE

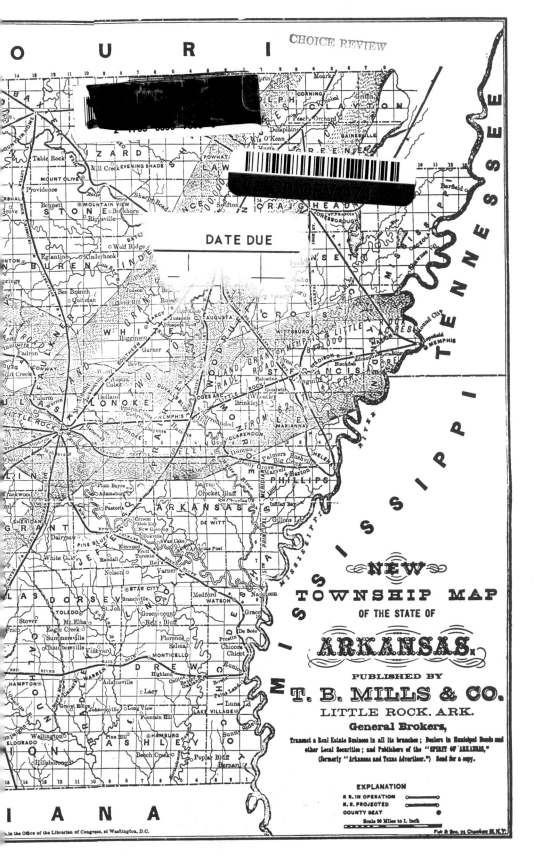

# NEW
## TOWNSHIP MAP
### OF THE STATE OF

# ARKANSAS.

### PUBLISHED BY

# T. B. MILLS & CO.

## LITTLE ROCK. ARK.

### General Brokers,

Transact a Real Estate Business in all its branches ; Dealers in Municipal Bonds and other Local Securities ; and Publishers of the "SPIRIT OF ARKANSAS." (formerly "Arkansas and Texas Advertiser.") Send for a copy.

### EXPLANATION

R R. IN OPERATION
R. R. PROJECTED
COUNTY SEAT
Scale 20 Miles to 1 Inch.

In the Office of the Librarian of Congress, at Washington, D.C.

Fisk & Son, 24 Chambers St. N.Y.

# ARKANSAS AND RECONSTRUCTION

Kennikat Press

**National University Publications**

Series in American Studies

*General Editor*

James P. Shenton

*Professor of History, Columbia University*

GEORGE H. THOMPSON

# ARKANSAS
# and
# RECONSTRUCTION

## *The Influence of Geography, Economics, and Personality*

National University Publications
KENNIKAT PRESS    //    1976
Port Washington, N. Y.    //    London

Manufactured in the United States of America

Published by
**Kennikat Press Corp.**
Port Washington, N.Y./London

**Library of Congress Cataloging in Publication Data**

Thompson, George H
   Arkansas and reconstruction.

   (Series in American studies) (National university publications)
   Bibliography: p.
   Includes index.
   1. Reconstruction–Arkansas. 2. Arkansas–Politics and government. 3. Arkansas–Economic conditions.
I. Title.
F411.T47        976.7'05       76-18192
ISBN 0-8046-9130-4

*FOR*
*SHARON*
*AND*
*MY PARENTS*

# CONTENTS

## PART THREE:
## CREDIT AND THE DEVELOPMENT OF RESOURCES

## PART FOUR: CONCLUSION

# FIGURES AND ILLUSTRATIONS

# TABLES

# ACKNOWLEDGMENTS

At the end of that journey on which this author has been carried by this study, a new appreciation of teachers, librarians, institutions, friends, and family has developed which needs to be expressed.

Most helpful in extending opportunity and encouragement when they were greatly needed was Professor Eric L. McKitrick, of Columbia. To him I am deeply grateful. Three professors at Hendrix College have also made their contributions. The late Dean Thomas S. Staples transmitted an interest in Reconstruction and provided the basis for understanding the Arkansas experience in his *Reconstruction in Arkansas*. Dean William C. Buthman personified the ideal scholar-teacher for me and, as a friend, has helped in innumerable ways during the course of the writing. Richard E. Yates accepted additional burdens within our department to provide the opportunity for research and writing.

Librarians were very helpful at every institution. The following are due my special gratitude: at Hendrix, Florence Carmichael Vardaman, Frances Nix, and the entire library staff; at the University of Arkansas, Marvin A. Miller and, especially, Grace Upchurch, Helen Jo Adkisson, and Richard Reid as well as Joe Hill, Sam Sizer, Gladys Felton, and Georgia Clark; at the University of Arkansas Law School Library in Little Rock, Ruth H. Brunson; at State College of Arkansas, Lee B. Spencer; and at Duke University, Virginia R. Gray.

Institutions also made their contribution. To President Marshall T. Steel and other members of the Hendrix College administration I am grateful for time and understanding while the work was proceeding. Gratitude must also be expressed to the University of Arkansas, Duke University, Columbia University, University of West Virginia, Chicago Historical Society, Rutherford B. Hayes Library, and to the Library of Congress. Of particular importance were the assistance and encouragement received from the Arkansas History Commission, its secretary,

John L. Ferguson, and his staff, Lois Jones, Clare Speer, and Frances Bowles.

Perhaps Walter A. Moffatt was the friend who made the most direct contribution. His innumerable suggestions improved the quality of the writing as he went through the manuscript with me. The thankless task of proofreading was shared by William C. Buthman, Robert W. Meriwether, and my wife, Sharon. Other friends who have helped in numerous ways include James H. Atkinson, Ted R. Worley, Walter L. Brown, Walter L. Lemke, and Margaret Smith Ross. I am especially indebted to Dr. Maude Carmichael for her fine dissertation, "The Plantation System in Arkansas, 1850-1876."

Nothing can help more than to have a congenial and efficient typist for that laborious task. Vicky Allen, who performed that role beautifully, has my sincere gratitude. Her husband, Harold V. Allen, also deserves thanks for his patience and cooperation. To Robert L. Campbell goes a special debt of gratitude for suggestions made during the revision of the manuscript. His assistance has made the reader's task more pleasant than it might have been.

# ARKANSAS AND RECONSTRUCTION

# INTRODUCTION

This study originally began as an attempt to write profiles of various individuals who were important as political leaders in Arkansas during the Reconstruction period. By utilizing their correspondence as the most important source material and by following a biographical approach, something of the historical significance of these individuals was expected to emerge. As the study progressed, however, more social involvement and less biographical profile appeared to be appropriate. The original intent of a biographical approach to political leadership is still present in the study, and the importance of that point of view should be kept in mind throughout.

Although a series of profiles has not resulted, the biographical materials accumulated during the research have made possible a biographical approach to leadership which has been fruitful in several ways. One example is the answer which this approach has given to the question of how much detail is appropriate for this kind of subject. Many readers may feel that too much detail has been included, but there is value in accompanying a few individuals rather closely during a period of time. Such intimate companionship can provide a corrective for generalizations which may have been founded on more distant acquaintance for a shorter duration. The tendency to simplify details under such inclusive labels as "Whigs," "Unionists," and "Confederates" may justify a tendency to complicate details through a consideration of a few specific Whigs, Unionists, and Confederates.

Another example of ways in which the biographical approach has proved fruitful was a rediscovery of the personal nature of leadership in the South. Party affiliation was far less important than personality of leadership. A man was influential in his locale because others knew him and respected his judgment, not primarily because of party loyalty. When to this personal nature of leadership is added the difficult problem of patriotism in a border state, one begins to understand why the Civil War and Reconstruction appeared as a local civil war and reconstruction within Arkansas.

Perhaps the most revealing result of the biographical approach has been the discovery of how much a given man's position could change throughout this period. Somehow Whigs, Unionists, Confederates, Refugees, Democrats, and Redeemers are expected to be different individuals; that is, one would not expect to find the same man in most of these roles; and yet, two of the main characters of this study confound that expectation.

David Walker and Augustus H. Garland serve well to illustrate the importance of personality of leadership and also the paradoxical nature of patriotism in a border state during the Civil War and Reconstruction period. Walker settled in Fayetteville, Arkansas, in 1830, and served as a delegate to the Constitutional Convention of 1836. Throughout the following years he became an influential Whig leader in the northwestern area and served as an associate justice of the Arkansas Supreme Court from 1849 to 1855. He was elected as a Unionist delegate to the Secession Convention in 1861, and then was elected president of that convention by the Unionist majority. During the Civil War, Walker joined the Confederacy and served as a military judge in the Confederate Army. When hostilities ended in Arkansas, he fled to Texas and remained there for some time as a refugee. After his return to Arkansas, David Walker was elected Chief Justice of the Arkansas Supreme Court in 1866, only to be removed from that office by Congressional Reconstruction. Refusing to take the voter's oath, he consistently opposed what he considered to be a *de facto* government. Then, in 1872, he joined a coalition of Democrats, reform Republicans, and conservatives in their attempt to elect Joseph Brooks governor. After a disputed election in which Walker believed Brooks had been elected, he remained loyal to Brooks' cause until the Brooks-Baxter War in 1874. Under the new state constitution of 1874, Walker used his political influence to bring the conservative voters of the northwest into the Democratic party and was elected an associate justice of the Arkansas Supreme Court on a ticket headed by Augustus H. Garland, candidate for governor.

Garland, a younger man than Walker, came to southwestern Arkansas as an infant in 1833. He inherited an excellent law practice in Little Rock when his law partner suffered an untimely death in 1857. This practice resulted in an opportunity for Garland to try a case before the United States Supreme Court prior to the Civil War, a fact of importance to him later. In 1861, he was elected as a Unionist delegate to the Secession Convention and was later chosen as one of the five delegates sent from Arkansas to the Provisional Congress in Montgomery. He served as a Representative in the Confederate Congress in Arkansas and was elected Senator in 1864. During the final days of hostilities in Arkansas, he served as an emissary of the Confederate governor to the Union general seeking terms of surrender. Garland received a Presidential pardon seventeen days after his application for amnesty, and this pardon extended an opportunity to him which led to *Ex Parte Garland* in January, 1867. The next month he was elected United States Senator only to be refused his seat in the Senate by Congressional Reconstruction. He became one of the leading Democratic spokesmen in the state who advocated taking the voter's oath and opposing the Republicans at the ballot box in 1868. Following the defeat in that election, he faded into a position of passive resistance to Republican rule until the Brooks-Baxter War in 1874. At that time he became the chief strategist for Baxter and used the struggle between Brooks and Baxter to secure a constitutional convention that would destroy the system on which the Republican power was based. The overwhelming vote which Garland then received for governor came as no surprise. He served as United States Senator from 1877 until 1885, at which time he was appointed Attorney General of the United States by President Cleveland.

In these various ways the biographical approach to leadership has proved helpful. But also of great value has been an attempt to view Reconstruction as part of a continuing development of the state rather than as a separate time period. To achieve this perspective, a time span extending from territorial days through the 1880's has been necessary. When Reconstruction is considered in such a context, the importance of certain continuing influences can be more properly appreciated. Among these influences are the personality of leadership, the importance of geography, and the significance of two failures to successfully use state credit as a means of financing the development of natural resources.

Perhaps enough has been said about leadership, but when leadership is biographically considered in an adequate time perspective, insights are possible which can be achieved in no other way. The continuing influence of geography also can be appreciated best when it is considered in this larger time span. Arkansas has been a border state geographically as well as politically, and the importance of geographical variations within the state, though always significant, was magnified during Reconstruction because of the effect these variations had on the incidence of the social reforms of the Reconstruction period. One of the major suggestions of this study is that the continuing influence of geography can best be understood when the state is thought of as having three sections—northwest, delta, and southwest—rather than the highland-lowland division usually found in Arkansas history.

A second major suggestion would consider Reconstruction, in part, as a second failure in the use of state credit to finance the development of natural resources. Following the initial failure of banks during the state's infancy, this second failure, associated largely with railroad construction, led to repudiation and seriously retarded the state's development.

The presentation has been divided into three parts. The first introduces the concept of the three societies—northwest, delta, and southwest—a concept which will be utilized throughout the entire work. Also contained in the first part is a consideration of the paradoxical nature of patriotism in this border state. Particular attention is paid to the dilemma felt by men of Unionist sentiment during those days in the spring of 1861 when they had to decide to which government their true allegiance was to be given. Similarly, the patriotic adjustments of men who had previously participated in the Confederate cause are considered at that time following the Civil War when they had to apply to the President of the United States for amnesty. In each of these situations something of the character of these men and the nature of their patriotism is revealed, which will provide an insight into their roles as leaders during Reconstruction.

The second part is devoted to a consideration of certain political aspects of Reconstruction. Seen from the point of view of leaders such as David Walker and Augustus H. Garland, the politics of the period were those of a struggle between *de facto* v. *de jure* forces. As the roles of these two men and others are contemplated, the focus on leadership in Arkansas Reconstruction will become clearer, and the significance of personality in leadership, of geographical influence on politics, and of patriotic allegiance will begin to converge.

A third part has been necessary to present an important underlying influence on the development of the state which it is necessary to comprehend in order to understand leadership during Reconstruction in Arkansas. During the early days of Arkansas, attempts were made to organize banks, backed by the faith and credit of the state, as a means of establishing a credit system and also of encouraging the expansion of the plantation system. These banks failed, and the state's credit was destroyed as a consequence. This ante-bellum financial legacy faced Governor Powell Clayton in 1868 with the necessity of funding a state debt over $3,000,000 before the credit of the state could be reestablished. The passion for railroad construction demanded that such refunding be done, however, and under the Republican administrations the state credit was once more pledged to encourage the development of natural resources, this time through railroad construction. When for a second time in the state's history there occurred a credit failure, the animosity felt toward a *de facto* regime was joined with economic grievances deriving from the failure in credit to encourage a sentiment for repudiation of the debts incurred.

As an illustration of railroad construction in Arkansas, the experiences of Asa P. Robinson, chief engineer for the Little Rock and Fort Smith Railroad, are considered. The financial disaster resulting from a contract with Boston capitalists, which required the railroad to pay the construction company 5.142 times the estimated cost of constructon, is used to indicate something of the disillusionment suffered by those who saw in railroad construction such great hopes for the future. The politics of that day encouraged many people to blame their own disillusionment on the unscrupulousness of the Republican regime. An historical understanding of this period must not be so simple.

# PART ONE

# THE LAND AND ITS PEOPLE

# CHAPTER ONE

# THE THREE SOCIETIES

Nature has done what she could in Arkansas to confirm the ideas held by Frederick Jackson Turner concerning the importance of environmental influences in society. The contrasting geographical divisions, the restrictive river system, and the various soil conditions influenced the social and political life of the state in many ways which historically resulted in the emergence of three societies. Any student of her history must keep in mind the interplay of these environmental factors as they contributed to the development of this "border state."

It is usually assumed that Arkansas is divided into two sections by a geological line, practically a northeast to southwest diagonal, which marks off the lowlands or gulf costal plain on the east and south from the highland area on the north and west. A division, however, which much more accurately describes the state geologically, and which is strongly reflected in the political activity and viewpoints of its inhabitants, is one which provides for three areas instead of the commonly accepted two. One area, according to this scheme, would take in the the low-lying "bottom" or "delta" land running irregularly north and south along the Mississippi River and extending west to include roughly one-fourth of the area of the state.[1] The part of the state west of this Mississippi bottom region is in turn bisected east and west by the Arkansas River valley. This valley and the Ozark Plateau to the north comprise a second area, the northwest. It is unsuited to large-scale farming; because of its rugged terrain roads are difficult to construct; and its waterways, except for the Arkansas, provide virtually no transportation. A third area, then, would be the territory west of the Mississippi bottoms and south of the Arkansas valley. In some respects this is the most interesting section of all. It is certainly the most varied in character. In the first place, the Ouachita Mountains, which occupy its northwest corner, match the

Ozarks of the northwestern area. Again, although there are no rivers comparable
to the Arkansas in size, there are a number of streams that have rather extensive
bottom stretches not unlike those along the Mississippi in the delta area.
Finally, the southwestern area contains an extensive forested coastal plain not
found in either of the other two. It is not strange, then, that the inhabitants of
this diversified region sometimes find their political and economic interests

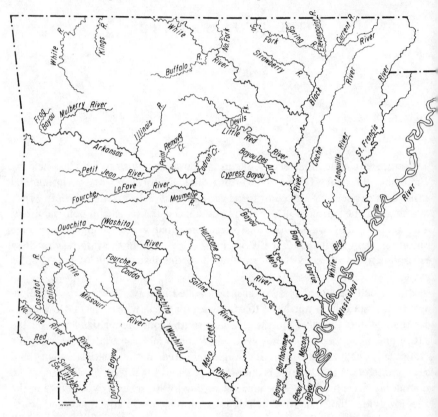

Figure 1.    Rivers of Arkansas

coinciding with those of the delta, sometimes with those of the northwest.

Leadership in Arkansas politics reflected this geographical variation. Although
it would be a mistake to over-emphasize social conflict between the lowlands
and the highlands, sectional interests did occasionally clash. One illustration of
such a disagreement occurred as early as the Constitutional Convention of 1836,
when the northwestern representatives opposed the inclusion of slaves as a factor

in determining the apportionment for representation in the state legislature.[2]

The river system provided another formative influence on social development. The Mississippi supplied the eastern lowlands along her banks with year-round navigation, but brought with this advantage the hazards associated with a winding and treacherous course, falling banks, and frequent inundations.[3] The remainder of the state was served by rivers flowing across her lands generally from northwest to southeast, ultimately emptying into the Mississippi. These rivers served to unite or isolate settlers largely on the basis of navigability. Most important among these were the White, Arkansas, Ouachita, and Red.

In northwest Arkansas the White—most beautiful of these streams—rose from three forks south and east of Fayetteville. David Walker came to this region of the state in 1830 and made his home there for the remainder of his life. East of Fayetteville, and along the west fork of the White River, Walker enjoyed the pleasures derived from a successful career as lawyer, judge, and farmer. It was here that part of his large holdings of land was located.

The White flowed northward into Missouri before reentering Arkansas on its southeastward journey toward the Mississippi. Although a beautiful stream, the White was of little value for navigation. Northwest Arkansas could not use it at all, and its service downstream was dependent upon the season. When the river was high, Batesville provided a good interior landing, but during most of the year boats could not be taken beyond Jacksonport, fifty miles downstream from Batesville.[4]  Residents along the White tried to improve their situation in 1854 by getting the government to establish a line of mail steamers from Memphis to Jacksonport. Had this venture been successful, there would have been regular steamboat service for a distance of 350 miles. But the Federal government refused to grant mail contracts to boats on rivers that were not navigable throughout the year; thus the residents had to continue living with irregular traffic on the White.[5]

The Arkansas also gave its share of trouble to the steamboat trade. On a river two thousand miles long, it would seem that navigation would not be a problem so far downstream, but the Arkansas was a wide and shallow river with a bed of yielding sand. Water during the summer months was often too low for regular boat traffic, and Pine Bluff or Little Rock would be as far as a boat could go upstream.[6]  Even in times of high water Fort Smith was considered the last good interior landing.[7]

Such concern with navigation problems led to the practice of unloading cargoes at Napoleon from the larger boats of the Mississippi trade and reloading them on shallow Arkansas River packets engaged in the Arkansas trade alone.[8] It also resulted in such humorous reactions as those reflected in the claim that people in Arkansas had a knack for constructing boats of ". . . amazingly light draft." As an example, it was said that the *Lucy Long*, built in Little Rock, ". . . [would] run anywhere that the ground . . . [was] a little damp. Usually she ... [came] to anchor if there ... [were] anything like a heavy dew."[9]

In spite of such discouragements as the river provided, trade along the Arkansas developed. Throughout the years acts of the Federal government served to stimulate the settlement and development of western Arkansas. White immigrants were allowed to go west on boats being used in association with the Indian removal policy. In time, the downstream voyage brought hides, pelts, and cotton for the markets in New Orleans, Louisville, or Pittsburgh.[10] The construction and supplying of Fort Smith and Fort Gibson served as a continuing stimulus to the development of river and other transportation. About 1835 the government improved the road passing through Fayetteville from St. Louis and designated it as a military road. This gave great impetus to trade in northwestern Arkansas. In particular, Van Buren and Fort Smith were stimulated now by being on two avenues of commerce. When the Butterfield Overland Mail Company began its regular runs through Fayetteville, Van Buren, and Fort Smith in 1858, Van Buren was further confirmed as the center of distribution for the northern trade.[11] Its location on the north side of the Arkansas, where the road from Fayetteville and St. Louis crossed the river on its way to Fort Smith, make it an important distribution point.

One of the leading merchants of Van Buren who participated in this growing commerce was David C. Williams. His historical significance to a large degree centers around his involvement as a Unionist during the secession crisis. His influence throughout northwestern Arkansas was magnified by the widespread distribution of his broadside "To the People of Arkansas," January 29, 1861. His friendship with David Walker of Fayetteville and with Jesse Turner of Van Buren will make his viewpoint of some importance, as these men held harmonious views concerning the problem of secession.

Because of the disadvantages inherent in the river transportation system, one should not be surprised to find that a man like Jesse Turner led his section in promoting the construction of the Little Rock and Fort Smith Railroad. Nor should it be surprising that men in other sections of the state were less than enthusiastic. Among the opponents of a bill to use the internal improvement fund to aid the road's construction were counted the members on the Mississippi, those from the back counties, a "class of politicians who wish to arm the Malitia [sic] with the surplus revenue," many members from the western section of the state who would not support railroad aid, and at least one who lived south of the Arkansas (the road was to go along the north bank).[12]

The Ouachita served the transportation and commercial needs of south-central Arkansas and north-central Louisiana. Arkadelphia provided a good interior landing in high water, while Camden could be used the greater part of the year.[13] As an avenue of commerce, it should be noted, this river tied south Arkansas to the river system leading to New Orleans markets rather than to eastern Arkansas.

Southwestern Arkansas was uniquely influenced by the Red River. Forming the border between Arkansas and Texas, it flowed eastward into Arkansas and then south into Louisiana, where it would receive the Ouachita before reaching the Mississippi. However, an obstruction known as the Red River raft, which was originally 128 to 160 miles in length, accumulated near Nachitoches. This hampered the flow of goods between Fulton and New Orleans and prevented dependable use of the river. Repeated efforts by Congress to remove the raft and maintain a navigable river were only partially successful, for as late as 1850 the Fulton trade still could be shipped only during the winter and spring months.[14] In 1855 the stockholders of the Cairo and Fulton Railroad had this geographic isolation of southwest Arkansas appropriately called to their attention:

The permanent opening of navigation, through the raft, is so uncertain and remote, that the immense region of territory in the Red River valley, above it, for a distance of 400 miles on a direct line, must of necessity be dependent on this and the Galveston road for the transportation of its products to market. None of this year's crop, upon this portion of the river, has, up to this time, been shipped, and no prospect of a rise this season. The value of last year's cotton crop alone, thus locked up, is sufficient to build one half of the Cairo and Fulton road.[15]

Perhaps this relative isolation strengthened the social and cultural ties among individuals in this area, while the national road, which cut southwest from Little Rock to Fulton, furthered their unity by increasing opportunities for mutual contact. The similarity of origin and kinship among the early settlers from Virginia and North Carolina contributed to their common cultural background. Commercial isolation invited smaller farms and prevented the extreme social contrasts that were a part of the delta culture of the eastern lowlands. All of these have been suggested by Miss Carmichael.[16] Two observations might be added.

This region had two things in common with northwestern Arkansas: geographical isolation deriving from its river system and similar reliance on a national road. On the other hand, the southwest shared with the eastern delta a common commitment to the continuance of slavery. It was reasonable to expect that southwestern Arkansas would become sympathetic with the northwestern section on such measures as railroad promotion; at the same time, a closer social affinity between southwest and delta made the two areas agree in maintaining the customary race relations. Whatever the validity of these views, this southwestern region had a uniqueness about it which distinguished it from the other two areas in the state and which revealed three societies rather than the usual highland-lowland division in Arkansas history. Brought to this southwestern Arkansas area by his parents as a one-year-old child in 1833, Augustus

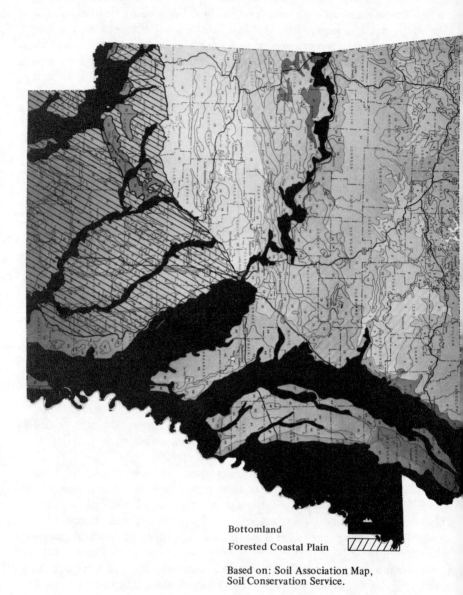

Bottomland

Forested Coastal Plain

Based on: Soil Association Map,
Soil Conservation Service.

Figure 2.        Soil Association Map Showing Bottomland and Forested Coastal Plain Areas

H. Garland would be greatly influenced by these regional attitudes until 1856, at which time he moved to Little Rock as a young lawyer twenty-four years old.

In addition to geography and the river system, soil conditions provided a third environmental influence which contributed to the development of a heterogeneous society in the state. Prior to the Civil War, the plantation system sought out the bottomlands, and presence or absence of this type soil marked the social and economic development of a given area. The lure of profits and social prestige associated with owning slaves might extend the system far beyond the bottomlands, but the soil would continue to define where the system would be most easily and most profitably developed.

The largest area of bottomlands in the southwest was a crescent area formed by the Red River as it went through that corner of the state on its way into Louisiana. The greatest width of this area was approximately eighteen miles. Three other bottomland areas forming narrow fingers along the Little Missouri, Ouachita, and Saline rivers had an average width of approximately five miles. Except for these limited stretches of river bottoms, this southwestern region, beginning at the western edge of the Arkansas valley bottomlands and extending west-southwest across the state, was predominantly a forested coastal plain. The composition of its soil proved a limiting factor on the size of farm units and gave another distinguishing characteristic to the southwestern area.

East of the forested coastal plain were bottomlands of the Arkansas River valley extending from the southeastern corner of the state upstream to Little Rock in a hugh crescent approximately thirty miles wide. Arkansas bottomlands west of Little Rock to Fort Smith narrowed to an area less than nine miles in width. In this valley, a few miles downstream from Pine Bluff, Powell Clayton had bought a cotton plantation south of the river and established himself there as a cotton grower prior to becoming governor.

Farther east the White, Black, and Cache rivers combined to produce a valley approximately twenty miles wide, which ran north and northeast toward the northeastern corner of the state. A delta region, extending from the Crowley Ridge area to the Mississippi, a distance of about forty-two miles at the greatest, filled out the northeastern section along the Mississippi and completed the bottomland areas of the state.[17]

The existence of bottomlands gave a rough indication of the location and intensity of operation of the plantation system. Counties having large areas in bottomlands were, to a significant degree, the same counties showing a high percentage of slaves in the total population and a high per capita of wealth in 1860.[18] Conditions here supported the conception of Arkansas as a Southern state, but caution should be given against considering the lowlands a homogeneous area. Bottomlands in the confines of the forested coastal plain of the southwest resulted in the emergence of a society of smaller economic units having a somewhat different social outlook which required recognition when compared with the wealthier and more expansive delta society of eastern Arkansas.

Two other factors contributed to the difference between the delta and the southwest: the influence of the river system, and the attraction of Texas. It will be remembered that rivers flowed generally southeast across the state on their way to the Mississippi. The White and Arkansas tied the economy to the Mississippi and made New Orleans, St. Louis, Cincinnati, or Pittsburgh ports of destination, while the Ouachita and Red transported goods downstream to New Orleans. On their upstream journeys, the Ouachita and especially the Red provided avenues of travel for people on their way to Texas from such states as Mississippi, Alabama, and Georgia.[19] Ouachita River travelers could go west from Camden on one of three roads leading into Texas: the Trammel Trace, which crossed the Red at Dooley's Ferry; the Mill or Washington Road, which led to Fulton; or the Fort Towson Road, which took them farther west to Paraclifta. Red River passengers could continue to Fulton or farther west on the river during high water, or they could take the Washington-Old Shreveport Road from Shreveport to Fulton and beyond when low water and the raft prevented their passage.[20]

Texas provided a continuing southwestern thrust across the state during the years before the Civil War. Four of the first five counties organized in Arkansas included major river crossings on the way to Texas.[21] This Southwest Trail, over which so many passed, would become the route of the Cairo and Fulton Railroad carrying migrants of a later era. The lure of hopes and promises of Texas must be included among the formative influences of southwestern Arkansas.

Just as the lowlands could easily be mistaken as being one homogeneous area, so also could they erroneously be considered as typical of the state. Soil conditions and environmental influences found in the highland northwest made it difficult to think of Arkansas as a Southern state. Two mountainous frontier areas, lacking in internal uniformity and separated by the trough formed by the Arkansas valley, encouraged the formation of small farm units, social isolation, and a resulting local-mindedness. These influences also produced a devotion to the Union, which would assert itself as the Civil War approached. Population influx from Northern states, Missouri in particular, and economic and social contacts with St. Louis over the military road perhaps encouraged pro-Union association. Whatever the causes, sympathy for the Union was strong in this area. Yet there were many here favoring secession and Southern independence. Indeed, it was this relatively mixed sentiment which made the Civil War and Reconstruction in Arkansas so much like a local civil war and reconstruction.

Arkansas was thus a "border state" in many ways. Varying environment contributed to its marginal character, as in the example of geological partition. The river system gave a general southeastern movement to its commerce and

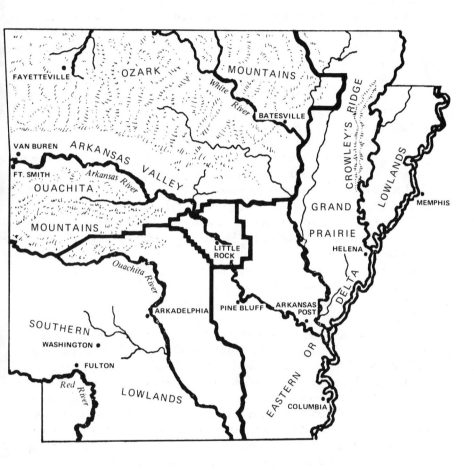

**Figure 3.    The River System and the Three Societies**

united or isolated areas according to availability of navigation. Soil types helped define the areas in which the plantation system could be most easily, profitably, and intensively developed. Size of farm units, kinds of crops grown, and, indirectly, the kind of social development occurring in a given region were also related to the soil.

Social variation complemented environmental as there developed what may be thought of as three societies: delta, southwestern, and northwestern. Each possessed its own heterogeneous characteristics, but some of these seemed more representative than others. The plantation system of cotton production, which was still expanding in 1860, gave the delta the highest concentration of social and political power and prestige.[22] Several counties in this area were distinctive for their large number of slaves and high per capita of wealth.[23]

The forested plain of the southwest provided mild to sharp contrast with the delta. A common culture, the absence of extreme social contrasts, and geographic and commercial isolation gave social cohesion to this area. Its rivers turned economics toward New Orleans, but also gave a reminder of the significance of the southwestern thrust toward Texas.

Ironically, as the *"Southern heart* [came to be] too much fired to reason"[24] residents of the northwestern region stood to bear a larger portion of military service than those of the delta, for in this area lived a majority of the white population.[25] Characterized by small farms raising a variety of products, by social isolation, and by a mixed population, this region produced local-minded provincials who paradoxically held a strong devotion to the Union, many becoming "mountain Feds" during the Civil War.

Despite all its variations the state had one quality common to all regions—it was predominantly rural. Even those exceptions to rural life, the towns, were not large exceptions. The Helena of Thomas B. Hanly had a total population of only 1,551 in 1860.[26] The Little Rock of Augustus H. Garland was the largest town in the state, having 3,727 people, while Washington, the southwestern town from which he had moved in 1856, had 480 residents. Van Buren, home of Jesse Turner and D.C. Williams, counted only 979, while David Walker's Fayetteville counted 972. But the rural society reflected itself in many ways other than in population totals. Attitudes and values such as those expressed below might lend a better appreciation of this rural society than census returns.

David Walker, certainly one of the most sophisticated men in his area, found some of his happiest hours in life at his farm or on the hunt as he described to a friend in 1857:

My negroes have for some years been upon the farm, except two kept for house work in Town. I have brought out an old family servant, my Mother's cook, to take care of my wardrobe and cook for me, have a small room fitted up with bed, table &c., which I occupy. My horse is caught every morning and hitched, ready for a ride over the farm, and where the hands are at work. By 11 o'clock I am in, reading and resting for evening, when I repeat my ride, or take a drive with some friends who are fond of hunting. I have good dogs and deer are plenty. I wish very much that you could come up and see my situation and take chase with me. Let me invite you into my room.

You will find two beds, one just between the window and door—what a fine draft of air for to rest at noon. There are a few of the last papers that have fallen near the bed, and a pile of them in one corner of the room. And there are three guns sitting in the corner next the door. I'll give you choice of them. That long barreled old-fashioned piece will do its work [at] 100 yards, will rarely miss air or fire, and as rarely fail to kick the huntsman over. That large double-barrel tools well, those are splendid locks, she carries a fine load and if you take *her*, you will carry one too. But see that short double-barrel. To shoot partridges you will say. Yes! to shoot anything within the range of 70 yards. You can ride half speed with it in one hand and fire too if need be, with a fair prospect of bringing down a Buck.

I will give you choice of them. But here are the dogs. They smell the powder, and know that a hunt is on hand. How restless they are! That old black tan is from the mountains of East Tennessee. He has a full mouth and will likely get up the deer, for in trailing he has the coldest nose this side of the North Pole. Those two young black tans are of his stock, both fleet and tough. That large blue dog with black speckled shots is the only real buck hound I have seen in Arkansas. You will distinguish him by his      full mouth. He will lead the chase. Be ready to shoot when he gets in 200 yards, the deer is rarely further than that from him. Earth has no *platform* wide enough for a deer to run on and keep out of his reach, and the water must be deep and wide to save him.

Here are cap, powder, and shot, and here is the best hunting horse in all the land. This spur, he may need persuasion. There, we are off, and back again. Here is water to wash the blood off your hands. Take off you[r] coat and rest a while, or would you rather take [a] smoke. Here is a pipe and here is a paper. I know you will not tear a letter off the edge as close as you may. Now your pipe is lit, tell us how far you shot, and all about it.

But then I am getting ————, and you will think me as nearly cracked as when I came upon the bench.[27]

Social conditions as they were prior to 1860 would be fundamentally changed. The Civil War would interrupt and Reconstruction modify three significant developments which made their appearance in the 1850's: a shift in the use of state credit from plantation expansion to railroad development; a transition from river system to railroad transportation; and the ending of an era of political oligarchy in Arkansas politics. These consumed a large portion of the energies of leadership during Reconstruction and will be of considerable importance to this study.

# CHAPTER TWO

# PATRIOTISM: SECESSION

*November, 1860        April 14, 1861*

*No man can renounce his allegiance to any government by proxy—no man can acknowledge allegiance to any government by proxy—...* [1]

It is ironic that Andrew Jackson's rise to political power, though popularly identified with the common man, was the basis for establishing an aristocratic dominance of Arkansas politics from its territorial days to the Civil War.[2] Federally appointed surveyors, led by relatives of Jackson, came to Arkansas in the early nineteenth century, made the survey, and laid claim to the best lands, which provided the foundation for their subsequent social influence. The party of fifty-two under William Rector included four of his brothers and four nephews, three of whom were sons of his sister, Ann Conway. Later, one of their kinsmen, Ambrose H. Sevier, married the daughter of Benjamin Johnson, from a prominent Kentucky family and brother of Richard H. Johnson, Vice President under Van Buren.[3]  Political prestige, power, and social influence thus concentrated in "the family," and from the names Rector, Conway, Sevier, and Johnson came two territorial representatives, two United States Senators, and three governors before the Civil War.[4]  Their political influence ruled the Democratic party, and candidates endorsed by "the family" were assured an excellent chance of victory.

A division among political forces in 1860, however, led to revolt against the currently dominant faction headed by Richard H. Johnson. Resigning his position on the Supreme Court, Henry M. Rector opposed Johnson for governor and won by 3, 101 votes out of a total of 60,795 in an exciting contest.[5] The cleavage created by this campaign would not heal, and the regular Democrats forced Rector out of office by November, 1862, two years short of his four-year term, by calling for another election to fill the governor's office under the new Constitution of 1861.[6]  Such dissension, augmented by the growing opposition to the political oligarchy, served notice that this disintegration of party unity was likely to bring significant changes in political loyalties in the immediate future.  When the effects of the Civil War are included, it becomes easier to understand why party organization was such an important item in the thoughts of men during Reconstruction.

It would be a mistake, however, to overlook the political significance represented by the Whig element in Arkansas.  As a measure of their political strength, it may be noted that from 1836 through 1856 the Whig canvass in Presidential elections never fell below 32.9% of the votes cast in Arkansas. This small canvass occurred in 1856 when Millard Fillmore ran on the American ticket.  The Whig's largest percentage was reached in 1848, when 44.9% of the Arkansas vote went to Zachary Taylor against the Democratic nominee, Lewis Cass.[7]  Socially and economically conservative, dominantly committed to the Union, many men of this political persuasion played significant roles in the secession crisis and during the Reconstruction period.  Especially in western and southwestern Arkansas were to be found men whose public roles helped to influence the course of events, but who in turn were changed by their experiences: David Walker and T.M. Gunter of Fayetteville, Jesse Turner and D.C. Williams of Van Buren, and in the southwest John R. Eakin of Washington.

The purpose of this chapter is to consider patriotism from the election of Lincoln to the end of the Secession Convention, June 3, 1861.  Lincoln's call for 75,000 volunteers, April fifteenth, may be considered a point of division between the time when those loyal to the Union, a natural majority of voters in the state, could express their patriotic feelings and one during which patriotism became entangled in the wartime passion for "simon pure" allegiance to the Southern cause.

In the canvass for Presidential electors in 1860 the Constitutional Union candidates, John Bell and Edward Everett, received all the help possible for a newspaper to give as the editor of the *Gazette* through editorials, stories, and make-up made the reader feel there were no other candidates.  Any speaker, meeting, or resolution worthy of note received publicity. The Union cause in western Arkansas was noticed, with flattering praise for the activities of David Walker, H.F. Thomason, T.M. Gunter, and J.P. Spring.[8]  The paper made note of Jesse Turner as president of a Bell-Everett Club in Van Buren and urged its readers to support Union papers throughout the state such as the *Washington Telegraph, Ouachita Herald, Helena Shield,* and the *Batesville Balance.*[9] Activities of A.H. Garland and Jesse Cypert were recognized as they campaigned for Bell and Everett.[10]  Across the state strenuous efforts were made in behalf of their political position as the election approached.

Speakers for the Breckinridge and Lane Democrats included an influential Whig, Albert Pike, whose course was lamented by John R. Eakin of the *Washington Telegraph.*[11]   Also prominently supporting these candidates were Thomas C. Hindman, Robert W. Johnson, Richard M. Johnson, and Henry M. Rector, advocating secession should Lincoln be elected.  One hostile critic observed that these men claimed to be Union men,"but there was a fearful 'if' in their patriotism."[12]

On November sixth, the Arkansas Presidential vote resulted in Breckinridge receiving 28,733 votes, while Bell totaled 20,094, and Douglas only 5,227.[13] Until November seventeenth the *Gazette* was almost entirely void of political material.  On that day Editor C.C. Danley began his post-election commentary. With the election of the representative of Black Republicanism, the hope of the country now was the Union party.  Being a party of one idea, the Republican party could not survive.  The Democratic party had already disintegrated, and now all conservatives must unite in opposition to the Republicans.  The best chance for saving the nation, therefore, resided in the Union party.[14]

During the remainder of November and December the *Gazette* continued to call for a watchful, waiting attitude toward secession.  Its editor would let Lincoln do something overtly injurious before seceding.[15]  Using an economic interpretation of current problems, he felt the basic solution lay in making the North aware of her economic interests in the markets and products of the South. As a means of teaching this lesson, he wanted the South to demonstrate her economic independence to the extent necessary to prove that the South could do better without the North than *vice versa.*  In order to take advantage of their position, Southerners should take control of cotton manufacture, commercial and financial matters associated with the cotton trade, and, while remaining in the Union, establish direct contact with European shipping centers.  Such actions would make the North realize that a dissolution of the Union would be disastrous to her.  At the same time, however, such a disunion would be ruinous to the South, and the editor urged the people to wait for calm, deliberate action. He warned his readers against becoming "followers of fanatics, let them be the descendants of Puritans or Huguenots."[16]

One of the leading voices speaking for the Union in western Arkansas was Jesse Turner, lawyer and prominent Whig.  Born in North Carolina in 1805, Turner settled in Van Buren in 1831, and made his home there until his death in 1894.  Prior to 1860, he had been state representative from Crawford County, Whig Presidential elector candidate in 1848, and United States District Attorney in the western Federal District, 1851-53.[17]  Since 1857 he had served as president of the Little Rock and Fort Smith Railroad and would in the near future represent Crawford County in the Secession Convention.

Describing himself as "a Union man, a Henry Clay Whig, who voted for Bell and Everett, and who intends to stand by the Union as long as it can be preserved in honor," Turner wrote the editor of the *New York Express* in December, ten days before South Carolina seceded. His letter was an attempt to make the readers of the Northern paper aware of the urgency of the crisis at hand. Only a liberal and enlightened policy by the North could avert the terrible consequences he foresaw. The liberty laws he felt were unconstitutional instruments intended to thwart the execution of the fugitive slave law. These must be "swept from the statute books—nothing less will satisfy the South, nothing less ought to satisfy them—." One thing Lincoln, as President, might do to restore harmony would be to recommend their unconditional repeal. Perhaps Turner's main reason for writing the letter was his fear that the Northern people were not seeing as clearly as they should the immediacy of the crisis. He cautioned them "that although we occasionally send blustering braggarts to Congress who threaten a good deal and do nothing, yet the honest yeomanry . . . are at last aroused and determined to insist on their constitutional rights—I beg you then to be deceived no longer—." Coming from such a conservative rather than from a Southern hot-head, these words, he hoped, would make his readers consider retracing Northern steps in order to prevent calamities anticipated by him.[18]

Such apprehension seemed justified when South Carolina seceded, December twentieth. Now the voices of secession would find more sympathetic hearing, while those supporting the Union might feel more on the defensive. One reflection of this was the expression of contempt for *submissionists* by Senator Robert W. Johnson in his message, December twenty-second. He felt the question of secession could no longer be put aside, and that the people should rejoice in the course taken by South Carolina.[19] "I do not believe that this Union will perish unless we consent to compromise and yield our rights away, or SUBMIT."[20]

On the same day Governor Rector recommended to the house of representatives immediate legislative action calling for a convention. In his mind the Union of the States could no longer be regarded as an existing fact. He also applied social pressure to the Unionists by asking them to speak out in order that the people could know those "who are deaf to the admonition of plain facts and reason, false to the honor, glory, and independence of their State which is their rightful sovereign."[21] The morale of those who wanted to preserve the Union must have sunk during these days, for from Washington came discouraging news of efforts made toward compromise.[22]

On January 15, 1861, six days after Mississippi seceded, the Arkansas legislature passed an act requiring Governor Rector to submit to the people the question of a convention to consider the political situation and what course the state should take. The following day the Governor issued a proclamation setting February eighteenth as election day.[23] In commenting on the developments, the *Gazette* thought well of referring political matters to the people at this time and pointed to two geographical influences which helped define Arkansas as a border state. The state was unlikely to secede alone, for its western border would be exposed to parties entering either from Indian Territory or Kansas. Also, should Tennessee and Louisiana secede, the editor felt Arkansas would have no choice. In the event Tennessee moved toward cooperation with the Northern slave states, however, he would want Arkansas to do the same.[24]

William Quesenbury, observer of the folly of men's actions and humorous writer under the pen name "Bill Cush," was well aware of the strange times they had fallen upon, but he thought some of the people—particularly one—were doing unaccountable things. He had in mind D.C. Williams of Van Buren, a merchant "of sugar and coffee, cold-water, theology, and idiosyncracies [sic], being a clear headed, clever, intelligent, good man, expounds politics to the people, and publishes a document at his own expense which is having considerable effect in the canvass."[25] The document referred to was Williams' broadside "To the People of Arkansas," published January twenty-ninth, and widely distributed, especially throughout northwestern Arkansas.

Beginning with an explanation of the election for a convention and the choice of candidates, Williams moved on to urge the people to vote, but by all means to question their candidates on where they stood. If they did not reveal their opinions, they were either demagogues or they had not made up their minds. Any candidate who had not made up his mind by this time "may be a very honest man, but he is totally unfit to represent you." As the author saw matters, *either* a person believed his rights could be secured in the Union, *or* he believed that those rights could not be secured in the Union. The question was which of these positions was held by a majority of the people in Arkansas. Therefore, things should be called by their right name and the issue clearly drawn between *Unionists* and *disunionists*. But one vitally important condition should be imposed: that they vote for no man who would not pledge himself to submit the decision of the Convention "*to the people for their approval, at THE BALLOT BOX—*." For an essential principle was at stake, "'the People are Sovereign' . . . Whether your allegiance shall be withdrawn from the Federal Government which we have been accustomed to recognize as the Supreme Government, or whether it shall remain unaltered; it can only be decided by yourself—and for yourself alone—no delegated body nor any other body of men under Heaven, can *decide* that question for you or me. No man can renounce his allegiance to any government by proxy—no man can acknowledge allegiance to any government by proxy—this is a principle, which is recognized in all enlightened nations of the world."[26]

Williams left no doubt in the reader's mind as to his sympathies with the Union. His hopes were not placed in Congress or the legislatures, however, but rather, in a "General Convention of Delegates from all the States in the Union." He wanted to see the National Constitution amended in such a way as to "settle forever that vexed question of slavery—," but his devotion to the Union was evident throughout the document. First appearing in the newspaper, hundreds of copies were printed and distributed in Arkansas and beyond the state.

While it is impossible to measure the influence of this one address during the weeks of the Convention canvass, it seems fair to conclude that Williams himself was a significant influence in that canvass. His correspondence from this period included letters from numerous northwestern Arkansas towns expressing agreement with his views, giving him encouragement in his work, and requesting copies of his address for community distribution. He was recognized in Little Rock as being one of the leaders of Union sentiment in western Arkansas, and from correspondents in Boston, St. Louis, and Oxford, Ohio came reassuring and sympathetic responses to his address. His work made him a center of influence for those supporting the election of Union candidates, and he aided the elections of these men, especially in northwestern Arkansas. His most significant contribution was found in the consensus held by representatives of his region of the importance of referring to the people whatever action the convention might take.[27] To recognize D.C. Williams, however, should not justify the neglect of other spokesmen for the Union. Northwestern Arkansas would be represented in the Convention by some of its strongest leaders, to a man advocates of remaining in the Union.[28]

On election day, February eighteenth, the people were asked to vote for or against a convention and for the candidate of their choice should there be a convention. The results of the canvass showed a majority of 11,586 for the Convention in a vote of 43,234.[29] The Union candidates won by a majority of 5,701, the vote being 23,628 for them and 17,927 for the secession candidates.[30] These results might lead to the conclusion that the state was almost evenly divided on the question of secession. These totals, however, must not be allowed to conceal the character of that division.

In the first place, there were large imbalances present in various counties. In the delta there were three counties in which secessionist candidates were elected without opposition; in three others large secessionist majorities overwhelmed their Unionist opposition. In northwestern Arkansas the reverse was true. In Crawford County, Jesse Turner and H.F. Thomason were elected by a majority of 800, and in Washington County the lowest Union candidate received 1,713 votes while the highest secessionist polled 410.[31] Despite such extremes, when the election results were in, the Union delegates to the Convention had a majority of five.

A further observation on the election was to note the sectional nature of the vote. To an unusual degree political allegiance reflected environmental influence. The three societies revealed their nature as party lines followed geographical lines. Except for three delegates, the northwest was solidly represented by Union men, while the reverse was true of the delta. From the southwest came ten secessionists and seven Unionists, reflecting the mixed nature of that area.

Party lines established in the election continued in the Convention. During the first session from March fourth to March twenty-first, almost every vote, which was a test of strength, followed the same pattern. Two examples may be taken to illustrate this. On March fourth, the opposing forces met in the vote to elect a president of the Convention. David Walker was the nominee of the Union delegates and B.C. Totten, of Prairie County, was the nominee of the secessionists. The resulting vote made Walker president by forty votes to thirty-five.[32] A second test of allegiance came on March eighteenth when the Hanly motion to secede came to a vote, and was defeated by a vote of forty to thirty-four.[33] The Unionists had been able to maintain their slim majority of five.

The preservation of that majority gave Jesse Turner no little concern, according to the letter he wrote his wife, Rebecca, in the early days of the Convention. It was smaller than he had expected and was being subjected to extraordinary pressure. He felt that all eyes were on Arkansas and that the secessionists feared there would be a reaction against secession if Arkansas remained in the Union. Therefore, they would try everything to get Arkansas to secede. On the other hand, news had come from Messrs. Crittenden and Douglas expressing a hope of a *"satisfactory adjustment of our difficulties"* if Arkansas remained firm. Turner thought she would do so.[34]

Accommodations at the Anthony House had been found abominable, and Turner moved to a Mr. Robbins' to board.[35] There he found the company of eight or ten Union delegates among whom were David Walker, T.M. Gunter, A.W. Dinsmore, Elias C. Boudinot, and A.H. Carrigan.[36] All of these were from northwestern Arkansas except A.H. Carrigan from the southwestern county of Hempstead. Spending all day at the Convention, these men would caucus with the Union delegates at night "exhorting them to unyielding fidelity." As Turner anticipated the forthcoming vote on secession, his confidence grew that the Union men would stand firm.[37]

Encouraging and sympathetic letters came to Turner from D.C. Williams, who was pleased with the composition of the Convention. Union men all over the state could draw encouragement from the example of the "noble forty" in the Convention at Little Rock. He hoped that the delegates would follow the lead of Virginia, for as that state went so would the border states go. Williams' desire to have a general convention of all states was somewhat dampened by Turner's reminder that such a convention would have to be called by Congress. This requirement was to be regretted, for politics was the source of their trouble; the politicians had taken control of public affairs and would oppose any procedure which might bring matters before the people. As he expressed it, "they have had the entire management of this country for many years—instead of being controlled by—they have controlled public sentiment—instead of carrying out the views & policy of the people as was the design in framing the government—they have used the people for carrying out their plans & have taught them that patriotism consisted in devotion to party—So I

Unionist [hatched]

(Numbers denote number of delegates.)

Calculated from: letter from
W. F. Holtzman to D. C. Williams,
Van Buren, Ark.; Little Rock,
February 25, 1861. Arkansas History
Commission, D. C. Williams Papers.

**Figure 4.    Counties Sending Union Delegates to Secession Convention**

cannot but believe that if there could be any mode by which Convention could be called without the intervention of Congress or politicians it would be a *present* blessing and a *good* precedent—. . ."[38]

On the night of March eighteenth, the Hanly motion to secede was defeated by a vote of thirty-nine to thirty-five.[39]   The drama and excitement of the moment was not lost, as Turner told his wife of receiving a beautiful bouquet thrown by a lady in the gallery when he gave his *"no with tremendous emphasis."*[40]   The significance of the vote was not lost to the secessionists either as several members left for home the next day.   A friend wrote D.C. Williams that his boat was taking disunionist members downriver from Little Rock.   He felt that "the disunionists have . . . given Arkansas up as a hard case, and are going home to seceede [*sic*] from Northern Arkansas.   Maybe they will, but they won't do to tie to."[41]

The work of the Convention was rapidly drawing to a close.   On March twentieth, an ordinance was passed calling for the submission of the question of "cooperation" or "secession" to the voters in an election to be held on August fifth, and on the next day the Convention adjourned to meet again on August 19, 1861.

Enthusiasm for the Union position in the forthcoming canvass combined with the eagerness of his youth prompted William M. Fishback, delegate from Sebastian County, to send D.C. Williams, April tenth, his ideas for the campaign. He had already secured sixteen subscribers for the campaign newspaper, which he hoped would have two leading objects that he had found effective with the people.   It should show "a *settled design* to break up the government on the part of the Secessionists and to prove their hostility to compromise."   The people should be taught not to look to Congress for an adjustment, for they were beginning to despair of solution by that body.   The organization of Union clubs in various counties would give an opportunity for demonstrating a show of zeal which would encourage the people.   Having speakers from other counties would give the appearance of activity also, and Fishback would be available for such service, especially against Robert W. Johnson, secessionist leader.[42]   The tone of his letter left one with the question of whether its author was writing as a patriot or politician.

Developments in Charleston Harbor on April twelfth and thirteenth ended the period when voices supporting the Union were heard by a majority of the people.   With Lincoln's call, issued April fifteenth, for 75,000 volunteers to put down the insurrection existing in South Carolina, the Union dialogue all but stopped in Arkansas.   The dilemma in which some Union men found themselves during these developments was expressively represented by William Stout as he wrote Jesse Turner from Dover on April fourteenth.   He had been one of the forty Union delegates in the recent Convention and held great respect for Turner's advice, for which he was now writing.   He perceived there would be war and was concerned that his patriotism be true. In unpolished, but sincere language, he expressed his feelings:

Should we union men change our position—Should we become Secessionists—I for one Say not yet.—I am not ready for that yet—and indeed I don't know when I ever Shall be, think I never will—I may possibly be too ultry [sic]—I think I have loved my country I have been proud to think that I was a citizen of the great United States of America—I have loved the flag of my Country I used to think So now I know it because that I feel it—but if in the dispensation of Providence I Shall have to become a citizen of the "Cotton Confederacy" I don't think it is ever possible that I can love it with the Same devotion on Earth—The thing that vexes me is this—I know there has been So much deception—So much rascality—and vilainy [sic] (hard terms these) used to bring about the troubles now upon the Country, by men who Stood high in the confidence of the people and professed to be their best friends—but have gulled deceived and ruined them—I can't but feel indignant when I contemplate the matter but what Shall we do what ought we to do is the question, oh I wish I could fully understand the matter and get right if I am wrong. I believe it is the President's duty to put down rebellion. I have always thought So. I have always thought that General Jackson was right in 33 if he was right then Lincoln is right now but it Seems that there is going to be war between the north & the South— for me to take the Side of the north against my brothren [sic] of the South that would brand me forever with valainy [sic] that would be too bad and roll up my Sleeves and go to killing off men that never did me any harm and never intends to do me any—that is too bad I declare Sir it troubles me I never have looked so Gloomy a future as I am looking at now. If I Pray to Heaven for help I can't feel like we deserve it and upon my honor Sir I don't know what to do, I would be glad to get a letter from you. I think it would do me good I know it would. The Secessionists here are rejoicing best pleased in the world a thousand times better pleased when they heard that Fort Sumpter [sic] was taken than they would have been to have heard that a plan was devised to put at rest forever all political differences and raised the Stripes and Stars again over a free contented happy and prosperous people—these are hard things to say but I believe in my soul it is So and can I ever cooperate with a people whose heart is so decidedly in the wrong place I think not I see no way to do that—I am certain that up to the time that the news came of Fort Sumpter [sic] that the union Side of the question was gaining all the time what influence that will have I know not for that has just reached us, and I am not prepared to Say yet what influence it ought to have.[43]

It was true, as D.C. Williams had said earlier, that no man could renounce his allegiance to any government by proxy or acknowledge allegiance to any government by proxy. During the weeks to come many Unionists would be compelled to face the dilemma expressed by William Stout.

April 15, 1861        May 8, 1861
*For weal or woe, my destiny is yours.*[44]

When the delegates arrived home from the Convention, which adjourned March twenty-first, they made preparations for the forthcoming political contest between "cooperation" (with the border slave states in an adjustment of the questions at issue between North and South) and "secession," anticipating the election on this question in August. The task for the Unionists was to maintain their majorities against secessionist encroachments. Senator Robert W. Johnson, who had become one of the chief spokesmen for secession through the *True Democrat*, planned a speaking tour of northwest Arkansas the latter part of April, and Unionists were being enlisted to answer his attacks. David Walker agreed to meet him in Huntsville; Jesse Turner was invited to speak in Ozark on April twenty-seventh; and, as has been seen, William Fishback volunteered his services as a speaker against the Senator.[45]

The steadfastness of some Union sentiment was questioned by W. W. Mansfield, of Ozark, as he abhorred the political wrangling and trickery he expected to face in days to come. He felt the Union majority would hold if they were not misled by such fallacies as that which argued that secession would secure rights which adhering to the Union meant to abandon. From Camden, a Unionist delegate, writing to Jesse Turner from an area in southwestern Arkansas surrounded by secessionist counties, observed that the real fight to maintain the Union majorities would occur in the northwestern section, for the southern and eastern counties were seccesionist or Unionist by small majorities. But he hoped Turner would aid his efforts by correspondence and material for his paper.[46]

These embryonic developments forecast an active political canvass leading to the election in August. But the attack on Fort Sumter and Lincoln's call for volunteers (April twelfth to fifteenth) interrupted and altered the direction of events and confronted many Unionists with a moment of truth concerning their political allegiance. The immediate effect of the news of these events should not be exaggerated, however, for in the rural isolation of most of Arkansas it took time for the citizens to know what had happened. In several letters there was expressed a skepticism over the validity of telegraphic reports, writers suspecting a secessionist trick. Before men reacted too firmly to the new situation, they were inclined to consult their friends to see what they were thinking. Perhaps the most important qualification on the immediacy of the effect of Lincoln's call for volunteers should be to remember that many delegates to the Convention had taken a position of watchful waiting, remaining loyal to the Union, but opposed to any coercive move by the Lincoln Administration. In their minds this call was such a move, and required a change in allegiance.

It is important to understand, however, that, as many Unionists changed their allegiance, they did so without embracing secession. This lack of positive commitment to Southern nationalism would be one of the basic weaknesses in Southern patriotism during the war. For many Unionists the change was a negative one, motivated by opposition to Northern aggression and domination by "Black Republicanism." One Union delegate wrote Turner an apologetic letter, anxious that he believe his correspondent's conscientiousness as he shifted his allegiance. He could not vote for secession and wanted Turner to understand he was not a secessionist, but he saw no plank upon which he could stand for the Union now. He expected to disagree with Robert W. Johnson and other secessionists, but he would console himself with the reflection "that while I was for the Union, I was sincere, and that when I was willing to yield, to a dissolution, I was honest in my convictions of the necessity for so doing—."[47] Others were more cautious and wanted to await the action of the border states. Another of Turner's correspondents was apprehensive that David Walker might be prevailed upon to reconvene the Convention before its normal August date. For this he could see no reason unless the purpose was to secede. It seemed to him the secessionists distrusted the people's decision of the matter at the polls and were trying to rush the state out of the Union.[48]

Circumstances turned attention toward David Walker, president of the Convention. Before the assemblage adjourned in March, commissioners had been chosen to represent Arkansas in a convention of border states in Frankfort, Kentucky, on May twenty-seventh. The decisions made there were to form the basis of the choice "cooperation" in the forthcoming election on August fifth. An ordinance of the Convention provided, however, that the president had authority to convene the Convention should an exigency arise before August nineteenth, justifying such action. Now that kind of emergency had occurred and men looked to Walker for his decision. On April seventeenth, Thomas B. Hanly, prominent secessionist whose motion for secession had been defeated, wrote Walker that, in his opinion, an exigency had arisen which demanded calling the Convention. He believed that the people would fully sustain Walker in a proclamation convening the delegates and that when the Convention met few voices would oppose secession. In an appeal to Walker's vanity, Hanly suggested that the course which he recommended would render Walker one of the most popular and influential men in the state and serve to advance his future aspirations.[49]

The sentiment in favor of issuing a call for the Convention was widespread. Governor Rector received a letter representing the views of several Arkansas planters in Memphis and urging him to use all means which could be devised to induce Walker to call the Convention. As for the August election, if one had to take place, let it be on the ratification of secession.[50] In an "Address to the People," dated April eighteenth, signed by 137 prominent men, including forty-five conservative delegates to the Convention, there was expressed the hope and belief that Walker would issue a convention proclamation.[51] It is unlikely, however, that any of these entreaties exerted direct influence on Walker, for before he would have heard of them he issued, April twentieth, a call for the Convention to meet in Little Rock on May sixth.[52]

As Walker took this action, he realized that, once in session, the Convention would vote to secede. This placed him in an awkward position with his own constituency, for he and other Union delegates had been elected pledged against voting for any ordinance of secession which did not refer that matter to the people for their approval. The convention bill had not contained this provision and Williams, Turner, Walker and others utilized the idea of pledging delegates to see that secession was referred to the people as a means of amending the original act.[53] Would it not be a breach of faith to support secession now, when it was highly unlikely that any referral to the people could be required?

A few days later (approximately April twenty-sixth), Walker published his "Address to the People of Washington County." In tones more rhetorical than literal he asked the advice of his people. The issue at hand was presented in a straightforward manner. He and others had been elected as delegates pledged to cooperate with the border states and under no circumstances to vote for an ordinance of secession not referred to the people for their approval. The Convention had passed resolutions declaring its intention to resist coercion of the states, however, and Lincoln had faced them with coercion. Under these circumstances he had called the Convention. What would they have him do now? In a consideration of the possibilities before them, Walker proceeded to clarify his own position in the minds of his constituents as he rhetorically asked them for instructions. Should the delegates adhere to their pledged position or vote for an ordinance of secession which would not be referred to the people? Should Arkansas remain connected with a government preparing to engage in war against the slave states or sever that connection with the old confederacy? If the state seceded, should it maintain an independent positon or join the Confederacy at once?

He touched on two matters of particular importance to the people in northwestern Arkansas. The dominant view was that under no circumstances should troops be taken from that area. With secession, it was believed the danger of attacks from Indian Territory or Kansas made retaining troops in that region essential for its defense. Walker reminded his readers of their obligation to provide troops wherever the Confederacy needed them. He also faced the unpopularity of this obligation by pointing out that since the northern and western counties had the largest white population in the state, they would bear a large portion of the military burden should they join the Confederacy.

In closing, he reminded them that his sentiments were known to them, that he had tried to avert the present calamity, and that his mind had not changed, but dwelling on the past was useless and improper. Now minds must be turned to the present and future as they tried to save the country from the calamity of civil war. *"For weal or woe, my destiny is yours."*[54]

These last words, though well intended, "will appear in judgment against him, a lasting commentary upon his utter faithlessness," wrote one of Walker's harshest Union critics in 1863.[55] Using language characterized by lack of moderation, A.W. Bishop considered Walker's actions during this period to have been motivated by circumstances and his "over-weening love of applause."[56] By simplifying the situation, he concluded that Walker could have averted secession by choosing not to call the Convention at that time.[57] While recognizing him as a man of magnanimous and generous nature, and one whose efforts in behalf of the Union had been admirable until he convened the Convention, Bishop believed that move initiated a series of actions, including Walker's address and his plea for unanimity in the Convention, which took Arkansas out of the Union and made Walker a member of the "Triumverate of Treachery."[58] Of particular offense to Bishop was the lack of time given to the people for responding to Walker's request for instruction. The address had been made public one day, and four or five days later Walker left for the Convention. Despite the lack of time, many tried to transmit to their delegate resolutions opposing secession.[59]

These criticisms of Walker were unfair. In part, they were inspired by the desire to discredit an enemy during wartime; in part, they were distorted by the omission of some of the circumstances pertinent to Walker's decision to call the Convention. Probably the most significant influence in his decision was a set of resolutions  concerning Federal relations which originated in the Union caucus and was thought to be unanimously supported by those delegates. These resolutions were introduced in the Convention by Jesse Turner, chairman of the Committee on Federal Relations, and passed unanimously on March twenty-first, last day of the session.[60] The fourth resolution read: "That any attempt on the part of the Federal Government to coerce a seceding State by an armed force will be resisted by Arkansas to the last extremity."[61] While it was true that delegate David Walker had pledged not to vote for secession without referring the question to the people, it was also true that president David Walker was bound by the actions of the Convention. By what justification could he refuse to call the Convention? Too much can be made of the importance of the call itself, for given the circumstances, the decision largely had been made by events.

It will be recalled that Virginia was looked to for leadership by the Union delegates. On April seventeenth, she passed her ordinance of secession. The following day the "Address to the People of Arkansas" was signed by 137 men, including forty-five conservative delegates to the Convention. It was true, as George C. Watkins wrote Walker on the nineteenth, that his name was on every man's lips.[62] The people looked to him to call the Convention. "Treachery" was hardly an appropriate word to describe his actions.

Events were changing the *status quo* and moving men more rapidly away from the Union. C.C. Danley, Constitutional Union editor of the *Gazette,* wanted conservative men in control of the forthcoming convention, but now favored war in the face of Lincoln's coercion. Indeed, as he wrote, he was cognizant of state military forces on their way to Fort Smith, which surrendered to them April twenty-third.[63] This "foolish and unnecessary adventure," Turner thought, as he prepared to leave for the Convention in Little Rock, was in keeping with the hysteria of the day.[64] With declining morale, D.C. Williams continued to hope that Virginia had not really seceded, despite telegraphic reports to the contrary, and that her people would reject the ordinance when it came before them. To the last, he hoped the Little Rock Convention would refer secession to the people.[65]

When the Convention met, May sixth, the momentum was overwhelmingly in favor of secession. By 3:00 P.M. the Committee on Ordinances and Resolutions presented an ordinance dissolving the Union. After one amendment requiring the submission of the measure to the people had been tabled, voting on the ordinance proceeded.[66] Only five delegates had voted against it when President David Walker rose to cast his vote. Noting the inevitability of Arkansas' secession, he appealed to these delegates to make the vote unanimous: " 'since we must go, let us all go together; let the wires carry the news to all the world that Arkansas stands as a unit against coercion.' "[67] But this and other entreaties were not sufficient to change the vote of Isaac Murphy, Unionist delegate from Madison County, and the final tally read sixty-nine to one in favor of secession.[68] The voting was over by 4:10 P.M. Waiting behind the State House for this news were men of the Pulaski artillery under Captain W.E. Woodruff, Jr. Upon its receipt, their guns rang out a salute across the Arkansas River.[69] The forces leading toward secession had overwhelmed and demoralized the Union sentiment. One man spoke of Union delegates on their way to the Convention as the "worst plagued set of fellows he ever saw." Another expressed the view of many that David Walker should have refused to be carried along by the excitement and left the Convention adjourned until August.[70]

Jesse Turner shared this demoralization as he wrote his wife about the action of the convention. His dominant reactions were to blame the Lincoln Administration for these tragic developments. Despite resolutions opposing coercion passed in the border states, where honest efforts were being made to preserve the Union, and notwithstanding the hope repeatedly expressed that forts would be evacuated, the Administration had chosen to hold and reinforce them. This policy led to the collision, which he realized had been initiated by the South Carolina troops. But beside the mere legality of the situation, he felt it to be "passing strange that any man who knows anything of the character of the people of this country could suppose that the . . . Union of these States can be preserved by force." His strongest condemnation of Lincoln lay in his neglect of the Union men in the border states. They had been looked upon as perfidious and treacherous, when, had they been supported and encouraged, they might have saved the Union. Lincoln chose "to act otherwise, *crushed* them and made secession triumphant."[71]

The pathos of Turner's position was revealed as he wrote Rebecca of his vote in favor of the ordinance of secession:

Perhaps you will think I done [*sic*] wrong in voting for this act of revolution. Would to God that it could have been otherwise. But a stern and inexorable destiny seemed to demand it—The people of the State demanded it, and I could not escape it without abandoning my post, which I could not do—God knows what is to become of our unhappy country. All is darkness and gloom ahead. Our people are thoroughly imbued with the revolutionary spirit. Madness and folly rule the land and I fear that the end of free government approaches. The conservative men who were for the Union cannot stay the rushing tide of revolution. I fear it can only be quinched [*sic*] in oases of blood.[72]

# CHAPTER THREE

# PATRIOTISM: AMNESTY

*May 8, 1861      April 23, 1866*

*One thing I do believe, "that we are" a very great distance from both the Confederacy and the Federacy, in fact, it seems like, we are a considerable distance from anywhere.*[1]

—October 16, 1864

A fundamental mistake could be made by emphasizing the contrast between Union and Southern patriotism in Arkansas. Each had its radical proponents as well as conservative, but given a moderate statement of both, the similarity of view outweighed the divergency. From the duality of citizenship in our Federal system had been inherited a duality of patriotism which was exposed to great stress during the Civil War and Reconstruction. For some, this duality of allegiance could be interpreted as a clear conflict between loyalty and treason. For others, defining the ultimate location of their political devotion presented a genuine dilemma. One issue or circumstance might compel commitment to the Union, while another situation could emphasize a person's local allegiance. This duality in patriotism was a shared experience by all citizens in the state and of course was most strongly reflected in the leaders. The period from the election of Lincoln to the vote on the ordinance of secession was one of trial for those holding dominant Union sympathies. Just as Lincoln's call for volunteers faced them with a moment of truth in which they had to make a commitment, so, in similar fashion, the closing years of the war presented Southern patriots and particularly the Southern leaders with a period of trial and the application for pardon under the Amnesty Proclamation a similar moment of truth.

Although they probably would not have used the term *laissez-faire*, that social philosophy was characteristic of their point of view. Freedom was strongly identified with local self-government. Nationality was seen as the enemy of free government, especially when that political force was in the hands of a hostile section.[2]

Southern patriotism was rent with internal divisions as it tried to express itself after the Secession Convention. In the first place, Southern nationality never completely captured the hearts of the people. References to "our country" (meaning the Confederate States of America) continued to have a hollow sound. There seemed to be more validity in reports concerning the reluctance of troops to go beyond the state line into Missouri and elsewhere.[3] During the war, provincial devotion to the state resisted the growth of genuine allegiance to the Confederacy.

In addition, these divided loyalties led to conflicts between state and Confederate officials and made the perfection of political institutions impossible. This in turn became a source of patriotic frustration. As an illustration, in 1861, General McCulloch of the Confederate Army was embarrassed by his inability to arm recruits under his command because the state had promised the same arms to the Arkansas troops under Colonel Hindman and the Governor had refused to transfer them to his command. Indefinite communications from Richmond only served to complicate matters.[4] Similar lack of unity between state and Confederate authorities continued to thwart the development of Southern nationality. In April, 1862, Governor Rector wrote Governor Pickens of South Carolina that the Confederate government had made several errors in administration. Among these, he pointed to the under-estimation of the valor of the Northern people and to the over-confidence placed in European responses to the Southern cause. He believed they were attempting an impossible venture, a defensive war, and had shown prejudice against men of valor in favor of West Point officers. His strongest criticism was for the incompetence of men in charge of the War and Navy departments. While he felt the people of Arkansas were willing to make "any sacrifice necessary to establish Confederate Nationality [,]" he hoped the governors could meet in the near future to discuss needed modifications in the central government.[5]

A third kind of division hindering the development of Southern patriotism was the conflict existing between military and civilian hierarchies. Men who were supported by political influence in Richmond were given military appointments in spite of opposition from their military superiors. Victory was often interpreted in terms of "good for old Arkansas" by men in civilian positions, while the military was blamed for defeats encountered. Nothing could have been better calculated to lower morale of the military hierarchy.

The position of the Negro in Southern society made him a part of Southern patriotism also. In its positive expression this patriotism was dominantly a white man's love of country. It was not based on hatred of the Negro, but rather on an exclusion of him from patriotic consideration. This view emphasized the necessity and propriety of the slave system in accomplishing the goals of free government in the South. The inherent inconsistency of this position was one of its greatest weaknesses. In its negative expression Southern patriotism found in slavery more than an economic system; it was also a solution to race relations. So long as the preservation of a caste system was not threatened, the more moderate and generous aspects of Southern society could express themselves. But threaten the future of racial separation and its underlying taboo against miscegenation, and a psychological poison seemed to spread among the people which could rapidly convert moderation into radicalism and generosity into vindictiveness. The political potential of this did not escape the politicians during the Civil War or Reconstruction.

The natural development of Southern patriotism was distorted and thwarted by excesses related to wartime emotions. P.B. Cox wrote Governor Rector in July, 1861, of a plan to discover and test disaffected persons in a community. On a given day all men were to register their names in support of the Confederacy. Suspected men would be required to take an oath of loyalty, and those who refused to do so would be tried for treason, made to leave the community, or forced to give some security against their aiding the enemy. He hoped this policy would reassure the soldier of the safety of his family during his absence from home and result in leaving only those of *simon pure* allegiance in the community.[6] A.W. Bishop spoke of militia or "Township meetings" to raise a company within the community. Any of the population showing reluctance to attend or enroll were given notice: From that time forward they might be subject to insult or abuse.[7] Hatred of the "Feds" was nourished by identifying the purpose of the Federal armies as being the imposition of social and political equality of the Negroes. Put as an inflammatory threat of placing Negroes in office over whites, this poison turned peaceful men into bands roaming the mountains "fighting a phantom."[8]

Hopes of achieving Southern nationality waned by the summer of 1863. Defeats at Vicksburg and Gettysburg in July lessened the Confederate chances of military success. And morale in Arkansas suffered with the news that Little Rock had surrendered on September tenth. Accompanying this surrender Federal troops gained control of the area north of the Arkansas River, and the state Confederate government moved southwest to Washington. From this time until the final surrender, Southern patriots would find increasing difficulty believing in the ultimate success of their cause. While it is true that expressions of faith in that victorious conclusion were voluminous, they came to have a growing quality associated with dogma.

There emerged for some a question of the fundamental validity of portions of their commitment. This presented the most uncomfortable kind of question, for it was introspective in nature. The institution of slavery itself came into question as some advocated freeing the slaves to fight for their homes and country. D.H. Reynolds thought this a strange recommendation from a people who had contended that slavery was "the true condition for the negro." Rather than abandon long-established doctrines, he felt that now was the time to "cling to them the firmer."[9]  A loss of confidence in the Confederacy was evident in the growing refugee problem as planters abandoned their homes in Federally occupied areas of the state and, with their slaves, cultivated crops in the Confederate area. With the first threat from Union forces, they tended to flee again, abandoning the newly planted crops, and trying to save what possessions could be salvaged.[10]

Monetary and fiscal failures contributed burdens to Confederate morale as currency declined and taxes remained high.  The government lacked constitutional power for regulating currency; and as the fortunes of the Confederacy waned, her money became worth less and less.  By the end of 1861, the value of a Confederate dollar was eighty-two cents in gold.  It had declined to thirty-three cents by the end of 1862 and brought only five cents by the end of 1863. Before the close of the Civil War, sixty-one Confederate dollars were required to obtain one dollar in gold.  After April, 1863, heavy direct taxation was utilized, which fell with large incidence upon the planters, as they were asked to pay 8% on all kinds of property, 10% profits from sales, a graduated income tax, and a 10% agricultural tax paid in kind.  Since the taxes were paid in currency which was depreciating, delay in payment was rewarded.[11]

The end of this social tragedy came with the termination of the Confederate government in Arkansas on May 26, 1865. Many men that day could join John MacLean in feeling they were "a considerable distance from anywhere."[12] Three days later President Johnson issued his proclamation granting amnesty to Confederates who took the oath of allegiance.  There were several excepted classes of men who had to petition the President for special pardon, the most frequent exceptions being men who had held offices in the Confederate government, and those whose taxable property was over $20,000. A moment of truth faced the petitioner as he wrote the President asking pardon.  How a man responded to that decision and the experience he had obtaining pardon revealed much about that individual and his milieu.  Five Arkansas men have been chosen to illustrate this transition in allegiance at the end of the Civil War.

### BRIGADIER GENERAL DAVID HARRIS REYNOLDS
#### Letter of Petition: August 22, 1865
#### Pardoned: November 13, 1866

Prior to the Civil War, D.H. Reynolds was a lawyer practicing in a southeastern delta county (Chicot).  His politics were those of a states rights Democrat who interpreted the election of Lincoln as an act of hostility against the

South. He therefore actively supported secessionist candidates in the election of
delegates to the Secession Convention in February, 1861. When the ordinance
of secession was passed in May, he assisted in raising the first military company
in his county, and becoming its captain, joined the Confederate service in June,
1861, serving until May 2, 1865.[13] In the First Regular Arkansas Riflemen he
received promotions through the rank of colonel, when in January, 1864, his
military career reached a crisis.

On January thirteenth, Reynolds and other officers in his division were
charged with incompetency and ordered to appear before an examining board at
a later date. Against this charge he vigorously protested through channels,
claiming illegality in ordering officers to appear before board members of
inferior rank, claiming injustice at wholesale charges of incompetency, and
charging that it was an injury to incentive in the army to be tried for incompetency after two years of loyal service.[14] These complaints were answered
in very brittle and precise military diction suggesting that Congress disagreed with
Reynolds as to what would "injure the army," and that when the board met
would be "quite time enough" for Reynolds to protest.[15]

Fearing the outcome of these developments, Reynolds turned to the political
hierarchy for an escape from his present troubles. He was especially anxious
about his situation, for not only did he want to avoid court-martial, but also he
had aspirations for promotion, and such a reverse would bar his advancement.
From January until March a race went on between the military hierarchy under
which he served, which was moving toward court-martial, and the political
representation of Arkansas in Richmond composed of Robert W. Johnson and
A.H. Garland, trying to secure promotion for Reynolds to brigadier general. On
March fourteenth, success of his Arkansas advocates was reported by Senator
Johnson: "You are appt*d* at last—by dint of your merits & the devotion esteem
& perserverence of your friends."[16] Apparently the appointment had come
none too soon, for A.H. Garland wrote on April eighteenth that the promotion
relieved General Reynolds of the penalty adjudged against Colonel Reynolds.[17]

During the closing days of the war, while serving in the vicinity of North
Carolina, General Reynolds was wounded by cannon fire, an injury requiring
the amputation of his leg. He was with the Confederate Army of General Joseph
E. Johnston when it surrendered to General William T. Sherman near Durham,
North Carolina, on April 26, 1865. He was paroled on May second and returned
to Arkansas.[18]

On August twenty-second, he wrote his letter petitioning President Johnson
for pardon. He had been excluded from the Amnesty Proclamation because of
his rank in the Confederate Army. In a letter, straightforward in manner, honest
in content, but especially pleading in tone, he stated his good faith in joining the
Confederacy and now again in giving his allegiance to the Union. With the
proper endorsements, the letter was sent to Washington, but no response was

forthcoming. On January 15, 1866, he wrote a duplicate and sent it to the President, fearing the first letter had been lost. Still no response came to him. On September 29, 1866, Reynolds wrote a letter to Henry Stanbery, Attorney General of the United States, asking him to call Reynolds' application to the President's attention. Under normal circumstances he would not bother the President, but in August the people of his district had elected him to the state senate and he wanted to avoid any confusion about his office before the legislature convened the first Monday in November.[19] Apparently, Reynolds had not been immune to the advice of a friend who urged him a year before not to "stand back & let the . . . lay outs & traitors rule your state. You deserve a first rate office & you ought to pick one to suit you & claim it."[20]

Adding endorsements from men in the North, Reynolds again wrote President Johnson, October 25, 1866. Excusing the intrusion by the factor of time, he called attention to the fact that the Arkansas Senate would meet on November fifth, and that should the President grant the pardon, his mail would reach him at Little Rock.[21] On November thirteenth, President Johnson referred the case to the Attorney General with an affirmative recommendation.[22] The pardon was issued that day, eight days after the Arkansas legislature convened.

### BRIGADIER GENERAL ALBERT PIKE
Letter of Petition: June 24, 1865
Pardoned: April 23, 1866

Albert Pike was one of the outstanding men in Arkansas before the Civil War. Born in Boston, Massachusetts, in 1809, he had come to Fort Smith in 1832 *via* Sante Fe. His breadth of experience and versatility of talents marked him as no ordinary man. For a time he taught school near Van Buren, anonymously writing articles and letters for Whig newspapers in his free moments.[23] In 1834, he was admitted to the Arkansas Bar and became the owner of the *Little Rock Advocate,* a Whig publication, in 1835.[24] His literary talents were evident early, and he continued to show strong interest in literature and scholarship throughout his life. He became something of a romantic poet, although at least one critic felt he did not fulfill the promise of his youth.[25] In fairness to his talent, however, it should be remembered that some of his poetry was published in *Blackwood's Magazine*, a British literary periodical of the day.[26]

He was attorney for the Real Estate Bank during the period of trustee control, and at that time performed an important role in the management of the affairs of the institution.[27] In 1850, he joined the Masonic fraternity and found there an interest of great importance to him for the remainder of his life. During the years to come he would attain the highest ranks of Masonry and become an authority on Masonic law and symbolism.[28]

Pike viewed the Civil War as a war for sovereignty and rights of the states. Although he believed in the right of secession under extreme circumstances, he had not favored its use in 1861; but when forced by necessity, he chose to go with his sister states. He accepted an appointment as Indian Commissioner and under that authority signed treaties with the Civilized Tribes stating that their warriors should not go out of their country. At the same time he insisted that the "wild bands" must not take up arms. In October, 1861, he became Brigadier General Pike in command of the Indian Country.[29] Protesting the action of Confederate authorities who failed to honor the treaty provisions mentioned above, he resigned his commission in June, 1862, at which time he became Judge of the Arkansas Supreme Court.[30] During this interim he endured the hostility of those who suspected him of disloyalty to the South.

On June 24, 1865, Pike wrote to President Johnson. His literary ability did not fail him as he presented his case. The letter conveyed the "manly but respectful frankness" its author intended. Although some of its content was unusual to be in a petition for pardon, the use of language was masterful, and the letter thoroughly persuasive. Making little of his claims to clemency, he proceeded to list them. Originally favoring the Union, he had only reluctantly exercised what he believed to be a right rather than an act of treason. Rather than accept military usurpation, he had resigned his commission, and he had always condemned all irregular kinds of warfare. Rather than attempt escape, he had returned east of the Mississippi and now presented himself for the President's judgment.[31]

Turning to the matter of allegiance, he considered the new circumstances without equivocation:

> I accept without reservation, that construction of the Constitution against which I contended. The war has hit home a little sooner that which the irresistible influences of Time were affecting. Power is as legitimate a source of government as contract. For the future, the States compose one Nation, and the Constitution of its government is enacted by the will of a Majority of the American people. Voluntarily accepting the Constitution as thus expounded, I have sworn to support it, and I will loyally keep the oath and bear true allegiance, I accept the decision as final, and shall never seek to disturb it.

As Pike wrote, his property was under threat of confiscation, a development which he was willing to endure, but he asked the President to spare his books, for he "need not tell him *how* dear the books of a scholar are to him, nor why."

Personal considerations behind him, Pike took the offensive to enter a plea opposing harsh reprisals against ex-Confederates:

> If convicted and sentenced, none now accused will feel, nor will the people of the South believe, that they have been guilty of Treason. Neither defeat nor

condemnation changes convictions. They will not seem to have atoned with their lives for the sin of failure, in assertion of rights, claimed, even if unreal by many States and by a great political party, since the beginning of the Government.

The President could immortalize himself by the use of mercy rather than follow those of his advisers, actually his worst enemies, who urged him to "use the hand of justice."

The sixth exception in President Johnson's Amnesty Proclamation barred persons who had engaged in any form of illegal treatment of Federal troops.[32] Rumor had been broadcast that Indians under Pike's command, and with his approval, had scalped Union soldiers. As a consequence, Pike was thought of as a vile and inhuman Rebel. Until the falseness of this rumor could be established, his pardon could not be expected. That Pike had been "belied" was argued by one of his Masonic brothers reporting an eyewitness account of an execution, ordered by Pike, of an Indian guilty of scalping.[33] On August 4, 1865, Pike himself submitted an affidavit pertaining to his military service and Indian relations.[34] The negative associations connected with his name persisted, however, and, when added to his military rank and property holdings, served to delay his pardon.

The importance of his position in the Masonic Order was a major factor in obtaining his pardon. Endorsement by fourteen Masonic Brothers in Memphis pleading for his pardon accompanied his petition to the President.[35] In addition, the Commissioner of Public Building in Washington, a Mason, wrote several letters in his behalf.[36] A memorial to the President signed by numerous Masons came from New York pleading for mercy and toleration in granting the pardon.[37] Delay continued and, prompted by proceedings against his Arkansas property, Pike wrote his Masonic Brother, B.B. French, in December that perhaps it was the proper season to press upon the President his need for pardon, for soon he would have no property remaining.[38] These efforts resulted in a parole for him, allowing him to return home without molestation, but not with a full pardon.

In April, 1866, Tal P. Shaffner wrote a letter marked "private," requesting the Attorney General to take action in Pike's case:

I am very anxious to have Albert Pike pardoned. He has a parole, full and protective, but a pardon is necessary for many reasons. Our Supreme Council of the highest degrees of Masonry is now in session, and it complicates many of us to sit in that body presided over by one who occupies Pike's position politically. We have nothing to do with politics, but we have in our midst some who do not conscientiously feel at liberty to meet in a body presided over by an officer tainted politically.

Please ask the President to grant the pardon.[39]

Figure 5.      Albert Pike
               Robert W. Johnson

Two days after this was written the President ordered a warrant for the pardon, and the following day, April 23, 1866, Pike was a pardoned man.[40]

He became editor of the Memphis *Daily Appeal* and argued in his editorial columns for a new party comprised of conservative men opposed to radicalism and Negro suffrage. By February, 1868, he had given up hopes for his new party and supported the Democratic organization.[41] Moving to Washington later, he joined Robert W. Johnson in a law partnership. There he was recognized as a superior lawyer, but practiced under the disadvantage of his Southern affiliation.[42] Prejudice against his having been a Rebel caused him to move to Alexandria, Virginia, in 1874, in search of a more congenial domicile.[43].

Echoes from the Rector land survey in Arkansas early in the nineteenth century were heard as Pike represented Henry M. Rector in his claim for the Hot Springs before the Supreme Court in 1876. Rector had inherited this claim from his father, Elias Rector, in 1822, when the former was a boy of six.[44] Litigation over the claim had intermittently dragged on through the years until actively resumed in 1870.[45] Pike argued the case before the Court in January 1876, and the decision, refusing Rector's claim, was handed down on April twenty-fourth.[46] Pike's disappointment over the decision was great, for he remained convinced he had won the argument. The Hot Springs were too valuable for an individual to own, the law notwithstanding, and this was the reason for the verdict of the Court.[47] Pike continued to point to this decision as reason for his lack of funds in future years, as he devoted himself to work for Masonry, his chief interest after the Civil War.

## SENATOR ROBERT W. JOHNSON
### Letter of Petition: June 27, 1865
### Pardoned: April 23, 1866

Adjectives descriptive of an ante-bellum planter aristocrat could be more appropriately used for Robert W. Johnson than for most any other man in Arkansas during the decade of the 1850's. One writer saw him as the most outstanding leader in Arkansas during the ten years prior to the Civil War.[48] His family connections, which made him an important figure in Arkansas politics, resulted in his being elected United States Senator in 1855. His economic position was equal to his social. By 1850 he was the owner of fifty-seven slaves, and by 1860 he had accumulated an estate between $700,000 and $800,000, which brought him an annual income exceeding $50,000.[49] His social views were similar to those of John C. Calhoun. He feared the dominance of majority rule and was sensitive to anything which endangered the interests of his section.[50]

With the approach of the Civil War, he became one of the leading spokesmen favoring secession and was opposed to the loss of rights through "submission." When the Secession Convention chose delegates to the Provisional Congress in Montgomery, Alabama, Robert W. Johnson was the only delegate sent who belonged to the original secessionist group.[51]   Later he was elected Senator in the Confederate Congress and served the state in that capacity during the war.

As the Civil War approached its conclusion, Johnson, with his family and slaves, went to Texas, considering for a time an exile in Mexico.[52]   Rejecting this course, he sent a letter of surrender to Major General Gordon Granger, Commander of the District of Texas, on June 19, 1865.  In surrendering to the United States authorities, he expressed the hope of being treated as a prisoner in a manner due his rank as a gentleman.[53]   From General Granger he received a temporary parole as he continued to live in Marlin Falls County, Texas, near Galveston.

On June twenty-seventh, he petitioned President Andrew Johnson for pardon.  His letter was free of embellishment and reflected an acceptance of circumstances as left by the outcome of the war.  He would leave his future to the judgment of the President, relying on his political and personal knowledge of the petitioner to grant him justice.[54]   General Granger's endorsement testified to Johnson's motives of good faith.[55]

Weeks passed without affirmative response from the President.  Johnson then sought assistance from other sources in obtaining the pardon.  He wrote Preston King, former Senator from New York, with whom he had served on a Senate military committee in the 1850's.[56]   Perhaps unknown to Johnson, King was now Collector of Customs in New York City, having been recently appointed by the President.[57]   William H. Seward was rejected by Johnson as an appropriate correspondent because of his cabinet position, but he hoped that King would show Seward his letter and expected the Secretary ot State to remember him with kind feelings.[58]

In this letter, which could not be read without enlisting pity for its author, Johnson declared himself bankrupt in a strange area and unable to make a living. Having freed his slaves, he was making plans to send them back to their old homes on the Arkansas River, where they thought they could be happy.  He had considered them members of his family, but now they would go in the care of his twenty-three-year-old son, who would help them as much as he could, but then must cut loose from Negroes and turn toward his profession, the law.

Johnson's own hopes were to go to New Orleans and begin a legal practice to support his wife and children.  An absence of twenty years from legal practice, plus the civil-law system in Louisiana, would prove to be barriers he had to overcome, but try he must, if he could secure the necessary pardon.  He hoped King would help him obtain the document.

Three days later, August nineteenth, Johnson wrote King again.  The content of that letter seemed more for emphasis than to transmit additional information.

(Perhaps it was insurance against the unreliability of communications.) His economic resources could see him through the fall, but beyond that he could see no future.[59]  He urged King to confer with Seward and see if they could not help him secure a pardon in order that he might go to work.

On September twenty-fifth, King sent Johnson's letter to the President, and three days later the case was referred to the Attorney General.  Again, on October second, King sent the President a letter from Robert W. Johnson (perhaps his second letter).[60]  One item which might have delayed the completion of pardon procedure was the absence of an endorsement from the Governor or Arkansas.  This was supplied on October twenty-eighth, as Isaac Murphy recommended Johnson's pardon.[61]  On November eighth, a Presidential parole was granted to him.[62]

After his parole, irregular proceedings against some of his Arkansas property were initiated.  By prompt and energetic action he was able to stop these measures, but not without some anxious weeks during March and April, 1866, as he tried to salvage what small portion of his ante-bellum holdings he could.

On April 23, 1866, Robert W. Johnson was pardoned by the President.[63]  He was never able to return to a position comparable to that which he enjoyed prior to the Civil War.  Moving to Washington, D.C., he joined Albert Pike in a law partnership, where he quietly practiced his profession.  In 1878, he made one effort to return to public life in Arkansas, but that ended in failure.[64]

### SENATOR AUGUSTUS H. GARLAND
Letter of Petition: June 28, 1865
Pardoned: July 15, 1865

As one turns from the experiences of Senator Robert W. Johnson to consider those of Senator Augustus H. Garland, the contrast is impressive.  Instead of requiring ten months, as in Johnson's case, Garland's pardon was completed in seventeen days.  Instead of destroying his social and economic position, the Civil War and Reconstruction lifted Garland to the highest position held by an Arkansan in the national government.[65]  Writers have been puzzled by the consistency with which circumstances seemed to work for his advantage.  Was he lucky, cunning, astute, or expedient?

One contemporary found a major part of his greatness in a "wonderful versatility of talent and accommodating sentiment."[66]  A later writer noted his capacity for work and "a happy faculty of adjusting himself to conditions."[67]  In the hands of a smaller man his actions might have appeared very opportunistic; however, there was a finesse and a political mastery in the manner in which he conducted himself that made the critic pause before pronouncing judgment.

In 1833, when he was one year old, Garland came to Arkansas with his

parents who left Tennessee and settled in the southwestern county of
Hempstead. After the death of his father, his mother married Judge Francis
Hubbard, under whose influence Garland read law and was admitted to the Bar
in 1853.[68] As a young man of twenty-four, he entered into law partnership in
Little Rock with Ebenezer Cummings, who had a large practice but whose health
was declining. In March, 1857, approximately one year after forming the
partnership, Cummings died, leaving this established practice to the young Gar-
land. Cases inherited from this practice gave him experience in the United States
Supreme Court prior to the Civil War, which proved of importance for *Ex parte
Garland* in 1867.[69]

His politics were those of an old-line Whig, but he was perhaps more flexible
and politic than most of his fellow Whigs.[70] In the secession crisis he offered
himself as a Union delegate and was elected by a majority of 557 votes.[71] With
the shift from Union to secessionist sentiment in the state after Lincoln's call for
troops, Garland voted for secession and received the largest number of votes as
one of the five delegates sent to the Provisional Congress at Montgomery.[72] He
served as Representative in the Confederate Congress until 1864, when, upon the
death of Senator Charles B. Mitchell, September 18, 1864, he was elected
Senator.[73]

The lawyer Garland was in command as he petitioned President Johnson for
pardon, June 28, 1865. The letter, written in the third person, was characteristic of the technique and brilliance of his ability as a lawyer. Reminding the
President of his being a Union delegate to the Secession Convention, Garland
pointed to the criticisms and abuse he had endured from secessionists prior to
his vote for secession on May sixth. On that day the majority of the Union in
the state was at least 15,000, he thought, but the hysteria of the moment made
resistance impossible, and Union men in the Convention had gone with that tide
in order to modify its force and return the state to friendly relations with the
Union at some future time. It was this hope of correcting evils in the future
which had motivated Garland in his own vote. His positions held later in the
Confederate government were based on election by this conservative element in
the state, the "ultra" party continuously opposing his election. He had merely
performed the duties of his offices, exercising a moderating influence whenever
he could.[74]

When he saw the war coming to a victorious conclusion for the Union, he left
his seat in the Confederate Senate in February, 1865, and came to Arkansas to
aid in the restoration of peace and an early return of the state to the Union. He
served as an emissary for Governor Flanagin to General Reynolds, seeking terms
for restoring peace.[75] About May twenty-second, he had drawn up an application for pardon, but this did not meet the requirements as stated in the
President's Amnesty Proclamation of the twenty-ninth; therefore, he applied to
take the amnesty oath, but was refused again because instructions for adminis-

tering the provisions of that proclamation had not yet reached the proper officials in Arkansas. He now attached his oath to this petition and sought a restoration of his rights through pardon. Once this pardon had been granted, he would encourage others to pledge their allegiance to the United States government.[76]

The thoroughness and effectiveness with which Garland prepared his case were impressive. In selecting those whose endorsements would accompany his petition, he further strengthened his argument and was able to appear before the President as a man whose pardon was needed immediately *for the benefit of the Union.* Elisha Baxter and William M. Fishback, who had been elected United States Senators in May, 1864, only to be refused their seats in the Senate, were among his witnesses.[77] Powell Clayton, then Brigadier General in the Union Army, and later to be Garland's adversary during Reconstruction, recommended his pardon.[78] Even General J.J. Reynolds, who was anything but generous in his recommendations for pardon, noted that, "universal good feeling and sympathy prevail in this community for Mr. Garland, and if any one who has occupied the positions that he has, can be pardoned, Mr. Garland is a fit subject for such clemency." Still, the General would withhold the elective franchise until after the state election in August, 1868.[79]

The editor of the *National Democrat,* C.V. Meador, earnestly recommended Garland's pardon, as did Robert J.T. White, the Secretary of State.[80] E.W. Gantt, an ex-Confederate who turned against the Southern cause as its future began to wane in 1863, and whose denouncements of things Southern had given him an exaggerated position in the eyes of Northern newspapers, joined the ranks of Garland's advocates.[81] In a letter to Secretary of State William H. Seward, he pointed out that "though holding an office in the Confederacy, he [Garland] represented that conservative sentiment which never lost sight of an ultimate return to the Union. . . . his pardon at this time would have a most salutary effect."[82]

Although Isaac Murphy had been generous in giving his endorsement to Arkansans seeking pardon, the wording in his endorsement of Garland was unusually strong as he recommended his unconditional pardon.[83] Judge Henry C. Caldwell, Federal District Judge in Arkansas, wrote a letter in Garland's behalf to the Secretary of Interior, James Harlan. That letter was carried to Washington by Garland and presented to the Secretary in person. Mr. Harlan then wrote a letter to the President on July tenth, testifying to the "practical sense and superior judgment" of Judge Caldwell and to the willingness with which he would follow the judge's advice.[84]

The collective effect of the testimony of these witnesses was enough to win Garland's case. On July 15, 1865, by special order of the President, Augustus H. Garland obtained an unconditional pardon.[85] This early post-war victory placed him in a position which ultimately led to *Ex parte Garland* by January,

Figure 6.     Augustus H. Garland
              David Walker

1867. The reputation he acquired from that success aided his election the following month as United States Senator from Arkansas.


COLONEL DAVID WALKER
Letter of Petition: September 14, 1865
Pardoned: October 9, 1865

Following the Secession Convention, David Walker returned to his home on the west fork of the White River. There the fortunes of war caught him in the middle, and as the contending forces swept across his area, his farm was laid waste.[86] The hostility bred by war could be seen reflected in a letter from a Union officer informing Walker that he could return to his home, and denying that Union troops were "thieves" or "marauders" or that the Union Army wanted his "Niggers or other property."[87] In various ways, the rising prominence of the Negro question served to alienate Walker from his natural devotion to the Union and ultimately influenced him in becoming an ardent advocate of Confederate victory.

In 1860, Walker had occupied an enviable position among men of northwestern Arkansas. Coming to Fayetteville in 1830, when the population there could be counted in six or eight families, he had, according to his testimony, only $2.75 in his pockets.[88] But over the years he had grown with the area, achieving a reputation as a lawyer, accumulating land as a farmer, and receiving recognition as a leader in public affairs. From 1833 to 1835 he served as prosecuting attorney. He represented his people as delegate to the Constitutional Convention in 1836 and as their state senator in the third and fourth General Assemblies (1840--1843). In 1844, he ran unsuccessfully against Archibald Yell as Whig candidate for Congress. After serving as an associate justice of the Arkansas Supreme Court from 1849 to 1855, he happily retired from public life to his farm and law practice during the years prior to the Civil War.[89]

Living in the most commodious house in his area, which overlooked a thousand-acre farm along the west fork of the White River three miles east of Fayetteville, Walker spent some of the happiest years of his life between 1855 and 1860.[90] His letters reflected the love of a farmer for his land as he spoke of crops of wheat, rye, corn, and fruit, especially apples, grown on his farm. Stock raising in hogs and cattle also held his interest as he spoke of his son's taking 432 head of cattle to the Kansas market, leaving 126 at home to replenish the herd.[91] Manpower for these farming operations was furnished by Walker's twenty-three slaves. The extent of his estate was indicated by the census enumerator, when he reported $50,000 real property and $40,000 personal property for David Walker in 1860.[92]

Retirement from public life did not end his interest in political affairs. The demise of the Whig party, however, left him as an observer without a party. Until May, 1860, he maintained a neutral position regarding the conflict between Democrats and Republicans. In a direct issue over slavery between Black Republicans and Democrats he would take the side of the Democrats without hesitation, although his relation to the infidel Republicans would be as a monk rather than as a crusader. But the question of slavery was not an issue among the Whigs, Americans, or Democrats in Arkansas, and his Whig background made the Democrats abhorrent to him. Nationally, that party was corrupt from longevity in positions of power; its platform was inscribed with the Kentucky and Virginia Resolutions and was permeated with the Calhoun construction of the Constitution. Locally, the Democrats had mismanaged the internal improvement, seminary, and swamp-land funds as well as the banks. If these objections were not enough, he was convinced that the leading Democrats were committed to dissolving the Union.[93]

By early May, Walker was ready to marshal Union forces of his area in opposition to the growing sentiment for disunion in the state. With the approach of the election of 1860, he and others still among "the corporals guard of Old Whigs" became increasingly active in behalf of the Constitutional Union party candidates, Bell and Everett.[94]  Putting aside his personal preferences for a private life based on his law practice and agricultural interests, he was carried by events into the Secession Convention as a Union delegate, became its president, and ultimately voted for secession for the sake of state unity.

Following the Convention, Walker went to Fayetteville and remained there through the fall of 1862.[95]  Exactly when or why he left is not known; however, three factors were probable influences on his thinking during this period. First, after the Battle of Prairie Grove (ten miles southwest of Fayetteville) on December 7, 1862, the Southern army retreated from that area of the state. With that army was his son, Charles W. Walker.[96]  Secondly, the unsettled loyalties of the time made Walker vulnerable to marauders from whatever source if he remained at home.[97]  A third factor was the threat to part of his property after January 1, 1863, represented by Lincoln's Emancipation Proclamation.

Leaving northwestern Arkansas, he went to Lewisburg, located in the Arkansas River valley some forty miles northwest of Little Rock. This geographic move indicated a political change as well, for he accepted a commission as Colonel of the Cavalry and Judge of the Military Court in the Confederate Army, May 1, 1863.[98]  That his experiences had changed his outlook was evident as he contemplated the future. He committed his thoughts to paper for future reference as he wrote the following in his notebook, May 26, 1863:

Whatever may have been the policy of the Federal Government at the outset, there can *now* be no doubt but that it is its fixed and settled purpose to free the negroes and to settle them permanently in the slave holding states, to assert and maintain for them equal legal and political rights with the white population. To secure this end, they will appoint civil officers to administer the laws, until the negro and abolition vote is sufficiently strong to elect to office their representative men. Most of the prominent Southern men would at once be arrested and imprisoned, after which a proclamation would likely be issued pardoning all such as give in their allegiance to the old government. Stringent laws touching treason and rebellion will be passed and the Federal Courts charged to enforce them. Under these laws they will proceed to arrest, imprison, try and execute the prominent and true men of the South and to confiscate their property until every brave spirited man will be cut down.

With negroes and white men promiscuously acting as witnesses, jurors, sheriffs and judges, an appeal to the courts for redress would be nonsense. Yankee adventurers will come in immense numbers to take possession of our vacant confiscated lands, and to stimulate the courts and assassins to vacate others. Our cotton fields are to be cultivated by free negro labour under the superintendence of abolition landlords or their agents, for the exclusive use of the Northern manufacturers.

Such in my opinion is substantially the policy of the Federal Government, one which they have contemplated and fixed upon in detail as above. And I have recorded them for future reflection.[99]

To consider Walker's point of view exclusively in terms of his apprehension of Federal policies regarding the Negro would be unjust. His conservatism was not so monolithic as that. He was also concerned about the future of civil government and constitutional rights in wartime as Southern people came to embrace military government as an alternate to chaos.[100] Gradually, he identified reunion with subjugation and believed there could be no protection from the prejudices of the Northern populace, who were flushed with success and who would demand punishment and indemnity. Therefore, he was pushed to a position strongly opposing surrender, for he wanted "a government in which our persons, property and rights will be in our own hands." He could not "trust these to others, least of all to the Federal States."[101]

He went to southwest Arkansas with the Confederate government following the surrender of Little Rock, September 10, 1863. As the prospects for that government faded, he continued to write of victory and resistance to the idea of surrender. In April, 1864, he could talk of regaining the whole state in thirty days and knocking "the Lincoln Arkansas government into a cocked hat."[102] Perhaps his apprehensions of the future were closing in by January, 1865, as he turned toward writing a short autobiography for his daughter.[103] Near the end of Confederate days in Arkansas, he wrote that a gunboat was in the Red River demanding surrender and that a council was then in progress between the generals and state officers to decide the question. He hoped they would not surrender, for in his view that meant becoming a conquered territory at the mercy of popular feeling in the North.[104]

In the closing hours of the Confederacy in Arkansas, Walker left Lewisville and became a refugee in Texas. The morning he departed he wrote a note to his friend and judicial colleague, George C. Watkins, who had chosen to return to his home in Little Rock. He had given Watkins a letter to Governor Isaac Murphy, which he now instructed him to destroy. But Watkins, using discretion born of their friendship, disregarded the request and presented Walker's letter to the Governor. Murphy was pleased to receive it and assured Watkins he would do all he could to help Walker.[105]

Writing Walker in July, Watkins told of his own arrest for treason upon his return to Little Rock and various harassments he had endured since then. Doubtless there was such an indictment against Walker awaiting his return, but Watkins continued to feel that Walker should have gone home the latter part of May rather than to Texas. The thing to do now was to get his application for special pardon to the President and pay back taxes on his property. Once he had done these things, Walker's position would be much better than his own, for the burden of debt was still heavy for Watkins.

On September 14, 1865, David Walker submitted his petition for pardon to the President. After reviewing his political background and Union sympathies, he gave three reasons for accepting his commission in the Confederate Army. The contending armies had laid waste his farm, removing his livelihood. The President, in Walker's judgment, had violated his constitutional rights in the Emancipation Proclamation. And Walker's sons were in the Confederate Army. His property before the war was worth over $20,000, but could not be sold for that now.[106]

Although Walker had known Isaac Murphy for thirty years, his circumstances led him to have Augustus H. Garland represent him in asking the Governor for an endorsement of his petition to the President. When the request was presented, Murphy enjoyed a moment of levity by pretending reluctance to give the endorsement. Judge Walker had been old enough to know better than to join the Rebel army and support its cause so actively. He should have stayed at home. Garland failed to see the humor and turned to go, but was called back. Murphy said to Garland as he signed the paper, "the Government must do something to prevent another rebellion! Now pardoning the head leaders is a bad way to begin."[107] Whether composed by Garland or Murphy, the endorsement of Walker was very strong, asking for an immediate and full pardon.[108] On October 9, 1865, such unqualified pardon was granted to David Walker.[109]

Perhaps anticipating the forthcoming election in the summer of 1866, Murphy wrote Walker in May, asking that he use his influence to prevent party and sectional agitation. He felt these should be avoided as if they were wild beasts. He hoped Walker would struggle against his despondent feelings, interest himself in the prosperity of the state, and cultivate kind feelings among the people. He advised letting political affairs in Washington pass without much

David Walker
J. J. Clendenin
F. W. Compton

*Gazette,* October 9, 1866, p. 3, c. 1.

**Figure 7.    Supreme Court Justice Election, 1866**

comment, for "our position there depends, on our behavior *here*—If we establish justice at home we can demand it with a good face, abroad. If we secure to all the good citizens of the state equal rights—the state is sure to obtain her just rights—"[110]

Walker offered himself as a candidate for Justice of the Arkansas Supreme Court that summer. His friend, John R. Eakin, editor of the *Washington Telegraph,* supported his candidacy by claiming it to be simple justice to remember the public services of such a man by granting Walker this judicial honor.[111] In the August election Walker led in a field of outstanding men and became Chief Justice of the Arkansas Supreme Court that fall.

# PART TWO

## DE JURE v. DE FACTO GOVERNMENT

# CHAPTER FOUR

# THE PROBLEM STATED

*... in the civil war just closed, there was but one great political question at issue, which was as to the power of the state to dissolve its connection with the national government—in which, by a conflict in arms, it has been settled that such power does not exist. That is the question, and the only question settled. In all other respects the compact remains just as it was previous to the war, and this change is but a change in the construction of a compact. The powers of the two governments, state and federal, remain the same—the rights of the people the same.*

*The national government, then, must exist, and that too, under the provisions of the constitution, in war as well as in peace; and if it must exist, it cannot destroy the state governments, which are indispensably essential to its existence. Nor can a state government be altered or changed by the federal government; nor can it rightfully compel the people of a state to make any change in their local government, because, by such compulsion, the act, in effect, would be the act of the federal government, not of the state.*[1]

In the May term of the Pulaski Circuit Court, 1861, Jacob Hawkins brought action against Lemuel M. Filkins to recover $450 owed him from a promissory note. The action was continued until the September term, at which time Hawkins received a judgment in his favor. On July 24, 1865, an execution based on this judgment was issued and a lien placed on Filkins' property to satisfy the debt. Filkins took action to stay and quash this judgment on the grounds that there was no valid judgment on record against him, for there had been no legal court held in Pulaski County in September, 1861. The judgment was, therefore, void.[2]

The question had been resolved in favor of Filkins before coming to the Arkansas Supreme Court during its December term of 1866. There, the decision of the lower court was reversed, and the debt had to be honored. But the legal significance of the case was to be found in the question of whether the judicial decisions, laws, and contracts under the Arkansas government during the Civil War were valid in the post-war period. What had the act of secession done to the state government and its institutions? What effect did the Constitution of 1864 have on the government under the Constitution of 1861? The importance of these questions enlisted two of the best legal minds in Little Rock, U.M. Rose and Augustus H. Garland, who argued for the validity of legal actions executed under the Arkansas Confederate government.[3]   Chief Justice David Walker rendered the decision, which he later judged to be among the most important of his career.[4]

Using an historical interpretation of the Constitution, Walker based his conclusions on the compact theory of the Union and on the existence of dual sovereignty between the two governments. As was indicated above, the Civil War had settled one question only, that of secession; in other respects the Union was exactly as it had been prior to the war. Nor could the Federal government alter a state government as it would a conquered territory, or compel the people to change their government, for this would exceed its authority. The war had not given the national government powers it had not possessed in 1860, for the Constitution defined those powers in wartime as well as in peace.[5]   The Arkansas government under the Constitution of 1861 was a continuation of the government established in 1836 and was altered by the Constitution of 1864 only in those matters in conflict with the United States Constitution; therefore, its legal institutions were valid, as well as continuous, and must be recognized.[6]

Judge Walker's decision may be taken as a statement of the nature of *de jure* government in Arkansas after the Civil War. Except for the abolishment of slavery and abandonment of the "right of secession," no fundamental changes in the ante-bellum government were recognized as being legitimate. From this point of view, the Reconstruction government under the Republicans from 1868 to 1874 could be seen only as a *de facto* regime and its establishment considered in terms of *de jure* v. *de facto* government. The chances of that regime's winning *de jure* recognition from the majority were never large; however, mistakes made by that government lessened those which did exist. The *de facto* character of the situation created a problem for men such as David Walker and A.H. Garland. Should they hold to their principles and refuse to participate in what they considered an illegitimate government, or should they accept the *de facto* nature of the situation and watch for opportunities to overthrow the Republican regime? If the latter course were taken, what means did that end justify? The following chapters will consider David Walker as he faced those choices; Augustus H. Garland will be the subject of two chapters on *de jure* v. *de facto* government.

In 1866, Chief Justice Walker, a man of sixty, could look back on a life closely identified with his section and one important to the development of his state. Indeed, few studies could be made of Arkansas between 1830 and 1878 without encountering his name.  As the preceding pages have indicated, his public life touched many of the significant phases of state history from territorial days through secession.  His importance as a leader among north-western conservatives continued during Reconstruction.  When Governor Garland sought a man to represent Arkansas at the Philadelphia Centennial Exposition in 1876, he could scarcely have made a more appropriate choice than David Walker.

It might be argued, however, that Walker is not an appropriate subject as a Reconstruction figure, for after his removal from the Supreme Court in 1868, he did not hold public office again until he was elected Associate Justice in 1874. Furthermore, according to one biographical account, he consistently refused to take the oath and become a registered voter.[7]  But if considered in terms of influence, Walker would rank very high in importance.  There is much truth in the statement of one writer that a collection containing all of Walker's correspondence would provide significant material for a history of the state.[8]  His ante-bellum career was most influential in forming his attitudes toward the Reconstruction government, as will be seen.

On April 15, 1867, Governor Isaac Murphy was directed by Brevet Major General E.O.C. Ord, Commander of the Fourth Military District, to inform the members of the Arkansas legislature that their reassembling on July eighth would be in conflict with recently passed acts of Congress.[9]  Thus setting aside the legislature, General Ord began the major transformations of Arkansas government under Reconstruction.  As the spring and summer passed, apprehensions were great among conservative men about additional interference with civil offices. Judge F.W. Compton wrote Walker about these fears in May, but took comfort in the hope that the moderate character of General Ord would spare them the worst elements of military despotism.[10]  John R. Eakin, a member of the legislature, regretted that some protest had not been made by that body, for the world would not know whether to blame Governor Murphy or General Ord for this outrage.  He felt that the only hope now lay in the judiciary and the moral force it could exercise.  Therefore, he hoped that the decisions of the Supreme Court would be allowed to stand and that Walker and his colleagues would be allowed to retain their offices.[11]

The justices were anxious about their positions also, as Judge J.J. Clendenin indicated in a letter to Walker, July thirty-first. There had been rumors in regard to removal which he had discounted, but the previous night he had learned that the state printer had received orders for blank commissions with the ironclad oath printed on them. Could this mean that all state officers were to be required to take the Oath or be removed?[12] Adding pertinence to this possibility was the announcement two days earlier that any officer trying to obstruct acts of Congress would be removed.[13]  Hearing of further efforts to bring about their

Figure 8.      Harris Flanagin
               Isaac Murphy

removal, Judge Clendenin wrote General Ord on August sixteenth denying any disloyalty or interference with Reconstruction under the acts of Congress on his part or by his colleagues, Justices Compton and Walker.[14]

Removal, however, was not the method used to deal with the judicial system. Instead, from September, 1867 to January, 1868, limitation on or substitution for civil jurisdiction, especially in serious crimes involving colored and white persons, was employed to assure justice for all citizens. Usually this meant substituting trial by military commission for trial in the civil courts.[15] During this period of restricted jurisdiction an executive decision permanently forbade payment to civil officers or others under authority of Walker's decision in *Hawkins v. Filkins.*[16]

Beginning in May and continuing throughout the summer and early fall, registration of voters for the forthcoming convention election proceeded.[17] In this registration the problem of *de jure* v. *de facto* government was faced for the first time during Reconstruction by men with social views similar to those of David Walker. His editor friend, John R. Eakin, who continued to advise his readers against registration, lamented the lonesomeness of that position in southwest Arkansas. Most men hoped to defeat the radicals at the polls, and principles relating to *de jure* government seemed far removed from the political realities of the day. Indeed, Eakin felt that men who had been original secessionists had never really forgiven the Union men who had been reluctant to join the secessionist ranks and consequently rejected advice from them now. But whatever the cost, he would hold to his position calling for a restoration of the Constitution and hope for a reaction against the Republicans to bring men to that position. In the meantime, he would withhold his recognition of the legitimacy of Reconstruction policies.[18]

On September twenty-sixth, General Ord issued the order which declared registration complete and established conditions for the election.[19] Voting would begin on the first Tuesday in November and continue until completed. The electorate of registered voters would vote "For Convention" or "Against Convention" and for the candidate of their choice should a convention be held. Delegates to the Convention were apportioned as nearly as possible according to the registration. From the point of view of Congressional Reconstruction, this was an equitable procedure for establishing the new government. Under the influence of social conditions in the state, however, the execution of this plan resulted in an inequitable distribution of registered voters and, consequently, an unjust apportionment. Ironically, those portions of the state which had been *least* inclined toward secession in 1861 were now to be penalized *most* under the new government. In order to understand the impact of this system on the state, one must recall something of the original construction of the state government.

The sectional nature of Arkansas found major expression in the initial formation of the state government. Social forces and individuals representing them came into conflict over the determination of legislative apportionment established by the Constitution of 1836. The northwestern highlands contained a small number of slaves and was, therefore, in favor of having representation based on free white male inhabitants. The southern and eastern lowlands, with large numbers of slaves in the population, advocated apportionment based on three-fifths of the slaves plus the white male population. These positions were discussed as a part of the campaign for delegates to the Constitutional Convention of 1836. In that Convention the argument continued as Absalom Fowler and David Walker, delegates from Washington County, became spokesmen for the northwestern area and James H. Walker, delegate from Hempstead County, for the southeastern areas.[20]

A district system based on areas of approximately equal white male population was proposed by the plantation areas after the three-fifths plan had not been well received. But David Walker and the northwestern delegates were able to win considerable concessions from their southeastern opponents. Out of a joint committee of representatives from the two areas (members of which included both Walkers), a compromise system was devised which ultimately became the basis for legislative representation.[21]

The senate was organized on a district system based on free white male inhabitants, each senator representing an equal number in so far as possible. A county system based upon free white male inhabitants, but assuring at least one representative for each county, was to provide the apportionment for the lower house. Every four years an enumeration was to be made to keep the apportionment current with population developments.[22] Thus the advocates of apportionment based on white male inhabitants had largely won the contest. On January 1, 1838, the first enumeration was to take place. Until that time, the representation in the northwest would be 32 1/3 legislators; in the delta, 22 1/2; and in the southwest, 13 5/6. Pulaski County would send 2 1/3.

By 1860 this system had resulted in the northwest's having 46%, the delta 28%, and the southwest 26% of the representation in the state legislature.[23] This rather accurately reflected the distribution of white population in the state. When registration of voters occurred in 1867 and 1868, a new basis for representation was presented which offered an unacceptable alternative to many men. The old system based on the principle of apportionment according to white adult male inhabitants was being superseded by another based on the principle of apportionment according to registered voters. The effects of this latter system were to add perhaps unintended burdens to the possibility of accepting Congressional Reconstruction as a *de jure* government.

The Convention election, which began the first Tuesday in November and lasted until December fifth, was based on an official return of 66,805 registered voters.[24] The distribution of those voters was important, for apportionment of representation in the Convention would be based on that registration. With approximately 40% of the adult male population, the northwest had 29.7% of the registered voters; with approximately 34%, the delta had 37.6%; and with approximately 26%, the southwest had 32.6%.[25]

## ABSTRACT OF RETURNS OF REGISTRATION
### IN THE
## STATE OF ARKANSAS,
#### UNDER THE ACT OF CONGRESS OF MARCH 23D, 1867

| COUNTIES. | Registered WHITES. | Registered COLORED. | TOTAL. | COUNTIES. | Registered WHITES. | Registered COLORED. | TOTAL. |
|---|---|---|---|---|---|---|---|
| ARKANSAS, | 498 | 1030 | 1528 | MARION, | ... | ... | 391 |
| ASHLEY, | 706 | 608 | 1314 | MISSISSIPPI, | 292 | 193 | 485 |
| BENTON, | ... | ... | 1009 | MONROE, | 525 | 551 | 1076 |
| BRADLEY, | 908 | 368 | 1276 | MONTGOMERY, | 492 | 26 | 518 |
| CALHOUN, | 422 | 184 | 606 | NEWTON, | 424 | 1 | 425 |
| CARROLL, | ... | 767 | 767 | OUACHITA, | 1084 | 870 | 1954 |
| CHICOT, | 268 | 894 | 1162 | PERRY, | ... | ... | 318 |
| CLARK, | ... | ... | 1576 | PHILLIPS, | 955 | 2681 | 3636 |
| COLUMBIA, | 1313 | 870 | 2183 | PIKE, | ... | ... | 565 |
| CONWAY, | 921 | 148 | 1069 | POINSETT, | 172 | 39 | 211 |
| CRAIGHEAD, | 522 | 41 | 563 | POLK, | 394 | 1 | 395 |
| CRAWFORD, | 704 | 147 | 851 | POPE, | ... | ... | 865 |
| CRITTENDEN, | 245 | 505 | 750 | PRAIRIE, | ... | ... | 1583 |
| CROSS, | 415 | 184 | 599 | PULASKI, | 1494 | 2402 | 3896 |
| DALLAS, | 668 | 337 | 1005 | RANDOLPH, | 848 | 59 | 907 |
| DESHA, | 231 | 592 | 823 | ST. FRANCIS, | 564 | 464 | 1028 |
| DREW, | 1081 | 576 | 1657 | SALINE, | 712 | 42 | 754 |
| FRANKLIN, | 741 | 102 | 843 | SCOTT, | 557 | 17 | 574 |
| FULTON, | ... | ... | 306 | SEARCY, | 574 | 1 | 575 |
| GREENE, | 921 | 5 | 926 | SEBASTIAN, | 1011 | 195 | 1206 |
| HEMPSTEAD, | 1307 | 1195 | 2502 | SEVIER, | 567 | 260 | 827 |
| HOT SPRING, | ... | ... | 825 | UNION, | 922 | 708 | 1630 |
| INDEPENDENCE, | 1458 | 142 | 1600 | VAN BUREN, | ... | ... | 896 |
| IZARD, | 762 | 31 | 793 | WASHINGTON, | 1813 | 81 | 1894 |
| JACKSON, | 849 | 283 | 1132 | WHITE, | 1278 | 156 | 1434 |
| JEFFERSON, | 1048 | 2733 | 3786† | WOODRUFF, | ... | ... | 1027 |
| JOHNSON, | 664 | 72 | 736 | YELL, | 731 | 150 | 881 |
| LAFAYETTE, | 560 | 931 | 1491 | | | | |
| LAWRENCE, | ... | ... | 753 | | | | |
| LITTLE RIVER, | 426 | 327 | 753 | Total, | 33,047‡ | 21,969‡ | 65,751‡ |
| MADISON, | ... | ... | 716 | | | | |

Figure 9.     Abstract of Returns of Registration

A rough estimate of adult male population in the northwest at this time indicated the possibility of there being as many as 12,000 to 15,000 unregistered men in that area.[26] Whatever the exact number, it was certain that the number of unregistered voters in the northwest far exceeded that to be found in the other two areas. One reason for this fact was the probability that larger numbers from this region had served in the Confederate Army because of the predominantly white population. Because of this service more men would have difficulty taking the oath necessary for registration. Another reason was the possibility that men expected this situation to be a temporary one and withheld participation in the hope of an overthrow of radical policies in the near future.

Perhaps many like John R. Eakin felt a principle was at stake and refused to compromise it for political expediency. But the most likely explanation for such a large number of unregistered voters in this area went back to the regional and racial nature of Arkansas politics. A registration including all adult males would place control of the government in the hands of those in control of the delta and the southwest. Just as Absalom Fowler, David Walker, and Jesse Turner had seen in 1836 that an apportionment based on total population would be detrimental to their section, so now men in the northwest could see that a government in which the radicals controlled the Negro vote in the lowland areas would bring what for them was an intolerable situation, "Negro domination."

Ironically, this lack of registration compounded their troubles and did much to confirm their apprehensions concerning radical policies, for apportionment to the Convention was based on registration. The northwest, accustomed to 46% of the representation in 1860, would receive 31.6% in the Convention of 1868.[27] That convention would draw up a constitution the features of which would further alienate men of the northwest.

The Convention election was declared completed on December fifth, the vote being 27,576 FOR Convention and 13,558 AGAINST, with approximately 24,950 registered voters not voting.[28] Georgraphical support for the Convention was rather widespread among the registered voters with only thirteen out of fifty-eight counties voting against it. In Washington and Benton counties, with 2,903 registered voters, the vote went against the Convention 1,054 to 418, but in the northwest as a region, out of 18,902 registered voters, the Convention won 6,224 to 3,640.[29]

From January seventh until February fourteenth the Convention held its sessions.[30] Constantly under editorial attack from the *Gazette*, the delegates wrote a new constitution which featured a strong executive, four-year terms of office, registration of voters, decreased representation from the northwest coupled with increased representation from the delta and southwest, political and civil equality for the Negroes, and a district system of apportionment which seemed likely to give the control of the government to those who controlled the Negro vote.[31] When it is recalled how fragmented party organization among the ante-bellum forces had become just prior to the Civil War and when allowance is made for the disorganizing effects of Congressional Reconstruction during the preceding year, it is understandable that this constitution was interpreted as a party instrument intended to create and establish dominance of the Republican party in the state while simultaneously denying party organization to their opponents. This statement does not leave out of consideration the resistance felt toward social reforms promoting Negro equality, but rather suggests that political exasperation in the face of instruments designed to perfect party organization was also an important factor in the hostility fel toward the Reconstruction government. The district system of apportionment may be taken as an illustration of such an instrument.

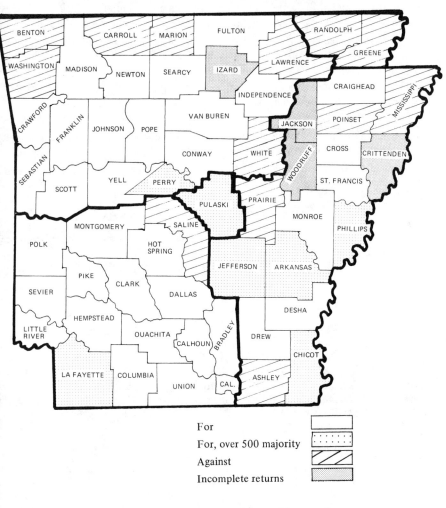

For

For, over 500 majority

Against

Incomplete returns

Calculated from: Abstract of
Returns of Election, *Debates
and Proceedings of the Arkansas
Constitutional Convention, 1868*
(Little Rock: J. G. Price, 1868),
p. 770.

Figure 10.    Constitutional Convention Election, 1867

By means of a division of the state into twenty-two districts, a system of apportionment was established patterned after the registration of voters for the Convention election.[32]    Again the northwest was affected by that small registration, and this time in a more permanent manner.   Until 1875 this apportionment would prevail; then an enumeration would be made and a new apportionment given on the basis of population.[33]    But in the meantime representation among the sections would remain 30.6% for the northwest, 38% for the delta, and 31.2% for the southwest.[34]

This apportionment could be defined as being equitable if the registration of voters were considered just, for distribution of representation was very closely related to the presence of registered voters. Choosing not to register, it could be argued, carried its own penalty, but that choice was not properly identified with the radicals.   One other characteristic of the system, however, appeared motivated by party principles rather than political idealism.  The districts were

## TABLE 1
## APPORTIONMENT STUDY BY AREA

|  | Total Population 1860[a] | Total Population 1870[b] | Gain or Loss 1860–1870 | White Population and as a Percent of Total White Population 1860[a] | White Population and as a Percent of Total White Population 1870[b] | Colored Population and as a Percent of Total Colored 1860[a] |
|---|---|---|---|---|---|---|
| NW | 165,070 | 194,547 | +29,477 | 151,365 | 184,468 | 13,583 |
| D | 133,335 | 138,242 | + 4,907 | 77,984 | 78,736 | 55,312 |
| SW | 125,346 | 120,277 | - 5,069 | 85,930 | 81,240 | 38,715 |
| TOTAL[i] | 423,751 | 453,066 | +29,315 | 315,279 | 344,444 | 107,610 |
| *% of Total* | *%* | *%* | *%* | *%* | *%* | *%* |
| NW | 39 | 43 | +17.8 | 48 | 53.5 | 12.6 |
| D | 31.5 | 30.5 | + 3.6 | 24.7 | 22.8 | 51.4 |
| SW | 29.5 | 26.5 | - 4 | 27 | 23.5 | 36 |

a.  Calculated from : U.S. Bureau of the Census, *Ninth Census: 1870. Population,* I, pp. 13–1
b.  *Ibid.*
c.  Calculated from: roster of thirteenth General Assembly (November 5, 1860 to January 2 1861) published in C.G. Hall, *Historical Report of the Secretary of State* (Little Rock: Sta of Arkansas, 1958), pp. 267–69.
d.  Calculated from: *Debates and Proceedings of the Arkansas Constitutional Convention, 18* (Little Rock, J.G. Price, 1868), p. 31.

so organized as to combine counties with a large Negro population with smaller ones in such a manner as to make probable control of the district through control of the Negro vote in one or more counties.[35]  Increasing the likelihood of such control was the election of representatives at large, a system which made it possible for all representatives to come from one or two counties within a given district.  Predominantly white districts were created in such a manner as to minimize their legislative effect.  These features led the *Gazette* to point to this system as an illustration of the unscrupulous character of the radical leaders. Perhaps these districts reflected a political dilemma faced by the Republicans at that time: they could not come into power without heavy reliance on the Negro vote, but by founding their organization so exclusively on the control of that vote, they forfeited what small possibility there was of winning *de jure* recognition as a government.

One development beyond their control, but which emphasized sectional

## TABLE 1 (CONTINUED)

| | Colored Population and as a Percent of Total Colored Population | Representation | Representation Constitutional Convention | Representation Legislature | Male Citizens 21 and Over | Representation Democratic State Convention | Representation Constitution of 1874 |
|---|---|---|---|---|---|---|---|
| | 1870[b] | 1860[c] | 1867[d] | 1868[e] | 1870[f] | 1872[g] | 1874[h] |
| NW | 10,018 | 44.5 | 22.5 | 31.8 | 37,355 | 37 | 46.3 |
| D | 59,406 | 27 | 27 | 39.7 | 31,245 | 24 | 38.7 |
| SW | 39,037 | 25 | 21.5 | 32.5 | 23,401 | 21 | 32.6 |
| TOTAL[i] | 108,461 | 96.5 | 71 | 104 | 92.001 | 82 | 117.9 |
| *% of Total* | % | % | % | % | % | % | % |
| NW | 9.2 | 46 | 31.6 | 30.6 | 40.6 | 45 | 39.3 |
| D | 54.8 | 27.9 | 38 | 38 | 34 | 29 | 32.8 |
| SW | 36 | 25 | 30.3 | 31.2 | 25.4 | 25 | 27.7 |

e.  Calculated from: roster of the seventeenth General Assembly (November 17, 1868 to April 10, 1869), Hall, *op. cit.*, p. 275-77.
f.  Calculated from: *Ninth Census, op. cit.*, p. 623.
g.  Calculated from: *Gazette, June 15, 1872*, p. 2, c. 2.
h.  Calculated from: Arkansas Constitution of 1874, Article VIII, sects. 1-2, Hall *op. cit.*, pp. 127-29.
i.  Pulaski County figures have been excluded.

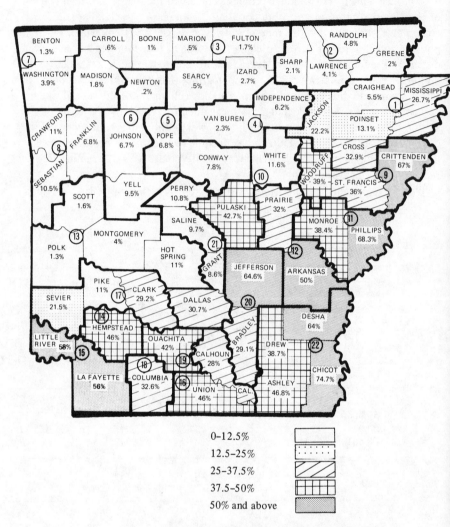

| | |
|---|---|
| 0–12.5% | |
| 12.5–25% | |
| 25–37.5% | |
| 37.5–50% | |
| 50% and above | |

Circled figures indicate voting districts

Calculated from: U. S. Bureau of the Census, *Ninth Census: 1870. Population,* I, pp. 13–14.

**Figure 11.    Colored Population as a Percentage of Total Population, 1870**

tensions and made the apportionment appear increasingly unjust, was the fact that migration between 1860 and 1870 resulted in the northwest's gaining over 17% in population while this loss in representation was occurring.[36] David Walker's district lost 2½ representatives while gaining 29% in population. Jesse Turner could report the same experience for his district. While maintaining approximately the same population, counties in Isaac Murphy's district lost 4½ representatives.[37] In the face of these experiences, *de jure* recognition would be difficult for many in the northwest.

The Convention continued its work throughout January while the political forces organized themselves for the forthcoming election. On January fifteenth the Republican state convention was held in Little Rock. A slate of candidates for state offices was chosen which included Powell Clayton for governor and J.M. Johnson for lieutenant governor.[38] The platform adopted included commitment to a system of internal improvements, free schools for whites and Negroes, and civil and political equality for all men. The Democrats met in Little Rock on January twenty-seventh for their state convention. Striving to unite "the opponents of negro suffrage and domination, and the friends of the constitution and civil liberty, in a combined opposition to the destructive measures of radicalism,"[39] they passed resolutions endorsing a white man's government in a white man's country.[40] Their immediate purpose, however, was to prevent the ratification of the new Constitution.

Its work completed, the Constitutional Convention adjourned February fourteenth, and preparations for the election, which was to begin March thirteenth, got under way.[41] As they looked toward that event, Walker and his friend, George C. Watkins, believed the Constitution would be defeated if they were allowed anything like a fair election.[42] Hope was placed in the decision of the McCardle case, then before the United States Supreme Court, to dispose of the Reconstruction laws entirely.[43] As days passed without word from Washington concerning this decision, morale declined and Watkins wrote Walker the day of the election that things had "been going bad to worse so rapidly, that there is no reliance on any hypothesis. It only remains for us not to be moved by sudden fears, and to possess our souls in patience."[44]

The election for ratifying the Constitution, which began March thirteenth and continued for more than two weeks, was followed by widespread reports of fraud and misconduct.[45] On March twenty-ninth, George C. Watkins wrote David Walker that men across the state should strive to collect evidence supporting the allegations of fraud such as Walker's own report of the suppression of three hundred voters in a township in his area.[46] This belief in fraudulent action during the election persisted and led to a statement of alleged irregularities being filed with General Gillem on April thirteenth by the Democratic Central Committee.[47]

On April first, the state board of election commissioners announced that the

Constitution had been ratified overwhelmingly at the polls under their authority.[48]   It was April twenty-second, however, before General Gillem received the completed returns of the election conducted under the military authorities.[49] Results of the vote left a genuine question as to whether the Constitution had been actually ratified. The southwestern and northwestern areas returned majorities against ratification with approximately 60% of those voting in each area being against the Constitution. In the delta the majority for ratification was comprised of approximately 60% of those voting in that

## TABLE 2

## VOTING STUDY BY AREA

|  | Total Population | Estimated Male Citizens 21 and Over (20% of Population) | Presidential Election | Supreme Court Election | White Registered Voters | Colored Registered Voters | Total Registered Voters |
|---|---|---|---|---|---|---|---|
|  | | | Nov. 6, | Aug. 6, | | | |
|  | $1860^a$ | $1860^b$ | $1860^c$ | $1866^d$ | $1867^e$ | $1867^e$ | $1867^*$ |
| NW | 165,070 | 33,006 | 22,231 | 10,319 (30,959) | 11,728 | 2,010 | 18,90? |
| D | 133,335 | 26,660 | 14,635 | 6,681 (20,043) | 10,140 | 11,393 | 23,89? |
| SW | 125,346 | 25,073 | 15,557 | 6,434 (19,402) | 9,775 | 6,119 | 20,72? |
| TOTAL^m | 423,751 | 84,739 | 52,423 | 23,434 | 31,643 | 19,522 | 63,52? |
| % of Total | % | % | % | % | % | % | % |
| NW | 39 | 39 | 42.4 | 44 | 37 | 10.3 | 29.7 |
| D | 31.5 | 31.5 | 27.9 | 28.5 | 32 | 58.3 | 37.6 |
| SW | 29.5 | 29.5 | 29.7 | 27.4 | 30.9 | 31.3 | 32.6 |

a. Calculated from: U.S. Bureau of the Census, *Ninth Census; 1870. Population*, I, pp. 13–14.
b. Calculated as 20% of total population.
c. Calculated from: *Gazette*, December 8, 1860, p. 3, c. 1.
d. Calculated from: *Ibid.*, October 9, 1866, p. 3, c.1.
e. Calculated from: Abstract of Returns of Registration, *Debates and Proceedings of the Arkansas Constitutional Convention, 1868* (Little Rock: J.G. Price, 1868), p. 769.
f. Calculated from: Abstract of Returns of Election, *ibid.*, p. 770.
g. Calculated from: Consolidated Report of Election Commencing March 13, 1868, *ibid.*, p. 807.
h. Calculated from: *Ibid.*

area.  Numerical results of this vote in the three sections indicated a majority of 2,606 against the Constitution, the totals being 25,600 to 22,994.  It was only when Pulaski County was added to these totals that a majority of 1,316 in favor of ratification was obtained.[50]   And there were questions about the Pulaski and Jefferson County votes which left the ultimate outcome in doubt.

Out of 54,510 voting, the registrars reported 27,913 FOR and 26,597 AGAINST the Constitution.[51]   As General Gillem reported, had the election been conducted according to instructions contained in General Order No. 7, the adoption of the Constitution would have been beyond dispute.  In Pulaski County, however, the returns showed 1,195 more votes cast than registered voters in that county.  The registrars explained this discrepancy by saying that

## TABLE 2 (CONTINUED)

| | Convention Election Vote | Registered Voters | Constitution Ratification Vote | General Election Congressional Vote | Male Citizens 21 and Over | General Election Governor | Estimated Adult Males By Race |
|---|---|---|---|---|---|---|---|
| | 1867[f] | Mar. 13, 1868[g] | Mar. 13–18, 1868[h] | Nov. 3, 1868[i] | 1870[j] | Nov. 5, 1872[k] | 1870[l] |
| NW | 9,864 | 21,235 | 15,338 | 11,996 | 37,335 | 21,428 | C  1,904 |
| | | | | | | | W 35,393 |
| D | 13,816 | 27,196 | 18,942 | 15,780 | 31,245 | 29,700 | C 13,435 |
| | | | | | | | W 17,810 |
| SW | 10,941 | 20,632 | 14,314 | 9,762 | 23,401 | 22,078 | C  7,582 |
| | | | | | | | W 15,796 |
| TOTAL[m] | 34,621 | 69,063 | 48,594 | 37,538 | 91,981 | 73,206 | C 22,921 |
| | | | | | | | W 68,999 |
| % of Total | % | % | % | % | % | % | % |
| NW | 28.5 | 30.7 | 31.6 | 31.9 | 40.6 | 29.3 | C  5.1 |
| | | | | | | | W 94.8 |
| D | 39.9 | 39.4 | 39 | 42 | 34 | 40.6 | C 43 |
| | | | | | | | W 57 |
| SW | 31.6 | 29.9 | 29.4 | 26 | 25.4 | 30.1 | C 32.4 |
| | | | | | | | W 67.5 |

i.  Calculated from: *Gazette*, January 9, 1869, p. 1, c. 2.
j.  Calculated from: *Ninth Census, op. cit.*, p. 623.
k.  Calculated from: *Gazette*, December 13, 1872, p. 4, cc. 4–5.
l.  This figure was obtained by calculating the percentage each race represented in the total population and multiplying the total adult male population by this percentage.
m. Pulaski County figures have been excluded.

For constitution
For, over 500 majority
Against constitution
Against, over 500 majority

Calculated from: Consolidated Report
of Election, *Debates and Proceedings
of the Arkansas Constitutional
Convention, 1868* (Little Rock, J. G.
Price, 1868), p. 807.

Figure 12.     Ratification of Constitution of 1868

they permitted persons registered in other counties to vote in the election in Pulaski. No record of these persons was kept, nor did the registrars check off other voters' names in the precinct books being used as a poll book, as their instructions had required. In Jefferson County there were 730 votes of persons registered in other counties involved in a similar manner.

Congress passed an act March 11, 1858, two days before the election began, which authorized "any person duly registered in the State to vote in the election district where he offers to vote," provided he had lived in that district for ten days prior to the election and offered the proper credentials. This act was promulgated in General Order No. 14 by the War Department on March fourteenth, but was not received in Arkansas until after the election.[52] Upon investigation of the election, it was found that the registrars in Pulaski, Jefferson, and Washington counties had unofficially heard of this act and had assumed responsibility for receiving the votes from registered voters of other counties. The 1,925 votes involved in the returns from Pulaski and Jefferson had not been recorded separately; therefore, no means existed for verifying whether the votes in question had been cast for or against the Constitution. If these votes, received by the registrars under a law for which they had no official notification, were considered valid, then the Constitution appeared to have been ratified by a majority of 1,316. Rather than attempt any further resolution of the dispute, General Gillem forwarded his report and supporting documents to General Grant for action by higher authorities.[53] This report became the basis for Congressional action which led to the readmission of Arkansas over the President's veto, June 22, 1868.[54]

David Walker and his judicial friends looked upon the Constitution with strong disfavor and considered the election fraudulent. They believed that in a fair election the Constitution could not have won ratification, but as this election had been conducted, the Republicans would have counted whatever number they found necessary to win.[55] George C. Watkins expressed the view that under the proposed Constitution not more than two thousand white men could or probably would take the required voter's oath, and he expected the system to work in such a way that bondholders, backed by the army, would live off the taxpayers.[56]

On April thirteenth, the Democratic Central Committee filed a statement of alleged irregularities with General Gillem.[57] The following day an officer met with that Committee and others to hear their complaints, giving them his assurance that the frauds would be investigated.[58] A portion of the report General Gillem submitted April twenty-third contained the results of an investigation of these charges by Colonel J.E. Tourtelotte. The conservatives claimed six weeks were necessary to prepare their case and months would be needed to complete the investigation. Such a long delay was considered unacceptable. What evidence was available at that time, however, was forwarded in General Gillem's report.[59]

The temper of conservatives in the state rose during the passing weeks.[60] As it became evident that Congress was going to recognize the newly elected regime under this distasteful Constitution, the issue of *de facto* v. *de jure* government entered a new phase. Whether justified by the facts or not, the disfranchised and their friends looked upon this government as alien and felt no moral obligation to support the constituted authorities.[61] On June twenty-fifth, three days after Arkansas had been readmitted to the Union, Judge F.W. Compton wrote David Walker:

The State is *"in,"* as the radicals term it, and we are for the time being, I suppose, under negro rule. How long this state of things will last, or whether we can bear it at all, it is not easy to say. Several of our friends have gone to New York to attend the national convention, with the *special* view of ascertaining whether any plan can be adopted by which our shackles may be speedily stricken off. If we are to be relieved, the relief must come from the north, for the simple reason that so many of our people are disfranchised in consequence of the infamous electors' oath and other provisions in the so called constitution, that I scarcely think it possible that a single Southern State will be carried by the democracy. Besides, if we had the strength to defeat the opposite party at the ballot box, who [is] so credulous as to believe that the unscrupulous men in power would hold a fair election?[62]

Under the circumstances, Judge Compton felt they should not decide upon the course to be pursued in the fall election until they had determined the tone and temper of the northern democracy. As an individual, however, he could not accept any platform which did not repudiate the Negro governments of the South as illegal and void.[63]

Because of their conception of *de jure* government and because of the circumstances in which the existing government had been established, David Walker and other conservative men throughout the state were confronted with a genuine problem. Should they hold to their principles and refuse to participate in what they considered an illegitimate government, or should they accept the *de facto* nature of the situation and watch for opportunities to overthrow the Republican regime? For David Walker the answer was to be the former.

# CHAPTER FIVE

# A DIFFERENCE REGARDING MEANS

With the "readmission" of Arkansas into the Union, the state government under the Republicans now had the task of trying to win *de jure* recognition from a population the majority of whom were hostile to that party's being in power. The opponents of the Republicans for their part had to choose the means by which they would attempt to modify or to overthrow the *de facto* government under which they lived. The struggle between these political antagonists was to lead to strange developments as the years of Reconstruction passed.

The impact of the Civil War upon post-war economic development in the state revealed once again the regional contrasts among the three societies. In the predominantly cotton-growing regions of the delta and the southwest, property values, both real and personal, dropped significantly between 1860 and 1870.[1] Reflecting the despair of men in his southwestern region, John R. Eakin, editor of the *Washington Telegraph,* wrote to David Walker in June, 1868, seeking advice about prospects for himself in northwestern Arkansas. "Our planters are all impoverished. My business has failed. I am every day getting poorer. My lands, being almost all swamp and unimproved, are wholly value-less."[2] A similar demoralization was reflected by the wife of a delta plantation owner in Phillips County, who wrote in 1865: "I wish I might go to some large town and live the remainder of my life, so utterly weary am I of plantations past, present and to come."[3] But the fate of the plantation lady who wrote the following can only be passed over in silence. "I have never before in my life ben [sic] obliged to wait on myself, and I am now forty-five years old."[4]

When attention is turned toward the northwest, however, one finds a different social and economic point of view. Cotton culture had not been a permeating factor here; therefore, the effects of the war, so devastating to the plantation system and property values in the other regions, were more easily overcome. New sources of energy and vitality were brought in with migrations from Missouri and other states, which increased the population during the decade after 1860 by almost 18%. (During the same period the delta had gained less than 4% and the southwest had lost approximately that same amount.)[5] Enterprising men in this region turned their attention toward dreams of a transcontinental railroad going across northern Arkansas and passing through Fayetteville on its way to the West Coast.[6] Other men more modestly worked toward the development of a north-south road which would connect the Arkansas River valley with the transcontinental road from St. Louis on its way westward.[7] Even the political picture seemed brighter here as the conservative forces regained control in Washington County by 1870.[8]

Evidence of expanding economic activity and improving economic conditions in Arkansas during the years of Reconstruction has been offered by students of business history. One such study reveals that the annual value of cotton production remained consistently above that of the best ante-bellum performance and that in five years of the decade 1866–76 actual cotton production surpassed the peak year of 1859.[9] In addition, this study suggests that business activity from 1870 through 1873 was well above the normal trend of economic development.[10] Another student, whose statistics are more conservative, nonetheless shows a steady growth in economic activity from 1866 through 1873.[11]

Benefit from this economic growth, however, varied greatly from one locality to another and from one individual to another. For those well placed politically, the opportunities were great for personal gain. For those well located geographically, the forthcoming railroad held promise of community development. For those fortunate enough to have credit available to them, great wealth could be accumulated. Those having the ability to utilize the credit of the state in support of their enterprises possessed additional possibilities. But many were not so well placed and suffered exclusion from these and other opportunities of the day.

Perhaps most tragic among the excluded was the Negro, who had gained his freedom, but had lost his position in society.[12] Because he failed to find an alternate place there, the economic forces of the plantation system aided by the social attitudes of the day placed him again at the bottom and held him there through his perpetual indebtedness. The planter, too, was displaced by past events and was hindered in finding a new place by the absence of money, labor, and morale. High cotton prices brought attractive profits to those men who were able to finance plantation operations, but many others who had enjoyed the status of an ante-bellum planter were now excluded from the opportunities of the day by the results of the Civil War. The old system had required flexibility in wages, dependability of workers, and stability in the work force; now slowly and painfully through trial and error these attributes were sought under the new conditions.[13]

Several experiments were attempted to fulfill these requirements. They included a lessee system, a wage system (which failed to give the planter flexibility in wages or dependability of workers), various share-tenancy plans (which failed to provide permanency), and, finally, what Miss Carmichael terms "debt slavery" (which reinstated the characteristics of the old system).[14] Under "debt slavery" the planter came to furnish his own credit, or to arrange for it through a local merchant. The results of this credit operation left the tenant in debt at the end of the year and tied him once again to the system. These adjustments developed slowly throughout the years of Reconstruction, however, and were not completed until the late 1870's.[15]

Amid such economic and social developments the Republican state government tried to win *de jure* recognition for itself. As this attempt was being made, the untenable position of the Republican party was revealed by the *Gazette* when that paper described the voting population in November, 1868, as having the following complexion:[16]

| | |
|---|---|
| White Voters | 70,000 |
| Negro Voters | 23,000 |
| Carpet-baggers | 1,500 |
| | 94,500 |

Despite this distribution, the house of representatives was comprised of eighty-two radicals and one Democrat.[17]  In the senate there were twenty-one and one respectively.[18]  Such an imbalance between voting potential and legislative representation was destined to correct itself at the first opportunity. In the meantime, the Republicans would rely heavily upon the control of the legislature, the Constitution of 1868, and, especially, the powers of the governor to perpetuate their regime.

As the Republicans attempted to strengthen their position, they found that powers granted the governor's office by the Constitution of 1868, augmented by legislative action, made the governor the key figure in the political structure.[19] By using his power to designate an official newspaper in which legal notices would appear in each county or district, he could guarantee his party a friendly press. By using his power of appointment, he could create throughout the state a group of assessors and registrars loyal to the party and ready to do its bidding. The Republican Governor, Powell Clayton, made clear his expectations from these appointments in a letter sent to all assessors in January, 1870:

... he [Governor Clayton] wishes to urge upon you the importance of giving the matter your personal attention and seeing that a fair and correct assessment be made. He hopes too that you will look after the interest of the party and keep him informed from time to time in reference to the political situation in your County. He trusts that you will do all you can for the Party. He would be pleased if you would make out at your leisure and send to him a list of the prominent Republicans in your County names and Post Office Addresses together with a list of moderate Democrats who may be led to work with us by means of Documents sent to them—as also the names of those who are likely to be candidates for Election to the [forthcoming] Legislature.[20]

Through his possession of the final authority in granting state credit to the railroads, the governor was in a position to exert tremendous influence on the future economic development of various regions in the state and to foster or impair the success of various corporate efforts to construct the roads.  In addition to the above powers, the governor could maintain significant control over public works, education, efforts to encourage immigration, and public printing.  He could also fill vacancies in state, county, and municipal offices as well as appoint county and township officers.[21]

Such concentration of power in the governor's office gave the Republicans many advantages in their battle to win *de jure* recognition.  This power proved to be a mixed blessing in practice, however, for the effectiveness of its use required a congenial relationship between the governor and party members, and this necessary harmony was often lacking.  One reason for its absence was to be found in the personality of Governor Powell Clayton himself.

In his letters Governor Clayton constantly called for loyalty to the Republican party, but the reader perceives that there was little difference in loyalty to the party and loyalty to Powell Clayton.[22]  General Clayton, the commander, seems always present in his communications. Factions which arose among the Republicans were likely based more on anti-Clayton motives than on ideological differences.  Utilizing his motto, "men that do the work shall have the rewards," Clayton distributed his patronage in such a manner as to develop loyalty to himself as he ran the party.[23]  This sense of being the commander of an army loyal to him was still characteristic of Clayton in the 1890's as, from his post as United States Minister to Mexico, he tried to control the Republican party in Arkansas through the office of his agent, Harmon L. Remmel, then active in the party in Little Rock.[24]

Factions within the Republican party, which were partially inspired by opposition to Governor Clayton's use of his powers, served to weaken the Republican potential in the state.  Such internal divisions could pose a serious threat to the party's future.  But an even greater threat to the Republican fortunes was ultimately to come from concentration of power in the governor's office itself.  This concentration meant that control of the governor's office carried with it the control of the state.  So long as a governor was sympathetic with the Republican party, that party could maintain its power.  But what would be the situation if a Republican governor became antagonistic toward one or more factions within the Republican party?  Could not this same concentration of power in the governor's office then be utilized to undo the Republican

Figure 13.    Powell Clayton

party's domination of the state? This very situation was to develop during 1873–74 when Republican Governor Elisha Baxter used his powers to thwart the aspirations of opposing factions in the Republican party and to maintain himself in the governor's office. His actions were largely responsible for a growth of Democratic power and a demise of Republican power in the state.

This heavy reliance on the powers of the governor's office might have proved successful in building a genuine party control for the Republicans if given the necessary time, but winning *de jure* recognition from the majority of the voters in the state would have been a much more difficult task to accomplish. The absence of a state-wide party among the Democrats and conservatives, who were seriously divided among themselves over such matters as the voter's oath and whose ranks were thinned by disfranchisement and voluntary refusal to vote, made the growing party organization of the Republicans appear particularly obnoxious. For in their thinking the Democrats and conservatives could not separate success in social reform from growth in the Republican party's consolidation. Nor were the Republicans oblivious to this connection, as Governor Clayton demonstrated when he wrote, "Our schools and internal improvements are building up for us a tower of strength everywhere."[25] Although schools and internal improvements were desired by most people in Arkansas, to have them become instruments for perfecting Republican-party control was another matter.

Perhaps the measure of the situation was taken by T.S. Staples when he noted that "whether warranted or not by the facts, the disfranchised whites and their sympathizers felt no moral obligation to support the constituted authorities. Republican rule, to them, was alien rule based on an ignorant negro electorate."[26] And in addition to this attitude, as the aims of the Republicans came to be realized, there would be an implied sacrifice of the "convictions, prejudices, and hopes on the part of the ex-Confederates wholly impossible in view of their temper at the time."[27] Given these circumstances, *de jure* recognition of the state government under the Republicans appears to have been a very remote possibility.

But if a majority of the voting population were in agreement in their opposition to the state government under the Republicans, it does not follow that the various elements in that majority were in agreement with each other as to the means by which that government should be changed. Democrats, Whigs, and other conservative opponents of the Republican regime were seriously divided among themselves over this question of means. In general, there were two directions of thought in pursuit of which men divided as they sought ways to overthrow the Republican government. The first position argued for the *de facto* recognition of the government followed by a flexible and pragmatic interpretation of means appropriate for successful opposition to the Republicans. The second position was far less flexible and argued for a refusal to grant even *de facto* recognition to the Republican regime. For men of this persuasion the hope of overthrowing the state government was to come from an effort to develop a national coalition of conservatives such as the Liberal Republican movement of 1872 rather than from political participation in state elections against an unconstitutional government.

The central figures of this study are representative of these two positions. Augustus H. Garland, political realist, may be considered an advocate of the former policy and David Walker, Whig jurist, an advocate of the latter. As divergent as these policies appear to have been, it is interesting to note that these two men maintained a mutual respect for each other throughout Reconstruction. The merging of their influence and the consolidation of their respective political following helped to unify the Democratic party in 1874. As attention now is turned to political developments which followed the ratification of the Constitution of 1868, the central position occupied by these two men in this study will be important to remember in this and in the following chapters.

Under authority of the new Constitution, the state legislature assembled April 2, 1868, and continued its sessions throughout the spring and summer.[28] Its work during the period from April second to July second was not impressive in terms of legislation passed, but its importance could be seen as a period of preparation for the twenty-day period following Governor Clayton's inauguration on July second.[29] During this short time much significant legislation was passed. Perhaps the most influential act was that which submitted to the voters at the general election in November a proposition to lend the credit of the state in support of the construction of railroads.[30] An act of more immediate consequence was the registration law, which provided for registration of loyal voters for the forthcoming general election. Under its provisions registrars were to be appointed by the governor before August first.[31] Such appointments could not fail to be interpreted as party patronage by Democrats and conservatives, but a matter of greater importance was the fact that the law forced these opponents of Republican rule to make a decision concerning registration. Should they advise their followers to take the voter's oath and try to register in the hope of defeating the Republicans in November?

The Democratic Central Committee chose its path on July thirtieth when the Committee met in Little Rock and issued an address to the people of the state recommending a vigorous campaign in the Presidential and Congressional elections that fall. Although the state government was regarded as being unconstitutional, the Committee urged all who could to register and try to elect conservative men to fill vacancies in the state legislature.[32] Augustus H. Garland wrote David Walker that day telling him of the decision to advise taking the oath and making a fight of it in the November election. Evidently aware of Walker's reluctance in this matter, Garland stressed the need for unity of action, "for now we are to be saved or ruined as one."[33]

The difference of opinion shown in this decision was indicative of the contrast between the two men. The political nature of Garland allowed him more flexibility as he moved with relative ease from his ante-bellum Whig background into a leading position among the Democrats. The legalistic nature of Walker made him less willing to grant *de facto* recognition to the Reconstruction government and more reluctant to abandon his Whig background in order to join the Democrats.

As weeks passed, Walker became despondent and probably felt that the apprehensions concerning post-war conditions in the event of a Federal victory, which he had expressed in his notebook in May, 1863, were now in some measure coming true.[34] His friend and former Confederate colleague, George C. Watkins, expressed concern for this despondency in a letter late in August. Although he was trying to console Walker, Watkins was himself full of apprehensions. Economically, he foresaw the creation of an aristocracy of wealth based on enormous public debts, state and national, guaranteeing railroad, corporate, municipal, and county stocks which would act as a mortgage on the industry and production of the country. The whole science of government would become a system of taxation allowing the bondholding aristocracy to live with ease off the taxpayers. How long this situation would exist without repudiation was an open question for him. Politically, Watkins felt that the Fourteenth Amendment would alter the Union of states and create a nation, and that the "best government the world ever saw" would be in danger of "being wrecked on this idea of nationality."[35]

In the expression of this last idea Watkins indicated an important characteristic of Unionist sentiment in Arkansas. Although a majority of the voting population in 1861 had been Unionist, it would be a mistake to equate that Unionist sentiment with nationalism. The nature of the Union to which many Arkansas Unionists were loyal was a decentralized organization which allowed local self-government among the states. Men such as Watkins and Walker, who were well placed in Arkansas society, observed the connection between social changes within the state and centralization of power in the national government and felt compelled to oppose these developments.

In the weeks preceding the Presidential election of 1868, the urgency of party organization was an important factor in the thinking of most Democrats and conservatives. Many felt as Watkins did that "Even if we do not succeed, we will have a party organization for our people to rally to."[36] Especially did the newspapers find their role in marshalling opinion in opposition to the Republicans. Their nature as party organs made them biased witnesses to the events of the day. That their means could become offensive even to those who opposed the radical regime was illustrated by a clash between David Walker and William E. Woodruff, Jr., editor of the *Gazette*.

Walker wrote Augustus H. Garland early in September, expressing adverse criticism of the *Gazette* for its provocative writing, which he felt was unnecessarily generating resentment among their friends. In the past Walker had twice discouraged strong denunciation of the paper by friends who disagreed with the course it had taken. He regretted seeing the alienation resulting from Woodruff's comments as the editor ridiculed and threatened in order to *"whip in* all who hesitated to follow." Indeed, this reminded Walker of the tactics used by the secessionists to insure unity for their cause.[37]

The course of the *Gazette* indicated a new direction in political action, which Walker felt should have come only after due deliberation and consultation with political leaders, but in such expectation he had been disappointed. For the *Gazette*'s editorials reflected the decision of the Democratic State Central Committee to recommend to its followers that they take the voter's oath and participate in the forthcoming election. Walker resented the fact that the decision had been made without calling a convention and that the July decision represented an abandonment of their previous position regarding the Reconstruction government.

Garland showed Walker's letter to Woodruff, who wrote Walker in defense of his paper's policy. Considering Walker's comments severe, he assured him that when the motives behind his actions were properly understood, Walker would again extend his good will toward the paper and its editor. Woodruff was in agreement with Walker's principles and admitted to him that the *Gazette* had cut loose from principle for the time being, but the nature of the circumstances made him believe that "the end arrived at will justify the use of any means." He was willing to accept the radicals at their word when they labeled the Democrats as rebels and claimed that war existed. Because of this situation he felt justified in using the tactics of war in the election canvass, the first of these tactics being the fundamental principle, "to destroy the enemy."[38]

Turning to the action of others for his defense, Woodruff reminded Walker that there were numerous other judges throughout the state who believed as he did that there was no "binding force in law or morals to an oath taken under duress." Among those Woodruff used to support his position were two former Supreme Court Justices, George C. Watkins (Walker's close friend) and E.H. English, and one of the leading Little Rock attorneys, U.M. Rose. The question was really a matter of conscience, Woodruff felt, with those of Walker's persuasion perhaps a little more conscientious than those of the opposite view.

Woodruff used two other considerations to justify his editorial policy in favor of taking the voter's oath. He believed he had excellent opportunities for knowing the conditions existing in the state; therefore, his actions were based upon considerable knowledge of the contemporary situation. In addition to this consideration, he was persuaded that if the white people of Arkansas could not vote as Democrats, many would vote as radicals; therefore, the course taken was the only one which would save the Democratic party.

Walker answered Woodruff's letter of September twenty-fourth, revealing the basis for his opposition:

I have believed and yet believe that we should have adhered to that plank in the democratic platform which treats the Reconstruction Acts, and the State Governments made under them as void. But it seems that we are to abandon this plank, and step off squarely upon the negro equality plank of the Radical platform, and urge its adoption, to swear never to abandon it, and to invite the negroes to get upon it and vote with us. Are you in earnest in all this? Do you realy [sic] intend to fasten negro suffrage and negro equality upon the State? If such is realy [sic] your intention, then I can see how in good faith the voters oath may be taken. But if it is intended that this position shall be assumed, and the negro vote used to enable us to get in power that we may disfranchise him. Then, then—no, I will give no utterance to my feelings.

I have thought it wrong to take any step which would commit us to this infamous state government, with its negro-equality provisions. But that step has been taken, and it is folly to oppose it *now,* for it has already gone forth, that in Arkansas at least, reconstruction is not a failure—that she has through her State Central Committee, consented to hold an election under the reconstructed state government, and has declared in favor of negro equality, and is ready to take an oath which the President said in his veto message, a majority of the Northern voters would not take. We stand in this degraded, humiliating condition before the world today, no effort which I or those who agree with me can make will change it. Seeing this I have upon all occasions refused to canvass, or speak against the policy which you urge. Though I have not, and will not advise any one who does not in good faith believe that negroes should have the same civil and political rights, with white men to take the voters oath and register.

You and those who think with you can have the full benefit of an open field here. I will not describe the meeting at this place, at which a resolution was passed advising all who *could* do so to register! A little time will undeceive all as to the real sentiment of our people.[39]

As the Presidential election of November, 1868, approached, the argument among Democrats and conservatives concerning the question whether they should register as voters continued. Governor Clayton's proclamation, October sixth, setting aside the registration in eleven counties, and the dramatic events associated with the steamboat *Hesper,* occuring nine days later, probably encouraged individuals who had been reluctant to take the voter's oath to remain unregistered.[40]

Efforts to secure full registration of those able to take the voter's oath were continued by various Democratic party advocates during September and October. Of particular discouragement to them was the influence of such prominent men as David Walker in the northwest and John R. Eakin in the southwest, who were advising men in their areas not to register. Ben T. DuVal, chairman of the Democratic Committee, wrote from Fort Smith to friends in Fayetteville of his regret that such a resolve not to register had captured so many in their area. He could not see how they could expect any outside power to help them if they failed to do anything for themselves.[41] The *Fayetteville Democrat* was also trying to encourage registration and lamented the actual number of registered voters in Washington County. With a population of approximately 2,700 adults, the editors estimated that at least 1,700 could have registered, but those who actually did totaled only 794, of whom 30 were Negroes.[42]

In post-election comment the general failure to register in the northwest was blamed for the defeat of the Democratic candidate for United States Congressman, T.B. Nash, and one paper pointed to the " 'do nothing' policy in the northwest" as reason for losing the entire state to the Republicans in the Presidential election.[43]  When one considers the election results, the conclusion that this failure to register was a major factor in the outcome seems valid.  Out of 41,230 voting, the Republican Presidential electors received 22,152 and the Democratic electors 19,078.[44]  Because of this small majority of 3,074, the vote of those able to register, but refusing to do so, might well have altered the result. One serious qualification, however, needs to be made.  The returns from fifteen counties were set aside in this election.[45]  Had all those able to register in the northwest done so, the possibility still remained that additional adjustments in other areas would have been made to carry the state for the Republican party.

During the Reconstruction years, David Walker from all indications enjoyed a comfortable and successful life in Fayetteville and its surrounding area as a prosperous farmer, augmenting his farm income with fees from his practice as a lawyer.  His friend, Trusten Polk, wrote from St. Louis in July, 1870: "I am particularly pleased to learn of the success of your farming operations and the easy circumstances that success has placed you in. I most sincerely and heartily congratulate you."[46]  Walker occasionally spoke of his farming achievements with a special pride uncharacteristic of the Whig reserve which he displayed in speaking of politics.  Apparently a good wheat crop such as that of 1874, when he thought he had raised sixty bushels per acre, gave him more pleasure than did success in politics.[47]  And yet at the same time that he declared himself to be so disinterested in politics, his correspondence was filled with references to political matters.   There can be no doubt that Walker continued to have a strong influence among the former Whigs throughout the state and among a larger following in northwestern Arkansas.

In August, 1869, he wrote his friend, John R. Eakin, who was still editing the *Washington Telegraph* in southwestern Arkansas.  Walker noted with regret Eakin's gradual retreat from his strong position taken in defense of the United States Constitution and expressed his admiration for the stand taken during the last Presidential election.  That stand commanded respect in a period when other men "seemed under the plea of necessity to have ignored all distinction between truth and falsehood, sincerity and deception."  At that time the issue of suffrage had been at stake; now, however, the matter had been settled for the time being, and they must submit to those terms of settlement no matter how distasteful. Therefore, Walker did not think Eakin's change of position could be held as an abandonment of principle.  Indeed, Walker had sufficiently shifted in his own thinking since the November election to believe that "under exhisting [*sic*] circumstances it is perhaps best that we should so far acquiese [*sic*] in results as to act together and cast as strong a vote as possible."[48]

Walker noticed Eakin's intimation that they might be able to pass a suffrage law which would be general in nature, yet would require educational qualifications for voting. Although he would favor such a development, Walker saw two disadvantages. The length of time required to enact such a law would make its passage extremely difficult. And secondly, equity would pose a problem, for it would be just as fair, if not more so, to include Negroes, Chinese, and women in the political element as to abridge the suffrage. The discouragement Walker felt as he observed the direction in which events were moving and the demoralization he felt as the old Whig principles of conservatism and personal integrity were overwhelmed by the expediency of the day had lowered his morale. Nevertheless, he wrote his friend Eakin that he still hoped "to be found all the while contesting every inch of ground, and when the final battle is fought, to die with a consciousness that I have at least not contributed to the downfall of free government."[49]

With the arrival of election year 1870, opponents of the Republican regime remained divided in their counsels. The choice of appropriate means by which the Democratic, former Whig, and other political elements could make their opposition to radical rule effective continued to be a problem. One line of thought advocated party organization in the counties followed by a state convention at Dardanelle. In this argument the *Fayetteville Democrat* joined, pleading for an early and thorough organization and indicating the party advantages even if the conservative forces were defeated in this particular election. The consequences of failing to organize in 1868 were pointed to as justification for present action.[50]

A second line of thought advocated the strategy of dividing the radical forces and winning concessions through this means. By refusing to place candidates in the field, the conservatives could support those radicals who promised the most moderate program and thereby could make their weight felt most effectively. Both Augustus H. Garland and David Walker advocated this course in 1870.[51] Although such strategy was effective politically, it was exposed to criticism by those who wanted more positive action and left its advocates vulnerable to attack.

The Congressional election in the third Congressional district in northwestern Arkansas served as an arena in which the merits of these two strategic plans were tested. This Congressional office represented Arkansas' newly acquired seat in the United States Congress and, therefore, carried with it a unique political interest.[52] David Walker remained opposed to conservative organization and a convention that year and wanted to support a radical who would advocate the restoration of political rights to the ex-Confederates. Conservative organization, he felt, could only bring the radicals closer together. It would also increase the stringency of registration and perhaps encourage frauds in counting the vote. In addition, the chances of obtaining a majority in the legislature, a goal of high priority, would be lessened. Even if a conservative candidate were elected, he would be harshly received in Washington, his seat would be contested, and some-one else ultimately would be put in his place. Efforts at party organization would also create strife and confusion in conservative ranks. Armed with these arguments, Walker defended his course, which he believed was directed toward the restoration of peace and quiet to the state.[53]

Consistent with these views, Walker agreed to support R.J. Rutherford, a northwestern radical who had split with the Clayton faction of the Republican party by openly advocating enfranchisement of ex-Confederates and removal of all political disabilities. Walker's political friend, John M. Harrell, active in the Democratic party, wrote him in reference to Rutherford: "[He] . . . is just the kind of *Republican* we want. Our people are hard to comprehend that we don't want *Republicans* of the *highest* abilities in places from which we hope soon to with-draw them."[54] Despite his feelings in the matter, Walker was later to offer his support reluctantly to a conservative, Sol F. Clark, who was following the political reasoning against which Walker had argued.[55] Neither strategy suggested by the opponents of the Republicans, however, was successful in pre-venting J.M. Hanks, the Republican candidate supported by the Clayton faction, from winning the Congressional election.[56]

In other races in the 1870 election the conservatives made moderate gains, which were celebrated by the *Fayetteville Democrat.* Of most importance to the editors was the redemption of Washington and Benton counties. Impassioned headlines reported a conservative majority of 250 over "the most foul and damning frauds ever perpetrated upon an outraged people."[57] They also noted the composition of the state legislature resulting from the election. In the senate the Republicans would have eighteen seats and the conservatives eight, a division representing a gain of seven for the latter. In the house of representatives the balance would be forty-four to thirty-three, a gain of thirty-two seats for the conservatives.[58] Although these gains did not threaten the dominance of a united majority, they were substantial enough to encourage hope of additional victories in 1872. The growing factionalism among the Republicans provided additional encouragement.

During the period between the election in November, 1870, and the state Democratic Convention in June, 1872, the impatience of those advocating party organization and open resistance became more pronounced. One editor in southwestern Arkansas expressed the feelings of many throughout the state when he advised:

Let the State Central Executive Committee issue the call for the Convention; and let there be no milk and cider platform arrayed to lead the Democracy of

Arkansas to defeat and disaster. We have tried doing nothing; we've tried con-
ciliation; we've tried fusion with liberals (so called) of the other party. We
reaped from the first unmitigated wrong; from the second shameless betrayal.
In god's name, then, let us plant ourselves firmly upon principle. With that for
our battle cry, asking no favors, seeking no affiliation, let us fight it out in the
campaign and at the ballot box, and success is sure in Arkansas.[59]

Part of this impatience was turned against men like Walker, who had been
trusted leaders in the past.   The Fayetteville editors wanted to know whether
these men were "so attached to their law-offices, counting-rooms, and doctor
shops that they feel no interest in trying to save the wrecks of our old ship of
State from utter ruin and desolation?"[60]   The editors hoped these men would
not rest easy and leave to the farmer and mechanic the burden of party
organization.   Such fears indicated a lack of understanding of the thinking of
established political leaders in the state.   As the spring and summer of 1872
passed, it would not be the farmers and mechanics, nor the editors, who would
determine the strategy of the various elements which hoped to overthrow the
radical regime, but rather such men as Walker, Garland, and ex-Confederate
Governor Harris Flanagin.

Although frequent reference has been made to the disunity among the
opponents of the Republicans, the factional situation existing among the
Republicans themselves as the campaign for the 1872 election  was conducted
should be noted.  The most powerful faction was that led by Senator Powell
Clayton.   Since Clayton's election to the United States Senate in 1871, this
faction had been headed in Arkansas by Governor Ozra A. Hadley, and Hadley
was the candidate many Democrats expected this faction to nominate for
governor.   The great advantage which this regular Republican, or "minstrel,"
faction possessed was its control of the registration and election machinery.[61]
A second faction, known as the reform Republican, or "brindletail," faction,
was led by Joseph Brooks.[62]   Control of the majority of the Republican vote in
the state gave to this faction its greatest advantage.[63]   Of particular political
significance was the fact that, on the one hand, Joseph Brooks was passionately
opposed to the Clayton faction and, on the other, his advocacy of equal rights
for Negroes had given him a large following among the Negro vote.   A third
faction, known as the liberal Republican, was a smaller group comprised of men
who opposed the "minstrels" but who were unwilling to go as far toward reform
as the "brindletails" under Brooks were advocating.

When one recalls the abnormal political circumstances in which the
Republican party was trying to maintain itself, it can be seen that disunity in
their own ranks presented an ominous threat to the party's success in the forthcoming election.  If the various political elements opposing the Republicans
could resolve their differences, or if these conservative forces could perfect a
coalition with the reform or liberal factions within the Republican party, then

the regular, or "minstrel," faction would be defeated in November. Of additional importance was the threat such a coalition would present to the Republican fortunes in the Presidential election. The national Liberal Republican movement would likely become the beneficiary of such a local coalition rather than the Republican party, and the state might be lost for Grant in that election.

The continuous appeals for party organization heard among the conservatives testified to the heterogeneous composition and disunited condition of the political opposition facing the Republicans. To refer to this opposition as Democratic is not entirely accurate, for some men carefully avoided that label. To refer to it as conservative is vague, and to refer to former Whigs as Whigs is also inaccurate. Perhaps their own label of Democratic-Conservative, although imprecise, has value in its descriptive nature of the situation. All this explanation is given to emphasize the fact that the fusion between Democrats and conservatives was not yet complete when on March 2, 1872, the Democratic-Conservative State Central Committee decided to call a state Convention in Little Rock for June nineteenth. Reflecting their conception of *de jure* apportionment, the Committee decided that representation and voting in the convention should be the same as that of the Conservative State Convention of January, 1866, with the modification that each county organized since that date would have one representative.[64] As a consequence of this decision, the distribution of delegates among the three sections was almost identical with that which existed in the Arkansas legislature of 1860. This meant that approximately 45% of the votes in the Convention would go to the northwest instead of the slightly more than 30% which it received in the legislature under the Constitution of 1868.[65]

Strategic thinking for the forthcoming convention and election campaign began as early as March and continued throughout the summer and fall. Correspondence from this period reflected political relationships of long standing as men exchanged ideas concerning successful opposition to the Republicans. Ex-Confederate Governor Harris Flanagin, of Arkadelphia, continued to be a center of influence in southwestern Arkansas as various writers discussed with him their thoughts on political matters.[66] The focal point of their thinking was similar to that which prevailed in 1870. Should the Democratic-Conservative party choose candidates and organize the party for an open battle with the Republicans, or should they refrain from nominating candidates and cast their votes for the Republican candidates promising the most concessions?

One southwestern correspondent wrote Flanagin in March expressing the belief that if the "rule or ruin hot heads" were not in charge of the Convention, something might be accomplished through "prudent counsel." His idea of prudent counsel was indicated by the alternate plans he suggested. If the Convention in June nominated candidates, they could be pledged to withdraw in

the event Republican registration practices were found to be unacceptable to the Central Committee. At that time the entire vote of the party could be cast for candidates opposing the nominees of Governor Hadley's faction. A second plan could be founded on the provisions of the new registration law. Since registration had to be completed during August, would it not be a "stroke of policy" to postpone nominating candidates until the fairness of the registration could be determined? As soon as a conclusion had been reached, the party could make its announcement of candidates, or refrain from nominating candidates, as the Central Committee might decide.[67]

Shortly before the Convention was to meet, Augustus H. Garland wrote Flanagin, giving his views on the situation.[68] Since Garland's active participation in the election of 1868, during which he had urged ex-Confederate voters to take the voter's oath and register, Garland had adopted a policy of passive resistance, stoically waiting for the appropriate time for action. His concern now remained "for our friends not to be committed to any course until the proper time, and then to go together as one man." He hoped the Convention would do as little as possible, appoint delegates to the Democratic Convention in Baltimore, and then adjourn until September, or delegate the power of making decisions to a special committee. By postponing action until the fall, the members could better judge what ought to be done or what might be accomplished. He would approve a caucus by the Convention on policy and candidates in June in the event that nominations were to be made later, but he wanted the Democratic-Conservative party to remain uncommitted for as long as possible to allow events to indicate the most profitable course.

For Garland, the chief objective was control of the legislature as a first step toward constitutional revision, and he perceived a threat to that control even if the Democratic-Conservative candidates won a majority of the seats. The current talk of a coalition between the Democratic-Conservative forces and the reform Republicans to support Joseph Brooks as a candidate for governor was particularly disturbing to Garland. A carpetbag minister from Iowa, Brooks had revealed himself as an ardent radical in the Constitutional Convention of 1868. That Constitution had given the governor's office such power and patronage that a man of force and will in that office could largely control the legislature. Recognizing in Joseph Brooks a man of such qualities, Garland felt it would be dangerous to risk him in that position. He believed, furthermore, that Brooks would have a special interest in returning B.F. Rice, a strong Brooks supporter, to the United States Senate; therefore, he would have a special reason for controlling the legislature. As a consequence of this thinking, Garland was not in favor of supporting the Brooks ticket, a feeling shared by many others as the Convention approached.

Garland expected the Republican faction to place two candidates in the governor's race—Governor O.A. Hadley, representing the "minstrel" faction, and Joseph Brooks, representing the "brindletail" faction. If the Democratic-Conservative Convention did not nominate a candidate, Garland felt that many of these conservative voters would not go to the polls because of their dislike for both of these Republican candidates. In this event the chances of electing conservative members of the legislature would be lessened considerably. Thus, what Garland considered the chief objective in the election would be lost.

Garland offered two suggestions to meet the necessities of the situation as he saw them. First, a candidate for the Democratic-Conservative party was needed who would command the admiration and respect of enough people to make them "come out & register & vote, & demand their rights." In Dr. Andrew Hunter, a Methodist minister inactive in party politics, Garland saw the candidate who could bring out the largest Democratic-Conservative vote under the circumstances. As these voters went to the polls to vote for Hunter, Garland expected the conservative vote for members of the legislature to increase proportionately.

His second suggestion proposed using the party's bargaining position to force the Republicans to allow some of the Democrats to run for state offices. He estimated that, despite the effects of registration, the conservatives would have 35,000 votes, the Negroes would have 23,000, and the white Republicans would have approximately 8,000. With the factional split within the Republican party, each faction would find it necessary to bid for the conservative vote in order to win. The balance of power would thereby shift to the Democrat-Conservative voters, and Garland wanted to take full advantage of that fact: "If we are so important, ought not those voters to be partially represented in the offices of the state?"

Flanagin did not share Garland's apprehensions concerning Joseph Brooks, nor was he persuaded by Garland's argument that Hadley as governor rather than Brooks would offer more promise to the Democratic-Conservatives as they attempted to gain control of the legislature. A week before the Convention, Garland wrote his estimate of the situation in more specific terms in a second attempt to persuade Flanagin of the correctness of his views:

From the tone of your letter, & from papers, letters & other sources of information the situation is unmistakably this, & of its certainty I have no more doubt than I have of my existence.
1st If your convention of the 19th inst endorse Brooks & his Ticket, the people will divide—some will vote for him, some for Hadley & most will not vote at all, & Hadley will beat him 6500 votes:
2nd If your convention makes a ticket & three run, your ticket will be elected:
3rd If your convention makes a Ticket and Brooks quits, & is passive Hadley is elected etc, etc—and Hadley gets the Legislature—this I feel satisfied he will do any how.
It is sheer nonsense for us to talk about getting a Legislature through Brooks Ticket.

4th If your convention will make a mixed ticket with Brooks you will beat Hadley 4200 votes.

The strong probabilities are then that Hadley is to have us & wring our necks again for four years—This is almost certain: God help us![69]

On June nineteenth, representatives of the various elements of the Democratic-Conservative party met in Little Rock. Bringing to the Convention divided counsels, the delegates too hastily passed resolutions which became the source of conflicting interpretations in the days to come. Central to this future controversy was the decision not to nominate a state ticket, but rather to endorse the "brindletail" Republican platform and to ratify the nomination of Joseph Brooks for governor. The Convention authorized its central committee to work with committees of the reform Republican organizations in the forthcoming campaign; a second duty was to choose delegates to the national Democratic Convention in Baltimore.[70]

If the party unity were the goal, the Convention's actions must be judged a failure. Reflecting the disappointment of those who wanted a Democratic ticket, the *Fayetteville Democrat* sarcastically suggested: "If the Democratic party is to *sell out*, let it sell to the highest bidder, by all means."[71] Apparently, there was some difficulty in understanding what the Convention had actually done. The Democratic-Conservative Central Committee's interpretation differed from that of the editor of the *Gazette* who acted as a spokesman for the more aggressive members of the Democratic Central Committee. Disappointed in not effecting a truly Democratic ticket which could be joined by the conservatives, Woodruff wrote an apologetic letter to David Walker assuring him that he had "no desire to bolt, or to put a new ticket in the field, or to effect a split, or to do anything except to get at the names of the persons for whom democrats are to vote."[72]

Observing the differing interpretations of the Convention's policy, Garland felt reassured in the correctness of his own views. This very difference he felt would go far in rendering almost useless the work done. He also believed that the confusion verified the wisdom of delaying definite action until all the facts were present. "As matters now stand I do not know what will be the result. I see very clearly our people are going to be greatly divided as to the policy of the convention."[73] The political talents of Garland were not failing him. Two weeks prior to this time his name had been suggested by John R. Eakin in the *Washington Telegraph* as a candidate for governor, and since then other papers had echoed the idea with favor. But in his own judgment Garland felt the time was not right for such a move, and in order not to jeopardize future possibilities, he had remained aloof from this Convention. Desiring some of his political friends to understand his position, he wrote Henry M. Rector a lengthy letter early in July:

Because I have been quiet I have had none the less a deep interest in our affairs and have always been ready & willing to do what I could—but determined never to go into or encourage our people to go into another fruitless fight—we have had too many of them. And now let [us?] see something that has any promise of relief to us—any hope that we may get out from this most terrible oppression that has about ruined us, and my time, pen, money & voice will all be at its aid & support, freely and fervently. But I must be excused from listening to every spirit that comes along to talk grandly & [largely?] & proposes to play the d    l with people with whom he has been one & continue[s] to be the blackest of them as long as they will tolerate him in their company—none of that.[74]

Joseph Brooks remained unacceptable to him.

Unlike Garland, David Walker supported the Convention and was chosen one of the delegates to the national Democratic Convention in Baltimore.[75] Other delegates to that Convention included John D. Adams, Harris Flanagin, J. J. Clendenin, Jesse Turner and H. F. Thomason, names which carried with them memories of ante-bellum and Civil War leadership in the state.[76] (It is interesting to note, however, that Harris Flanagin was the only secessionist among these names.)

Although Walker strongly opposed running a Democratic-Conservative ticket, he found the reform Republican ticket headed by Joseph Brooks unsatisfactory as it was and hoped it could be modified sufficiently to be made acceptable. Indeed, he believed that if some alterations were not made, the conservative forces would fall far below their full vote in the election. He favored leaving Brooks on the ticket as candidate for governor, but insisted that until other modifications were made, the Democratic-Conservative, Reform Republican coalition would not have a stable ticket. He appealed to Harris Flanagin to have the matter definitely settled.[77]

In early August, a joint campaign committee comprised of three members from each of the opposition parties—Democratic-Conservative, reform Republican, and liberal Republican—was organized to perfect the coalition.[78] When this committee met on August twenty-fourth, the reform Republicans refused to make the general modifications expected. In resentment of this treatment, the liberal Republicans organized a ticket of their own with Dr. Andrew Hunter as their candidate for governor. Disappointed also was the Democratic Central Committee (not to be confused with the Democratic-Conservative), which published an address asking all Democrats to support Dr. Andrew Hunter.[79] From the Democratic-Conservative party came such strong reaction to this move by the Democratic Central Committee that ten days later a second address urged an end of the Hunter movement and a return to the original plan of a coalition support of Joseph Brooks.[80]

The regular Republicans did not neglect their opportunities to undo the plans of their opponents. If division of opponents was good strategy for Democrats, liberal and reform Republicans, it could also be used to advantage by the "minstrel" Republicans. Passing over O.A. Hadley, who was their obvious candidate for governor, on August twenty-first the Clayton faction, or "minstrel" Republicans, drew up a platform as attractive as that offered by their opponents and chose a candidate more acceptable to many Democrats that the carpetbagger, Joseph Brooks. Because of his appeal to the native white Republicans and his ability to divide the Democratic-Conservative vote, Elisha Baxter, an Arkansas Unionist, was nominated as the "minstrel" candidate for governor.[81]

Factional division among the Republicans and controversy over means among the Democratic-Conservative forces had thus led to this situation. Ironically, the gubernatorial contest would be conducted by two men untypical of their supporters, who had been chosen largely for their ability to divide the vote of the opposition party. Elisha Baxter had been nominated by the "minstrel" Republicans in the hope that he would be able to divide the conservative vote in northwestern Arkansas. His background as an Arkansas Unionist from that area was a factor in his being chosen, and the favorable platform offered by that faction was calculated to help win votes in the Democratic-Conservative ranks. A similar calculation had been behind the "brindletail" coalition with the Democratic-Conservative party. Joseph Brooks hoped to receive support from the Democratic-Conservative ranks as a result of his attacks on the "minstrel" Republicans. In turn, the Democratic-Conservatives hoped to use Brooks' following among the Negro Republicans as a means of unseating the "minstrels."

Under such circumstances political loyalties could easily become blurred and party regularity terribly confused. The opening skirmishes of the Brooks-Baxter War of 1874 are to be found in the political strategy of the 1872 campaign rather than in the comic-opera events transpiring in Little Rock in the spring of 1874.

# CHAPTER SIX

# JOSEPH BROOKS WINS THE ELECTION

During May and June of 1872, there had been several encouraging indications that political disqualifications against ex-Confederates were about to be removed. One such indication was the platform adopted by the Liberal Republican party in Cincinnati on May first which demanded "the immediate and absolute removal of all disabilities imposed on account of the Rebellion, . . . believing that universal amnesty will result in complete pacification in all sections of the country."[1] Another indication was the Amnesty Act, passed by Congress during the latter part of May, which removed political disabilities from all but approximately five hundred of the most prominent leaders.[2] In Arkansas the "brindletail," or reform Republicans, echoed Congressional action by calling for "universal suffrage, universal amnesty, and honest men in office."[3] On June eighteenth the Cincinnati platform of the national party was endorsed by the liberal Republicans, a second reform faction in Arkansas.

Ironically, state sovereignty would be used to prevent the extension of this liberality to the Arkansas state elections that year. On July twenty-third, Governor Hadley announced that the registration would be made under the 1868 laws; and on August twenty-first, the "minstrel" Republican State Convention, although endorsing the Amnesty Act passed by Congress, insisted that the act did not have authority to remove disabilities imposed on the ex-Confederates by the state Constitution of 1868.[4]

Garland wanted to bring this conflict before the Federal District Court, but was unable to do so in time for a decision to be rendered prior to the November election. He was optimistic, however, concerning the manner in which registration was being done. As a joke, he attempted to register and was not refused. Although he had never been disqualified, the registrars believed him to have been; therefore, he interpreted this action as an indication of liberality in the registration procedures.  He had not heard of anyone who had been refused.[5]

David Walker, however, did not share Garland's optimism.  In an open letter published in the *Fayetteville Democrat*, he reminded his readers of the resolution passed by the "minstrel" Convention the previous month stating that the Amnesty Act did not alter the Arkansas Constitution, nor did it enfranchise any citizens disfranchised by the latter document.[6] His conclusion was somber as he warned his friends that they would have to submit to the provisions of the state Constitution as interpreted by the "minstrel" party.  This basic conflict between national legislation and the state Constitution provided a basis for controversy over the registration and the outcome of the November election even before a vote was cast.

Opponents of the "minstrel" Republicans during the election year of 1872 were divided over two dominant political attitudes as November fifth approached.  The first looked toward the election of Horace Greeley and the success of the national Liberal Republican movement as the ultimate means of rescuing the state from the radical government in power.  Hope of bringing conservative men, North and South, together in a new political alignment appealed to such men as David Walker and John R. Eakin.  Liberal Republicans, together with former Whigs and conservative Northern Democrats, could abandon the radical measures of the day and bring political relations back to their proper condition.  Coalition appeared to them as political principle, not as expediency, the latter being the charge which they leveled against Democrats more inclined toward the immediacy of their party's success.

These considerations made Joseph Brooks acceptable as a candidate for governor to men of this persuasion.  Under normal circumstances he would not have been acceptable, for this carpetbag minister from Iowa had been strongly associated with the creation of the Constitution of 1868, had been a staunch advocate of equal rights for Negroes, and, as a result, had a large Negro following in the Republican party.[7] If this vote could be combined with that of the populous northwest, however, success in November was assured.  His ability as a speaker and his determination to expose the corruption and evils existing in state affairs made him a formidable candidate.  One contemporary said of his campaign, he "went through the State like a fiery cross, . . . denouncing Clayton and Dorsey, and all of them, telling the people if they would elect him governor he would fill the jail so full of them that their legs would stick out the windows."[8]

Advocates of the second political attitude were oriented more toward the immediacy of state political affairs.  Short of electing a Democratic governor (an impossible task), a strong legislative majority which could begin the process of reducing the governor's power was the only alternative.  Although they preferred to think in terms of a purely Democratic ticket rather than a Democratic-Conservative coalition, government under the Constitution of 1868 made it necessary for men of this persuasion to consider regaining control of the state legislature to be their essential goal. If they gained this control for the Democratic party, the legislature could be used as a means of modifying some of the powers of the governor's office and could serve as a check on the manner in which other powers were exercised. In addition, through legislative action such party instruments as the registration law might be modified. But of paramount importance to men of these views was the hope of ultimately holding a constitutional convention to rid the state of the Constitution of 1868, on which the present system was based.

Chances of gaining control of the legislature appeared to lie in a large Democratic vote in November, in a popular ticket to bring out that vote, and in a thorough party organization. Holding the end to be so important as to justify the means, spokesmen for this point of view, W.E. Woodruff. Jr., as an example, embraced a much more expedient approach to the forthcoming election than that of Walker and his political associates.

Among the prominent Democrats supporting the Brooks reform ticket was ex-Governor Harris Flanagin. In response to an invitation from B.F. Rice, chairman of that coalition campaign committee which represented the Democratic-Conservative, reform Republican, and liberal Republican coalition, Flanagin actively spoke in behalf of the ticket in his area. His influence was important enough to cause him to be invited to become Presidential elector in his district.[9] When the Hunter movement made its attempt to divert Democrats from the reform coalition, he was among those of the Democratic-Conservative party to speak out in opposition.[10]

The Hunter movement was apparently an expression of reaction against the direction matters were developing under the Brooks reform ticket. On October first, the liberal Republicans proposed a ticket headed by Dr. Andrew Hunter. Perhaps sharing the disappointment felt by the liberals over the meager concessions they had received from the reform Republicans, the regular Democratic Central Committee issued an address asking all Democrats to support the Hunter ticket instead of that headed by Brooks.[11] When one recalls Garland's suggestion to Governor Flanagin, made four months earlier, that Dr. Hunter would be the candidate having the ability to bring out the largest vote among the Democrats and also Garland's emphasis on the importance of that vote to gaining control of the legislature, the question of Garland's relationship to the Hunter movement arises.[12] That he found the idea of Brooks as governor so unacceptable in the light of his hopes for effective control of the legislature was also of interest. Unfortunately, evidence for answering these questions has not been found. A fair conclusion seems to be, however, that Garland was sympathetic to the Hunter movement, and that the movement itself was an expression of that political attitude referred to above which wanted Democratic party organization directed toward gaining control of the state legislature.

Whatever the motives behind the Hunter movement, reaction against it was swift among the Democratic-Conservative members. By October tenth, the Democratic Central Committee issued a second address urging Democrats once again to support the Brooks ticket as was originally agreed upon in the Democratic-Conservative convention on June nineteenth.[13] The negative response to their first address was based on resentment of the committee's action in assuming authority which had not been granted. They were also embarrassed by Dr. Hunter's declining to become a candidate. When Hunter withdrew his name, B.F. Rice jubilantly telegraphed Harris Flanagin on October eighth: "Hunter's letter of declination just received in this city. Grand rally tonight of the friends of reform.[14]

In the northwest this attempt to introduce a new ticket at such a late hour served to unite the conservatives behind the Brooks cause. James Mitchell wrote

## TABLE 3

## GOVERNOR'S ELECTION 1872 – STUDY BY AREA

|  | Male Citizens 21 and Over[a] 1870 | General Election (Governor)[b] Nov. 5, 1872 | Official Baxter Vote[c] | Official Brooks Vote[c] | Reform Baxter Vote[d] | Reform Brooks Vote[d] |
|---|---|---|---|---|---|---|
| NW | 37,335 | 21,428 | 9,399 | 12,029 | 10,158 | 15,27 |
| D | 31,245 | 29,700 | 18,425 | 11,275 | 18,370 | 12,76 |
| SW | 23,401 | 22,078 | 10,760 | 11,318 | 9,825 | 12,50 |
| TOTAL | 91,981 | 73,206 | 38,584 | 34,622 | 38,353 | 40,54 |
| *% of Total* | % | % | % | % | % | % |
| NW | 40.6 | 29.3 | 43.9 | 56.1 | 40 | 60 |
| D | 34 | 40.6 | 62 | 38 | 59 | 41 |
| SW | 25.4 | 30.1 | 48.7 | 51 | 44 | 56 |

a. Calculated from: U.S. Bureau of the Census, *Ninth Census: 1870. Population,* I, p. 623.
b. Calculated from: *Gazette,* December 13, 1872, p. 4, cc. 4–5.
c. *Ibid.*
d. Calculated from: Reform convention address, *Gazette,* January 23, 1873, p. 2, c. 3.

David Walker that, although many in the Cane Hill region had been slow to support Brooks, they were coming behind him now and would stand firm, "as you say our honor is at stake in this matter. We have pledged ourselves in the most solemn manner—in conventions—by the press, on the stump, everywhere to stand by Brooks in this canvass. We cannot now stultify ourselves—cannot violate every obligation and desert him. We are irrevocably committed to the Reform movement and must rise or fall with it."[15] The *Fayetteville Democrat* echoed the observation that the Hunter episode had helped unite reform Republicans and Democrats in that area.[16]

On October eleventh, the day after the collapse of the Hunter movement, the *Gazette*, which had been chief spokesman for the new ticket, revealed something of its disappointment in its editorial pages. Unless the party obtained control of the legislature, the outcome of the governor's election would be of little importance. The editor had nothing to say about how that control should be won, but he wanted the people to gain it "regardless of everything else."[17]

The election took place November fifth with results unknown for several days. Hugh F. Thomason wrote Walker in despair over the farce that the election had been, but part of that despair came from the inability to contest the result successfully.[18] The confusion must have been great, for the *Fayetteville Democrat* on November thirtieth claimed the election of Brooks and a conservative legislature[19] Of particular interest to David Walker was the newspaper's announcement that his friend, T.M. Gunter, had been elected United States Congressman from the third district.[20] The elation over these announcements was destroyed, however, when the *Gazette* published the official returns on December thirteenth.[21] They revealed that Elisha Baxter, the "minstrel" candidate, had received 41,681 and Joseph Brooks 38,415 votes. The entire "minstrel" ticket was declared elected, with the exception of the three Congressmen at large. Even T.M. Gunter had not been elected.

That Brooks was actually elected would be impossible to prove, but the testimony of men of integrity such as David Walker, Hugh F. Thomason, Isaac Murphy, and James Mitchell of the northwest, U.M. Rose of Little Rock, and Harris Flanagin and John R. Eakin in the southwest would argue that he was.[22] The distribution of votes and the absence of returns from four counties would place suspicion on the validity of the official totals.[23] The persistence of Brooks and the loyalty to his cause of numbers of people for over a year, the unusual maneuvers to deny him a fair hearing before the legislature, and the reorganization of the legislature itself cast doubt on his opponent's claim. The fact that T.M. Gunter, defeated on the same ticket with Brooks, was ultimately able to win his contested seat in the United States Congress also adds credibility to the proposition that Joseph Brooks was elected at the ballot box in November, 1872.

This evidence supports the unquestioned belief of David Walker that Brooks

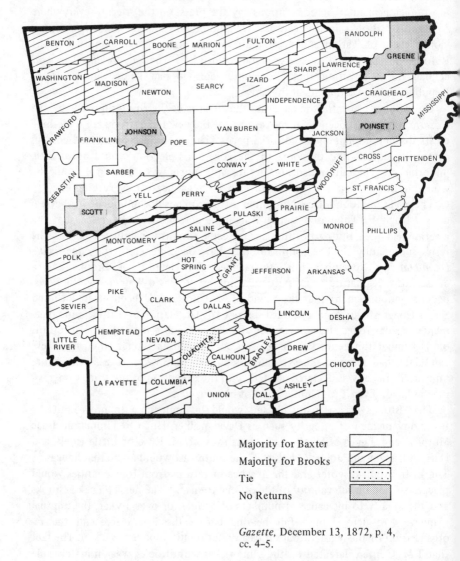

Majority for Baxter
Majority for Brooks
Tie
No Returns

*Gazette,* December 13, 1872, p. 4,
cc. 4-5.

Figure 14.    Governor's Election, 1872: Official Returns

Majority for Baxter
Majority for Brooks

Reform convention "Address to the
People," *Gazette,* January 23, 1873,
p. 2, c. 3.

Figure 15.    Governor's Election, 1872: Reform Convention Returns

was elected governor and also explains the loyalty given to Brooks' cause by many people from November, 1872, until his own resort to expediency as a means for accomplishing his purpose in April, 1874. Considering the Brooks-Baxter War out of this context will lead to a misunderstanding of it. Brooks had a legitimate cause for which he could not get a fair hearing. The Constitution of 1868, in the construction of which he participated so energetically during the Convention, provided that disputed elections for the governor's office would be decided by the legislature.[24]   In one of the strongest ironies of Reconstruction in Arkansas, that instrument would be used to deny him a fair hearing because the legislature was in unfriendly hands.

The official returns indicated that Brooks had received 56.1% of the votes cast in the northwest, 51.3% of those in the southwest, but only 38% of those in the delta.[25]   The Negro vote in the delta had gone to the "minstrel" rather than to the reform ticket, and in the northwest the vote was much lighter proportionately than in the other sections. The voters there either were denied registration, or refused to accept the tickets offered, or were indifferent to the outcome in the absence of an attractive candidate, as Garland had expected them to be. When the "minstrels" insisted on conducting the election according to the disqualifications imposed by the Constitution of 1868, the Democratic-Conservative party resorted to the use of affidavits by those who had been refused registration.[26]   In many places two polls were conducted. Besides the regular ballot box there was a second one for those using the affidavits to vote. Many voted in both polls, an action which added to the confusion and resulted in charges of fraud during the election.[27]   The calculations involved in the strategy of choosing Baxter and Brooks for their ability to divide the opposition increased the confusion as to the actual outcome of the election both for people of that day and for students in days to come.

On November eighteenth, leaders of the reform Republicans called a Convention in Little Rock for January 4, 1873, to consider what course might be taken.[28]   The need for calm and experienced men to gather evidence of frauds perpetrated during the election and to decide what legal recourse should be taken was stated by the *Fayetteville Democrat.*[29] Delegates to this Convention, which met two days before the new legislature was to convene, took little immediate action other than to pass resolutions and appoint a committee to prepare an address presenting their position to the people.[30]

The dilemma faced by this Convention was related to the nature of the state Constitution. Although that document gave exclusive right to the legislature to resolve disputed elections, the candidates of the reform ticket could scarcely expect to obtain a fair hearing in that tribunal, for the judges there would be the newly-elected legislators, their "minstrel" opponents during the election. Brooks and the "brindletail" legislators briefly considered organizing a second legislature, inaugurating Brooks as governor, and letting Congress settle the matter.[31]   But this course of action was ultimately abandoned as being unwise. After passing several resolutions and appointing a committee for the purpose of preparing an address to the people of Arkansas, the reform convention adjourned.[32]

The committee and Mr. Brooks busied themselves with collecting evidence of fraud and making their own estimation of the election results.  Their findings were published in an "Address to the People" carried in the *Gazette* on January twenty-third.  In their judgment, justice for their cause could be obtained only from the Federal government through its constitutional responsibility for assuring the states a government republican in nature.  They hoped to reach a Congressional committee with the claim that the frustration of the people's will, expressed at the ballot box in November, had denied them a republican government.[33]

According to their tabulation of the election returns, Baxter had not won the governor's office, but had received 41,394 votes to Brooks' 43,802.[34]   Their distribution showed that 60% of the vote in the northwest went to Brooks, 56% in the southwest, and 41% in the delta.  Returns from all counties were included, and their count gave Brooks majorities in ten more counties than the official returns had done.[35]

The address made a strong appeal for the support of the reform movement. Noting that the Democratic party had added "conservative" to its name in order to appeal to the "old line Whigs," the committee hoped "reform" might also be added in order to consolidate the opposition to radicalism and make an effective party out of these elements.[36]

Under the circumstances such appeals were weaker than they might have been.  Although the legitimacy of Brooks' claim to the governor's office was recognized by many men throughout the state, the possibility of obtaining a fair hearing for that claim before the legislature was very small.  If Baxter conducted himself with any degree of wisdom, the probability was strong that he would be able to establish securely his tenure in the governor's office.  That tenure would likely come to be recognized by more and more people with the passage of time.  And as this development took place, the Brooks forces would become demoralized and disintegrate.

## TABLE 4

## ARKANSAS VOTING RECORD AND POPULATION

| Date | Identification | Number Voting | Adult Males | Registered Voters | Aggregate Population |
|------|----------------|---------------|-------------|-------------------|----------------------|
| 1860 | U.S. Census | | 98,845[a] | | 435,450[b] |
| Nov. 6, 1860 | General Election (Pres.) | 54,000[c] | (87,090)[d] | | |
| Aug. 6, 1866 | Supreme Court Election | (24,790)[e] 74,372 | (91,992)[d] | | (459,960)[f] |
| Nov.-Dec. 5, 1867 | Convention Election | 41,134[g] | (92,972)[d] | 66,805[g] | (464,862)[f] |
| Mar. 13-18, | Constitution | | (93,953)[d] | | |
| 1868 | Election | 54,510[h] | 93,500[i] | 73,784[h] | (469,764)[f] |
| Nov. 3 1868 | General Election (Pres.) | 41,230[j] | (94,933)[d] | | (474,666)[k] |
| 1870 | U.S. Census | | 104,083[l] | | 484,471[m] |
| Nov. 5, 1872 | General Election (Pres.) | 79,000[n] | (119,861)[d] | | (548,081)[k] |
| June 20, 1874 | Convention Election | 88,866[o] | (133,669)[d] | | (594,595)[k] |
| Oct. 13, 1874 | Constitution Election | 103,504[p] | (135,641)[d] | | (611,691)[k] |
| Nov. 7, 1876 | General Election (Pres.) | 97,000[c] | (151,419)[d] | | (673,701)[k] |
| 1880 | U.S. Census | | 182,977[q] | | 802,525[r] |

a. U.S. Bureau of the Census, *Eighth Census: 1860. Population*, I, pp. 12-17. Adult males 2 and above.
b. U. S. Bureau of the Census, *Ninth Census- 1870. Population*, I, pp. 13-14.
c. U.S. Bureau of the Census, *Historical Statistics of the United States Colonial Times to 195* (Washington, D.C.: Government Printing Office, 1960), pp. 688-89.
d. Estimate of adult male population 21 and over shown in parentheses. Calculation based o 20% of total population for that year.
e. *Gazette*, October 9, 1866, p. 3, c.1. In this election 74,372 votes were cast, but the electio chose three judges for the Supreme Court out of four candidates. It is believed that the vot was asked to vote for each of the three positions to be filled thereby reducing the number o actual voters to perhaps nearer one-third of the votes cast.
f. Estimate of total population calculated as 50%, 60%, and 70% respectively in the yea 1866, 1867, 1868 of the difference between total population 1860 and total populatio 1870. Allowance for war casualties explains the 10% lag in population increase in those yea
g. *Debates and Proceedings of the Constitutional Convention, 1868* (Little Rock: J.G. Pric 1868), pp. 769-70.
h. *Ibid.,* p. 807.
i. T.S. Staples, *Reconstruction in Arkansas* (New York:Longmans Green & Co., 1923), p. 27 This is Staples' estimate in November, 1868.
j. *Ibid.,* p. 287.

k. Calculation of estimated total population based on 10% per year of the difference in total population figures 1860–1870 and 1870–1880. Exception to this is the estimate for June, 1874. Here the 1874 estimate for June, 1874, was lessened by 33% to allow for the four month time interval between June and October.

l. *Ninth Census, op. cit.,* p. 623.

m. *Ibid.,* pp. 13–14.

n. *Gazette,* December 13, 1872, p. 4, c. 4.

o. *Ibid.,* July 14, 1874, p. 1, cc. 5–6.

p. *Ibid.,* October 31, 1874, p. 1, cc. 5 – 6.

q. U.S. Bureau of the Census, *Tenth Census: 1880. Population,* I, p. 648.

r. *Ibid.,* p. 3.

Note: Estimated figures used in this table should be taken with extreme caution. They are intended as rough approximations rather than as precise statistics. Skepticism concerning their accuracy arises in relation to the size of the vote reported in the election ratifying the Constitution of 1874. The total of 103,504 appears abnormally large when compared with the estimated number of adult males (135,641).

# CHAPTER SEVEN

# ELISHA BAXTER WINS THE OFFICE

While the reform convention was trying to solve Brooks' problems of strategy, the legislature convened on January sixth, and Elisha Baxter was inaugurated governor. A formidable candidate himself, Baxter had been chosen to run on a liberal platform calculated to appeal to the Democratic voters and to win their support away from the reform ticket. His attractiveness as a candidate was related to his Unionist background and to his residence in northwestern Arkansas, an area in which the "minstrel" faction needed votes. Although born in North Carolina, he had lived in Arkansas since 1852. A resident of Batesville, he had engaged in the mercantile business, had learned the newspaper business, and later had established a law practice with James Hinds in Little Rock prior to the Civil War. He was elected a member of the legislature from Independence County in 1854 and again in 1858.[1] Baxter had been elected United States Senator under the Murphy government in 1864, together with William M. Fishback, but their credentials were refused in Washington.[2]

Beginning his term of office under the clouds of a disputed election, Governor Baxter wisely delivered a conciliatory inaugural address in which he promised to restore friendly relations among the whole people, to stimulate industry, and to encourage the development of natural resources. He also expressed his desire to enfranchise those disfranchised by constitutional limitation and predicted "that from the present indications it is safe to presume that before another general election shall be held, this last vestage of the late civil war will have been completely obliterated."[3] If he meant what he said, this statement announced the beginning of the end of Republican rule in Arkansas, a fact which did not go unnoticed.

The period from Governor Baxter's inaugural on January sixth until March fourth was of vital importance to future political developments in the state.

Figure 16.  Joseph Brooks
Elisha Baxter

During these weeks political realignments began which promised a fundamental change in the *status quo*. One of two major issues of the period was the election of a United States Senator. A constitutional amendment providing for the removal of political disabilities for ex-Confederates was the second. In the process of resolving these issues new political relationships emerged.

It will be recalled that Senator B.F. Rice had been a leading supporter of Joseph Brooks in his campaign for governor and that Augustus H. Garland had believed that "the whole end and object really of Brooks fight is to continue B.F. Rice in the U.S. Senate first, & therefore all their energies will be directed to getting and governing the Legislature."[4] This belief had been one of Garland's chief objections to Brooks becoming governor. Now, however, prospects for the election of Senator Rice had been practically eliminated by the results of the election, and the choice of another man had to be made.

The leading candidate for the office was Stephen W. Dorsey, who enjoyed the support of Governor Baxter. Next in order of strength was Augustus H. Garland, favorite of the Democrats.[5] Thomas M. Bowen was the favorite of the Republican faction headed by Senator Powell Clayton and received the active support of Chief Justice John McClure, who was now the most active leader of that faction in the state. On the first ballot these men received the following vote: Dorsey, forty-three; Garland, thirty-five; and Bowen, twenty.[6] As long as the legislators remained loyal to their candidates, no choice could be made; therefore, the factions had to do some bargaining in order to break the deadlock. On January eighteenth, this bargaining resulted in the election of Stephen W. Dorsey, as United States Senator.[7] The Democrats had shifted their support to him—a change which brought about a final tally of Dorsey, eighty-seven; Garland, eleven; Walker, three; Newton, one.[8]

The next day the *Gazette* offered several reasons why the Democrats shifted to Dorsey. They realized that they could not elect Garland without Republican help; therefore, that possibility was eliminiated. They opposed Bowen's election because of his support by Senator Clayton and other members of the "minstrel" faction of the party. And, finally, they saw hope in the policy laid down by Baxter in his inaugural address.[9]

An additional reason very likely influenced their actions as well. A joint resolution and act for submitting a franchise amendment to the vote of the people had been introduced in the senate on January the eighth.[10] The Democrats were naturally quite interested in seeing this act passed. Therefore, it is quite probable that its passage was their price for the voting support which Dorsey needed.[11] The timing of the two occurrences would lend credibility to this connection, for on January eighteenth the election was completed, and on the twenty-third Governor Baxter signed the act which called for the submission of the constitutional amendment to the people in an election to be held on March third.[12]

Two political coalitions could be perceived in the November governor's election by noting their leading political figures. Supporting the reform ticket were to be found the following leaders:

| | |
|---|---|
| Joseph Brooks | candidate for governor; |
| B. F. Rice | candidate for United States Senator; |
| Harris Flanagin | ex-Confederate governor and Democratic leader in south-western Arkansas; |
| David Walker | former Chief Justice of the Arkansas Supreme Court and Whig leader in northwestern Arkansas; and |
| Augustus H. Garland | (former Whig) Democratic leader reluctantly supporting Brooks as candidate. |

Supporting the regular Republican ticket were these leaders:

| | |
|---|---|
| Elisha Baxter | candidate for governor; |
| Stephen W. Dorsey | aspirant candidate for United States Senator; |
| Powell Clayton | Republican leader and United States Senator; |
| John McClure | Chief Justice of the Arkansas Supreme Court and active party leader; and |
| Thomas M. Bowen | aspirant candidate for United States Senator. |

As a result of the outcome of the November election and of the political experience since the legislature convened, three coalitions could be identified by January twenty-third. One of these was comprised of the Baxter-Dorsey-Garland forces, which had come together, at least temporarily, to elect Stephen W. Dorsey United States Senator and to secure Governor Baxter's aid in passing the Franchise Amendment Bill. A second coalition was comprised of the McClure-Bowen-Clayton forces, which had suffered defeat in the election of Dorsey and who would feel increasingly estranged from Governor Baxter as he came under the influence of Democratic leaders. A third political coalition was comprised of the Brooks-Rice-Flanagin-Walker forces, which continued to represent the cooperation established in the 1872 campaign between the Democratic-Conservative party and the "brindletail" Republican faction and who remained faithful to the conviction that Joseph Brooks had been elected governor in November.

The significance of the Baxter-Dorsey-Garland cooperation should not go unnoticed. Through this action the Democrats in the legislature recognized the legitimacy of that political body and consequently reduced the chances of Joseph Brooks being able to make a successful contest of the results of the November election. In addition to this consequence, Governor Baxter, by approving the act which called for an election on the Franchise Amendment, demonstrated his good faith in honoring pledges expressed in his inaugural address and thereby encouraged the Democrats in their hope that he meant to honor other conciliatory pledges made during and since the campaign. The growth of this good will toward him would be important in months to come.

The defeat of the McClure-Bowen-Clayton forces in their efforts to elect Thomas M. Bowen United States Senator was indicative of their future troubles in the legislature. When the Baxter forces combined with the thirty-one Democratic members, they could control the legislature by placing the McClure-Bowen-Clayton faction of the Republican party in an enclave. The frequency with which this maneuver might be carried out placed that Republican faction in a vulnerable position. It should be emphasized, however, that Senator Clayton maintained his good relations with Governor Baxter, for he above all others realized the importance of the powers of that office and the necessity of having the Governor's good will in political matters. His open break with Baxter did not occur until sometime after the November election of 1873, but open hostilities between Baxter and Chief Justice John McClure, who was assuming an aggressive leadership of this faction of the Republican party within the state, could not be contained beyond early April.[13]

The "Address to the People" of the Reform Convention published on January twenty-third indicated something of the plight of the Brooks-Rice-Flanagin-Walker forces. They had endured and would endure in the future the frustrations of a just cause denied a proper hearing. After the Reform Convention had decided not to establish a separate government and not to submit a petition before the existing legislature, Brooks initiated a suit in the Federal District Court on January eighth, only to be refused a hearing there because the court lacked jurisdiction.[14] On January twenty-second, the house indicated its disinclination toward an investigation of election frauds by organizing its election committee along strictly partisan lines. There were no Democratic members on the committee, and a majority of the members held seats which were contested by the Brooks forces.[15] A further discouragement was the fact that the chairman of the Senate Election Committee was John M. Clayton, the brother of Senator Powell Clayton.[16] Under these circumstances it should not be surprising to see the Brooks forces look toward a Congressional committee as their only hope for a fair hearing.

Senator Rice did what he could in Washington, but his efforts proved to be insufficient to obtain Federal aid. The first week in February, he introduced a resolution in the Senate calling for an inquiry by the Committee on Privileges and Elections into the question of whether or not Arkansas had a legal state government. Senator Furry of Connecticut objected, saying that: " 'on reflection,' he had become satisfied 'that the senate exceeded its power in attempting to carry out a similar resolution in regard to Louisiana.' "[17] The resolution failed to pass. But one final effort by Senator Rice late in February was successful in preventing the acceptance of the Presidential vote in Arkansas because "the election returns showed that persons certified by the secretary of state were not elected as electors."[18] With the expiration of his term of office on March fourth, however, the Brooks cause lost its chief spokesman in Washington.

In Arkansas a surprisingly small number of voters cast their votes in the March third election which was to decide the fate of the Franchise Amendment. In comparison with some 80,000 votes cast in the last governor's election, there were less than 28,000 votes cast in this one. From those voting, however, the Amendment received an overwhelming majority, there being 24,203 for and only 3,694 against removing the constitutional restrictions on the franchise. Chicot and Perry counties were alone in returning majorities against the Amendment.[19]

The political significance of this development would be hard to overemphasize. For the Brooks forces this Amendment lessened the vitality of the support they could expect from the Democrats in any future effort to overturn the Baxter regime in favor of Brooks' claim to the governor's office. For the Democrats this Amendment signaled a change in the political tide in their favor. If they could maintain their good relations with Baxter, this tide would continue in their favor and bring them control of the legislature in the 1874 election. No one was more aware of this probability than John McClure, who had become increasingly important as an active leader of the "minstrel" Republican faction in the state during Senator Clayton's absence in Washington. McClure had been directly involved, as a member of the Apportionment Committee, in creating the political system under the Constitution of 1868 by which the Republicans had established their power. The demise of that system now must not be allowed to happen without a struggle. For the McClure forces this Amendment brought home to them the political shrewdness with which the Democrats had bargained with the Dorsey men in the legislature. It was true, as Garland had observed in June, 1872, that the legislature was the great objective for the Democrats; and with this Amendment, which had been secured, in part, through the cooperation of the Dorsey and Baxter men in the legislature, the means for accomplishing that objective had been established. Despite these reverses for the McClure forces, the present legislature offered conditions more favorable to them than those they might anticipate in the future. Consequently, if defensive moves were to be made to save the system, they had to be made soon.

The nine months following passage of the Franchise Amendment witnessed a political struggle for control of the legislature during which awareness of the existence of this Amendment acted as a continuing influence on the combatants. It is important to bear in mind that the objective of this nine-month struggle was the control of the legislature. Although one might question the singleness of purpose among the factions involved, control of the legislature was the prize any group had to possess before attaining success. Without that control Brooks could not become governor, McClure could not check Baxter's use of the powers of his office, nor could the Democrats secure reform of the Constitution through calling a convention.

Throughout most of this period two Little Rock editors acted as spokesmen for the Baxter Republican-Democratic forces and for the McClure Republican forces. William E. Woodruff, Jr., editor of the *Gazette,* and John McClure, Chief Justice of the Arkansas Supreme Court and editor of the Little Rock *Republican*, vigorously represented the interests of their supporters. Their verbal exchanges were calculated to enlist support for their political point of view, and, as the editorial repartee between them grew warmer, distortions of the passing events undoubtedly crept into their writing. The student must attempt to understand those events through the maze of these exchanges.

To the editor of the *Gazette,* the legislature, which had been in session since January sixth, appeared to have accomplished little by the end of February. "The general assembly has been in session now nearly two months, and has passed during that time perhaps a half-dozen bills. There seems little desire to do anything."[20] The last month of that session, however, would supply the interest the editor found lacking in this earlier period. Controversy centered on three bills advocated by the McClure forces: an election law, a militia bill, and a railroad-aid bill. The *Gazette* would perceive in these schemes a conspiracy by a ring of politicians and speculators headed by John McClure, Thomas M. Bowen, C.W. Tankersley, and a half-dozen other men.[21]

The passage of the Franchise Amendment threatened one of the vital parts of the system by which the Republicans had maintained their control of the state—the elective franchise. The attempt to pass a new election law may be interpreted as an attempt to strengthen the power of the election commissioners' control over elections as a means of cushioning the impact upon the Republican party of the enlarged franchise. It is certain that John McClure, who had been so active in constructing the system, fully appreciated the danger this change represented. Losing control of the franchise and simultaneously losing favor with the governor's office could prove disastrous. The new bill called for concentration of power in the hands of the lieutenant governor and two election commissioners and for an enlargement of the role usually played by the election commission.

The second of the three controversial measures, the Militia Bill, called for an appropriation of $400,000 to pay for property alleged to have been taken from citizens during the course of various militia raids throughout the state. In the eyes of the *Gazette*, a claim of fraudulent militia vouchers previously issued to members of the ring of politicians and speculators made this bill a vehicle for their own enrichment, and no one outside of the ring might expect any benefit from the appropriation.

The third measure, the Railroad-aid Bill, or "railroad-steal" bill as the *Gazette* partisanly referred to it, would permit the railroads to honor their obligations to the state for the bonds they had previously received by using stock of their own railroad as currency. This exchange of stock for bonds would release them from their present obligation to pay off approximately $5,200,000 in state bonds as they came due.[22]   Through the eyes of an adversary this scheme appeared to be an outright gift to the railroads of the amount of the bonds.

This Railroad-aid Bill was introduced in the house of representatives on March twenty-fifth, and was passed ten days later.[23]   Whatever smooth sailing this development might have promised the McClure forces was deceptive, for those forces were on a collision course with Governor Elisha Baxter.   The importance of the powers of the governor's office now came into prominence as Baxter began to use them to thwart the hopes of the McClure faction of the party.

Before the end of January, Governor Baxter was being exposed to Democratic influence. Especially in the exercise of his appointive powers did the Democrats constantly make themselves available to assist him in his choices. As early as January twenty-eighth, E.H. English, who had been Chief Justice of the Arkansas Supreme Court from 1855 to 1864, transmitted to Baxter letters of men who had written to him seeking help in securing positions.[24]  Although English did not presume to plead their cases, his letter to Baxter was characterized by political subtlety and psychological persuasion. Noting certain newspaper criticisms of Baxter for appointing to office men who were illiterate and also noting Baxter's inability to answer these jibes directly, English offered himself to Baxter as a confidential adviser and recommended a method by which Baxter could anonymously respond to these criticisms. English suggested to Baxter that "when any matter is thus publicly stated, that you desire contra-dicted, if you will furnish me with the facts, I will publish them through communications to the *Gazette,* in a manner that will be satisfactory without its appearing that you had anything to do with the matter."[25]

The continued vulnerability of Baxter to Democratic influence was indicated when, on March thirty-first, U.M. Rose wrote Harris Flanagin in regard to political appointments in the southwest. He urged Flanagin to see the Governor personally about these and other matters, adding, "if you would yourself see the governor and talk with him the effect would be good. It would certainly be well for you to do so with reference to general results, if nothing more."[26]

In his appraisal of Baxter, Rose expressed a guarded optimism:

> It is needless to say that I make very great allowance for the situation in which he is placed and the great difficulty of combating the corporation of sharks that have got hold of the body politic. I am persuaded however that he would like to promote an honest and economical administration of the government and to make such appointments as would secure a fair administration of the laws and reflect credit on himself . . . it follows from what I have said that he is not insensible to the good opinion and advice of others.[27]

The growth of Democratic influence on Baxter did not go unnoticed by John McClure. Ten days after the letter above was written the public rupture in the relations between McClure and Baxter occurred. In an article appearing in the *Republican* on April tenth, McClure attacked Baxter for the use he was making of his appointive powers to oppose passage by the legislature of the Railroad-aid Bill.[28] As he commented on the situation, the party politician was evident in his thinking. His comments also revealed the partisan nature of the political system established by the Constitution of 1868:

> We are getting sick of this one-man power. It was given the executive to hold the republican party in power. No man in the executive chair before this time ever threatened to use it to carry out his personal wishes; nor did any previous executive attempt to use it for any other purpose than that of strengthening the party.[29]

It was as if the system, which had concentrated powers in the governor's office, had become a political boomerang which was now coming full circle toward the McClure forces. The great power and patronage of the governor's office, which had been designed in part to give him dominance and, if need be, control over the legislature, were being used against the McClure faction of the party by Governor Baxter.

The opening guns in what the *Gazette* billed as the "McClure-Baxter war" had been fired.[30] Chiefly verbal and political, this "war" did not appear to threaten open military hostilities. Before the ironies of political developments during Reconstruction were completed, however, another challenge to Baxter's tenure in office would lead to a *coup d'état* and to a brief skirmish known as the Brooks-Baxter War in 1874. These two "wars" should not be confused with one another.

As if to press what advantage there might be in this split among the Republican forces led by McClure and those supporting Baxter, on April fifteenth the *Gazette* criticized the Republican majority in the legislature for not carrying out the promises contained in their August platform.[31] Except for the Franchise Amendment, nothing had been done by them to honor those pledges, although the legislature had been in session for three and one half months. The particular action desired by the editor was an election law which would submit to the people the election of officers not prohibited by the Constitution and would fix the time for that election. Three days later the editor continued his attack by pointing to the fact that the conservative press "unitedly and unreservedly denounces" the Railroad-aid Bond Bill and that the Republican press "either does the same thing or remains silent," the only exception being the Little Rock *Republican.*[32]

The lengthy session of the legislature was approaching its conclusion thanks to a joint resolution which had designated April twenty-fifth as the date for adjournment. The hostility among political groups was rising, and the press of business associated with the final week of this unusually long session was adding tension to the conduct of affairs. In the house on Friday afternoon, April eighteenth, at three o'clock representative Thrower (Ouachita and Nevada) rose to a question of privilege. In his hand he held the petition of Hon. Joseph Brooks seeking to contest the validity of the late governor's election![33] Given the situation, a worse context in which to consider the merits of Brooks' claim to the governor's office could scarcely be imagined.

Several members rose to a question of order. Representative Warwick of Pulaski was recognized and stated that the order of the day had been set and that this matter was not a privileged question. The presiding officer ruled that it was, and Mr. Thrower was allowed to make his motion that the petition be read and the prayer be granted. An appeal from the ruling of the chair was called for and on that vote the decision of the chair was not sustained. The vote to sustain the ruling of the chair read: twenty-nine ayes, thirty-six noes, and thirteen not voting.[34] This was as close as Joseph Brooks ever came to obtaining a hearing of his case before the legislature.

If John McClure faced a political boomerang in the powers granted the Governor by the Constitution, Joseph Brooks faced one in the authority granted the legislature to decide contested elections for the office of governor. The irony of this present situation was not only that the Constitution was working against his success, but also that some of his former Democratic supporters would be responsible for denying him a hearing before the legislature. Several factors contributed to this denial.

He reaped now the hostility which he and his supporters had sown in January when they placed by name upon a "roll of infamy" and denounced as traitors to their party those Democrats who had taken their seats in the legislature. These were largely the same men who now were being asked to receive the plea of Brooks. A second factor working against his cause was the lack of moral commitment to the Constitution of 1868 felt by many of these men. One Democrat, representing the expediency argument of the day, commented that "the constitution cuts no figure in the case, and all constitutional arguments may as well be left out of the discussion."[35]

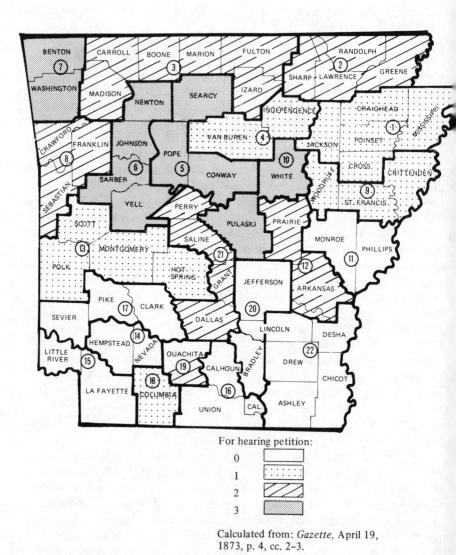

For hearing petition:

0
1
2
3

Calculated from: *Gazette,* April 19,
1873, p. 4, cc. 2–3.

**Figure 17.    Vote on Presiding Officer's Ruling to Hear Brooks' Petition**

Other legislators, however, were caught in a dilemma and voted against considering the petition with far more reluctance. One man felt it was a most trying ordeal and "that this contest should have come on at the time the governor was in the midst of a war with corruption and public plunderers, and whilst his fame is glowing among the people, is to me grievous."[36] One representative from Benton County justified his negative vote because he believed that "we have not time to try the cause, and for the further reason that I do not believe a fair trial before this general assembly can be had."[37]

Perhaps the judgment of James L. Witherspoon, who was a Democratic member of the nine-member joint campaign committee supporting Brooks and who was one of six men over whose signatures the Reform Convention's "Address to the People" had been issued, may be taken as representative of the thinking of the Flanagin-Walker-type loyalty which Brooks still possessed at this time. In a letter to Flanagin on April twenty-first he commented on these developments:

A majority of the Democrats in the Legislature on Saturday [Friday] refused Brooks a hearing, and thereby say they prefer Baxter to Brooks. Their excuse that certain Republicans had fallen out with Baxter and were now willing to put Brooks in, will not do. They will not be able to sustain themselves before the people.[38]

It was becoming increasingly difficult in the state of Arkansas to tell which was the *de jure* and which was the *de facto* government.

Four days after the vote concerning the Brooks petition the *Gazette* gave its interpretation of the conspiracy at hand. By associating the Brooks claim with the schemes of the McClure faction, the editor discredited the legitimacy of Brooks' claim and also laid the basis for enlisting support for Baxter among his readers. The description of the plot below appeared in altered form on several future occasions, but the essentials remained the same for all good Democrats to read. The struggle was between the evil forces of McClure using Brooks for his own purposes and the heroic efforts for good being made by Governor Baxter:

People living outside the capital, and unacquainted with the inside working of the ring politicians at Little Rock, can form little conception of the nature of the fight which Gov. Baxter has recently made, and is now making, against the ring of desperate politicians and speculators who have controlled this state for the past five years. The announcement that if it passed he should veto the railroad release bill, and other kindred and supplemented measures planned by the ring has called down upon his head the united opposition of the most powerful ring that ever cursed this state. The bringing in of the petition of Hon. Joseph Brooks, asking to contest the right of Gov. Baxter to the position he occupies, was a movement on the part of the very ring that put Gov. Baxter in the position he occupies today, and which denounced Mr. Brooks a short time since in the severest of language. . . . It was never the intention of the ring that Mr. Brooks should be installed governor, but, it has been developed, having promised him enough republican votes (twenty-two it is reported) united with the democrats to have his petition received and referred to a committee, it was then the programme to secure from one of the supreme judges (probably the chief justice) an injunction restraining Gov. Baxter from exercising the duties of governor while the contest was going on, and let V.V. Smith (lieutenant governor) act as governor *ad interim.* The legislature would have adjourned, and the case not being adjudicated, it would have gone over and Smith remained as acting governor.[39]

Although the McClure-Brooks combination would appear to have more validity in the months to come, there was an exaggeration in detail of the circumstances at this time which was more characteristic of political propaganda than of historical accuracy. The correlation between those voting for hearing the Brooks petition and those voting for the Railroad-aid Bond Bill was rather small. Out of a membership of eighty-two only nine members of the legislature voted both for hearing the Brooks petition and for passing the railroad bill.[40] These nine votes were cast by members who came from regions affected by the Little Rock and Fort Smith Railroad, a fact which would suggest economic interest as much as political conspiracy, for it should be recalled that this had been, for the most part, a Brooks territory in the election. Most of the remaining votes in favor of the Railroad-aid Bond Bill came from representatives of southern Arkansas, whose action reflected an economic interest in the promotion of the Mississippi, Ouachita and Red River Railroad.[41] Again it would seem that the economic interests of a region without the service of a railroad were a major factor causing these southern representatives to vote for the bill. Little Rock had enjoyed railroad service from Memphis since April 11, 1871, when the last spike in the Memphis and Little Rock Rail Road had been driven; and as recently as February 10, 1873, the first through train from St. Louis had arrived over the Saint Louis, Iron Mountain and Southern Railroad.[42] Perhaps the editor did not appreciate the economic isolation suffered by these other areas.

Politically, the situation might be more accurately described as follows: a portion of the Republicans under the leadership of McClure hoped to use Brooks' claim as a means of combining with Democrats in the legislature to place Baxter forces in an enclave and to gain control of the legislature, to remove Baxter from office, or to throw matters into a contest in which Federal intervention might be enlisted to save the system. The disastrous context in which the Brooks petition was presented gave his cause little chance of success on its own merit. The Democrats were placed in a political situation in which a majority of them responded politically. Their coalition with the Baxter forces had been successful in securing the Franchise Amendment, Baxter's opposition

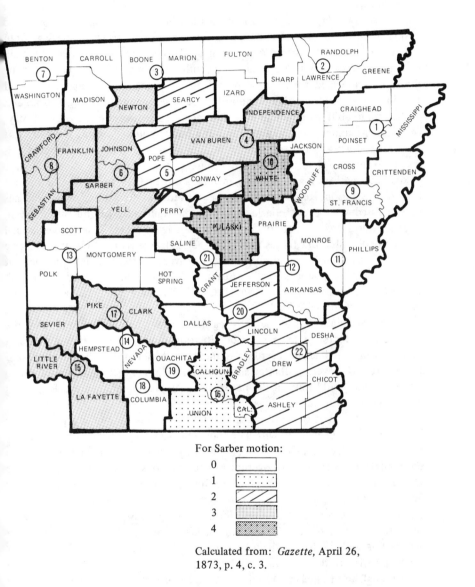

For Sarber motion:

0

1

2

3

4

Calculated from: *Gazette*, April 26,
1873, p. 4, c. 3.

Figure 18.    Vote on Sarber Motion to Consider Railroad-Aid Bond Bill

to the schemes of the McClure forces was much to their liking, and the reforms they desired had a better chance of success with Baxter as governor than by risking a change which might lead to Federal intervention. Time was in their favor now, and they believed waiting under Baxter would be better than risking the unknown.

The last two days of the legislative session provided the finale to this second period of Governor Baxter's administration. The house received a message from the senate during the afternoon session of April twenty-fourth that the Railroad-aid Bill had passed the upper house with amendments.[43] The next morning the house convened for its final session in an atmosphere of excitement and anticipation, for twelve o'clock noon had been set for the time of adjournment.

The militia-bill vote, which had gone against the measure the previous day, was brought under consideration, and the ballot counted again. The tally this time read thirty-eight ayes and thirty-nine noes. Great applause greeted this result. From this time until the adjournment at noon the house was in a state of disorder, with as many as thirty members out of their seats. Within the last hour of the session, Representative Sarber moved that the reading of the journals be dispensed with and a consideration of the Railroad-aid Bond Bill be given. That motion lost by a vote of forty-seven to twenty-eight. This signaled a final defeat for the McClure forces during this legislative session. Now disorder gave way to chaos as the hour of adjournment arrived. "After the announcement of the adjournment, a series of yells, screams and other oaths were made. The mob called for Tankersley, Neal Brown, Kent, Erwin and others, and went out the door singing, 'Old Black Joe'!"[44]

At the termination of this lengthy legislative session of over three months, the *Gazette* saw Baxter as master of the situation if he chose to be. Expressing praise for his stand against corruption, the editor believed that the people should be grateful to Governor Baxter and give him their support regardless of party. The Governor could rely on the newspaper's support in the future as long as his course remained unchanged.[45]

By the latter part of April, Elisha Baxter could look back on the period since his inauguration in January with a considerable degree of satisfaction. Beginning his term of office under the handicap of a disputed election he had been able to consolidate his position as governor and to win considerable support from the Democrats. His candidate, Stephen W. Dorsey, had been elected United States Senator, and the cooperation gained from the Democrats in that election had continued with sufficient strength during the legislative session to repeatedly place the McClure forces in a political enclave. Defeat of the Election Bill, the Militia Bill, and the Railroad-aid Bill provided testimony of the effectiveness of this opposition to the McClure forces.

Although the Franchise Amendment indicated a shift in the political tide in favor of the Democrats, by sponsoring this act Baxter gained significant support from Democratic forces and proved himself trustworthy in their eyes. By the time Joseph Brooks' claim came before the legislature many Democrats preferred to take their chances with Baxter and wait rather than to risk Joseph Brooks and the unknown. To be sure Baxter's tenure of office would be challenged in the future, but by the end of April it could be said that he had won his office.

# DAVID WALKER WRITES A LETTER

Governor Baxter and his Democratic supporters were not given time to enjoy their victories over the McClure forces. In Democratic eyes the Brooks petition had been an effort by the McClure forces to gain control of the legislature and to overthrow Baxter's domination of the government. The legislature's refusal to consider that petition should have brought the fruits of victory; namely, a recognition of Baxter's possession of the governor's office. Instead, by the middle of May the possibility of a *coup d'état* through other means appeared to be imminent. Rumors of such a revolution circulated throughout Little Rock in the weeks following the adjournment of the legislature.[1]

An application for the issuance of a writ of *quo warranto* was expected to be made by the attorney general and issued by the Supreme Court. The rumors predicted that once the writ had been issued, Chief Justice John McClure would as an individual member of the Court, enjoin Baxter from exercising his powers as governor while the inquiry authorized by the *quo warranto* was being conducted. The lieutenant governor would act as governor, and order would be maintained by the militia under the command of General Upham. The inquiry would be allowed to lie neglected for four years, during which time the McClure faction would run the government.[2]

These rumors seemed to be coming true by Monday, May twelfth, the day appointed for Attorney General T.D.W. Yonley to apply for the *quo warranto* before the Supreme Court. Because of the lack of a quorum on the bench the Court adjourned until the following Monday, May nineteenth. Prior to that date, however, Governor Baxter took the necessary steps to preserve his power.

On the evening of May fifteenth, Governor Baxter established a guard around his office and initiated action to reorganize the militia forces in such a way as to remove those officers who he had reason to believe were not loyal to him,

General Upham being one, and to appoint men on whom he could rely.[3] The consequent result of this fear of revolution was to move him increasingly into the hands of the ex-Confederate and Democratic forces. His appointment of Colonel Robert C. Newton as major general of the militia may be taken as an illustration of this development.

On May sixteenth, Newton wrote Harris Flanagin from Washington, requesting aid in securing a fresh horse to deliver a dispatch from the Governor, if the need arose, and indicating his awareness of the importance of these exciting developments in Little Rock:

We should not under-estimate the importance of what is going on. I understand it fully, and if with you could lead you into the light of it. Were I not actually *chained* here, in old Col. Lige Ferguson's case I should start at once for Little Rock! As it is, if Gov. Baxter telegraphs Block that I *must* come at once anyhow, I go.[4]

It is ironic to remember that Confederate troops under the same Colonel Robert C. Newton had placed the Unionist Elisha Baxter under arrest in 1863.[5]

That Baxter's actions had checked those moves against him was indicated in a letter from George A. Gallagher to Flanagin on May nineteenth. He reported that the Supreme Court had met that day without a *quo warranto* or a suggestion of one. "Baxter seems determined to be governor. Sup Ct met to-day no quo warranto or suggestion to that effect. Clayton & Hadley both gone to Washington—Think the present Govr master of the situation."[6]

To his credit, the editor of the *Gazette* brought to the attention of his readers an injustice then being done to Joseph Brooks by newspapers which were identifying him with this recent attempt to depose Baxter. Editor Woodruff felt that, in relation to Baxter, Brooks adhered firmly to his rights in his quarrel over the disputed election, but that, when faced with an attempt to execute this kind of *coup d'état*, Brooks earnestly desired the success of Baxter.[7] Also coming to Baxter's aid were many of Brooks' supporters throughout the state, including the editors of the *Washington Telegraph* and the *Fayetteville Democrat*.[8]

Baxter's success over his adversaries in this brief encounter gave his friends a sense of victory marred only by the apprehension of additional maneuvers which might threaten Federal intervention. The editor of the *Gazette* presented a persuasive argument intended for the supporters of Brooks who might be tempted to listen to political overtures from the McClure forces:

It would be well for those democrats and liberal republicans who are disposed to listen to McClure's emissaries, because they believe a foul injustice had been done Mr. Brooks, to consider well the consequences of inviting congressional interference. Of course, in voting for Mr. Brooks their idea was to accomplish their own deliverance. Is it likely that a radical congress would be more disposed to deal fairly with the people than Gov. Baxter?[9]

Each time a political crisis appeared the persuasiveness of this argument became stronger.

On June second, Attorney General Yonley made application for a writ of *quo warranto* against Governor Baxter before the Arkansas Supreme Court.[10] The irony of such an application against Baxter by Yonley, a man whose claim to office was weaker than the Governor's, was not missed by Woodruff. "When the latter says he appears in behalf of the people—as their representative—to declare Elisha Baxter a usurper, and that he does it for the good of the people, who can believe him? Have some peanuts, Yonley."[11]

On June third, Senators Dorsey and Clayton telegraphed their support for Baxter from New York.[12] Clayton appeared especially interested in disassociating himself from this effort to oust Baxter. Admitting that he had disapproved of Baxter's actions in calling the militia during the crisis in May and urging him now to avoid the use of any kind of force, Clayton assured Baxter of his belief that he was the legitimate governor and should stand firm regardless of the decision.

On June fourth, at five o'clock the Court met and Justice Gregg delivered the opinion of the Court. All of the judges, with the exception of the Chief Justice, denied the writ of *quo warranto* because the Court had no jurisdiction in such a case.[13] Ironically, as a means of denying the writ, former justices E.H. English and F.W. Compton, who in many ways opposed the Constitution of 1868, presented effective arguments upholding the provisions of that Constitution in this case. The denial of this writ of *quo warranto* signaled the failure of the maneuver to oust Baxter and to place Lieutenant Governor V.V. Smith in the governor's office as acting governor. The McClure forces had lost another battle in the "McClure-Baxter war."

With this decision the second portion of the nine-month struggle for control of the legislature came to an end. Once again, as it had done in April, the *Gazette* could rejoice over a Baxter victory, which made Baxter master of the situation. Now that matters had been settled, the people could turn their attention to their private interests in peace.[14] At this time Baxter enjoyed a growing popular support, the continuation of which would prove conclusive against any remaining hopes possessed by Brooks.

As a celebration of these days of victory and as an indication of his popularity, the capitol guards and the city cornet band gave Baxter a serenade at the state house on June ninth to which he responded with a glowing speech.[15] The *Augusta Bulletin* took notice of the transference of popular sentiment to Baxter which had been so marked during the last sixty days. "Nine-tenths of the whites voted against Baxter for governor. Not one negro in one thousand voted against him. . . . But both parties misjudged the man."[16]   All papers did not observe this popularity with pleasure, however, as the Fort Smith *Independent* revealed when it turned its editorial criticism against the *Gazette*.   "The influence of the Little Rock *Gazette* over the minds of democrats did more to break down the claims of Brooks and bolster up Baxter than anything else."[17]

A part of the change in attitude toward Baxter might well have been due to developments in the press throughout the state.  Beginning in May, Baxter had designated a few Democratic papers to carry the public printing.  In June, the *Gazette* was made official organ for state printing, and the influence of its position on politics was magnified as its articles became used throughout the state.[18]   This development was embittering to those papers loyal to Brooks and to those few remaining independent papers.  Representing the Flanagin-Walker, Democratic-Conservative point of view, the *Fayetteville Democrat* stubbornly remained loyal to Brooks and criticized these Baxter papers for having bound themselves to only two principles: Baxter and public printing.[19]   The implication was clear.  Although editors of the papers favored by Baxter knew that Brooks had been elected, the papers needed public printing to prosper; and as they accepted this form of patronage, editorial interpretation changed in Baxter's favor.  With the passage of time the number of papers in Baxter's column grew, while the number of papers listed in Brooks' column diminished. By late August the *Gazette* would count thirty-nine for Baxter and ten for Brooks.[20]

His morale declining as this shift in journalistic support was occurring, Joseph Brooks filed a complaint on June sixteenth in Pulaski Circuit Court against Baxter, claiming that Baxter had usurped the office of governor without authority.  Baxter demurred in response, and *Brooks* v. *Baxter* rested without a decision for ten months.[21]   It would be a revival of this complaint and a speedy, illegal decision in Brooks' favor that led to the events known as the Brooks-Baxter War in April, 1874.

On Friday night, June twenty-seventh, Brooks made a fiery speech in the grand opera house in Little Rock.[22]   During the course of that speech he denounced the *Gazette* for its role in the struggles of the past and by his attack brought forth a hostile reaction from the paper's editor.  Now in unequivocal terms Editor Woodruff identified Brooks and McClure as one.  "The heads of the brindles and minstrels are united—the wicked, bad and unscrupulous men of both sides."  In a revealing passage defending the course taken by the paper, reform was pointed to as the end by which the means were to be measured:

He [Brooks] now abandons his late supporters and returns to the organization he deserted a year ago in order to get into office. He has lost sight of the
great object which the people have had in view—*reform*, not *men*. He forgets
that the masses of the people do not care the snap of their fingers who is
governor, so they get the reforms [of which] they so much stand in need. And

there is where Mr. Brooks and many of *our* good friends have made their mistake. The people do not want *Brooks* for reform or *Baxter* for reform, but they want reform for its own sake, no matter from where it comes. . . . Like a commander of an army, we have had but one objective point, to secure the prize—reform; not to put this man or that man in position. A general uses his material sometimes in one direction, sometimes in another, We have won the battle—that is, secured for the people what they and we, for we are of them, have been demanding—that there should be an honest administration of the affairs of this government.[23]

Machiavelli could scarcely have expressed this position more effectively.

Brooks' speech brought forth a different reaction in the northwest. In that section Brooks still held the loyalty of many former Whigs and conservative Democrats who had supported the Democratic-Conservative coalition with the reform Republican ticket during the governor's election. The fire of his speech and his evident determination to secure his office were well received among those supporters. On July first, James Mitchell wrote David Walker, expressing his determination to fight Baxter to the bitter end.[24] Brooks seemed to him to be desperately determined to secure his office, and they should remain loyal to him. His political sense pointed to the effectiveness of the *Gazette*'s strategy as he advised: "We must above all things scout the idea that Baxter in his war with McClure is for the people." He saw in the *Gazette* their most formidable enemy and interpreted that paper's actions as an attempt to form a political party of Baxter and other elements of both parties. In the weeks to come the *Fayetteville Democrat* reflected his views in its scorching attacks on the editorial policy of the *Gazette*.[25]

A calmer and more detached attitude toward the developments of the day is reflected in the letter which U.M. Rose wrote to Harris Flanagin on July first.[26] He did not doubt that the present government was a usurpation, but he felt that Baxter was doing as well as their friends could have expected Brooks to do had he become governor. If one considered the present allies of Brooks, there would be more cause to fear the results of his being governor than those which the present circumstances threatened. Rose's sympathies were not strong for either side, and he did not feel the present danger was very great. He thought, however, that this was an extremely trying time for the McClure forces, who in his opinion were wavering painfully between the alternatives of force and the slower means of party organization.

Appointments by Baxter and resignations by several legislators had created vacancies in the legislature for nine seats in the senate and for forty-one in the house. November fourth had been named as the date for a special election to fill these seats.[27] The provisions of the constitutional amendment which had been passed in March would be in effect as these representatives were chosen, and the results of the election based on this enlarged electorate were expected to give the Democrats control of the legislature. Anticipating that development, the Democrats became enthusiastic for the idea of calling a constitutional convention as soon as the new legislators were elected.

The Democratic enthusiasm for a convention was taken up by Editor John McClure in one last effort to gain control of political affairs before his opportunity disappeared with the November election returns. Throughout the weeks of July and August the editorial repartee concerning a constitutional convention went on repititiously.[28]

The hope of McClure was to have the Constitutional Convention before the November election, or failing in this maneuver, to use the Convention as an excuse for bringing in Federal intervention in behalf of his political forces. The task of Woodruff was to persuade his readers to be patient, to let well enough alone, and to wait. Time would give victory to the Democrats if they could only avoid Federal intervention.

The major threat to the Democratic victory in November was the requirement of registration for voting. Governor Baxter did much to remove that threat, however, by suggesting his "happy idea," which was made public by the *Gazette* on July thirty-first. In each county one leading Democrat and one leading Republican were jointly to suggest names for a board of registration.[29] This bipartisan approach seemed to assure the kind of electorate promised by the constitutional amendment. It came as good news to the Democrats.

By this time McClure's defeats had left him with little but threadbare points of strategy to propose. Perhaps the Constitutional Convention of 1868 could be recalled and could be used as the new Constitutional Convention, he suggested.[30] The improbability of this course of action may be taken as a measure of how close he had come to the end of his role as a political power in the state.

With McClure's decline in power, Woodruff felt increasingly confident of the security of his own party's position. On August twenty-first he wrote: "About the best thing that all good people can do would be to continue as at present— support the Governor in all his praise-worthy acts, and let other questions take care of themselves."[31]

Elisha Baxter's position as governor became increasingly secure with the passage of time. On September fourth, he wrote President Grant inquiring about the status of his office. The matter was referred to Attorney General George H. Williams, who responded to Baxter on September fifteenth. He assured Baxter that "there would seem to be little room for controversy about . . . his right to the office." What was more important to Baxter was Williams' opinion that Federal interference with his office would not be forthcoming because both the state legislature and state Supreme Court had decided that he was the lawful governor.[32] In any maneuver to overthrow him which might grow out of *Brooks* v. *Baxter* in the Pulaski Circuit Court Baxter had reason to believe that if Federal intervention were brought into the contest, it would be on his side.

Encouraged by this opinion and other favorable developments, Baxter accepted the resignations of Generals W.W. Wilshire and R.C. Newton on September twenty-ninth and decided to muster the entire militia force out of service.[33] For a third and final time during this nine-month period Elisha Baxter was master of the situation.

Confidence in Democratic victory in the forthcoming election had grown during the weeks of July and August. One possible development, however, could rob the Democratic party of its anticipated victory. Those forces identified as the Flanagin-Walker forces in the coalition which supported Brooks had remained loyal to his cause. This was especially true in the northwest, where men like James Mitchell had made a vow to fight Baxter to the end.[34] If these conservative Democrats and Whigs refused to join now in the effort to gain control of the legislature, that lack of unity might rob the party of its expected victory.

William E. Woodruff, Jr., participated in an editorial duel with some of the Brooks papers in an attempt to bring these political forces in line with the course taken by the Little Rock Democrats. As these exchanges continued, editorial remarks grew warmer and at times seemed to equal the heat of those directed against the McClure forces. Exchanges between the *Gazette* and the *Fayetteville Democrat* were especially vehement, and the name of David Walker was referred to in public print—at first indirectly and then openly.[35]

As has been seen, one of the most effective bits of strategy used by Woodruff was to associate the Brooks cause with the McClure schemes. By this stratagem, Democratic support could be enlisted for Baxter in his fight against McClure, and by a process of guilt by association discredit of Brooks and his supporters could be achieved by identifying them with McClure. Men such as Walker and Flanagin, who remained loyal to Brooks because of honest belief in his election rather than unscrupulous maneuvering, vehemently resented Woodruff's insinuations.

Harris Flanagin wrote to Woodruff on August twenty-sixth to complain about some of his recent comments regarding frauds committed by Brooks' supporters in the governor's election. After apologetically explaining that Flanagin had misunderstood his writing, Woodruff went on to reveal something of his thinking during this period:

We supported Baxter because we believed him preferable to Brooks, but especially, because we believed his legal tenure of office impregnable—however little founded in right.—This view is fully supported by the decision of the supreme court in the M.S. opinion which has just been filed & which cuts off Mr. Brooks, till the next legislature meets, from all hope of getting his office.

I am sorry to think you have no hope of electing a conservative legislature. It seems to me plain that such an accomplishment is easy if conservative people will work together. Possibly the senate may not be saved. In such case there will be no extra session.

Whatever may be the opinion generally entertained of the wrong done Mr. Brooks, from my stand point it is a sad thing that the small wrong done to such a man should be allowed to stand in the way of the mightier and numberless wrongs done the conservative people in Arkansas. It may be an unworthy prejudice, but in my mind Mr. Brooks' wrongs are merely poetic justice or merited retribution for the injuries done our people.—It is not in me to feel a single regret for his misfortunes.

In the course of his editorial exchanges with the *Fayetteville Democrat*, particularly during July and August, Woodruff on several occasions made reference to David Walker. Some of these references were not overt, but their indirectness does not mean that they were indefinite. Walker was a reserved, conservative man for whom principle and dignity were important. Perhaps his his popularity suffered because he was too conscious of these qualities, for he frequently gives the impression of having a rigid and proud personality. These traits had probably made him a leader of men, however, and he continued to exercise a strong political influence in the northwest throughout Reconstruction because of his reputation for integrity. When Woodruff adversely criticized the Democratic "brindle" reform opponents of Baxter who "rear back on their dignity and state that it is not Brooks but a principle they are contending for," it is quite likely that he made reference to Walker and his followers.[37] The bitterness of the attacks on the *Gazette* by the *Fayetteville Democrat* prompted Woodruff to charge that the Fayetteville paper was "controlled by one who has an insatiable desire for office, and has been disappointed. He belongs to another generation."[38] These words could not fail to wound the sixty-seven-year-old Walker.

As if to vindicate himself before his people, Walker wrote a lengthy open letter to Woodruff which was dated November eighteenth and first published in the *Fayetteville Democrat*.[39] It amounted to a review of Walker's thinking on developments during the past year and revealed much about his political position.

In the campaign for governor Walker had consistently supported Brooks. When the Hunter movement appeared, he openly condemned it as an abandonment of pledges given to their candidate. After the election of Brooks, a fact of which he had no doubt, Walker insisted upon exposing the frauds by which Brooks had been denied his victory and insisted upon his being inaugurated as governor. In an effort to defeat these aims, the *Gazette*, in Walker's opinion, had used its influence to stifle this investigation of fraudulent activities and to uphold Baxter in his office, although that office had been secured through fraud.

Senator Rice and Joseph Brooks had withdrawn from other radicals; had made a platform, liberal and just in nature, in order to appeal to the Democrats; had declared for Horace Greeley; and had formed a state ticket with Brooks at its head. These actions had been influenced by assurances given to them by the Democrats that a joint canvass would be made, both state and national, and that Brooks would head the state ticket as their candidate for governor. As an additional means of binding this agreement, the ticket had been remodeled and several Democrats placed on it as candidates for important state offices. Under these circumstances Walker considered it to be a duty on the part of Democrats to act with fairness and liberality toward the Brooks faction. Indeed, Walker thought it dishonorable to abandon this ticket and to offer another one such as the Hunter ticket.

Walker's regard for Hunter was high, and he was unacquainted with Brooks, but when support had been pledged to Brooks by the Democratic Convention, he felt obligated to honor that pledge. Walker saw in the Hunter movement one more effort by the *Gazette* to discourage and to embarrass the reform ticket's canvass.

Walker charged that Woodruff and his confederates had been in correspondence during the campaign with prominent men throughout the state, trying to get these men to withhold their support from Brooks. Indeed, word had come to Walker that he should say nothing in favor of Brooks that he was not prepared to take back. For his denouncing the Hunter movement as being dishonorable, Walker had been accused of having received assurances from Brooks of his support of Walker for the United States Senate. This was an unfounded charge, for Walker intended supporting Garland if there was any chance of his being elected.

Walker's friendship for T.M. Gunter was evident as he continued the letter. Instead of respecting the integrity of the people and their desires to have the frauds exposed, the *Gazette* had followed the opposite course. In trying to suppress investigation, the newspaper had made matters more difficult for such Congressmen-elect as Gunter in his efforts to expose the frauds by which he had been defeated. Because Gunter had run on the reform ticket, the same frauds and misconduct which had denied Brooks his office also denied T.M. Gunter and others their victories.

With the passage of time Woodruff had watched Baxter perfect his means of staying in office and had even encouraged him as he achieved his purpose. Through the patronage of public printing four-fifths of the state's press had been purchased and silenced. And in the meantime Woodruff had "badgered, ridiculed and abused" the small number of independent editors who refused to betray the people.

Next Walker turned to the personal references Woodruff had made to him. Perhaps the charge of an "insatiable desire for office" had stung Walker most.

A similar charge had been made against him by A.W. Bishop, Unionist critic of his activities during the secession crisis.[40] Walker's response to this charge was to point to his own loyalty to the Whig party and principles at a time when, by joining the Democratic party, he might have increased his chances of political success had he been motivated by an insatiable desire for office. He expressed his feelings in this manner: "Ever in a hopeless minority, I battled under the leadership of Clay and Webster, until the whig party ceased to exist, after which time I was only twice a candidate for office; ran and was elected both times without nomination."[41] If this were the editor's idea of an insatiable desire for office, he could make the most of it.

Another accusation of Woodruff's which had stung concerned the inconsistency of Walker, the Unionist, voting for secession. Walker responded with the following words: "I could not have supposed that so gallant a gentleman, one at whose request I had cast that vote, would taunt me with inconsistency for having done so."

Woodruff had also taunted him for his support of a carpetbagger as governor. Walker's response was that "This cry of carpetbaggers, after-all, had rather too much of the demagogue about it to meet my approval; mind and morals are much fitter tests of man's worth than place of birth or transition."

Bringing to a conclusion his remarks on their dispute, Walker had this to say to Woodruff:

I apprehend that the difference between us is as to the means of obtaining redress, not as to the necessity for it. I hold that the end, however desirable it may be, must be reached by honorable means. I could not consent to a breach of good faith in order to reach the most desirable end; while I infer, from your course, that you hold the end justifies the means, and hence the difference between us.[42]

Ending his letter in a conciliatory mood, Walker remarked that he had for long years been a faithful supporter of the *Gazette* and that "The integrity of its purpose has never been questioned by me; but the means used by it to accomplish that purpose in the recent canvass have met my unqualified disapprobation."

Walker's letter, requiring more than three newspaper columns to print, was published in the *Gazette* on December tenth. He received several congratulatory letters from friends throughout the state, who had read it with pleasure. His feeling of patriotic demoralization had been shared by many men during these years, and his letter seemed to give expression to their feelings as well as to his own. His old friend, John R. Eakin, wrote to Walker two days after the letter's publication:

My course has been the same as yours. Unlike yourself, I have not been sustained by *any* sympathy of my neighbors. Almost without exception they have followed the lead of the Gazette throughout, and gradually, little by little I have been "cold shouldered" out of all political consultation. That concerns me but little. It produces no resentment nor abates one whit of the sympathy I feel with their ultimate purposes, nor of the warm and friendly interest I have in their welfare. I calmly await the better time, which will succeed I hope, the demoralization of the war; when patriotism will revive, and great National Parties be again formed upon great principles and with noble aims. That time is not yet. May not be for you and I. But, looking to it, I will not allow myself to be annoyed by the petty and temporary shifts for relief to which my friends resort although I cannot go with them, and a political coolness results.[43]

Reflected in these comments by Walker and his friend Eakin was a lament for one of the casualties of *de facto* v. *de jure* government—the loss of that longing for political principle and integrity as represented by the old-line Whigs.

# CHAPTER NINE

# AUGUSTUS H. GARLAND

*That is a very bright man—that man Garland. What a pity he is a lawyer!*[1]
—*Isaac Murphy*

*His success in life is founded on his artful avoidance of friction.*[2]
—*John Hallum*

*Because I have been quiet I have had none the less a deep interest in our affairs & have always been ready & willing to do what I could—but I determined never to go into or encouage our people to go into another fruitless fight—we have had too many of them. And now let [us] see something that has any promise of relief to us—any hope that we may get out from this most terrible oppression that has about ruined us, and my time, pen, money & voice will all be at its aid & support, freely and fervently. But I must be excused from listening to every spirit that comes along to talk grandly . . . & proposes to play the d    l with people with whom he has been one & continue to be the blackest of them as long as they will tolerate him in their company—none of that.*[3]
—*Augustus H. Garland*
*July 3, 1872*

*I do not suppose, in point of fact, Brooks wants a convention. But my chief idea . . . in having a Legislature, is to get the convention. I believe this very trouble we are having will make the members a unit almost for a convention. Baxter will favor it outright. It is of small moment really who is Govr. of these two, but it is of great moment to settle these troubles and get a government by & from the people.*[4]
—*Augustus H. Garland*
*April 20, 1874*

Congressional Reconstruction together with the legacy of party disintegration, which occurred just prior to the Civil War, made party organization a major concern for the opponents of radical Republican rule in Arkansas. That concern was made more urgent because the struggle for party organization had to be made during a period when another battle between *de jure* v. *de facto* government continuously confronted the combatants with questions related to means and ends. As has been indicated, various tactics used in each of these contests served to unite, divide, confuse, and demoralize men. Among political leaders in the state, Harris Flanagin, David Walker, and Augustus H. Garland appear to have been the most likely men under whose leadership a successful party organization and a return to *de jure* government might have been accomplished.

Both Flanagin and Walker were strong leaders in their respective areas, and either might have been able to lead a successful coalition of political forces throughout the state. But each one brought liabilities with him to such a statewide political leadership. Flanagin had been a secessionist and had served as Confederate governor during the Civil War. For this reason the native Unionists in the northwest would likely find his leadership undesirable. Walker's adherence to Whig principles and his adverse criticism of the shift in Democratic support from Brooks to Baxter cost him political strength in the other areas of the state. Indeed, the security of his leadership in the northwest was threatened by the influx of new population into that region. For these and other reasons neither Flanagin nor Walker would be the man under whom the various political fragments could unite. In the end, Garland would become the leader of a state ticket in 1874 which brought together the various elements of the Democratic party. This chapter will consider Garland as he faced problems associated with *de jure* v. *de facto* government and as he moved toward redemption of the state from Republican control.

Augustus H. Garland, the youngest child of Barbara Hill and Rufus King Garland, was born in Tipton County, Tennessee, on June 11, 1832.[5] Shortly after the infant's birth, Rufus Garland, while drunk, nearly killed a man. Fortunately, the victim recovered from his knifing, and Garland was not prosecuted. Embarrassment to the family over this affair, however, encouraged them to leave Tennessee, and they migrated to southwestern Arkansas in 1833.[6] There they settled on a farm in LaFayette County overlooking the Red River. But tragedy struck the family that year with the death of Rufus Garland on July seventh.

Mrs. Garland rented the farm, and it is believed that she, with her children, moved to Spring Hill in Hempstead County. In 1837, she married Thomas Hubbard, lawyer, judge, and later a candidate for governor, whose influence on young Gus was to be significant. The family moved to Washington, the county seat, in 1844, and at age fourteen, Garland was sent to Bardstown, Kentucky, for his education.[7] There he attended St. Mary's College and graduated from St. Joseph's College in 1849.[8]

Following graduation, he spent a year teaching in Sevier County before returning to Washington, where he accepted a clerical position in the county clerk's office.[9]    The Whigs wanted him to be their candidate for county treasurer, but the influence of his step-father and his mother persuaded him to enter Hubbard's law office instead to begin his study of law.[10]  Garland proved himself to be a bright young man, and his parents believed his caliber to be worthy of more than such a county office.   In this belief they were to be justified.

In 1853, at age twenty-one, Garland married Sarah Virginia Sanders, was admitted to the Arkansas Bar, and formed a partnership with his step-father. He was now a young man on his way. In 1856, his speeches helped elect Edward A. Warren United States Congressman from the second district.[11]  Also during this year he made a change which would prove very beneficial to his career.

On June 26, 1856, a partnership was formed between Garland and Ebenezer Cummins of Little Rock.  Cummins had formerly been the partner of Albert Pike and had a large practice in the capital city.  The new firm was advertised in the *Gazette* for the first time on February 28, 1857.  Twelve days later, on March eleventh, Cummins died, leaving the young lawyer before his twenty-fifth birthday with one of the best legal practices in Little Rock.[12]  Garland was properly aware of his good fortune, as is indicated in the letter he wrote to his friend, Dr. Roscoe J. Jennings, on July second:

He [F.W. Compton] is on a cold trail for law—there are six or eight new ones coming in here, in the last few months.  The business mainly is in four offices here & will be until the country is settled up—new population—new things occur—different impetus given to matters—new channels of business created—the thing strikes every one at once, who has any sense.  For a moment see, the business in all of our offices here is inherited, except [Absalom] Fowler, who has been here from the beginning.   [George C.] W[atkins] & [George A.] Gallagher have descent cast on them from [Chester] Ashley—[Samuel H.] Hempstead from old Ben Johnson with state patronage—I of [Albert] Pike & [Albert] P[ike] & [Ebenezer] C[ummins].  This is in short the way things are.[13]

The inheritance of this legal practice provided the talents of Garland with unusual opportunities.   Fortunately, those talents proved to be equal to the challenges offered. In December, 1860, the twenty-eight-year-old Garland went to Washington, D.C., for the first time to file several cases before the United States Supreme Court.  With the assistance of Reverdy Johnson in making his preparations, he was admitted to practice before that Court on December 26, 1860.[14]

Garland was elected as a Union delegate to the Secession Convention representing Pulaski County.   But after Fort Sumter and Lincoln's call for volunteers, he joined those members of the Convention who wanted David Walker to reconvene that body for appropriate action. Garland had been out of town on April eighteenth when the "Address to the People of Arkansas" had been signed by 137 men including forty-five conservative delegates to the Convention.[15] But he joined J. Stillwell, another Pulaski County delegate, in endorsing that address on April twenty-sixth. Their language expressed more than token support for the direction in which events were then moving. "We are now bound to raise our flag of resistance—of rebellion, and whether it floats to the breeze, or trails in the dust, follow it to the last, and write our resolve with the sword and seal it with blood."[16]

Garland served the Confederacy well and held several responsible positions in its government. He was one of five delegates sent to the Provisional Convention in Montgomery, Alabama in 1861.[17] In November of that year he was elected as a Representative in the Confederate Congress. The following year he was narrowly defeated by Robert W. Johnson, the incumbent, for the office of Senator. On the twelfth ballot the victory had gone to Johnson forty-six to forty-two. In 1863, Garland was unopposed for reelection to his seat in the Confederate Congress. He was joined there by his brother, Rufus K. Garland, who had been elected to represent Arkansas from the second district.[18] Senator Charles B. Mitchell died on September 18, 1864, and Garland was chosen to replace him. Albert Pike was Garland's leading competitor when the legislature chose a successor to the late Senator Mitchell, and Garland's margin of victory was very small.[19]

In February, 1865, he left his seat in the Confederate Senate and returned to Arkansas. He served as one of Governor Flanagin's emissaries to General Reynolds in the closing days of the Confederate government in Arkansas, seeking terms for restoring peace.[20] Garland applied for his pardon from President Johnson on June 28, 1865, and was successful in obtaining it seventeen days later.[21] Although his law practice had been disrupted and would have to be painfully restored, Garland appears to have been fortunate when compared with other ex-Confederate leaders in July, 1865.

Garland possessed two outstanding advantages over other leaders in Arkansas during Reconstruction. The first was the fact that he was a person who, although identified with Arkansas, had demonstrated his ability to deal effectively with the Federal government prior to the Civil War and who had access to that government at the present time. The second advantage was the fortunate combination of qualities he possessed as a man, which attracted other men to him and enlisted their voluntary acceptance of his leadership. Attention will now focus on these peculiar advantages as Garland's leadership during Reconstruction is considered.

More than anything else Garland's victory in *Ex parte Garland* served to identify him as a man who could successfully stand up before the powers of the Federal government. His admittance to practice before the Supreme Court, obtained in 1860, coupled with his early pardon under the Amnesty Proclamation now provided him with the opportunity to challenge the constitutionality of an act of Congress of January 24, 1865. This act barred from practice before the Supreme Court any person who could not take an oath that he had never fought against the United States.[22]  Should the act continue to be enforced, many ex-Confederate lawyers would be faced with professional disaster. Acquiring the assistance of Reverdy Johnson and Matt Carpenter and joining forces with R.H. Marr, a Louisiana lawyer who was in a similar situation, Garland petitioned the Supreme Court to declare the act unconstitutional.[23] On March fourteenth, and again on December 15, 1866, the case was argued before the Court.[24]

Garland made two telling arguments in his presentation. The first was that the power of the President to pardon was an unqualified power which could not be limited by Congress.  When Garland received his pardon from President Johnson in July, 1865, this instrument protected him from any Congressional interference related to his participation in the Confederacy.  Any act which would alter the powers of the President to pardon was in conflict with the Constitution.  Should the Court not uphold this argument, his second one was based on the Fifth Amendment.  In depriving him of the right to practice before the Court, Congress had placed a penalty upon him which was in violation of that amendment.  He possessed a "property" in his right to practice his profession which Congress was denying him without "due process of law." Therefore, the act which imposed a penalty in violation of this principle, a principle which was as old as the *Magna Carta* itself, was unconstitutional.

On January 14, 1867, the Supreme Court, in the first five-to-four decision in which an act of Congress was held unconstitutional, granted the prayer of the petitioner.[25]  This was a significant victory for the South and a personal victory for Garland.  The following month, in the wake of this victory, Garland was elected United States Senator to fill the vacancy created by Andrew Hunter, who had declined the office.[26]  On February twenty-fifth, Garland wrote Alexander H. Stephens, former Vice-President of the Confederacy, of his recent election.[27]  Garland felt that the election was "a doubtful, if not an empty honor," but if he could do any good he was more than willing to try.  His political astuteness predicted that which events would demonstrate within a week—that he would not be able to cope with Congressional Reconstruction. For Garland was to be one of the Senators whose credentials were refused by the Senate.

He arrived in Washington, D.C. on March twenty-first to find "things all confused & much 'mixed up.' No one, even the wisest seems to have any very well defined ideas of our fortune." But Garland had not lost his own bearings enough to overlook an occasion to point out the irony of contemporary judicial developments. *Ex parte Milligan* had attracted much attention in recent weeks, and Garland wanted Alexander H. Stephens to set the record straight in his book which was then being written. Garland felt credit should be given where credit was due:

> In your books if you can give my Minority Report on Habeas Corpus a notice I would like it—as upon that I must live hereafter, and especially so as now Judge Davis in the *Milligan* case is being immortalized for stating what I did there, & what you & all of us in the C.S.A. that agreed on this subject, situated time & again. To you & myself & others they were plain truths then—& not made any more so now by the case alluded to above. And to us (few) who stood forward on this question against all the influences that were brought to bear, a good place in history is due.[28]

During his stay in Washington, Garland was clandestinely associated with *Mississippi* v. *Johnson*, a case presented to the Supreme Court on April fifth, which sought to enjoin the President and General E.O.C. Ord from enforcing the Reconstruction Acts. The bill was submitted to Garland for his approval before going to the Court. Lawyers promoting the case secured eminent counsel from the North to appear and argue the case, and what Garland and his associates were able to do was done behind the scenes.

Garland shared the apprehensions about the future held by Stephens, but he had already begun to think about what might be done. "The chief point now with me is, should we of the South touch the present scheme of reconstruction at all? Of course it is going to be carried into execution, but should we act at all?"[29]

Four years after *Mississippi* v. *Johnson*, Garland took advantage of an opportunity to set the record straight on the slavery question in *Osborn* v. *Nicholson*.[30] The case itself was not very important. The problem involved a promissory note for $1,300 dated March 26, 1861, payable on December 26, 1861, with interest at 10%. The consideration of this conveyance was a young Negro slave, Albert, then about twenty-three years old. On February 10, 1869, Henry T. Osborn brought suit against A.G. Nicholson *et al.* in Federal District Court in Arkansas in an effort to collect the money due him on the note.[31] That Court denied his plea for two reasons: because it would be contrary to the spirit of the provisions of the Fourteenth Amendment; and because it would be against public policy.[32] The *ex post facto* character of this reasoning provided Garland with his opportunity.

The decision was appealed to the Supreme Court, where Garland argued the case on November 8, 1871.[33] Early in his argument Garland corrected two errors concerning the Constitution and slavery. Instead of arguing that "the right of property which existed in the service of a slave was the creature of statute law," Garland argued that slavery had never been the creature of law, but was rather the creature of custom, deriving the force of law from its operation.[34] Instead of insisting that the Constitution did not recognize property in slaves except in its provision for the rendition of fugitive slaves, Garland pointed to a more significant recognition in the provision for the importation of slaves. "Property in slaves was thus not only recognized in the Constitution, but was guaranteed by it; and with the exception of property in inventions, it is the only species of property expressly recognized."[35]

Through his argument Garland established the fact that a contract had existed which was protected by laws and the Constitution and that the obligations therein could not be violated by any act of the government. Garland admitted that the Thirteenth and Fourteenth Amendments had been properly adopted and that they were to be enforced by the Supreme Court. The question was whether "they invalidate the note in question and bar a recovery in the courts of the United States?"[36]

In regard to the effects of the Thirteenth Amendment, which declared that slavery should not exist in the United States, Garland posed the guarantees of the Fifth Amendment that no person should be deprived of his property without due process of law. With this logic he had answered the lower court's decision and now asked, "how can it be said that the spirit of the latter demands a violation of the former Amendment? . . . A solemn guarantee in the fundamental law cannot be thus frittered away."[37]

The fourth section of the Fourteenth Amendment declared that "neither the United States nor any State shall assume any debt or obligation incurred in aid of the insurrection or rebellion against the United States, or any claim for the loss or emancipation of any slave."[38]   Garland pointed out that this section dealt with claims arising from Emancipation and did not apply to past contracts for slaves emancipated later. Silence on these contracts was conclusive evidence that they had been excluded from the provisions of this section.

The lower Court had claimed that the contract was against public policy, but in response to this contention Garland presented the Supreme Court with a difficult question: "Can it ever be against public policy to enforce a contract which was protected by the laws when executed? This we presume is the first instance in which such a doctrine had been announced by a judicial Tribunal."[39]   In its decision on April 22, 1872, the Supreme Court reversed the decision of the lower Court and honored the terms of the contract, Chief Justice Chase dissenting.[40]

Garland's personal thought on this subject was revealed in a letter to Henry M. Rector on November 12, 1871, written four days after his argument before the Court:

I am greatly pleased that you approve my *slave contract* argument. The law part of the case is in the smallest possible compass:—but I did this to give the lie to so much abuse & villification our people are receiving from these devils, & their perjured courts, on the subject. And while I will not be surprised, if the *higher law*! doctrine will carry that court, I concluded to go down to the bottom, & vindicate our people [of?] all such flings as all these saintly fellows could or can throw at us. There never was on earth a subject which has drawn out or brought about more humbuggery than this one upon which we are now tortured & put upon the wheel:—and as it is or may be, let[it?] go, but I was determined to put it on record in complete and tangible shape, & I have appealed to impartial & disinterested historians—none of our own—but all theirs or authors opposed to us. And if I have put our people right, then I am content, rebation may be the judgment of the court in this case.

You are quite right, in my judgment, as to their morals, when they are attempting to put aside the − −. They would have one hundred armies—They would put negroes back in slavery—They would sell their mothers and daughters virginity & purity & all their souls—to make money. We are in one terrible condition when they are our rulers. We can do nothing, but I will put it on the record everytime I can, what and where we are, & let them make the most of it. This is all that's left us.[41]

*Ex parte Garland*, election to the United States Senate, his actions in relation to *Mississippi* v. *Johnson*, and his slave contract argument in *Osborn* v. *Nicholson* all served to identify Garland as an Arkansas man capable of successful relations with the Federal government. The stature he gained by this recognition gave him a strong advantage over other political leaders in the state. A second advantage was to be found in his personal characteristics. There can be no question as to the brilliance of Augustus H. Garland. He had distinguished himself as a youth with his bright mind, and he continued to win recognition for his mental powers throughout his life. He was a fine lawyer, but his intellectual strength seems to have displayed itself to greatest advantage in the field of politics. There were other brilliant men in Arkansas at the time, but the patterns of their personalities did not allow political expression to the same extent as did Garland's. David Walker, as an example, was certainly bright enough, but his Whig reserve and legalistic turn of mind were political liabilities in attracting widespread popular support. U.M. Rose was a brilliant man and a fine lawyer, but his interests were so dominantly literary in nature that he lacked the appeal necessary to become a popular political leader in Arkansas. It was Garland's good fortune politically to possess a combination of traits which could best be utilized in the field of politics.

Garland was essentially practical and realistic, but he made these qualities appear so attractive that he never needed to apologize for his lack of idealism. His most severe critic, John Hallum, felt he was very expedient. Indeed, he believed that Garland's success in life had been founded "on his artful avoidance of friction."[42] But such condemnation is perhaps too severe, for Garland had far more integrity than this would imply. The milieu in which he practiced his profession constantly tested a lawyer's integrity, and, if his own words are to count for anything, he was very jealous of protecting his good name. Commenting on this problem, he wrote to Henry M. Rector on July 3, 1872:

I can say too what some who are clamoring for certain things & are exercising their suspicions can not say:—With my practice here & my status at the bar, there is no illegitimate fee found its way on my books or in my pocket, and I have refused hundreds of them when I needed money badly, & found afterwards that self constituted censors of morals & ethics readily took them. I have a list of them & can put them all down—some of them you know of.[43]

An important part of Garland's power as a political leader was to be found in the informal nature of his personality. The ability to show himself as a plain-spoken, folksy man was a definite asset for any political leader in a rural state such as Arkansas. With all his brilliance, Garland possessed these informal characteristics which drew men to him. He loved to hunt deer and was a good fisherman, two interests which are still cultivated by many Arkansas men.[44] His humor could be as homely as the occasion demanded, or his wit could be as subtle as propriety required. In short, his brightness was coupled with other traits which drew men to him rather than separated him from popular support.

Two additional advantages which Garland enjoyed over such men as Walker and Flanagin were his age and his place of residence. In 1874, Walker was sixty-eight years old, Flanagin was fifty-seven, and Garland was forty-two. The advantages of youth went to Garland, and, furthermore, when one compares his political experience with theirs, he does not seem to be at any disadvantage in this category either. Perhaps the greatest advantage Garland enjoyed over these two men, however, was the fact that he was at the scene in Little Rock where so much of the political maneuvering took place.

Garland's first reaction to Congressional Reconstruction was to leave it alone. Four days after the second Reconstruction Act of March 23, 1867, he wrote to Alexander H. Stephens: "To my mind the South should not, by word or deed make herself a party to this proceeding—but should stand still and leave it to those who got it up."[45] In taking this position, Garland displayed one of his political characteristics during Reconstruction. All signs pointed to trouble for men of his political views. The time was not right for political exposure; there- fore, the answer was withdrawal and conservation of strength until the appropriate opportunity in the future. Perhaps this was what Hallum meant when he pointed to Garland's success as being based on the "artful avoidance of friction."[46]

The one miscalculation Garland made, if he were trying to follow this strategy, was his participation in the campaigns of 1868. The Constitution of 1868 was voted upon in an election which began on March thirteenth; and Garland was among those Democratic spokesmen who advocated making a fight against the Constitution at the polls. In addition to Garland, the leading spokes- men included E. H. English, U. M. Rose, Thomas C. Hindman, Sol F. Clark, S. W. Williams, Albert Pike, and George C. Watkins.[47] Their counterparts in the

Republican party were James Hinds, Joseph Brooks, Powell Clayton, B.F. Rice, Asa Hodges, and Logan H. Roots. With the ratification of the Constitution completed in April, the franchise provisions now led to a voter's oath being required before the voters could participate in the forthcoming general election in November. The Democrats once again had to decide whether to participate in these *de facto* proceedings.

After some hesitation on the matter, the state Democrats decided to make a contest of it with the Republicans in November. On July thirtieth, Garland wrote David Walker of this decision and pleaded with him to join in the campaign. "I write now simply to say, that after long and mature deliberation and discussion, our friends have agreed to advise the taking of the *oath* and to make a fight; and we have agreed to run candidates for Congress in all the Districts. . . . Whatever may be the individual opinions of persons, we must all unite in this, and make it as one action. For now we are to be saved or ruined as one."[48] The more politic nature of Garland gave him a flexibility which allowed him to recommend taking the oath as a means of fighting a *de facto* regime. Walker's legalistic integrity could not permit him to do so.

The extent to which Garland's faith in the strength of political persuasion went was revealed in a letter to Alexander H. Stephens written six days after the Presidential election in November, 1868. Grant's victory was no surprise to Garland, and he was keenly aware of the great influence and weight of character Grant would possess in his new office. So much power would be his that the new President would be able to destroy the liberties of the country, or to arrest the tide of events and to restore peace. If Grant followed the influence of his party, the former effect would occur; but, if he followed his own judgment and governed according to the Constitution, a "broad, deep, and permanent" foundation for the future could be created. Which of these alternatives he chose was all important.

Garland wanted to increase the probability that Grant would make the right choice, and it was his belief that Grant's ambition provided the key. "If his ambition is at all purified and well directed, the idea of saving the constitution of his country and living hereafter by the side of Washington might move him in a direction altogether different from that desired or expected by his *party* friends."[49] To lead Grant toward such a moderate and conservative position was the ambition of Garland, and he had a plan to accomplish this result—a plan which he wanted Stephens to consider:

One or two *representative* men of true *conservatism* in each of the *10* secession states should, by private agreement, meet with Genl. G about 1st of January next and lay before him the parts as they are in these states, and promise & work for the peace & order & obeying of the laws on the part of the people here if the government is properly conducted. By representative men I do mean neither active democrats or republicans in the late contest—but men who have been quiet and have been looking to the peace & quiet of their people, and who have not stirred up strife & bitter feelings among their people. For as you well know, we have been for the last three months ground in between the upper & nether mill rocks—conservatism proper had been strangled, and bad men on both sides, desiring trouble & commotion have kept the country on fire, just as the late [still?] born war was inaugurated in *1860-1*. And I do not believe I mistake the facts, when I say, that our people South—I mean those of social, pecuniary & moral responsibilities—desire peace earnestly, & are ready & willing to conform to rules under any one if they can be protected in their rights as given them even in the general terms of the constitution; and I believe this assurance full & ample can be made to Genl. G, & strictly within the bounds of truth. These things properly laid before him by men who are known to be conservative men must make him pause, & reflect, and then act as a man of sense & of patriotism, & they will do so, unless he is a fool or a fiend, or both, which I do not believe at all.[50]

In Garland's opinion Stephens was the man to initiate and to carry out this plan. Names of other men whose influence might cause Grant to change his expected course of action were suggested by Garland to be included in the plan. Those mentioned were General Robert E. Lee, ex-Governor William Alexander Graham of North Carolina, Governor James L. Orr of South Carolina, and General Joseph E. Johnston.[51] Garland was also willing to help, but he believed his own influence in Washington had been destroyed by his connection with *Ex parte Garland, Mississippi* v. *Johnson,* and his election as a United States Senator during the previous year. He appraised his influence in Arkansas, however, in more favorable terms. If Stephens and his colleagues could obtain from President Grant an assurance that he would follow the course of action which they advocated, then Garland said, "I could quiet Arkansas in ten days, I believe, and it would give me the greatest pleasure & joy to do this."[52]

But circumstances developed beyond the manipulative powers of such political techniques, and Garland, following his political judgment, withdrew from an active participation in politics. He was a person of such a political nature, however, that men found his withdrawal hard to believe, and they continued to suspect that he was clandestinely at work. In a letter to his friend Henry M. Rector, written in July, 1872, Garland explained his inactivity in politics since 1868.[53] These years from 1868 to 1872 had been difficult for him financially, and he had worked very hard to regain some of his previous affluence. Days, nights, and Sundays he had spent at this effort, excluding himself from society while this work was being done. Political matters had gone beyond his control or influence, and his immediate responsibility had been to pay his debts and to provide for his family. He had spent $1,760 on *Ex parte Garland* and had spent an additional $750 during his days in Washington in 1867. These debts, added to the loss of his legal practice, represented a sufficient contribution to the public for a while. Therefore, he had withdrawn from active participation in politics and had been quietly at work.

The occasion in 1872 which brought forth this explanation from Garland was the suggestion that he become a candidate for governor in the November election. He was anxious for friends, such as Rector, to understand his position. He had never aspired to be governor, but to run for that office now would be impossible. In the first place, financial considerations would prevent his entering the race. If he ran and was defeated, the result would be financial disaster. If he ran and won the election, even this victory would be disastrous, for to quit his practice and to live on the $2,500 salary of the governor's office would be financially ruinous to him. Secondly, Garland's political astuteness told him that for a man of his political position to run for governor was unsound policy at this time.

His political inactivity, however, did not mean that he was disinterested in political affairs. He had been willing, and was willing now, to do what he could to improve the political situation. But the fruitless battles of the past had taught him caution. If a genuine opportunity to rescue the Arkansas people from Congressional Reconstruction and Republican control presented itself, then, his "time, pen, money, & voice will all be at its aid & support, freely and fervently." Until such an opportunity came, he asked to be excused from what he considered to be false hopes. Both his proposed candidacy for governor and the current coalition of the Democrats with Reform Republicans in support of Joseph Brooks for that office were, in Garland's judgment, examples of fruitless efforts.

In his overt actions Garland remained consistent to this position throughout 1873 and until April of 1874. The legislative bargaining, however, which resulted in the election of Stephen W. Dorsey as United States Senator and which secured the Franchise Amendment in March of 1873, tempts one to credit Garland with the covert action behind this strategy. His strong opposition to Brooks as governor, because he believed that Brooks would make gaining control of the legislature more difficult, seemed justified as Baxter proved himself susceptible to Democratic influence during 1873. When one remembers that Garland's chief objective was to regain control of the legislature, there appears more consistency in the actions of the Democrats during this period. Unfortunately, evidence to validate Garland's role in these developments has not been found, and, therefore, although consistent with his political views and style of leadership, his direct participation must remain no more than conjecture.

It was not until the Brooks-Baxter War in the spring of 1874 that Garland was provided with the kind of opportunity to which his talents could fully and openly respond. By the time the consequences of that fiasco were finally over, Brooks' claim to the governor's office had been permanently set aside, a new Constitution had been adopted, and Augustus H. Garland had been elected governor. To these developments attention is now directed.

It became increasingly evident with the passage of time that Governor Baxter was influenced less and less by his Republican associates and more and more by his Democratic supporters. By April 1, 1874, it was true, as Thomas S. Staples has reported, that Republican control of Baxter had come to an end.[54] Evidence of this situation could be found in the publication of Governor Baxter's refusal on March sixteenth to issue additional railroad-aid bonds. The occasion for this refusal was politically revealing, for the company requesting the bonds was the Arkansas Central, a company in which Senator Dorsey was interested.[55] When one recalls Senator Dorsey's active interest in promoting the sale of state bonds during the previous years, the shift in his political support from Baxter to Brooks within days after this decision comes as no surprise.[56]

Since February 21, 1873, Baxter had authorized the issuance of bonds amounting to $300,000 to the Arkansas Central Railroad Company and bonds amounting to $100,000 to the Little Rock and Fort Smith Railroad Company.[57] Now he announced his belief that, as governor, he had no constitutional or legal authority to issue additional bonds. To Republicans under whose administration the credit of the state had been used to issue bonds since 1868 the portent of this decision, should it stand, was clear. If it was unconstitutional for Governor Baxter to issue bonds now, it had been so for Governor Clayton and for Governor Hadley before him. Nothing could destroy the bondholders' equity or the credit of the state, with which the Republicans were identified, faster than the acceptance of this interpretation of the governor's authority.

In his letter to the president of the Arkansas Central Company, Governor Baxter gave three reasons for believing that he had not any authority to issue the bonds then under consideration.[58] The first pointed to the fact that the election which authorized the issuance of the bonds in 1868 was invalid because that portion of the act which contemplated the election was not in force on the day of the election. Thus there had been no real authority for conducting the election because no prior law granting the authority was in existence at that time.[59]

A second challenge to the validity of the act authorizing railroad-aid bonds was the fact that the Constitution of 1868 had vested the power of making laws exclusively in the general assembly. When this legislation was referred to the people, the Constitution had been violated, for that document contained no provisions authorizing the passage of legislation in the manner which would be identified in the future as the referendum.[60]

A third objection expressed by Governor Baxter was related to the timing required to put an act in force. Normally, an act became law ninety days after the expiration of the legislative session in which it had been enacted. Since there were no stated provisions to the contrary in the Railroad Aid Bond Act of July 21, 1868, that act could not have become law until ninety days after the legislative session closed on April 10, 1869.[61]  In violation of this requirement, the election in which the people voted for railroads by a majority of 23,984 to 5,210 had taken place on November 3, 1868, eight months before it could have been authorized.[62]

Such an obvious difference of opinion over so basic a concern as the use of state credit for the promotion of railroads could not be ignored. The forthcoming split with Baxter should not be interpreted simply as a "falling out among thieves" over the spoils of railroads.  The Republican party in Arkansas, the reputation and integrity of numerous men who had sponsored the sale of the bonds, and the economic interests of the bondholders were all at stake when the constitutionality of these bonds came into question.  No mere "railroad steal" will suffice to explain the political developments in the following weeks.

Three days after Baxter's refusal to issue these bonds, the Republican State Central Committee met in Little Rock.[63] Besides members of the Committee, other Republicans from throughout the state converged on the city March nineteenth, the day of the meeting.  An unusually large number of radicals were reported in town including Senators Powell Clayton and Stephen W. Dorsey.[64]

It was indeed a time for making decisions of fundamental importance to the future of the Republican party in Arkansas, for the party had both lost control of Elisha Baxter and witnessed with increasing embarrassment the growing liason between Baxter and conservative Democrats.  Not only had Baxter's decision to stop the issuance of bonds prevented the Arkansas Central from receiving additional state support, but previous bond issues also had been threatened by that decision.    In addition to these concerns, the future apparently threatened further dangers to the very existence of party power in the state. The Franchise Amendment of March, 1873, made it likely that the Democrats would overwhelmingly dominate the legislature after the fall election of 1874. In anticipation of that victory the Democrats were already clamoring for a constitutional convention to undo the system established by the Constitution of 1868 upon which Republican power had been based.[65] Clearly, some course of action had to be found to prevent these developments. If that course could not be found in the political potentialities within the state, then perhaps those political potentialities found in Washington could be used to save the party.

Awareness of the importance of the Republican State Central Committee's meeting was indicated by the *Fayetteville Democrat* in its editorial columns:

> In our opinion, the only hope of success for the plunderers is to either obtain guarantees from Baxter that he will run the election machinery next Fall in the interests of the Ring, or endeavor in some way to displace him.  As we said before, time will soon develop the move, whatever it may be.[66]

Less than four weeks later events revealed the Republican decision to utilize the legitimacy of Joseph Brooks' claim to the governor's office as a means of deposing Elisha Baxter and of seeking assistance from Washington to regain the party's power in Arkansas.

On April fifteenth, as Governor Elisha Baxter was sitting in his executive office in the state house, he was faced with a *coup d'état.* As he described the experience: "Mr. Brooks, in person, with an armed force of a dozen or twenty, took possession of my room, and I was permitted the alternative of forcible and unseemly ejection, or of such arrest and punishment as he might see fit to inflict. Before I could take measures to reoccupy the statehouse it was filled with armed desperadoes."[67]

Moments before this action Brooks had secured a decision from Judge John Whytock of the Pulaski County circuit court which recognized Brooks as governor of the state. It will be recalled that ten months earlier, on June 16, 1873, the case of *Brooks* v. *Baxter* came to rest without a decision in this same circuit court.[68] Now, without notice to Baxter or to his attorneys, the case had been reopened, Judge Whytock had overrruled Baxter's demurrer and had declared Brooks to be entitled to the office of governor.[69] Without hesitation the oath of office was secretly administered to Brooks by Chief Justice John McClure, and Brooks, with his associates, proceeded through the rain to the state house armed only with such authority as that derived from a copy of the minutes of Judge Whytock's action supported by the questionable ceremony of the oath-taking which had followed.[70]

The legal maneuvering of these moments did much to destroy the legitimacy of Brooks' claim to office. Any review of these proceedings would find them in violation of due process. It was true that the Republican strategy in this action was to enlist aid from Washington in regaining control of the state for the party. But the crux of the matter in the future would be whether Washington would go behind these moves of expediency to the legitimate claim of election in November, 1872. Unless Attorney General Williams could be persuaded to consider that part of Brooks' claim, these current developments would throw his case out of court. Brooks had always had the problem of obtaining a fair hearing for his claim, but now his expediency had added an additional burden to his cause.

The exciting events which occurred during the month following April fifteenth are usually referred to as the Brooks-Baxter War.[71] To call them a "war" over-dramatizes events, and yet on four occasions during the month actions did reach the intensity of military engagement. All the elements of a melodrama were present during this period as Joseph Brooks occupied the governor's office in the state house secure behind barricades erected on the grounds. Three blocks to the east, down Markham Street, Elisha Baxter, still claiming to be the legitimate governor, made his headquarters at the Anthony

House. Main Street, which ran south from the Arkansas River, served as a dividing line between the hostile camps. United States troops were stationed along Main from the river to Ninth Street in order to prevent the outbreak of hostilities.[72]

At the intersection of Markham and Main on Tuesday, April twenty-first, there occurred the first of these dramatic encounters between the opposing forces. Late that afternoon, while Brooks' troops were on dress parade in front of the state house, they received news that Baxter's men were on their way. Brooks' troops took their position behind the breastworks on the state-house grounds. In Baxter's area, east of Main Street, Negro troops from Jefferson County were turned out for a parade about this time. Their commander, King White, halted this parade on Markham just east of Main Street with the troops facing westward toward the state house.[73]

Overlooking this scene from windows above were armed followers of Brooks and Baxter. In spite of efforts of Colonel T.E. Rose, United States Army, to prevent hostilities, a shot rang out, and for five minutes indiscriminate shooting followed from which one man died and several others were wounded. The disturbance was quickly terminated by United States troops.[74]

The most costly skirmish of the war occurred near Pine Bluff on April thirtieth. Two white men had gathered about one hundred Negro troops at New Gascony in Jefferson County to aid the Brooks cause. It was rumored in Pine Bluff that these men were to be used to burn and pillage that city. King White, leading about one hundred Baxter troops, left Pine Bluff to meet these Brooks forces near New Gascony. In the fight which followed, nine Brooks men were killed and twenty were wounded. Nine Baxter men were wounded.[75]

On May eighth, a third encounter took place at Palarm, sixteen miles upriver from Little Rock. Before dawn, several Baxter men left Little Rock on the steamboat *Hallie* to intercept a flatboat loaded with arms which were being sent to Brooks from the University armory at Fayetteville. Brooks' men in Little Rock learned about the *Hallie's* departure and left by train at 6 A.M. to overtake the Baxter men. Arriving at Palarm about 8 A.M., they found the *Hallie* downstream replenishing its fuel. When the boat reached the place along the bank where the Brooks men were hiding, a fight ensued which resulted in the capture and return of the *Hallie* to Little Rock.[76]

A final skirmish of note occurred in Little Rock on May twelfth when Brooks troops attempted to intercept Baxter reenforcements on their way into the city. Both Baxter and Brooks sent troops to contest the other's presence, and a genuine battle appeared in the making. Fortunately, United States troops broke up the disturbance before hostilities could develop beyond their initial stages. Two of Baxter's men were wounded, and eight of Brooks' men were killed or wounded.[77]

Figure 19.    Brooks' Troops at the Old State House During the Brooks-Baxter War

The primary interest of this study is not in those events, but rather in the political consequences deriving from this last attempt of the Republican party to regain its control of the state during Reconstruction. The realignment of political forces which brought together the various elements of Republican opposition under the leadership of Augustus H. Garland was the most significant development of these and subsequent days during 1874.

Elisha Baxter had retired to St. John's College immediately after his eviction from the state house on April fifteenth. There he gathered advisers for a conference to decide what was to be done. About midnight a group of armed men led by U. M. Rose went from St. John's to Garland's home on Scott Street to summon him to their council. Rising from his bed, Garland went with them to St. John's and found there such other members of the bar as Henry C. Caldwell, Sam W. Williams, and F.W. Compton.[78] With U.M. Rose and Garland included in this list, Baxter's cause appeared to have the advantage, if legal talent were the basis of comparison.

Initially, it was Baxter's idea to go to Washington and to settle matters through a personal conference with President Grant. Garland promptly opposed this idea, for he was afraid that, once Baxter was in Washington, the Republicans would find some means of keeping him there and thereby of maintaining Brooks in office in Little Rock. Therefore, under no circumstances should Baxter leave the state. His presence would be a great asset in the forthcoming legal struggle. And for that contest Garland now volunteered his services and took up his residence with Baxter at his headquarters, which were established the next evening at the Anthony House, located three blocks east of the state house. There Garland lived for the next six weeks, and it is true, as Professor Shinn has noted, that "Down at the Anthony House . . . Garland's judgment was supreme, and that judgment won out."[79] At last Garland found himself in a situation which demanded the full use of his political talents.

Three actions taken on the first day of the Garland-Baxter collaboration placed Brooks on the defensive. Elisha Baxter, as governor, issued a proclamation declaring martial law in Pulaski County.[80] And in the meantime, at a meeting of some thirty members of the Little Rock Bar over which Garland presided as president, a resolution was passed condemning Judge Whytock's decision in favor of Brooks. This resolution, which was signed by those present, declared that the decision was wholly null and void and that it gave no authority to "the revolutionary proceedings based upon it."[81] A third action was an address to the people, calling for their support of Baxter as governor and urging them to rally at the Capitol to sustain him in his power and authority. The prominence of the men who signed this document was meant to add influence to its contents.[82]

Four days later, on April twentieth, Joseph Brooks made a formal appeal to President Grant for aid to suppress domestic violence.[83] This appeal was accompanied by a paper, signed by Chief Justice John McClure and Associate Justices Searle and Stephenson of the Arkansas Supreme Court, stating that they recognized Brooks as governor of the state. Circumstances of the case which had brought the matter before the Court, and which had resulted in the statement of the two justices, were such that United States Attorney General Williams saw through the artificiality of the dispute under consideration. When time came for Williams' own opinion to be rendered on the merits of Brooks' appeal, these maneuvers would damage Brooks' cause.[84]

On April twenty-second, Governor Baxter issued a proclamation calling for the legislature to convene in Little Rock on May eleventh for the purpose of settling the dispute between Brooks and himself. Earlier that day he had proposed such a solution to President Grant and had received assurances that the President would "heartily approve any adjustment, peaceably, of the pending difficulty in Arkansas—by means of the Legislative Assembly, the courts or otherwise."[85] By approving this proposal of Governor Baxter, the President unknowingly assisted the strategy of Augustus H. Garland in his efforts to end Reconstruction in Arkansas.

The special election held in the fall of 1873 to fill vacancies in the legislature had given the Democrats a majority of the seats. Any consideration of Brooks' claim to election as governor in the general election of 1872 would now be conducted by a Democratic legislature sympathetic to Baxter. In all probability Brooks' cause would be lost under these circumstances. But in Garland's thinking the possibilities of the future went beyond this immediate result. Which of these two men, Brooks or Baxter, won the immediate contest was of secondary importance to him. Garland's real objective in calling the legislature was disclosed in a letter to Harris Flanagin written on April thirtieth:

I do not suppose, in point of fact, Brooks wants a convention. But my chief idea . . . in having a Legislature, is to get the convention. I believe this very trouble we are having will make the members a unit almost for a convention. Baxter will favor it outright. It is of small moment really who is Govr. of these two, but it is of great moment to settle these troubles and get a government by & from the people.

I do not think Brooks wants a Legislature, but, if it is protected by the federal government in its meeting, Mr. B. will have to stand aside & submit to it:—if the U.S. Government will not protect it in meeting then Brooks opposes it, we are put where we are, & no government is here at all.

I hope you may find it consistent with your views to urge the members, all of them, to come & meet here in May, 11th:—This is the only way out of it for us.[86]

Appropriately enough this letter was written on stationary marked "Executive Office, State of Arkansas."

As Garland was closing this letter, at approximately nine-thirty in the morning, an encouraging word came from U.M. Rose, who had gone to Washington to represent Baxter's interests before the President. "Everything favorable—Atty General will receive written arguments on both sides—President will decide speedily—be firm."[87]

With Garland in command in Little Rock and with Rose in charge in Washington, assisted there by Albert Pike and Robert W. Johnson, Baxter's case was in the hands of some of the finest legal talent the state could offer at that time.[88] In this legal association could also be seen the coming together of some of the political elements which would unite under Garland to redeem the state from Republican control.

The *coup d'état* executed by Brooks and his followers required a political reappraisal by almost everyone, and that action resulted in a realignment of political forces. The realignment was not without its ironies. President Grant was asked to sustain the legitimacy of Brooks' election in 1872, but in doing so he would place doubt upon the legitimacy of his own victory in the Arkansas Presidential canvass. Senator Clayton would have to forget many hostile exchanges during the campaign of 1872 before he could genuinely accept Brooks as governor. Senator Dorsey had received his own certificate of election from Governor Baxter, the man he now had to renounce as the legitimate governor of the state. And Chief Justice John McClure had administered the oath of office to Baxter as solemnly as he had administered that oath to Brooks.[89]

Circumstances were also awkward for those Congressmen who had run on the Brooks ticket in strong opposition to the Clayton and McClure forces in the Republican party. Their plight was expressed by T.M. Gunter on April sixteenth when he wrote to David Walker from Washington, where Gunter was still contesting for his own seat in Congress: "I am not well pleased with the apparent combination, but cannot and will not go back on Brooks and the expressed will of the people in their choice of Gov. The same frauds that put Baxter in as Governor, put [M. L.] Bell, [L. C.] Gause, and myself out as Congressmen, and it would be inconsistent in us not to sustain Brooks."[90] Gunter expected David Walker to write and advise Joseph Brooks concerning Brooks' course of action.

On April twenty-second, David Walker received a letter from Sam W. Williams, one of the conferees present with Baxter at St. John's College, who was apparently trying to enlist Walker's cooperation and support for the Democratic efforts to reinstate Baxter in the state house. Walker promptly answered Williams' letter, indicating his continued support for Joseph Brooks even though Walker had publicly denounced the Whytock decision as "a corrupt and infamous abuse of power." Walker's evaluation of the facts seems to have pronounced a curse on both the radicals and the Democrats:

Radicals are holding the man in office who was in fact elected but who they by fraud had kept out of office whilst the Democrats are trying to reinstate, the man who they voted against, and who was not elected, over their own candidate who they know was elected. And thus the Radicals today are sustaining the popular will, by upholding its rightfully elected officer, and the democrats are for forcing a man into office who took it confessedly in defiance of the popular will.[91]

Despite his apprehensions concerning the perpetuation of Republican rule should Brooks remain in office, David Walker continued to be loyal to the legitimate claim of Joseph Brooks to the office of governor.[92] By no means was Walker ready to become a part of the Democratic strategy.

In this position Walker was not alone. A significant portion of the state's press advocated Brooks' cause. As many as nine Democratic and ten Republican and independent papers throughout the state were enlisted on Brooks' side.[93] These editorial exchanges revealed a touch of irony which William E. Woodruff, Jr., editor of the *Gazette*, easily perceived. Just as he had spoken of "poetic justice" when referring to Brooks' defeat in 1872, so now his old adversary, the *Fayetteville Democrat*, commented, "there is a vast amount of poetic justice in the way in which Baxter had been disposed of."[94] Thus the positions of the advocates of principle versus expediency had been reversed, as Woodruff was quick to remind his editorial colleagues:

How do the powder-begrimed democratic veterans of the campaign of '72, Wheeler of the Independent, Barry of the Monticellonian, Hobson of the Star and [sic] of the Fayetteville Democrat, like the company some of their leaders keep as they are sandwiched above? Were they for measures or men then or now; or then *and* now? Will they continue to work the guns of the great, good and honest democratic convention of '72 under the joint leadership of Brooks, Clayton and company? or will they politically strengthen their recreant leader and the traitorous few who hoodwinked and misled the honest sentiment of the convention of '72 as we have a thousand times said, and as their present companionship proves was the fact. Let them consider whither a further support of Brooks will lead them.[95]

On May first, lawyers for both sides of the dispute presented their written arguments to Attorney General George H. Williams. Brooks was represented legally by T.D.W. Yonley, Attorney General of Arkansas, and Brooks' cause was advocated in Washington by the Arkansas Senators and Representatives in Congress, with the exception of W.W. Wilshire.[96] In addition to this number, Brooks received support from ex-Senator B.F. Rice and from the three Congressmen who claimed to have been elected on the Brooks ticket in 1872 and who were currently in Washington contesting for their seats.[97] And as has been noted, Baxter was represented legally by U.M. Rose, Albert Pike, Robert W. Johnson, and W.W. Wilshire.[98] On the next day in Little Rock, the Democratic-

Conservative State Central Committee announced its support for Baxter stating that: "We stand where we stood in June, 1872, battling against the same enemy, and as Brooks has entered their camp we cannot follow him."[99]

By May ninth, an agreement for settling the dispute had been accepted by the attorneys and agents of Brooks and Baxter in Washington. The plan called for a full hearing of Brooks' claim before the Arkansas legislature to be followed by a thorough investigation by that body of the allegations made. In the meantime, both sides were to send their troops home with the exception of one company each, and all belligerent actions were to cease. During the time required for making the investigation the man President Grant designated would exercise the functions of the governor's office, a choice to be based on the arguments previously submitted on May first.[100]

This proposal was acceptable to Brooks, and he so informed the President on May tenth. Accordingly, on the following day Brooks issued his own call for the legislature to convene on May twenty-fifth.[101] The President's proposal was not so well received, however, by the Baxter strategists in the Anthony House.

Governor Baxter refused to consent to anything that would directly or indirectly recognize Joseph Brooks as governor of Arkansas.[102] Garland reported this decision to one of Baxter's supporters on May eleventh: "We consent to nothing affecting our interests—our response if accepted puts us level as a yard stick."[103] The nature of this response was revealed in another telegram to Baxter supporters in Pine Bluff later that day: "President Grant had ordered Brooks to retire with forces as far west of the State House as we are east—building to be turned over to Secy Johnson—Legislature to meet therein unmolested and their judgment to be sustained. Bully."[104] Baxter and his advisors knew they had won an important concession. The legislature's judgment was to be sustained by Grant, but now there was no stipulation that an investigation of Brooks' allegations would be conducted. With a Democratic legislature arriving in Little Rock that same day, Baxter's yardstick appeared far more level than Brooks'.

After two days during which a quorum was not present and a third day spent in organization, the legislature began its business on May fourteenth.[105] That day the two houses jointly telegraphed President Grant, requesting him to clear the state house and other public buildings and jointly received the Governor's message. In that message Governor Baxter recommended a constitutional convention.[106] Understandably, the morale in the Baxter camp was high. Anticipation of victory was at hand. "You can assure the people that [the] job is about complete—We are making it too hot for them—not a Brooksite to be found outside the State House—Rats to their holes—Expect good news Tomorrow."[107]

True to these expectations the good news came. In response to the recognition of Baxter as governor of Arkansas by the state legislature, President Grant proclaimed his own recognition of Baxter and ordered Brooks to disperse his forces within ten days.[108]  Secretary of State Hamilton Fish had the President's proclamation telegraphed to the President of the Arkansas Senate.[109]  A short time later, at approximately two o'clock, the proclamation was read aloud by Augustus H. Garland from the balcony of the Hewitt building just across from the Anthony House.[110]  The large crowd assembled in the street below responded as might be expected:

... the cheering was tremendous and long continued. Hats were thrown in the air and men shouted themselves hoarse with every manifestation of rejoicing. The crowd then surged into the Anthony House, where Baxter was, and overwhelmed him with handshakings and congratulations. The general assembly met at three o'clock, and it [the proclamation] was read aloud to the body by acting President Frierson amid great excitement. From that time on till night the city was a scene of intense excitement and rejoicing in the Baxter lines, and a feeling of great relief prevailed that the difficulty had at last been settled.[111]

Attorney General Williams' opinion on the arguments submitted to him on May first was also announced on May fifteenth and served as the legal basis for President Grant's proclamation. The decision considered only the legal aspects of Brooks' actions during the preceding month and refused to go into the legitimacy of his claim of election in November, 1872.[112]  Thus this aspect of the Republican attempt to bring intervention from Washington to save the party in Arkansas had failed. In addition to this result, the morale of those who had remained loyal to Brooks during all those months since November, 1872, had suffered a fatal blow from these developments, as was reflected by the *Fayetteville Democrat* in its columns:

From the canvass of 1872 up to the present time we have not swerved from the course marked out by a rigid adherence to what we conceived to be right in principle and for the best interests of Arkansas. It makes little difference that we have been defeated. It matters not that the wrong has triumphed and truth crushed to earth—we are still for the right as we see it, and against the wrong. ... If a rigid adherence to truth and principle will give success, we propose to gain it—if on the other hand, expediency and vile complicity with fraud and villainy are to succeed, as they seem to be now succeeding, we shall always prefer defeat.[113]

With the day of victory, May fifteenth, there began a period of harvesting the fruits of that victory by the Democratic forces. The legislature refused to honor Brooks' request that the vote of the 1872 gubernatorial election be recanvassed and proceeded to rush through a bill calling for a constitutional convention election to be held on June thirtieth.[114]  Even B.F. Askew, Senator representing Columbia and Nevada counties, who had introduced the bill on May sixteenth, was impressed by the speed with which it had passed. He wrote Harris Flanagin the following day that the bill "was passed by both branches of the legislature within two hours. I do not approve running things so fast as that was done—but I feel elated at the passage of the bill for I offered it as an olive branch of peace for the State and its citizens."[115]

The prospect of a new constitution was not the only harvest made by the Democrats during the remaining days of May as many state offices recently held by Republicans were filled by Democratic appointees of Governor Baxter. By June first the following changes had been made:

| *Republican Office-holder* | *Democratic Replacement* |
|---|---|
| Chief Justice  John McClure | E.H. English |
| Associate Justice M.L. Stephenson | J.T. Bearden |
| Associate Justice John E. Bennett | F.W. Compton |
| Attorney General T.D.W. Yonley | James L. Witherspoon |
| Treasurer Henry Page | Robert C. Newton[116] |

In these appointments could be observed a further consolidation of the various elements of the Democratic party which would unite under Augustus H. Garland in the near future.  Both E.H. English and F.W. Compton had served in these positions on the Arkansas Supreme Court before the Civil War and during the Confederate government.  Compton was elected again in 1866 and had been removed from office by Congressional Reconstruction.[117]   James L. Witherspoon had been a member of the Democratic-Conservative State Central Committee and a Democratic member of the coalition committee supporting the Brooks campaign in 1872.[118]   Robert C. Newton had been a friend of "the family" before the Civil War and had been a prominent Democratic spokesman for secession in 1861, together with Robert W. Johnson and T.C. Hindman. Newton had served Baxter during the preceding weeks as the commander of his military forces during the Brooks-Baxter War.[119]

Awareness of the debt owed to Garland for the favorable outcome of the Brooks-Baxter contest was indicated on May twenty-ninth in a letter to Jesse Turner from one of his long-standing Whig friends living in Little Rock: "Garland has worked hard & deserves all we could say of him."[120]

# CHAPTER TEN

# THE PROBLEM RESOLVED

The legislature adjourned on May twenty-eighth and thoughts turned toward the forthcoming election on June thirtieth in which the voters would decide whether to have a constitutional convention and would choose candidates for the convention should there be one. The momentum of political events appeared to be moving toward an early return of local control of constitutional government. There was only one factor which posed any significant threat to this eventuality—the Poland Committee.

On May twenty-seventh, a House resolution had created a five-man Congressional Committee under Representative Luke P. Poland of Vermont to investigate political affairs in Arkansas.[1] As long as this Committee was in existence, there was some danger that Republican influence in Washington would be successful in securing the intervention of the Federal government in behalf of Republican interests in Arkansas. Hearings before this Committee began at once in Washington. Some of the most pertinent questioning was directed toward the actual need for a new constitution. On June tenth, chairman Poland asked witness Robert A. Howard a question which revealed the crux of the matter: "Do you think that these defects that you have named in the constitution are the real occasion for calling this constitutional convention, or is it because it furnishes an opportunity to make an entire change in the government?"[2] Governor Baxter's lawyers were successful in obtaining the promise of the Committee that it would visit Arkansas before making its final report.[3]

In Arkansas the threat represented by the existence of the Poland Committee was relegated to the background as preparations were made for the election. Garland accepted chairmanship of the state board of election supervisors as a precaution against possible irregularities which might rob the Redeemers of their anticipated victory.[4] From the Democratic point of view June thirtieth was a glorious day.    In the election the Democratic-Conservative party had polled 80,250 votes for the Constitutional Convention to 8,607 against.[5]   In addition to this fact, out of the ninety-one delegates to the Convention more than seventy were to be Democratic delegates.[6]    There could be little doubt in Democratic minds that the return of *de jure* government was at hand.

At noon on July fourteenth, the Convention met in the hall of the house of representatives.[7]  As will be seen, the Convention brought together delegates representing the various elements of state politics from ante-bellum days to the present, and the opening session must have had the atmosphere of a homecoming as acquaintances were renewed.    One person's absence, however, was conspicuous—David Walker was not there.

As early as May thirtieth, Walker had offered himself as a candidate for convention delegate.[8]   Having enjoyed a position of leadership in his county for so many years, he quite naturally expected to be sent to the Convention.   To his surprise and chagrin he suffered the worst defeat in his political experience. With the influx of new population into Washington County there had come the Granger movement.   In this election for delegates to the Convention the local Granger organization had offered three candidates who thoroughly defeated their political opponents, David Walker included.[9]   In disappointment mixed with anger Walker attempted to explain his defeat to his friend W.W. Mansfield, who had been sent to the Convention as a delegate from Franklin County:

I was beaten by clever gentlemen two of them strangers who came in since the war, never canvassed held no office or put forth their views in any way, not half those who voted for them ever saw or herd [*sic*] of them only that they were "grangers," no one wished to hear from the candidates [and] in parts of the County refused to hear *Lawyers.* In short it was rendered in secret council to elect them, and they were elected with the solid Radical vote, which I neither expected nor desired.

And worse than all I did not meet with ten men in the whole County outside the radical ranks who did not think that I was best qualified and was the proper man to send, but with all, I was beaten, and Wilson much worse. Well after all when I consider the fatigue, the warm weather, and my advanced age, I am glad to be at home with my children and at rest.[10]

Once the Convention turned its attention to the business of writing a new constitution, two areas were paramount in the delegates' thinking: the powers of the governor and the system of apportionment. These two features of the Constitution of 1868 had served as the foundation for Republican control of the state, and to undo this system had been the real reason underlying the desire for a new constitution. There were other areas of concern. For example, the desire for economical government led to a restriction of the taxing power and to a limitation of the government's ability to contract debts. But the dominant motivation for the delegates' actions came from their concern over the powers of the governor's office and over the system of apportionment.[11]

By concentrating power in the hands of the governor and by relying heavily on executive patronage, the Republicans had been able to utilize a strong executive for party purposes. To insure against a repetition of this experience, the delegates created a weak executive who had powers adequate for frugal government but who was dependent upon the legislature for powers which went beyond those usually required by minimal government. To lessen the powers of the governor's patronage, the Convention reduced the number of state officers and, at the same time, provided for the selection of those officers through popular election. An additional limitation of the governor's power was the reduction of his term of office from four to two years.[12]

It will be recalled that the apportionment which resulted from the system provided by the Constitution of 1868 led to an over-representation of the delta area and to an under-representation of the northwestern area.[13] Furthermore, the district system of the 1868 Constitution had maximized the influence of the Negro vote at the expense of the whites.[14] The new Constitution would try to correct these inequities through the use of a county-based system of apportionment which closely reflected the distribution of adult male citizens throughout the state.[15]

The reduction of the governor's term of office to two years posed the problem of selecting a governor to serve under the new Constitution. In the northwest, where political forces were somewhat disorganized as a result of the outcome of the Brooks-Baxter contest, men began to suggest David Walker as the candidate under whom these forces could rally. As early as June third he was mentioned as a candidate for governor.[16] But when, to his embarrassment, Walker was not elected as a delegate to the Convention, this defeat placed the northwestern men in a weak bargaining position. The one thing men of the northwest did not want was a continuation of Baxter in the governor's office. L.C. Gause reflected this attitude in his letter to Walker on July eleventh: "There is one thing however unalterably fixed in my mind. I never will support Baxter for Governor and if our party friends are so foolish as to drive that entering wedge into the democratic party they will split me off for one, and if nothing but a chip I will still oppose the unnatural alliance."[17]

Harris Flanagin was also suggested as a candidate for governor. Jesse Turner believed that Flanagin's stature throughout the state would make him a candidate under whom the various elements of the Democratic-Conservative party could unite. The most likely alternative to Flanagin was Baxter, according to Turner's evaluation of the prospects.[18]

There were two particular reasons for seriously considering Baxter as the proper governor to serve under the new Constitution. In the first place his four-year term of office would normally have continued until 1876. To terminate his occupancy of the governor's office now would appear far more revolutionary to the Poland Committee than to allow him to serve under the new Constitution. A second reason could be seen in the obligation Democrats felt toward Baxter for the manner in which he had opposed the radical elements in the Republican party. John R. Eakin well represented this thought when he wrote David Walker prior to the Convention:

> I cannot but think Baxter entitled to some high and appropriate recognition for his services, but *"what to do?"* If nominated for governor, he is almost certain to have arrayed against him so determined an opposition of conservatives as will divide the party. If not nominated, I cannot feel we will be absolved in the worlds eyes, of ingratitude. And what else is there for him? Not Senator certainly! He is not fit for that, whilst he might do for governor.
>
> On the whole I have concluded to take no decisive stand in the matter, but wait until the delegates come up to the political convention. They will come advised of the temper of the people from all sections. If they think Baxter can be elected, and that the people desire to tender him that recognition of his services, they will nominate him, and I will think it right. But if they find too great opposition existing in different parts of the state (on a comparison of views) to make his nomination a sweep, then I would favour taking up any good man of unquestionable patriotism. The state is full of good material.[19]

The conservative opposition to which Eakin referred was strongly represented in the person of David Walker. The threat to the unity of the party which Baxter posed was clear in Walker's mind as he wrote to W.W. Mansfield during the Convention:

> I very much dislike the movement of the Gazette to force Baxter upon the Democrats as candidate for governor. I do not feel very deeply under obligations to him for calling the convention, because I am confident he never would have done so but for Brooks puting [*sic*] him out of office, he was thrown into the army of the Democracy and acted at their biding. [*sic*] I assure you that I do not know of a democrat in the County who will support him for Governor. We desire a nominee of our own party wholly disconnected with either Brooks or Baxter. In no other way can the unity of the party be preserved.[20]

The Constitutional Convention, which had begun its sessions on July fourteenth, completed the task of writing a new constitution by September eighth and adjourned until October twentieth. Election day for the ratification of the Constitution and for the choice of officers to serve under the new document was set for October thirteenth.[21]

September eighth had been designated as the time for a Democratic state convention to meet in Little Rock, and for three days, September eighth through tenth, the various elements of the party met, compromised their differences, and consolidated party unity. In this Convention the traditional two-thirds rule for choosing a nominee for governor was abandoned despite objection from northwestern delegates and replaced by a simple majority vote.[22] On September ninth, Elisha Baxter was nominated on the first ballot, in which he received fifty-two of the seventy-two votes cast.[23] A committee was then appointed to inform Baxter of his nomination.

In the meantime the Convention turned its attention to the choice of a candidate for chief justice of the Supreme Court. E.H. English was nominated first, and his name was immediately followed by the nomination of David Walker. A delegate from Washington County reported that David Walker "could not accept the position, and therefore did not desire the same."[24] With this withdrawal of his name Walker served notice that there would not be party unity with Baxter leading the ticket.

Baxter's response to the Convention's nomination read like an acceptance until its concluding paragraphs. Then Baxter expressed his declination: "under the peculiar circumstances which exist, I deem it better and more honorable to decline a nomination dictated, in some measure, by a feeling of gratitude as well as a regard to the public good."[25] By this act Baxter had done a magnanimous thing for which the Convention was appropriately grateful. Great cheering and cries of "He's the biggest man in the state" followed the reading of his letter. To express this gratitude in some tangible form, the Convention nominated him a second time—this time by acclamation, but that nomination was also rejected. Near the close of the session someone called for Augustus H. Garland, and the name was greeted with cheers.

The following morning Augustus H. Garland was nominated for governor. Several nominations of favorite sons were also made, but each of these names was withdrawn, and Garland was nominated by a unanimous vote. Perhaps there were reservations to this unanimity, as was indicated by one county when its vote went for "Boss Garland," but there was overwhelming support for Garland and for the party unity which was possible under his candidacy.[26]

One of the most important elements contributing to the party unity which developed was the joining together of the northwestern Whig and conservative Democratic forces under David Walker with those Democratic forces radiating from Little Rock under the leadership of Augustus H. Garland. When to these are added the conservative Democrats and Whigs of the southwest, the dominant forces of party consolidation could be accounted for.[27]

After Baxter had removed himself as a candidate, Walker was willing to have his name placed in nomination as an associate justice of the Supreme Court. In the balloting which followed, David Walker and William M. Harrison (of Jefferson County) were nominated for the two positions on the bench.[28] The relationship between Walker's nomination and the unanimous vote which was received by Garland in his own nomination for governor was hinted at in a letter written by Garland to David Walker two days after the Convention had adjourned:

During the hurry & fuss of the few days you were in this place recently, I had no opportunity of talking with you. I received through my brother your expressions of willingness to go upon & aid the ticket if I would go on it for Gov.:–This I agreed to do, upon the express idea, that I was not a candidate, & the convention [tendering?] it so unanimously, I could not decline it, whatever the sacrifices might be, if I was in earnest at any time about serving the people.

I am very glad indeed you consented to take a place on it. As far as I can see & hear, the Ticket is entirely satisfactory![29]

The candidates on the Democratic-Conservative ticket reflected the distribution of political forces which were components of this party. Of the eleven major state offices, four candidates were from the northwest, three were from Little Rock, two were from the southwest, and two were from the delta.[30] The conscious desire for a regional balance among these offices was reflected by the delegates from the delta when they pleaded as a matter of justice for the two delta candidates. In the political adjustments of the day these delegates were afraid the delta regions were in danger of being slighted.[31]

The election was held on October thirteenth. Republicans, denying the validity of the Constitutional Convention, refused to offer candidates in this election. They did participate, however, in the voting. By a vote of 77,461 to 24,592 the Constitution was overwhelmingly ratified, and the largest electorate the state had ever known cast over 103,000 votes in the election.[32] The distribution of those votes discloses a strong correlation between the distribution of Negro voters throughout the state and the vote cast against the Constitution. There is a similar correlation between the distribution of white voters and the vote cast for the Constitution.[33]

The government to be formed under the new Constitution would be a *de jure* government for the greatest number of the white population; therefore, they could freely give their allegiance to it. For the Negro, however, allegiance to the new government would be more difficult to give, for, although the Constitution guaranteed his rights in a liberal manner, political, social, and economic factors would soon exclude the Negro from effective participation in the new government.

Garland received over seventy-four thousand votes for governor, and the absence of opponents for the other major candidates made the election a mere formality for them.[34] The political result of the election for the legislature was disastrous for the Republican party. The composition of the new legislature would have thirty-one Democrats and two Republicans (whose seats were contested) in the senate and eighty Democrats and ten Republicans in the house of representatives.[35] The loss of radical control was that complete.

It was time for celebration by the Democrats, and yet, on November twelfth, Garland was very quietly inaugurated as governor. The reason for such a subdued inauguration was to be found in the presence in Little Rock of

## TABLE 5

### RATIFICATION OF CONSTITUTION, 1874

| | *For Constitution of* 1874[a] | *Against Constitution of* 1874[a] | *Male Citizens 21 and Over* 1870[c] | *White Adult Males (Estimated)* 1870[d] | *Colored Adult Males (Estimated)* 1870[d] |
|---|---|---|---|---|---|
| NW | 31,910 | 3,444 | 37,335 | 35,393 | 1,904 |
| DELTA | 23,625 | 13,963 | 31,245 | 17,810 | 13,435 |
| SW | 18,844 | 6,013 | 23,401 | 15,796 | 7,582 |
| TOTAL | 74,379 | 23,420 | 91,981 | 68,999 | 22,921 |
| *% of Total* | % | % | % | % | % |
| NW | 42.9 | 14.7 | 40.6 | 51.2 | 8.3 |
| DELTA | 31.8 | 59.6 | 34 | 25.8 | 58.6 |
| SW | 25.3 | 25.7 | 25.4 | 22.9 | 33 |

a. Calculated from: *Gazette,* October 27, 1874, p. 1, cc. 5–6.
b. Calculated from: *Gazette*, December 13, 1872, p. 4, cc. 4–5.
c. Calculated from: U.S. Bureau of the Census, *Ninth Census: 1870. Population.* I, p. 623.
d. This figure was obtained by calculating the percentage each race represented of the total population and multiplying the total adult male population by this percentage.

| | *Total Number Voting* 1874[a] | *Total Total Voting in Election* 1872[b] | *Total for Augustus H. Garland* |
|---|---|---|---|
| NW | 35,354 | 25,433 | 30,310 |
| DELTA | 37,588 | 31,137 | 22,550 |
| SW | 24,857 | 22,322 | 18,320 |
| TOTAL | 97,799 | 78,892 | 71,180 |
| *% of Total* | % | % | % |
| NW | 36.1 | 32.2 | 42.6 |
| DELTA | 38.4 | 39.5 | 31.7 |
| SW | 25.4 | 28.3 | 25.7 |

e. Pulaski county figures have been excluded.

representatives of the Poland Committee.[36]    Garland was not willing to risk the victory so recently won by indulging now in cheap theatrics.

There was a minor threat to Garland's tenure of office when Volney Voltaire Smith, who had been lieutenant governor under Baxter, claimed that he was the proper successor to Baxter as governor. His claim was set forth in a proclamation which was circulated on the streets of Little Rock on November fourteenth.[37]    This action resulted in the issuance of a call for his arrest, but he had previously gone to Washington to plead his case. His efforts to get a hearing in Washington led to nothing, as the position of President Grant and his advisers was that until the Congressional Committee had completed its investigation the Executive branch should not interfere.[38]    The real threat to the continuance of Garland's government remained the Poland Committee.

Created on May twenty-seventh, the Poland Committee had conducted hearings in Washington during May and early June, and members of the Committee came to Little Rock for an on-the-scene investigation in July and again in November.[39]    Once again in Washington the Committee conducted hearings during December.    Weeks went by during which those interested anticipated the submission of the Poland Committee's report to Congress, but it did not come.[40]

In Little Rock the legislature remained in session awaiting the decision of Washington.    Morale among the members began to decline as their personal expenses accumulated.    Jesse Turner reflected the mood of the legislature in a letter to his son: "Our work of more than three months may be of no avail. We have been here at great expense.    Have to pay our own way.    The State Treasury being empty and the credit of the State too low to borrow money—the State government is for the present being run on the private means of the officials.    Another break up, and more reconstruction would hopelessly ruin the State for the next fifty years."[41]

The cause of Turner's despondency was a message by President Grant in which he indicated that the evidence from Arkansas favored the claims of Joseph Brooks.[42]    Should the Federal government intervene now in behalf of Brooks all would be lost.    Behind Grant's message was the influence of Senator Clayton, whose Senate resolution had requested information on affairs in Arkansas. Should Grant follow the urgings of Senator Clayton, a serious threat was at hand.[43]

The Poland Committee submitted its reports to the House of Representatives on February sixth.    The majority report, signed by four members, concluded that it was improper for the Federal government to interfere with the existing government in Arkansas.    The Louisiana experience, in which the principle had been established that the Federal government should not go behind the record of election returns submitted by state authorities, became a deciding influence in the Arkansas case.    In Louisiana the decision had sustained a Republican

# FRANK LESLIE'S
# ILLUSTRATED
## NEWSPAPER

No. 1,016—Vol. XL.]   NEW YORK, MARCH 20, 1875.   [Price 10 Cents.

HALT THERE, GENERAL BOUM!

JUDGE POLAND TO GEN. U. S. G. BOUM—"*By the Constitution of the United States, and by your oath of office 'to preserve, protect and defend' it, you are estopped from going further in this direction. The existing State government in Arkansas should not be interfered with, either by Congress or by any department of the National Government, which has no more right to interfere with it than has England or France.*"

Figure 20.   Cartoon Depicting the Poland Committee and Congress Preventing
President Grant from Intervening in Arkansas

administration, and now consistency demanded that Baxter and thus Garland be sustained in Arkansas.[44]    The minority report, signed by Representative Ward, insisted that Joseph Brooks had been elected governor in 1872 and was still the legitimate governor.[45]    Until the House of Representatives acted on these reports, Garland's government could not feel secure.

As he had done before in times of trouble, Garland now turned to his friend, Alexander H. Stephens for assistance. Stephens was a member of the House of Representatives and could use his influence there to win acceptance of the majority report. On February eleventh, Garland wrote to Stephens in response to the danger represented by Grant's message. Garland defended his government against charges that it had been established through violence and intimidation and against the charge that it was a revolutionary government. Garland also described the danger of unseating his government: "To turn us back here will be to remit us to chaos—There will be nothing but anarchy here, and Mexico will be a paradise compared with it. This is true as preaching."[46]

In time Garland came to fear that Congress would adjourn before it took action on the Poland Committee's report and that the continuing threat represented by President Grant's message would perpetuate the insecurity felt by Garland's government. He pleaded with Stephens to use his influence with Grant to relieve Arkansas from this discomfort:

The general interpretation of the Pres'ts. message to the Senate, on the Arks. matter is, that Congress not acting, he will set the present government aside and put in Mr. Brooks. I confess I have never so interpreted that message, nor do I yet believe it is the Prest's. intention to so act. I believed when I first read it, and yet believe, I could see in it a desire on the part of the Pres't. to get Cong. to act, for [reasons?] and on grounds entirely consistent with the true interests of the country. Now if I am correct in this, . . . I think the Pres't owes it to himself to Arks. and to the country to say so publicly & officially when Cong adjourns without action! Why?

Because, no one ever dreamed he would interfere unless Cong so said, until his message came out—his message raised this impression all over the country & it still exists to a great extent. Then if we are left here in this condition, people are uneasy, uncertain—business is checked and we are crippled in every way—in fact the difficulties will be almost, without number & of the most serious character. You see them at once. One word from the Pres't would settle all that. As he raised the trouble by public expression, does it not follow he should allay it in the same way, if he really intends not to interfere. It looks so to me very plainly to be his duty. It seems to me from your high toned & conservative course since the war towards the Pres't & his party, you could approach him on this subject and have him to say so. . . . If he can be brought to announce this direct & publicly, all will be relieved and we can go ahead & prosper. I wish you would consider of this & see if it can be done. We have, as you see, to rely on gentlemen of other states there to aid us.[47]

Garland did not have long to wait before the resolution of his difficulties was accomplished.  On March second, the Poland Committee report was called, and, after a prolonged debate, the majority report was adopted by the following vote: one hundred fifty for and eighty-one against, with fifty-six not voting or being paired.[48]

In a message of final surrender Powell Clayton advised his followers that "The action of Congress on Arkansas affairs is conclusive. The validity of the new constitution and the government established thereunder ought no longer to be questioned.  It is the duty of Republicans to accept the verdict, and render the same acquiescence which we would have demanded had the case been reversed."[49]

The response to these developments was unrestrained in many parts of Arkansas.  Exuberant from the excitement of the moment, E.H. English wrote David Walker of the reaction in Little Rock:

The long-looked-for 4th March has come and gone, and our political agony is over. . . .
When the news of the adoption of the Poland resolution got here, there was quite a hurrah in the city, and it was kept up all night—Next day the whole population turned out in the streets to shake hands and congratulate each other. Even the pretty ladies were tripping along the side walks nodding smilingly at the rejoicing men.  Garland and his legislature were all *mouths.*  The farmers are in purchasing plows, and say they will now plow deeper and longer. No body hurt, and only a few drunks.  Little Rock had not been so happy since the day that Grant ordered Brooks out of the State House.  There are of course a few long and gloomy faces, but not many. . . .
I think Arkansas will begin now to hold up her head, and look the world in the face, and after she makes another crop will be able to lift her *tail* into the air, and snort![50]

In a more sober mood Augustus H. Garland expressed his gratitude to Alexander H. Stephens: "I shall strive hard to have Arks. deserve the confidence bestowed by our friends in Cong of both parties.  We are silently happy—prudent and forgiving, & we will try to let nothing mar the victory."[51]

# PART THREE

## CREDIT AND THE
## DEVELOPMENT OF RESOURCES

# CHAPTER ELEVEN

# BANKS:
# THE FIRST ATTEMPT TO USE STATE CREDIT

*However reluctant to acknowledge the fact, it is nevertheless true, that our treasury is not in a condition, nor will it be, to pay the interest on the State bonds, which is now, or will be soon, due, for the next few years. However much the people of Arkansas may be disposed (and none are more so) to sustain her faith and credit, in the payment of all just, legal claims, she would nevertheless be unworthy of the character of a sovereign State, if she tolerated, for a moment, the idea of paying for bonds illegally and fraudulently disposed of.*

*—from Governor Yell's message to the Arkansas
General Assembly, November 7, 1842.*[1]

One of the most important of the continuing factors which influenced Reconstruction in Arkansas was the failure throughout the state's history to successfully use state credit as a means of encouraging the development of natural resources. During Reconstruction, economic development seemed guaranteed by the development of railroads, and the desire to use state credit for their construction proved irresistible. Before this credit could be utilized, however, state credit had to be reestablished, for during the early days of her history Arkansas had pledged her faith and credit for a different enterprise. Banks appeared irresistible in those days as railroads did during Reconstruction, and the faith and credit of the state were pledged to endorse their development. Unfortunately, this first attempt to establish a credit system failed. A significant part of Reconstruction in Arkansas comprises a second attempt to establish a credit system for the development of the state's resources. Handicapped as this effort was by the ante-bellum experience in financing economic development, it will be the purpose of the present chapter to consider that legacy.

When the General Assembly met, November 7, 1842, Governor Archibald

Yell expressed in his message the disillusionment resulting from the failure of the state's first attempt to establish a credit system for the development of her resources.  To be sure, he had not been a proponent of the system and had encouraged the election of anti-bank members in the present assembly during recent months; therefore, his lament did not lie in the failure of the banks themselves, but rather in his realization as governor that, plans having now gone wrong, the state might become obligated to pay for the failure of others.  His remarks, quoted above, not only expressed a judgment on the fortune of the first six years of statehood, but also expressed a theme which carried through Arkansas politics from 1842 to 1884. Words honoring the "faith and credit" of the state, yet finding intolerable "the idea of paying bonds illegally and fraudulently disposed of," sounded political overtones which would not be finally silenced until repudiation won its victory with the Fishback amendment in 1884.

The first state legislature met in Little Rock, September 12, 1836. The need for an adequate circulating medium and the desire for a source of credit for the expansion of the plantation system led to an early consideration of state banking institutions.  Pride of a new state and enthusiasm of a young, expanding economy persuaded the legislators to endorse the creation of the Bank of the State of Arkansas as a means of providing an adequate circulating medium, and of the Real Estate Bank for the promotion of the development of agricultural interests.  The state was to sponsor the creation of these institutions by allowing them to sell state bonds to provide the original operating capital, but it is important to remember that with the successful banking functions promised, the state expected the banks themselves to pay the interest as it came due and also to retire the bonds out of their profits.  The state did not expect to become responsible for the debt.

The day's optimism left advocates of the banking system unaffected by certain signs of caution which might have dampened the assurance of a more prudent group of men.  As an example, by 1836 Kentucky's banking system had failed, but Arkansas legislators quickly pointed to mismanagement rather than to any defect in the system as the cause of the collapse.[2]  Nor were they warned by the danger of over-expansion of banking facilities.  A rural society having a population of less than 100,000, no railroads, and much of its territory inaccessible would hardly seem justified in launching nine banks.[3]

Sectional division of the state also promised complications for the dreams of these men.  The question of political representation had brought out the sectional nature of Arkansas politics during the Constitutional Convention in 1836.  This geographic influence continued to express itself as efforts were made to establish a banking system.  Dominant among the goals of the planters was a bank to aid the expansion of the plantation system.  Using their political power in the legislature, they succeeded in establishing the Real Estate Bank to provide credit for the anticipated development of planting areas. There should be no surprise in finding branches of this bank located at Helena and Colombia (both in southeast Arkansas) and Washington (southwestern Arkansas), while the main bank was situated in Little Rock.[4] For northern and northwestern Arkansas the Bank of the State of Arkansas would bring the benefits of banking institutions to that area. As if to represent a sectional compensation for the Real Estate Bank, the branches of the State Bank were located at Fayetteville and Batesville, with the main bank at Little Rock.[5]

Optimism and faith in the potentialities of state banks as a means of economic development triumphed in that first General Assembly of 1836. By November, 1842, however, these expectations had been replaced by the pessimism and frustration born of a system which had failed in a state which was becoming liable for that failure. The present purpose is not to write a history of the banks or of this period, but rather to consider matters in this first effort to establish a credit system germane to the second attempt during Reconstruction.

Arkansas in 1836 was a rural, frontier society with slightly over 50,000 inhabitants and a total wealth estimated at approximately $15,000,000. This wealth was chiefly in the form of land, and "how to convert [its] potential value into ready capital was the outstanding problem confronting the first legislators."[6] The authors of the state Constitution had authorized the creation of two banks, "one to provide long-term credit to farmers and planters and to promote the agricultural interests of the State, and the other to serve the State as a depository and fiscal agent."[7] It was to further this latter function that the General Assembly created the Bank of the State of Arkansas, November 2, 1836.[8]

The State Bank, as it was called, began its existence with an authorization of $1,000,000 in state bonds, the authority to make loans and negotiations, and the expectation of additional funds coming to it in the future to add to its operating capital.[9] Initial expectations predicted one million dollars from the sale of the bonds and $382,333.32 "in specie, or its equivalent, from the state's share of the surplus revenue of the United States."[10] Experience was not kind to these expectations, for disposing of the bonds proved more difficult than anticipated. Other state banks were suspending specie payments, and the consequent downward trend in the state bond market of 1837 seriously damaged the State Bank's hopes of selling its bonds.[11] By August 6, 1837, this State Bank opened its doors for business, but as late as November 6, 1837, the amount of capital paid in was considerably less than expected.

| | |
|---|---|
| Sale of state bonds | $100,000.00 |
| U.S. surplus revenue | 286,156.49 |
| Five per cent fund | 26,725.00 |
| Seminary fund | 96.30 |
| Saline or salt spring fund | 127.50 |
| | $413,085.29 |

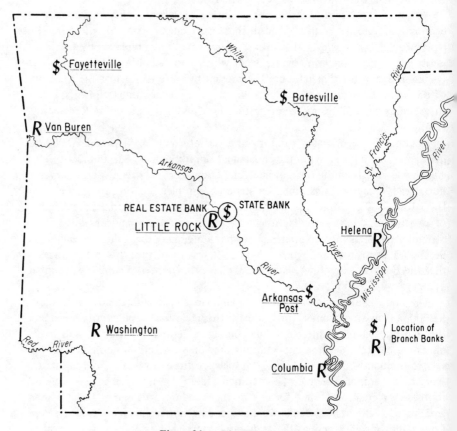

Figure 21.    The First Banks

Of this total $216,725 was specie and U.S. Treasury drafts and $196,881.29 paper of non-specie paying banks.[12]    The legislature aided the bank in December, 1837, by authorizing it to issue $200,000 in post-notes and by authorizing a second issue of state bonds, these placing $300,000 at the bank's disposal.[13]

Despite the early disappointments, with this additional support the bank continued to operate, and the central bank and its branches were able to redeem their circulation with specie. As late as October, 1838, the State Bank was considered sound. Contrary to appearances of affluence, however, this bank was approaching financial difficulties, and on October 31, 1839, the branch at Arkansas Post suspended payment of specie. The next day the main bank and the remaining branches followed that example.[14]   Economic conditions progressively worsened from the time of these developments.

Depreciation became severe as bank notes continued to be issued. About $750,000 came into circulation before liquidation proceedings were ordered in 1843, but their value declined as low as thirty cents on the dollar.[15] The extent of this depreciation indicated the failure of the State Bank to serve as a depository and fiscal agent for the state. The social effects of this failure were significant. Credit and business activity were severely curtailed, and, as an illustration of the effect on consumer prices, a barrel of flour, which cost three dollars elsewhere, required twenty-two dollars to buy in Arkansas.[16] This failure of the circulating medium was particularly felt by the state as it tried to conduct public affairs, and by various public officers, who received their salaries in state currency. The consequent reduction in salaries led to numerous embarrassments and extended even to difficulty in paying postage for state business. Salaries of $1500 paid in Arkansas paper came to be worth $500 of $600 in specie.[17]

By 1841, Governor Yell, whose initial opposition to the banks was strengthened by recent experience and rumors of mismanagement, began an investigation of the State Bank. Reports from the Batesville and Arkansas Post branches failed to reveal mismanagement, but indicated that these banks could not collect their debts, that the demands of interest payment were draining them of their best deposits, and that their supply of specie would be exhausted during the coming year.[18]   The Fayetteville branch, however, revealed many irregularities to its investigators and, for that reason, the report on it was most influential. Of additional importance to this study is the fact that David Walker was one of the commissioners appointed by Governor Yell to examine the Fayetteville bank.[19]

A few days before R.C. Byrd and David Walker began their examination of the bank, the account books were allegedly stolen. All were later recovered, but the one most valuable to their concern had had the pages containing cash transactions and other entries cut out.[20] The minutes of the directory were of no assistance, nor could the commissioners "ascertain that any account of the cash, bills or notes discounted, . . . [had] ever been made from the organization of the bank, until within the last ten days."[21]   Under questioning about specie in the bank, the cashier, William McK. Ball, admitted misrepresenting the true condition of the bank from the fall of 1838, in order to prevent a drain of the specie and to save the bank's credit. The examiners were unable to determine the exact specie deficit, but their report did show $35,350 worth of blank impressions of notes unaccounted for. Their conclusion charged William McK. Ball with the issuance of these notes.

At the time of their appointment as commissioners, Walker and Byrd were senators in the third General Assembly, representing Washington (Fayetteville) and Pulaski (Little Rock) counties respectively.[22] The directors of the Fayetteville bank showed some resentment toward this examination when, on June fourth, they instructed their attorney to inquire into the commissioners' authority.[23] This challenge, however, did not prevent the completion of the commissioners' investigation, and on June twentieth, a report presented their criticism of the cashier. But in August the directors decided that any proceedings against William McK. Ball should be suspended until Mr. Boileau, attorney for the bank, could make a thorough report on the bank's condition. On October fourth, the time and extent of this inquiry was enlarged, resulting in an investigation which began on August 22, 1841, and lasted until April 29, 1842.[24] The conclusion of this examination also found William McK. Ball a defaulter, but for a somewhat smaller amount than that mentioned in the Walker and Byrd report.[25]

During this period the directors planned a move which would help their financial position considerably. Arkansas bonds were quoted in New York at thirteen to seventeen cents. By taking $10,000 in specie from their bank and buying bonds at even twenty cents, they would be able to reclaim $50,000 worth of bonds used to put the Fayetteville branch in operation. Their agents, sent to New York to execute this plan, were unable to carry out the desired transaction, and trustingly, they left $9,934.36 with S.J. Silvester, a New York broker, who was to execute their exchange. By September 4, 1842, no word had come from him, and other agents were sent to New York. There they found Silvester had instructed his London agent to make the bond purchase, but no word had been heard from him. After the failure of an attempt to recover the Fayetteville currency from Silvester through legal means, a Philadelphia company having a claim against the Fayetteville bank was successful in securing some relief from Silvester for itself.[26] The Fayetteville financiers were left wiser, but somewhat less solvent. The days of the Bank of the State of Arkansas were ending as the legislature convened in November, 1842. A membership influenced by economic failure of the bank voted for liquidation, and by July 21, 1843, the main bank and the branches were in the hands of the receivers.[27] Final settlements would take years, but banking functions were at an end.

Leaving the State Bank for the moment and turning to the Real Estate Bank, one finds in its characteristics some of the reasons for the greater influence it played in Arkansas politics. In a day when enlarging the individual plantation and extending the plantation system to new lands were looked upon as the best means of promoting the economic development of a society, an institution providing the credit for such expansion would naturally have its enthusiastic supporters. Such a real estate bank could be considered an ideal solution to the problem of converting into operating capital the potential value which land represented. The importance of this theory to the planter-dominated first General Assembly was indicated by its first legislative act, the creation of the Real Estate Bank, October 26, 1836.[28]

Its charter followed the pattern of the Union Bank of Louisiana, and its operating capital was to come from the sale of $2,000,000 in state bonds, which were secured by real estate mortgages given by stockholders or borrowers "on land unencumbered by debt and in cultivation."[29] The bank was responsible for paying the interest on the bonds and retiring them as they matured; the faith and credit of the state would become involved only after the bank had failed in its responsibilities, a development which seemed remote due to the optimism of the period. Loans were available to anyone with sufficient security. The requirements regarding loans, however, were somewhat more favorable to stockholders than to others. The profits from the bank's operations would be used to retire the bonds and other debts, and any surplus assets at the end of the charter's life (twenty-five years) would be divided among the stockholders.[30]

Many aspects of the bank made it the basis for a system of economic privilege. In the first place, the Constitution and the legislature made the agricultural interests the beneficiaries of its operations.[31] But the distribution of those benefits was affected by the sectional nature of the plantation system and the aristocratic character of the stockholders. As was noted in the first chapter, the plantation system flourished most in the eastern delta and the southwestern bottomlands. Locating its branches in Helena, Columbia, and Washington, the bank reflected this geographical influence. The regional nature of its stockholders also reflected this sectionalism.[32] But the exclusive nature of the bank was best indicated by the fact that there were only 284 men who became stockholders.[33] This economic aristocracy controlling the bank was to a large degree an extension of the political aristocracy dominating the politics of the day. Credit based on the sale of state bonds would actually be at the disposal of a relatively few men. Contributing to this position of privilege were weaknesses in the nature of the bank itself. The appraisers, appointed by the governor, usually were men of means who were prone to over-value land.[34] Because the portion in cultivation of land offered as security for a loan was not specified, the danger of over-appraisal and fraud was always present.[35]

The experience of this bank from its charter in 1836 to the meeting of the hostile legislature in the fall of 1842 may be divided into two parts with October 4, 1839, marking the suspension of specie payment, as the date of division. The first period was filled with reckless loans and discounts; the second was a period of expansion of paper money and its consequent depreciation.[36]

In September, 1838, the Real Estate Bank sold 1,530 of its bonds at par and opened its doors for business, December 12, 1838. Thus began a period of rapid extension of loans and discounts which, by the end of October, 1839, amounted to $1,585,190.80.[37]  On October fourth the cashier of the main bank announced that in order that a "prudent expansion" of the currency be achieved a suspension of specie payments would be the policy of the bank.[38]  The expanded circulation of paper in addition to the circulating specie put Gresham's law into operation, and in a short time specie did not circulate. Depreciation of the paper was the consequence. The extent of these developments may be seen by noting that from November first to January 1, 1840, a period of two months, paper issues by the Real Estate Bank expanded from $153,910 to $328,400 and loans and discounts from $1,585,190 to $1,830,259. By May, 1840, the bank's paper totaled $759,000, five times what it had been in November. The decline in value resulting from these actions saw the paper fall to 35 and 40% below par.

Matters were coming to a climax for the bank with the approach of January, 1840. Interest coming due on the bonds could not be paid unless some special means were found. Bowing to the pressure of these circumstances, those in charge resorted to a tactic to get around the charter's specific restriction against selling any of the state bonds below par. On January 1, 1840, the Real Estate Bank clandestinely hypothecated 500 bonds still in its possession to a New York agent, the New York Trust and Banking Company. The Arkansas bank put up this $500,000 in bonds as collateral for an expected $250,000 loan. Actually received by the Real Estate Bank was the sum $121,336.59, which was used in the financial emergency.[39]  On December 1, 1840, the New York Trust and Banking Company transferred these bonds in bad faith to an innocent third party, James Holford, a London banker for $350,000. These actions would haunt Arkansas history for decades to come.

As the fortunes of the Real Estate Bank waned, questions about the future of the state bonds arose. In February, 1841, the *Gazette* indicated a willingness to submit to direct taxation for state purposes, but "that we should be taxed to pay the debts of the most *aristocratic* monopoly of land holders in the United States is unbearable."[40]  As Worley indicates, however, the large planters themselves would have borne too heavy a burden from such a taxation to allow that solution of the debt problem. By July, 1841, Governor Yell was prompted by the questions, rumors, and uneasiness concerning the bank's condition to write a letter to C. A. Harris, president, seeking information.[41]

Governor Yell's inquiry was directed to the 500 bonds represented by the bank in its November 1840 report to the legislature as "on hand and unsold." He referred to the general impression that some disposition of the bonds had been made but not reported, and he specifically wanted to know whether the bonds had been hypothecated, or otherwise disposed of, and especially whether the present bondholders considered the stockholders of the state liable for their redemption. Mr. Harris did not respond to the Governor's July letter until

October twenty-fifth, at which time he gave the excuse of having been on a protracted absence, and even then did not respond to Governor Yell's questions because the central board of directors was to hold its semi-annual meeting the next Monday at which time Yell's letter would be considered.[42]

On October twenty-ninth, Governor Yell wrote a letter characterized by suppressed anger to the President and the Board of Directors of the Real Estate Bank. News had broken concerning the hypothecation of the bonds in January, 1840, and the transfer to Holford in December, 1840. The Governor had received letters from Holford and Talmage, President of the North American Trust and Banking Company, which persuaded him that they would attempt to hold the state liable for the bonds and interest. His position defined that of many men to be faced with the debt problem in years to come:

> Believing as I do that the *Hypothecation* of the Bonds is without authority of law—or the sanction of the Charter and will opperate [*sic*] as a fraud upon the State and stockholders (If any liability has been incurred) I shall as the Executive of the State, *protest* against the illegal and unauthorized assignment— and will resist all attempts from *any quarter* for the collection of either principal or interest—from the People of this State.[43]

The interest on the bonds had not been paid and had been or would be protested; therefore the Governor wanted an immediate consideration of the liabilities involved.

Governor Yell received three letters from Messrs. Talmage and Holford during September and October. On November tenth, he answered them in a letter denying the state's liability because (1) the bank authorities had exceeded the authority given them by their charter; (2) the agreement made with the North American Trust and Banking Co. gave the bonds to them as collateral only and was not intended to be a sale of the bonds; and (3) since the bank did not have the authority, it could not delegate authority to commissioners and bind the state. He promised to transmit their communications to the legislature, but extended no hope to his correspondents.[44]

As the hostility toward the bank increased during the early months of 1842, the bank officials made a move to protect their position and remove the threat of state interference with the control of the bank. On April second the board made an assignment of all the bank's assets to a group of fifteen trustees, making certain that none of the state-appointed trustees were included in that number.[45] This assignment was contested in the courts, but ultimately upheld by the Supreme Court. Ironically, then, the assignment went to the debtors for their own benefit while the state and the bondholders, having an even larger interest in these affairs, were excluded from the trust.

Conditions of the State Bank revealed in Governor Yell's letter to the people in August, 1841, and those developments in the Real Estate Bank made public later led to the possibility of a bond and anti-bond party in the election of 1842. David Walker apparently was concerned that Governor Yell might encourage a repudiation sentiment present in the state, for he wrote warning against the support stockholders might give Yell in a temporary crusade against state credit, pointing to the more lasting and valid support of those men for whom the credit of the state was still sacred, stating that "there are Democrats here true as ever shaded under a hickory, or, cursed hard cider, or shouted the name of Jackson, who still hold the credit of the state as sacred, and on that issue will rally to a man in support of the credit of the state."[46] The dissatisfaction felt toward the Real Estate Bank had become statewide, and the election of 1842 resulted in a strong victory for the anti-bank candidates.[47]

The failure of the first attempt to use the faith and credit of the state as a foundation for developing resources was almost complete when the General Assembly met November 7, 1842. The State Bank had not made an interest payment on its bonds since January 1, 1841, and the Real Estate Bank had defaulted six months later.[48] The consequences of this failure returned the liability to the state as the hostile legislature convened, for the state's credit had been pledged to the payment of $3,206,000 to redeem bonds upon which the unsuccessful system had been founded.[49]

In his address to the assembly, Governor Yell forcefully described the unfortunate circumstances. No reliable conception of the condition of either bank could be obtained from their reports, for the deceptions indicated by the hypothecation and Fayetteville branch episodes destroyed faith in the validity of the banks' records. Taxation would have to be used if the present system was to be sustained without loss of the faith and credit of the state. Yet it was clear that $80,000 to $100,000 in specie had been lost through mismanagement or embezzlement and that the state treasury was unable to pay the interest due on the outstanding bonds. Faced with the consequences of an unsuccessful attempt to provide credit for the development of the young state's resources, Governor Yell defined his position and expressed a theme recurrent in Arkansas politics. He would sustain the faith and credit of the state for those debts which were just and legal, but would not tolerate "for a moment, the idea of paying bonds illegally and fraudulently disposed of."[50] Since the Real Estate Bank had willfully violated its charter, that charter should be revoked.

After investigating the circumstances before them, the legislature passed an act calling for the liquidation of the State Bank, and that institution went into the hands of the receivers in June and July, 1843. They also passed an act on January 31, 1843, looking to the settlement and liquidation of the Real Estate Bank. The latter accepted the assignment of the preceding April and increased the power of the trustees. but called for five of the fifteen trustees to be chosen by the General Assembly. The affairs of the Real Estate Bank resisted settlement, however, and continued to be a factor in Arkansas politics until the Civil War.

From 1843 to 1853 no legislative act dealt with the bank, but it was a topic at each legislative session. The fifteen trustees of the bank chose not to obey the provisions of the Liquidation Act of January, 1843, and as a consequence their banking charter was forfeited by a decree of the Supreme Court, July 29, 1844. This decree also provided that, should the stockholders refuse to accept the Liquidation Act, the circuit court of Pulaski County was to appoint ten trustees and the General Assembly elect five to conclude the affairs of the bank.[51] The provisions of this decree were not carried out, however, and five trustees chosen in April, 1844, from the fifteen bank trustees, continued to manage the bank's affairs. Thus, from 1844 to 1855 a five-man trusteeship managed the assets of the bank seemingly beyond responsibility to the state.

A Senate report on the Real Estate Bank of 1852 expressed surprise and astonishment that the people had been kept in such ignorance about the bank since the 1842–43 legislature. The committee writing the report searched the journals of the intervening years and found nothing to help them in their quest for information.[52] The report's conclusion as to the financial condition of the bank on October 2, 1852 read as follows:[53]

| | |
|---|---|
| Liabilities | $2,984,887.18 |
| Assets or credits | 2,174,296.87 |
| Total deficiency | $   810,590.31 |

But its authors questioned the assets as shown because they believed the lands included were worth less than when originally taken by the trustees, and that many of the notes, bonds, and bills of the bank were worthless. Therefore, they felt the assets should be reduced at least $400,000 in value, a change which would make their calculation of the total deficit approximately $1,300,000.00[54]

Because of the individuals involved the committee members were reluctant to criticize the trustees, but the evidence they found made them feel that their report provided grounds for removal. They charged the trustees with mis-applying and wasting trust funds and with mismanaging trust property. Under the circumstances, the report recommended that the state either take action to secure the assets, settle with the creditors and retire the bonds, or fund the debt as Governor Roane was then suggesting. Either of these "would be far prefer-able, in the estimation of the committee, to the seeming indisposition which has distinguished former legislatures to provide for our State debt, or even the interest accruing thereon."[55]

On January 12, 1853, the legislature passed an act calling for court action to divest the trustees of the assets.[56] On January 15, 1855, an act was passed calling for a genuine accounting, and a separate court of chancery was established to settle claims related to the Real Estate Bank. Under authority of these actions the assets were taken from the trustees by a decree of the Court of Chancery, April 20, 1855, and they were transferred to a court-appointed receiver five days later.[57]

Governor Elias N. Conway, younger brother of Governor James S. Conway, who had sponsored the creation of the banking system while serving as the state's first governor, initiated suit against the trustees May 1, 1854, and continued throughout his eight years in office to redeem the bonds through application of the assets of the bank. The record of the trustees from April 2, 1842 to May 1, 1854, was damning testimony, for during that period they had not redeemed a single bond. Perhaps under the spur of the Governor's action of May first, they collected on that day $487,958 of bonds and interest, but instead of cancelling them had them re-issued at a sacrifice of $133,813, thereby leaving $354,145 as the total amount of bonds collected by the trustees during this twelve-year period. In addition to this negative commentary on their management was the fact that when the trustees assumed their role in April, 1842, the excess of assets over liabilities was $30,930; when the assets went to the receiver on April 20, 1855, the deficiency of assets was $1,394,165.[58]

The Governor's policy of reducing the outstanding debt had progressed by May, 1860, to the following extent:

| | | |
|---|---|---|
| Bonds and coupons paid into the treasury— | | |
| | Real Estate Bank | $1,278,273.33 |
| | State Bank | 946,425.03 |
| Total | | $2,224,698.36[59] |

By the continuation of this policy until the entire assets were exhausted, the debt on account of the Real Estate Bank would be reduced to $1,394,165. Beyond this amount, Richard H. Johnson, nephew of one stockholder, and son of another, urged that proceedings be initiated against the lands mortgaged by the stockholders. By paying their pro-rata share of this debt, the stockholders could guarantee its settlement, and the bonds, which would come due on October 26, 1861, could be honored.[60]

The Holford claim against the state continued to be a controversial part of the debt question. James Holford came to Little Rock in 1850 in an unsuccessful attempt to have his claim honored. After his death the matter was pursued by his estate's lawyers. Only a technicality prevented the legality of his claim being decided by the United States Supreme Court.[61] In 1862, his claim was considered by the Arkansas Supreme Court in a decision written by Judge E.H. English. That the officials had exceeded their authority by hypothecating the bonds made that action illegal and void; therefore the state was not liable. But since the bank had accepted and used that portion of the money advanced for its wn purposes, the bank became liable in equity to repay the money received. Governor Archibald Yell might have written the same decision in 1842.

With the collapse of the Real Estate Bank in 1843, state-sponsored financing of plantation development was at an end. Planters now relied more on the services of commission merchants in New Orleans and elsewhere, who became bankers as well as merchants for the plantation system.[62] By the late forties these cotton factors had extended their economic ties to local merchants, who recruited business near the various cotton-shipping points in Arkansas.[63] The failure of the Real Estate Bank as a source of agricultural credit forced the planters to rely increasingly on these other sources, while the problems associated with the initial failure to establish a credit system remained for the state to solve in the form of the public debt. That problem would be part of the legacy inherited by Reconstruction. And what might be said about this ante-bellum legacy?

The desire for credit for agricultural development and financing a new government motivated the leaders of the state to look into banking institutions to meet these needs. The times led to over-optimism, for the exaggerated expectations of a new state and a young economy seemed to be confirmed by the general prosperity and speculation preceding the panic of 1837. This optimism brought about an over-expansion of banking facilities, an over-valuation of land, and too rapid an expansion of debt. The effects of the panic of 1837 altered the course of events, however, and seemed to change certain success into inevitable failure. The stringency of money circles made it difficult to sell bonds or to keep specie in hand, and a long period of low agricultural prices discouraged what optimism may have remained.[64] The fixed nature of bonded debt became increasingly evident as value of the paper and other assets declined. When to these general developments were added other factors contributing to the failure of the banks, the optimism so firmly held appeared increasingly naive. Easy credit led to unwise borrowing, and borrowers found themselves unable to repay their debts. A delay in the payment of debts followed by a decline in scrip would be to the benefit of the debtor, and by dumping land on the state, or avoiding payment of debt, the borrower might take advantage of the state. To these might be added the inadequacy of laws and dishonesty of management as factors contributing to the failure of the banks.[65]

The results were threefold. In trying to establish a credit system to aid agriculture and finance the government, a privileged group of individuals benefited from the pledges of the faith and credit of the state. Secondly, the attempt to meet these needs for credit through state banking institutions failed. And last, as the banks failed, the problem of public debt arose to plague the political scene and hamper further economic development. As a consequence, those making a second attempt to use the credit of the state had to begin with

an initial handicap of $3,363,509.19, representing the bonded debt inherited b
Reconstruction from this ante-bellum experience.[66]

If one were to substitute "railroads" for "banks" as the panacea for problem
of economic development and make the necessary qualifications appropriate fo
the Funding Bill of 1869 and the Railroad Aid Bill instead of the State Bank an
the Real Estate Bank, then there would be a strong parallel between the firs
and second attempts to make use of the faith and credit of the state for th
promotion of economic development. The actors were different, but the pla
seemed somewhat familiar.

# CHAPTER TWELVE

# JESSE TURNER
# AND THE
# LITTLE ROCK AND FORT SMITH RAILROAD

*The question of State aid to railroads, is much mooted just now, and there
re some who advocate the issuing of State bonds to raise the necessary means to
uild them. While it is evidently the interest of the State to aid the construction
f railroads, I very much question the propriety of issuing new bonds until the
ld ones are redeemed.*

*The bonds of the State would be worth very little in the market just now, if
deed they could be disposed of at all. They would not be worth exceeding
ifty cents on the dollar, and at such a discount, instead of furnishing assistance,
he use of them would destroy any company in the world. For instance to raise
unds by means of State bonds to build a road costing $2,000,000, would
equire the sale of $4,000,000 worth of bonds, and the interest on this sum, at
ix per cent. would be $240,000 per annum. Could any company afford to pay
uch an interest; an interest in fact equal to 12 per cent. on the actual cash
eceived for the bonds? I think not, and were I a member of a railroad company
 certainly should vote to refuse any such aid—aid that would certainly destroy
he company entirely. When the State of Arkansas is untrammeled with debt—
ich and prosperous as she will then be—the question of issuing bonds of the
tate to build railroads with might, with great propriety be brought before the
eneral Assembly. But such aid now would not only destroy the railroad
ompany that received it, but would involve the State in a ruinous debt from
hich she would receive no compensating benefit.*
                                    —Richard H. Johnson, *"Address to the People of
                                    Arkansas," May 31, 1860*[1]

*Arkansans, like the rest of the nation's citizens, had more money to spend
han ever before during 1959, according to a Commerce Department report
ssued yesterday. But a per capita income figure of $1,322 still left the state
n next-to-last position, one notch above Mississippi.*[2]

When one considers how rich and varied the natural resources of Arkansas have been throughout her history, it seems puzzling that her development ha been so unimpressive in comparison with that of other states. Certainly no single factor can be used as an adequate explanation. Neither social conditions economic factors, nor geographic influences can be omitted from any judiciou consideration of why Arkansas is found near the bottom of most comparative evaluations today. But are there historical factors which served as a continua and a cumulative discouragement to economic development? That the failur to use state credit successfully as a means of financing the development o natural resources may have been such an historical factor is the major suggestio of part three of this study.

Just as the creation of banks seemed to be the means through which th economic potentialities of Arkansas could be released during her infancy as state, the construction of railroads seemed to present the same kind of promis in the 1850's. The Civil War interrupted the aspirations of ante-bellum railroa builders, however, and left for those men in power during Reconstruction th attempt to use state credit as a means of encouraging the construction of rail roads. The financial consequences of this second attempt to use state credi were as disastrous to the future development of the state as the consequences o the first had been. Economic development would have to be accomplished with out benefit of adequate credit for financing, and the problem of the public deb would be transmitted through the decades as a continual burden to futur economic development.

The use of land to promote economic development was attempted in severa ways before the Civil War. Fourteen million acres had been granted to the stat for various purposes, but by September 1, 1858, most of these lands had bee disposed of.[3] The economic development resulting from the disposal of thi vast acreage, however, was not as great as it should have been.

A Federal land grant of 500,000 acres was given to Arkansas in 1841 to b used for internal improvements.[4] The legislature decided that the land was to b sold at a minimum of two dollars per acre, but the legislature made th administrative mistake of placing the management of these lands in the hands o an agent who was to be elected every two years. Under these circumstance political and speculative influences could easily combine to determine th selection of a man who was responsive to various land-speculation ventures.[5] By 1844, only 136,000 acres had been sold at the two-dollar-per-acre price.

As a means of selling the land, Governor Thomas S. Drew suggested minimum price of $1.25.[7] This reduction initiated a series of price reduction over the years which resulted in the state's receiving less than the full potentia value represented by the Federal grant. Some lands were sold on longterm pay ments, and sympathy for the debtor led to extensions of time being granted. A failure to levy an effective property tax may also be added to other mistakes i management which lessened the economic return to the state from this internal-improvement grant. With the lands gone and after an expenditure of some 476,278, the editor of the *True Democrat* voiced the complaint in 1858 that he "state was miserably deficient in regard to good roads."[8] The only roads maintained in fair condition were the military roads which were maintained by the Federal government.[9]

Another attempt by the Federal government to assist in the development of natural resources was the swamp-land acts which began in 1849 and which gave to the state approximately 8,600,000 acres of swamp and overflowed lands.[10] Arkansas used a large portion of these lands to promote levee construction and to increase the acreage available for agriculture. Construction was to be financed with state scrip, which in turn could be used to purchase land contained in the Federal grant. Between 1852 and 1860 over $2,500,000 in scrip was issued and levees were built which extended along most of the Mississippi River and along a large portion of the Arkansas.[11] Unwise location and the effects of the floods in 1858 and 1859, however, resulted in the destruction of many miles of these newly constructed levees.[12] Neglect during the Civil War caused additional losses.

In one sense it is incorrect to say that Arkansas as a state utilized the land resources granted her by the Federal government. Local improvement districts were formed in each county and the determination of levee projects and other internal improvements were decided at the county level.[13] The creation of too many swamp-lands boards led to the issuance of too much scrip and its consequent depreciation. In turn, this situation encouraged speculation in land based on the depreciated paper.[14] In the absence of coordination at the state level these numerous local projects diluted the economic benefit of internal improvements which had been expected from the transfer of the land grants. By the time of the Civil War these land grants had largely been spent, but the economic benefits which the state had derived from their expenditure were disappointing. David Walker expressed that disappointment in 1860 when he criticized the Democrats for their mismanagement of the banks and the internal improvement funds as well as for their tendency toward secession.[15]

In an earlier chapter the observation was made that the river system flowed across the state in a southeasterly direction.[16] One of the unanswered questions as men began to contemplate the construction of railroads was whether railroad construction would complement the river system and continue the southeastern flow of Arkansas trade to markets such as New Orleans, or whether railroad construction would replace the river system and change the direction of Arkansas trade east to Memphis or beyond and northeast to St. Louis. A related question was which town on the Mississippi River would become the terminal for the Arkansas trade. Would it be Memphis, Helena, or Napoleon? For the northwestern section of the state a third question remained to be answered.

How could the railroad be utilized best to release that section from its geo
graphic isolation?

Eventually railroads would change the direction of the flow of economic goods
and Memphis and St. Louis would gain as New Orleans lost portions of the Ar
kansas trade. Better wagon roads in Arkansas and railroad construction beyond
Memphis initiated this development, however, rather than railroad construction
in Arkansas itself.[17] As Miss Carmichael has noted, the effects of this change in
direction could be observed in the increase of cotton shipments to Memphis, an
increase which grew from 35,000 bales in 1840 to 391,918 bales in 1860.[18]

Efforts to maintain New Orleans as the shipping destination of this trade in
the Mississippi Valley were unsuccessful. One plan recommended Memphis and
Natchez as railroad terminals for cotton, which would then be shipped down
river to New Orleans.[19] Another plan called for the Mississippi Valley Railroad
Company to pass south through the central part of Arkansas and Louisiana
going from Iron Mountain, Missouri, through Jacksonport, Little Rock, and
Camden on its way through Monroe, Natchitoches, and Alexander to New
Orleans.[20] Economic developments did not favor the fulfillment of these plans
however, and New York via Memphis or St. Louis increasingly competed with
New Orleans as a final destination for the Arkansas cotton trade.

The choice of a terminal city on the Mississippi River caused some rivalry
between Memphis and Helena during the 1850's.[21] To Helena's disadvantage
her leaders concluded in 1851 that the construction of a railroad from Memphis
through the St. Francis River swamp lands was almost an impossibility. Over
confidence in the advantages Helena enjoyed in the rivalry was perhaps a fac
tor in making the decision not to send delegates from Helena to the railroad
convention held in Little Rock February 13-15, 1852.[22] The omission proved
to be unfortunate for Helena, for at that convention a decision was made to
provide financial assistance for constructing a railroad from Memphis via Little
Rock to Fulton in southwestern Arkansas.[23] From this time forward Memphis
was favored in her rivalry with Helena, in spite of the difficulties represented by
the St. Francis swamp lands. Ironically, the rail line between Little Rock and
Memphis was the only line on which any rails were laid before the Civil War
The swamp lands did prove to be a barrier, however, and construction of the
section between the St. Francis and White rivers was not completed until after
the Civil War.[24]

In southern Arkansas railroad dreams were associated with the Mississippi
Ouachita and Red River Railroad which was chartered in 1853.[25] This road was
to run west from the Mississippi at Eunice in Chicot County through Camden
and on to the Texas border, Passengers moving west on the road would get to
Texas with greater comfort. Products moving east on the road would be
transported to the Mississippi with greater facility, thereby freeing the southwest
from its geographic isolation.

The most important railroad development of the 1850's was the Federal land grant on February 9, 1853, given to the Cairo and Fulton Railroad Company for a road which was to move diagonally across the state beginning at the Mississippi River opposite the mouth of the Ohio and extending to the Red River at Fulton.[26] Branches from this trunk line were to extend from Little Rock west to Fort Smith and east to Memphis. There could be no doubt now that Memphis and St. Louis were to be the beneficiaries of railroad development in Arkansas. In 1855, the president of the Cairo and Fulton told stockholders that the extension of the road through Texas and Illinois would be to Arkansas what the Erie Canal was to New York—"the nucleus of her internal improvement enterprises."[27]

The land grant included land given to the state as well as that given to the railroad (see end-paper map). Every alternate section on either side of the right-of-way extending a width of six sections was granted to the state. Provision was made to prevent waste of the land by restricting its sale. The railroad was to be built in twenty-mile stretches, and the sections in that distance had to be sold and the railroad completed before the next twenty-mile stretch could be developed. At the end of ten years the land would return to the Federal government if the road were not completed by then.[28]

With this Federal grant railroad sponsors were now faced with the problem of what Professor Goodrich refers to as "developmental" enterprise.[29] Instead of promising a quick return on investment, as an "exploitive" venture did, railroad building in Arkansas must be described as a developmental undertaking which "depended for most of its traffic on the settlement that its own construction was to bring about."[30] This meant a delay in economic return for those men promoting the railroads. Indeed, one is impressed more by the expectations these men held for the development of natural resources than by the profit they expected from railroad construction itself. Where to secure the initial financing and how to pay operating expenses until future economic potential could be developed were the real problems men such as Jesse Turner, who had become president of the Little Rock and Fort Smith Railroad Company, three years after its charter had been written in 1854, had to solve.[31]

By July 31, 1860, three years later, the company had reached a financial crisis. J.H. Haney, chief engineer for the road, wrote Turner a polite letter, but a letter which revealed a man at the end of his patience. He had stopped work on the road except for minor construction of masonry foundations. Haney's purpose in writing was to inquire about the future intentions of the board. If they were not making financial provisions for the future and did not intend prosecuting their project with greater energy in the future he wanted to know, for he felt it was necessary for him to practice his profession.[32] Haney had good reason to inquire about the future. A financial statement of conditions at that time revealed an excess of liabilities over assets of $2,875.45, and $2,088.72 of this amount was owed to Haney on his salary.[33]

Turner and the board were trying to obtain capital from New York. In May the company authorized Robert J.T. White to go to the East in search of funds.[34] On his way there White contacted capitalists and railroad men in Alexandria and Baltimore. With recommendations and introductions from these men, White sought interviews with several concerns in New York. His reception there was cordial, but his efforts ended in failure. Turner's dream of a railroad extending from the headwaters of the Arkansas River and passing through Little Rock on its way eastward to the Atlantic coast was an attractive idea to the capitalists, but the idea did not fall within the normal business operations of those firms. Furthermore, since the panic of 1857 these capitalists had not granted loans on railroad lands alone, and in no case had they become financially involved before a significant portion of the road was completed. White felt confident that assistance could be obtained in a later stage of the railroad's development, but the need for money in Arkansas was more immediate than that distant prospect.

This situation provides an illustration of the kind of circular causation among economic forces which continually discouraged the development of natural resources in a state during its early stages of economic growth, as was Arkansas at that time.[35] The Little Rock and Fort Smith Railroad could not obtain capital for financing its development until the company had completed a signifi cant portion of its own construction. The bitter irony was that the company could not construct its road until the capital was made available. By 1860, of course, the financial reputation of Arkansas had been affected by the fate of the banks and the controversy over the Holford bonds. This reputation became an additional factor in the circular causation among economic forces.

Failing to obtain capital from New York, Turner and his friends turned to the state legislature for financial assistance. In the legislative session, which began on November fifth, the aspirations and financial difficulties of railroad projects from various sections of the state confronted each other. At that time there was approximately $380,000 in the state treasury which legislators considered surplus revenue. In an internal-improvement fund known as the "five percent" fund there was approximately $120,000, and in the swamp-land fund of the Clarksville district there was thought to be about $60,000.[36] The goal for the representatives of the various roads was to secure as much of this money for their respective roads as possible.

Letters to Jesse Turner from J.H. Haney, who was in Little Rock to look after the interests of the Little Rock and Fort Smith Railroad, and letters from members of the legislature who were advocates of the railroad give some indica tion of the extent of the bargaining carried on during the session.[37] The three dominant contenders for portions of the state money were the Memphis and Little Rock Rail Road Company, the Little Rock and Fort Smith Railroad Company, and the Mississippi, Ouachita and Red River Railroad Company.

The devotion of the legislators to the local interests of their own sections illustrates well the existence of three societies.

The Memphis and Little Rock advocates wanted to complete that section of their road between the St. Francis and White rivers. To finance this project, the company wanted to exchange $100,000 in state bonds, which were then selling for approximately fifty-cents on the dollar, for $100,000 cash from the "five percent" fund.[38]   If this exchange could be made, the money would not only help to pay the construction costs, but would also double the economic value of the bonds then in the company's possession.

The Mississippi, Ouachita and Red River Railroad Company wanted to get $120,000 from the "five percent" fund to finance construction of its road. Delegates from southern Arkansas and those from northwestern Arkansas agreed to vote for each other's projects in order to achieve their objectives.[39]

The Little Rock and Fort Smith company hoped to apply the resources of the swamp-lands fund of the Clarksville district to the construction of that road. Estimates of the value of these resources varied from $40,000 to $60,000, and opposition from Senator George W. Lemoyne, who lived in that district but on the south side of the Arkansas River, was dreaded because, of the unsold swamp lands in this district, one-third was located to the south—across the river from the railroad.[40]

Application of these state funds, which were intended for general distribution among the counties, to special projects such as railroads was resented by some representatives from counties in which the roads were not to be located. Senator Thomas B. Craighead of Mississippi and Crittenden counties spoke strongly against railroads in general and against the economic interests of the west in particular.  Not only were many delta representatives disinterested in railroad construction, but their growing concern over relations with the Federal government made these men want to conserve the state's financial resources for use in a possible future emergency.  The advocates of railroad aid felt the pressure of time operating against them in another way, for these men were conscious of the approaching expiration of their ten-year land grants in 1863. If this legislature did not help the railroads, any assistance given them by the next legislature would come too late to save those grants.[41]

By mid-January, decisions had been made by the legislature.  The Memphis and Little Rock Rail Road was loaned $100,000 from the "five percent" fund at 8% interest.  This loan was secured by a mortgage on the property of the company and was granted with the understanding that the project would be completed within twelve months.[42]

The Mississippi, Ouachita and Red River Railroad and the Little Rock and Fort Smith Railroad were granted respectively the proceeds from the overflow and swamp lands in the Champagnolle and Clarksville districts, which were to be used to purchase stock in each of the respective roads.  A similar arrangement granted the lands in the Fayetteville district to the recently chartered North-western Border Railroad Company.[43]  In immediate funds this allocation meant a grant of $38,000 to the Little Rock and Fort Smith Railroad and a grant of $6,000 to the North-western Border Railroad.[44]  One interesting aspect of Turner's plan for using this money was his intention to start construction on the west end of the line and to move eastward to Little Rock rather than to begin in the reverse direction, a procedure which might have been normally expected.[45]

These plans, of course, were interrupted by problems associated with secession.  As early as December tenth, Jesse Turner was writing letters to New York papers about the future of the Union; by January twenty-ninth, a petition had been signed by his fellow townsmen asking Turner to become a Union delegate to the Secession Convention; and on February eighteenth, two weeks after the state auditor had written to inform him of the $38,000 grant to his railroad company, Turner was elected as a delegate to the Convention.[46]

The Civil War delayed railroad construction and the post-war conditions provided an abnormal setting in which that construction would take place, but one is most impressed by the intensification of interest in railroads during Reconstruction.  Confidence which men held in the railroad as a vehicle for economic development can only be compared with that confidence which men held in the banks as a similar vehicle during an earlier period. If propaganda to lure emigrants into the state may be taken as any indication of current thinking, there were very few counties which did not expect to have a railroad.[47] Exaggerated expectations created by the prospects of a railroad coming through a county, or a section, made the realities of railroad construction difficult to accept.  Disillusionment easily led to cynicism, and "conspiracy" was easy to discover.

The initiative for resuming efforts to build the Little Rock and Fort Smith Railroad was taken by J.H. Haney in January, 1866.  On the twelfth of that month he wrote Jesse Turner a letter in which he urged Turner to call a board meeting, to conduct a new election, and to reorganize the company.[48]  Haney believed that the time was right and that they must take action at once. He also sensed that requirements for railroad building had changed.  No longer would the private subscriptions from men who lived in the area and who were primarily interested in the benefits which the road would bring to their section be of much importance.  In this new era Northern capitalists and favorable state legislation were to be the sources of capital.  In the efforts to reorganize and to negotiate for new money, however, the company was fortunate to have in its possession the funds granted to it just prior to the Civil War.[49]  Once the company had acquired the full-time leadership it needed, Haney was very optimistic about the future prospects.

The expiration of the Federal land grant in 1863 was the cause of much concern to these men. Whether that grant would be renewed was of major importance to the future of the railroad. Turner and Haney were at a great disadvantage in trying to obtain assistance in Congress, however, for Congressman-elect William Byers had been refused admission to Congress, and Byers' lack of knowledge about Arkansas railroads served as an additional handicap.[50] The urgency of their situation was noted by Haney when he reminded Turner that because the land grant and their charter had expired, their company faced the necessity of liquidation in behalf of their stockholders. Under these discouraging circumstances Haney recommended that the promoters apply for a new charter as an expedient to protect their interest in the road.[51]

By July twentieth, a bill reviving and extending the Cairo and Fulton land grant, which included that of the Little Rock and Fort Smith road, had passed the Senate and had gone to the House Public Lands Committee.[52] Byers believed that the bill would have been reported to the House and passed except for the opposition expressed by Governor Fletcher of Missouri, by Gratz Brown, and by others from St. Louis. The Chairman of the Committee was George W. Julian, a radical Congressman from Indiana, who was instrumental in refusing to report the bill to the House, and the measure seemed destined to die in the Committee. As Byers interpreted these events, the radicals were determined to refuse granting anything to the Southern states until they were represented in Congress. By thus exerting political pressure, the radicals expected to gain ratification by the Southern states of the Fourteenth Amendment, which had been proposed the previous month by the Joint Committee on Reconstruction.[53]

Contrary to Byers' expectations, Congress passed an act on July twenty-eighth which revived and extended for ten years from that date the grant made to the Cairo and Fulton line and its branches on February 9, 1853. This new act required that at least one twenty-mile section of road be completed on each of the Cairo and Fulton, the Memphis and Little Rock, and the Little Rock and Fort Smith lines within three years and that another twenty-mile section be completed on each of these roads each year thereafter. A failure to perform this minimum requirement would cause the land grant to revert to the United States. Because of the association of Arkansas with the Confederacy special requirements had to be met by companies in that state. Before this act would go into effect there, the Secretary of Interior had to file a certificate in his office and in the office of the Arkansas Secretary of State which verified that the board of directors had been reorganized and that the company had rescinded all acts or proceedings carried out under the authority of the Confederate government.[54]

Railroad enthusiasts in Arkansas were not content to rely on Congress alone; perhaps some encouragement could be obtained from the state legislature.[55] As one could have anticipated, enthusiasm for railroads led to the passage of a

Railroad-Aid-Bill on March 18, 1867.[56] The most important features of this act included the requirement that the road have at least forty miles of construction completed before any state bonds could be received. With that mileage completed, $10,000 per mile would be given to the railroad in the form of state bonds bearing 8% interest. As additional ten-mile sections were completed, the company could obtain additional bonds at $10,000 per mile.[57] In order to protect the state's interests, the legislature stipulated that a first mortgage should be placed on all property, rights, and credit of the railroad company.[58]

On March nineteenth, the day after this act was passed by the legislature, Governor Isaac Murphy wisely vetoed the measure. In his veto message, which was reminiscent of Richard H. Johnson's message to the people in 1860, Governor Murphy pointed out the weaknesses of this legislation.[59] The faith and credit of the state, which had been dishonored since 1841, must be redeemed before they were pledged for additional millions. To place bonds on the market without first redeeming those of earlier days would mean that "they could not be sold in the market for any fair price, but, if sold at all, it would be of but little advantage to the road, while the attempt to put them on the market would utterly destroy the credit of the State among capitalists, and be the means of retarding the building of the other important roads in the State."[60]

The operation of this act would have worked exclusively for the benefit of the Memphis and Little Rock company, for that railroad was the only one with construction enough to qualify for state aid. The probabilities were that before that road had received $1,500,000 in state aid, which represented $10,000 a mile for its entire length, other roads would not be able to qualify for their first $10,000. Governor Murphy did not accuse the legislature of intending this result, but his analysis of the probabilities seems correct. The veto message also raised a significant question about whether Arkansas aid should be given to promote a railroad the terminal of which was Memphis rather than to develop another road the terminal of which was within the state—Helena, for example.

Even if all the roads did qualify themselves for state aid under the terms of this act, "the people would be saddled with an amount of debt that would cripple the energies of the State for generations, without any corresponding benefit to the State, as the depreciation of the bonds would be such that their influence would not advance the completion of any of the contemplated roads an hour."[61]

Governor Murphy continued with words concerning the importance of credit which could have been written by Richard H. Johnson, or for that matter, by Governor Powell Clayton. "No individual or community can prosper without credit. Credit can only be maintained by acting with honor and good faith. The statesman whose aim is to build up a happy and prosperous State, will use all his talents and energies in placing the faith and credit of the State on a basis that cannot be doubted or impeached. Arkansas does not stand on that elevated position, but wise statesmanship might soon place her there."[62]

Rather than risk the consequences of the act proposed by the legislature, Governor Murphy recommended that the present indebtedness be funded, new bonds be issued for principal and interest, and that a special tax be levied to provide for accruing interest and for the retirement of the debt at maturity. If with these measures a strict economy was practiced in the operations of state government, then citizens could look forward to the redemption of the faith and credit of the state and to a genuine prosperity.

Unfortunately, this message did not receive the support it deserved from the legislature.  On March nineteenth, the vote in the House of Representatives to override the Governor's veto failed to receive the necessary three-fourths majority, the vote being 35 to 20.[63]  But a second vote on the following day resulted in an overthrow of Governor Murphy's veto by a vote of 43 to 11.[64] The passion for railroads proved to be too strong to be subdued by wisdom.

Concern about the future of the Little Rock and Fort Smith company was expressed by J.H. Haney in May when he sent Jesse Turner copies of letters from General John C. Fremont and R.C. Brinkley, President of the Memphis and Little Rock Rail Road Company. These letters led Haney to suspect that an organized effort was being made to overthrow the board's control of the Little Rock and Fort Smith Company. Haney was especially anxious that these maneuvers not persuade Turner to resign his leadership of the company. A few days later Haney received a letter from the Secretary of Interior which stated that the Secretary had filed in his office and had transmitted to the secretary of state in Arkansas the necessary certificate related to the company's land grant.[65] This was good news, for with the land grant renewed and the charter recognized, Turner and Haney could make their future plans with greater confidence. Their company had until July 28, 1869, to complete the first twenty-mile section in order to comply with the provisions of the act of Congress. With this encouraging development, Haney began to write with a fresh optimism about the future. During recent weeks he had been in the field making a survey for the railroad. That survey had now progressed to Palarm Bottom, a distance of twenty-four miles from Little Rock, and Haney expected to be at Lewisburg, an additional twenty-nine miles, by the middle of June.

In the fall of 1867, Haney went to New York in search of funds for the railroad.[66]  There he encountered the objections of the capitalists to the features of the state Railroad-aid Bill which had passed over Governor Murphy's veto in March. The forty-mile requirement was too large, the first-mortgage lien was unacceptable, and the authority for the governor to seize the road in case of nonpayment was unthinkable to these capitalists.[67] Haney believed that no contract could be made with respectable capitalists which did not include the conditions that the state's mortgage would be a second lien on the railroad and that, in case of default in payment, a receiver would be appointed who would have

charge of the company's earnings until the defalcation was made good. In the
meantime the railroad would remain in the company's hands. To Haney's mind
the conclusion was simple. The law would have to be changed to incorporate
some of these demands before that legislation could be of any benefit to the railroads. In its present form the law served only as a stumbling block to negotiations and should be amended at the first sitting of the General Assembly.[68]

The weakness of Haney's bargaining position and the high price which
capitalists would demand for constructing the road were revealed in an offer
made to Haney by Ambrose W. Thompson of New York, who claimed to be an
agent for European capitalists. In return for building the railroad the company
was to transfer to Thompson all property, rights, and franchises. In addition, a
new board of nine was to be created with five members comprising the
"financial board," who were to be chosen on Thompson's nomination and who
were to live in New York, and four members comprising a "local board," who
were to live in Arkansas. Securities could be issued only on the vote of
two-thirds of the board. Officers of the company were to be Thompson as
president, General C.B. Stuart as engineer in chief, and J.H. Haney as chief
engineer of construction. The present stockholders were to be given $240,000
in stock with no further claim upon the company.

Exercising an appropriate caution in the conduct of his business, Haney asked
Thompson to reveal his associates, to have them endorse his proposal, and to
submit bond as security for the performance of any contract on which they
might agree. When Thompson refused to comply with these requests, Haney
broke off negotiations. In that day of *caveat emptor* Haney was well aware that
he could make a contract in a very short time with parties "whose only object is
to manipulate the securities of the Company & who are men without responsibility or backing." To negotiate a contract with responsible parties, however, was
most difficult under the existing circumstances. Haney concluded from his experience that their company could "hope for nothing without more liberal terms
on the part of the State or securing some further aid from Congress."[69] Indeed,
he had come to favor some kind of reconstruction—certainly not the kind then
being advocated by Congress, for he considered that unjust—but he thought that
it was "nevertheless a fact that a reconstruction in any shape & representation in
Congress would be a powerful aid to the development of our State."[70]

By January, 1868, affairs of the company had reached a turning point. In
the stockholders' meeting held in December a new board of directors had been
elected, and a reorganization of the company was anticipated.[71] W.P. Denkla
was in New York trying to conclude negotiations with Eastern capitalists, and, if
those negotiations were successful, Haney believed Denkla would expect to
become president of the company. If the negotiations failed, however, Haney
urged Turner to continue as president in the interest of the company, despite
Turner's personal desire to resign.

At this point in the company's history there entered a factor associated with the $38,000 in gold which the state had granted the company just prior to the Civil War. Members of the old board were embarrassed by a shortage of funds, and this embarrassment would continue to make the position of the new board vulnerable in relation to the Eastern capitalists with whom they were negotiating and with whom they would contract to build the railroad.

On January seventeenth, Joseph Brooks introduced a resolution in the Constitutional Convention to appoint Thomas M. Bowen, W.C. Adams, and G.W. Smith commissioners to investigate the affairs of the Little Rock and Fort Smith Railroad.[72]  Although such a resolution would have been more appropriately introduced in a legislature than in a constitutional convention, the resolution passed forty-one to twenty-one.[73]  In response to this action Haney wrote a letter to R. S. Gantt. a member of the Convention, in defense of the company.[74] The Convention, under the influence of John McClure, rejected Haney's letter by a vote of forty-three to eighteen.[75]  And the threat of an investigation by a hostile commission was added to the company's troubles.

It is doubtful that the action of the Convention was based on any specific knowledge about affairs within the company.  But three days after the Brooks resolution Augustus H. Garland, as lawyer for Philip Pennywit, sent an account of claims due Pennywit by the company.[76]  Philip Pennywit had been treasurer of the company from the time of its original organization. In his care had been placed the funds granted to the company just prior to the Civil War. Pennywit had been stricken with paralysis in 1865, and he had found it necessary to hire a reliable man to serve as clerk to assist him in caring for the company's resources.  For expenses incurred during these years Pennywit now submitted a claim against the company of $7,800 in gold.[77]  About ten days after signing the document drawn by Garland, Pennywit died, and now Garland submitted the claim in the hope of doing justice to his estate.[78]

At the board of directors' meeting, held in Clarksville in February, a committee, headed by Jesse Turner, was appointed to audit and to settle the Pennywit account. Except for one voucher, the committee found an exact correspondence between the account and the vouchers recorded. This one voucher was for $2,010, which had been allowed Captain Pennywit for "services" rendered to the company. Actually, this amount had been allegedly stolen by a Negro girl living in Charles G. Scott's family, and the board had decided in 1866 to allow this amount to be charged to Pennywit for "services."

When the committee considered this $2,010, and added to it the $7,800 claim currently presented in Pennywit's behalf plus the difference between $17,000 in currency and $17,000 in gold in which the vouchers had been paid, the total amounted to more than $15,000. This amount was not approved by the committee, and the matter was returned to the board of directors for their action.[79]  This matter continued unresolved for years to come and remained a source of embarrassment for members of the board of directors of the original company. These men, with the exception of J.H. Haney, were part-time officers of the company, and they had tacitly agreed to contribute their services to the company without remuneration, except for essential expenses. The submission of Pennywit's claim under these circumstances, and especially the fact that it remained unsettled, placed the board in a vulnerable position.

The company entered a new era in February, 1868, with the resignation of Jesse Turner as its president.[80] This event is somewhat symbolic of a decline in power and control of those local men whose primary interest in building the railroad was for the benefit of their localities. Circumstances now required the new board under its president, Charles G. Scott, to seek the help of men whose interest in the road would be somewhat different.

By the first of July, W.P. Denkla and J.P. Robinson of New York were in Little Rock actively engaged in promoting the interests of the railroad.[81] More specifically they were trying to get the kind of railroad-aid bill they wanted passed by the legislature. Robinson represented the parties—Warren Fisher, Jr., contractor, and Josiah Caldwell, capitalist—with whom the Little Rock and Fort Smith company had contracted to build its road. There was thus active participation by representatives of Northern capitalist interests in the creation of the Railroad-aid Bill which was approved by the General Assembly on July 21, 1868.

Haney wrote Turner on July fifteenth of his approval of the forthcoming legislation and stated that he expected the law to "satisfy our Co. & be such as to enable us to carry out every provision of the Contract on our part." With a note of caution, Haney added: "All this information is solely for you & the other directors at Van Buren as it will not do to have it publicly talked about. It would be well for Gran [sic] Wilcox or whoever runs the *Press* now to keep quiet on Railroad matters—We do not want the subject discussed while the legislature is in session—especially by 'rebel' sheets."[82]

The influence of capitalist interests could be seen in the provisions of the new Railroad-Aid Act as one by one the major objections which capitalists had expressed in regard to the 1867 Railroad Act were satisfied in the new one.[83] State bonds would be available after ten miles were ready for iron rails rather than after forty. No first-mortgage lien to protect the state's interest in the venture appeared in the new bill, nor did the governor have the authority to seize the road for non-payment of interest on the state bonds. Instead, a method for settling non-payment was provided which was more congenial to the capitalists but was less protective of the state's welfare. This method called for a tax to be imposed upon the railroad from time to time which was equal to the interest due on the bonds which had been issued to that company. If the company failed to pay this tax, the treasurer of the state was required to take possession of the income and revenues of the company by writ of sequestration until the defaults were paid. Once this obligation had been satisfied, the revenues returned to the company.[84] The railroad and its land grant, however, would not be lost to the company, an arrangement which was much more satisfactory to the capitalists than the older one had been.

The Pennywit account continued to disturb J.H. Haney. By August, newspapers were insinuating that the funds of the company had been misappropriated, and Haney feared the effect which knowledge of this unresolved matter would have on the contractors if they found out about it. "Our contractors I believe are men of honor & fully able to perform the work & it will not do to let them know anything of this affair."[85] There is about Haney's concern over the Pennywit account an urgency which hinted at more than the available evidence explains.

During the early weeks of 1869, two challenges to the current control of the company appeared. Jesse Turner sought proxies to prevent a "miserable set of carpetbaggers and scallawags" from obtaining control of the road at the directors' meeting held on January twenty-third.[86] These men wanted the road to be located along the south side of the river and were without the financial means of building the road even if they should gain control. On the other hand, if that control were retained in the hands of its friends, Turner was assured that work would begin within six weeks. This first challenge was defeated, but a second challenge to the control of the road by its old friends was not to be denied.

At the meeting on January twenty-third, an election of new directors to replace some of the older directors of the company was insisted upon by W.P. Denkla representing the wishes of the Northern capitalists. Another step had been taken by the contractors in achieving control of the road. With resignation Haney wrote Turner: "We have yielded every point demanded by the Contractors, reserving nothing at all but the little stock belonging to us, 5/6 of which is yet to be paid for should they see fit to make additional calls. I see nothing to regret in this respect. If they should fail to build our road we shall have the satisfaction of knowing that we have done our whole duty."[87]

In these transactions the financial controversy associated with the Pennywit account continued to curse the company. The whole affair had become the subject of public talk and had seriously damaged the company's position. On February fifth, Haney wrote Turner: "We have not credit in Little Rock to-day for $100 and it will not be long before contractors as well as the Company will be involved in the public mind in this scandalous affair."[88] The vulnerability of the company and of some of the old directors in relation to the contractors was indicated when Haney wrote Turner eleven days later: "I only regret that we should have permitted our treasury matters to get into such a muddle, but the Contractors know all about it now and they threaten a fierce war upon Mr. Scott and will wring the last dollar from him should he refuse to surrender every point & place his claims entirely at the discretion of the Board as he should have done in the first place."[89]

It will be recalled that Congress revived the land grant of the Cairo and Fulton and its branches on July 28, 1866.[90] One of the provisions of that act was that at least twenty miles on each of these three roads had to be completed by July 28, 1869, or the land grant would revert to the United States. An extension of time was needed to provide a margin of safety for the contractors. Congressman Logan H. Roots and other Arkansas Congressmen were trying to obtain that extension of time in the House of Representatives during the closing days of the 40th Congress.[91]

Root's experience was similar to that of Congressman-elect Byers in 1866, for this second bill also encountered the opposition of Congressman George W. Julian, Chairman of the Public Lands Committee. During the last hours of the session, March 3, 1869, the bill was being debated. An amendment to the bill had been offered by Julian which would likely have killed the measure in the Senate. Roots appealed to Speaker James G. Blaine for assistance in getting the measure passed without the amendment. Blaine advised Roots that the amendment was out of order. But when Roots confessed that his knowledge of the rules was insufficient to tangle successfully with the experienced Julian, Blaine sent his page to Congressman John A. Logan of Illinois, who raised an objection to the amendment. Of course Speaker Blaine then sustained the objections, and the measure passed 91 to 17.[92] This victory meant that the contractors had until April 28, 1870, to complete the first twenty miles in order to preserve the company's land grant.[93]

Three actions during the month of April completed the preliminaries for the construction of the Little Rock and Fort Smith Railroad. On April tenth, the General Assembly approved a bond bill to provide for paying the interest of railroad-aid bonds granted to the various companies.[94] On April twelfth, an act was passed reincorporating the Little Rock and Fort Smith Railroad Company.[95] This reincorporation signified the end of the interference with the company which had been threatened by the investigating commission appointed in 1868. And on April twenty-eighth, the Little Rock and Fort Smith Company was awarded $1,500,000 in state bonds, which represented $10,000 per mile for the entire length of the road.[96] The fate of the railroad was now in the hands of the contractor and the Northern capitalists who were behind the venture.

# CHAPTER THIRTEEN

# ASA P. ROBINSON
# AND THE
# LITTLE ROCK AND FORT SMITH RAILROAD

For the efficient construction of railroads in Arkansas there was a need not only for capital but also for men experienced in railroad building. This latter need was fulfilled for the Little Rock and Fort Smith company by Asa P. Robinson. Although J.H. Haney held the title of chief engineer, Asa P. Robinson was engineer in fact and had been placed in charge by Josiah Caldwell, Boston capitalist, and Warren Fisher, Jr., also of Boston, in whose name the contract to build the road had been granted. Robinson had been told by Caldwell: "You have full and absolute control of all the business appertaining to the business in Arkansas."[1] With this authority, Robinson ignored Haney, for the most part, and proceeded to build the railroad.

In many ways the construction benefited from Robinson's energetic leadership. He was forty-seven when he came to Arkansas in 1869. Born in Hartford County, Connecticut, in 1822, he had grown up in Newburgh, New York, and was later educated as a civil engineer. His railroad experience had been gained from the Erie Railroad, for which he was a rodman on the first forty-five miles west of the Hudson River, and from the Missouri, Kansas and Texas Railroad Company, for which he was working prior to coming to Little Rock.[2]

A reading of Robinson's letterbooks, which cover with some thoroughness the period from October, 1869, through December, 1871, reveals an efficient engineer hard at work trying to construct a railroad. These letterbooks also reveal a most loyal employee, who never deviated from what he considered to be the best interest of his employer. It is important to remember, however, that his immediate employer was Josiah Caldwell and that Robinson worked for Warren Fisher, Jr., contractor for the railroad, and not for the Little Rock and Fort Smith Company itself.

To follow Asa P. Robinson from October, 1869, when his letterbooks begin,

Figure 22.    Jesse Turner
              Asa P. Robinson

until December, 1870, by which time the forces he had brought together were capable of laying two miles of track per day, cannot fail to make the reader respect his ability as an engineer. The degree to which railroad construction was a matter of solving logistical problems and the extent to which geographic, climatic, and social conditions complicated the solution of those problems might easily be overlooked were it not for the record left by Robinson.

His first concern was to stop what he considered the exorbitant costs of labor. Negro labor was only half as productive as white, Robinson believed, and therefore he began to make plans for importing labor from Chicago to provide the bulk of his labor force. These men were to be transported from Chicago to Memphis at their own expense for a fare of $8.50. From Memphs to Little Rock the company paid a fare of $3.50 per man, which was later taken out of their wages. By October twenty-fifth, about three hundred Danes and Irish had been hired and Robinson expected five hundred men to be at work in a few days.

When Robinson arrived in Arkansas, the men were being paid by the day, and board was included in their wages. Robinson immediately changed this arrangement to one by which the men were paid two dollars per day and were charged four dollars per week for board. Paying the laborers by the day was a great mistake, Robinson felt, for that policy resulted in costs to the company which were two or three times fair value. As soon as possible he shifted payment of labor to a sub-contractor on a contract basis in order to know more precisely what labor costs really were.

Robinson learned how hot a summer can be in Arkansas when stifling weather during June of 1870 almost stopped the work entirely. He complained that his men and teams were used up. "We are endeavoring to lay track . . . , but the Rails are so hot that during the day they cannot be handled without mittens—Men cannot perform half labor some are leaving and others demanding increased pay." Robinson continued his remarks to Caldwell: "You can have no conception of the heat in our clearing for we have not had a two mile breeze in a month. . . . Unless the heat moderates we shall be obliged to cease work entirely." The climate was harshly teaching Robinson that the season for constructing railroads in Arkansas ran from October first until June first.

Perhaps the most frustrating problem Robinson had to endure in his efforts to coordinate the application of men, materials, and equipment to the construction of the railroad was the unreliability of river transportation. Most of the heavy freight, such as iron rails, had to come up river from New Orleans. Frequently the Arkansas River was too low for such freight, in which case the cargo had to wait for a rise in the Arkansas or had to be transported up the White River to DeValls Bluff and then shipped to Little Rock over the Memphis and Little Rock Railroad. This latter procedure made freight costs high and made arrival of the freight slow, for several trips were required to deliver the entire cargo.

An illustration of the havoc this transportation system could create for Robinson's efforts at coordination can be seen in a letter he wrote to Caldwell in September, 1870. Robinson was surprised to learn that Caldwell was relying entirely on one boat, the *Colossal,* and her barge to transport rails from New Orleans. On one trip the *Colossal* could bring enough cargo to lay six miles of track; but by this time the organization had progressed to the stage that a mile of track per day could be laid if all materials were on hand. Robinson reminded Caldwell that a round trip for the *Colossal* required at least twenty days. Therefore, three such ships and barges would be required to keep the work going.[3]

The river could threaten a greater loss than a mere disruption of plans. When the first twenty miles of the railroad were almost complete, news came which required Robinson to write Caldwell: "The steamer *Guidon* started from the mouth of White River on Saturday last with our Barge in tow containing the Locomotive No. 1 and twelve cars. About 10 miles this side of Pine Bluff night before last the Capt. reports that she struck a sharp clay point of a shoal knocking a big hole in her. She went over the point into very deep water and he hauled her as far as possible toward shoal water. She sunk in about 10 feet water. Everything is reported out of sight except the bell and Smoke Stack and cab of the Engine. . . . This is a most unfortunate occurrance and will delay us seriously."[4]

Eleven days later a wrecker was at work raising the engine, and Robinson believed that it could be put in order by the time the irons arrived. The falling river, however, threatened to prevent their arrival in time for the April Twenty-eighth deadline, by which time the first twenty miles of track had to be laid in order to keep the land grant. Fortunately, circumstances improved, and the first twenty miles were completed on April twenty-third.

Robinson had to endure certain problems which derived from faulty administration, but they were problems which were beyond his control. The first of these occurred in the accounting office. Mr. Stackpole, who was put in charge of the records, did not seem to understand double-entry bookkeeping well enough to make the proper original entries. As a rule, he did not keep a blotter, and for that reason journal entries were made from his check stubs by a bookkeeper who was unfamiliar with the original transactions. Errors and omissions were very difficult for Robinson to correct.

This faulty bookkeeping easily provoked a second problem for Robinson. He was frequently led to believe that there was more money available in the bank than was actually there. In one case he thought that $45,000 was on deposit and therefore felt secure to draw on that amount for payment of $19,000 to accounts due. To his dismay, he found there was less than $9,000 in cash. By February, 1870, banks in Little Rock had heard some injurious statements about Josiah Caldwell, and bankers were "disposed to be shy in advancing much on drafts before they have notice of their payment." Rather than have their credit damaged in Little Rock by such erroneous practices, Robinson suggested the need of an account in New York on which he could draw directly. But his suggestion was not heeded. Indeed, one of the questions which repeatedly presents itself is why Caldwell did not keep Robinson better informed about money available to him. Throughout the entire period of the Warren Fisher, Jr. contract Robinson continuously had to report his own expenditures to Caldwell without having a sufficient knowledge of the funds which Caldwell had available to cover those expenditures. For Caldwell to treat such a loyal employee in so responsible a position in this distrustful manner seems inexcusable.

By May, 1870, Robinson had come to question the entire mode of operation existing between Caldwell, Robinson, and Steacy. Peirce, Steacy, and Yorston, sub-contractors under whose supervision the actual work was being done, were fine contractors in Robinson's judgment. He raised a protest to Caldwell "against the whole arrangement simply that you may not bye and bye hold me responsible should results not meet your expectations." The source of Robinson's complaint was that he could not analyze the expenditures of the sub-contractors for which Caldwell was paying. Robinson was wisely attempting to limit the area of his personal responsibility to that area over which he could exercise control.

Expectations had been high as work began on the construction of the road in October, 1869. Budd and Decker, the first sub-contractors, were to have five hundred men at work by November first and were to complete the first twenty miles by April first. These men had not met the terms of their contract, however, and Robinson terminated their connection with the project on November twentieth. Peirce, Steacy, and Yorston, who were subsequently employed as sub-contractors, proved to be capable and experienced men, however, and now the expectations of the future could be realized.

The laying of track began during the second week of January, and plans were to be so coordinated that the track could be laid without cessation. Despite some delays in these expectations, Robinson wrote in May that he thought the road could be opened to Lewisburg, a distance of fifty miles, sometime in July. By July, however, the heat had slowed the effort considerably, and Robinson reported to Warren Fisher, Jr. on July twenty-ninth that the fifty miles to Lewisburg could be ready for operation by September first, seventy-five miles by October first, and one hundred miles by December first. Robinson thought that the entire road, some one hundred and fifty miles could be completed by the fall of 1871.[5]

When one compares these expectations with the progress actually made, a slower scale must be used to make the comparison. The first twenty miles of track were completed on April 23, 1870. The unusually hot weather in June caused a cutback in the work, and the summer heat continued to be a major factor in retarding the progress of the road. By the end of July only twenty-five miles of track were completely finished, but the road was graded and was ready for tracks for a distance of seventy-eight miles, except for a few minor bits of work. The surveys had also been completed, except for minor refinements.

On September fourth, Robinson was able to run a passenger train up the road for thirty-three miles, and he reported that the track was almost to Cadron, a distance two miles beyond that point. There was a large supply of iron on hand, and he expected the track-laying to continue without hesitation. Trains were able to run thirty-seven miles out by September twenty-ninth, but the track-laying had been seriously delayed for want of bolts for laying the heavy rails, and there was also need of both plates and bolts for the last shipment of rails. As a temporary expedient to keep the track-laying going, Robinson reported that "All the heavy rails have been laid and 1750 of them without splices."

Josiah Caldwell and a party of twenty-five left New York to visit Arkansas on October twenty-sixth. This trip was largely a promotional excursion, although there were other motives involved. Local businessmen in Arkansas offered their hospitality and were flattered to be playing host to Josiah Caldwell, to Warren Fisher, Jr., and to other men of such financial stature. John D. Adams, for example, was their host in Memphis and offered the visiting party the use of one of his best steamboats. As if to return the compliment, Caldwell invited Adams to confer about future business connections while the visitors were still in Arkansas. Caldwell, Fisher, and a few other interested parties, including John C. Pratt, the new president of the Little Rock and Fort Smith Railroad Company, left for the East on November twentieth, the eve of the opening of train service from Little Rock to Lewisburg.[6]

The next day, November 21, 1870, was an exciting day for people from Little Rock to Fort Smith. At last, regular passenger and freight service had begun on the Little Rock and Fort Smith Railroad! A person could be picked up at his hotel in Little Rock now and transferred across the river to the station at Huntersville, from which the train departed at 8:30 A.M. The trip to Lewisburg, a distance of fifty miles, took three and one-half hours, the passenger arriving there at noon. Stage connections from Lewisburg to Fort Smith were available for the passenger whose trip was to continue. On the return trip the passenger could reverse these steps, departing from Lewisburg at 1:00 P.M. and arriving at Huntersville at 3:52 P.M.[7]

The status of the road was reported by Robinson to the Commissioner of Public Works and Internal Improvements on December third. By this date fifty miles of the road had been completed, forty-five additional miles had been graded, and there were sixty-one miles yet to be completed. The road had received $800,000 in state railroad-aid bonds, and the state owned $38,125 in stock. With the train in operation and with the public view of the future so bright, the reality of actual circumstances was hard to accept, for the railroad company and its contractor were in grave financial difficulties.

At the board of directors' meeting, held on November fifteenth while Caldwell and his associates were in Arkansas, the Boston financial interests took over the control of the Little Rock and Fort Smith Railroad Company.[8] John C. Pratt of Boston was elected president, although his election ignored the fact that he was not a stockholder, a prerequisite stated in the charter. The "Boston board," as it was referred to, ran the business of the company from November fifteenth until their authority was challenged by the members of the "old board" in August, 1871. This challenge was followed by Pratt's resignation the next month. Actually, the executive committee of the "Boston board" was in undisputed control, and this meant, in reality, that Josiah Caldwell was in control.

One of the early decisions made after this change in administration was to delay the construction of the Little Rock and Fort Smith road. At the time of the directors' meeting, November fifteenth, the need for money had already become a pressing problem, and seven days later application was made to Governor Clayton for $100,000 in railroad-aid bonds for the ninth division, that section of the road eighty to ninety miles from Little Rock. Governor Clayton refused to grant the bonds on a section of the road so far ahead of the fifty miles of track then in operation. This decision of the Governor was probably the reason for the frantic race against time Robinson appears to have run in December.

With the irons on hand and with the desperate need for money, Robinson tried to lay enough track to qualify for another $100,000 in bonds before the decision to delay was put into effect. His position at this time was reflected in his telegram to Caldwell on December fifth: "Please instruct me about funds. It is impossible for me to get along unless provision is made for deficiencies and Freights immediately—say—Fifty Thousand dollars—I must have it." That the financial condition of Caldwell, Fisher, and their interests was desperate at this time is verified by the fact that Robinson was instructed to send the remaining $2,200,000 in land-mortgage bonds to Caldwell on November twenty-eighth and, again on Caldwell's instructions, Robinson sent another package containing unsigned first-mortgage bonds (estimated to be $1,000,000) to Caldwell on December tenth.

In his race against time, Robinson reported that eight miles of track had been laid by December seventh and that the men were able to lay two miles of track per day. With twelve miles of track laid, bad weather added an additional handicap to his efforts because a storm of several days' duration stopped work on the road. But Robinson still believed that there was plenty of time remaining and that there were plenty of rails to meet their deadline. But he added desperately: "For God's sake let me have money faster."

The need for money was strangling Robinson's efforts by December twelfth. No longer could he get currency in Little Rock on Boston drafts until after they had been collected, an action which required ten days. At the rate at which Caldwell told him he could draw money, Robinson could pay for nothing, for the momentum of the operations had become too great. Three boats were on their way with rails, the work had been interrupted by the storm, the fourth and fifth engines had arrived, and the *Colossal* was at DeValls Bluff waiting for money.

Work resumed on the tracks, and sixteen and one-half miles of track had been laid by December fifteenth. Robinson continued to believe that they would get through in time. But his desperation for money continued to increase. In the absence of Caldwell, who was in Maryland, Robinson sent a dispatch to Warren Fisher, Jr. informing him that protests of Robinson's drafts on Boston had denied him funds for daily needs. A sum of $85,000 for November bills had been promised Robinson, but Boston had not provided the money. "These repeated protests completely cripple me and leave me no resource—Colossal has been laying at De Valls Bluff for one week for want of funds."

In what must have seemed the most bitter of ironies to Robinson, $40,000 was deposited, but was to be spent for pay rolls only. The restrictions placed on the use of the money served to deny Robinson its use, for that cost which appeared on the pay rolls was but a fraction of the total labor cost, and to pay such a small portion of what was owed to labor would cause trouble. "We can't pay a d    d cent to any one for anything except the balances which appear on P.S. & Y.S pay Rolls. No contractor can get a dollar and we have them hanging around us clamoring for something to relieve their men. They cannot get supplies to feed them for the contractors have no credit except through us—If this sort of thing cannot be amended the work had better be stopped entirely."

The end of this frantic period came with the closing of the year. On December thirtieth, Robinson wrote to Governor Clayton that the road was ready for another $100,000 in railroad-aid bonds. The twenty miles of track had closed the gap between the last section of completed track and the section for which the railroad asked state aid and thereby qualified the road for another grant from the state. On New Year's Eve, Robinson wrote Caldwell a letter in which he indicated something of the interdependence of all factors involved in the construction of a railroad.

"I was in hopes when you left here from the numerous assurances given us by Mr. Pratt that the 1st Jany would see us with clean Books & good credit and prepared to commence the New Year with everything in shape. But we are in the most deplorable condition. Everything is in arrears." Robinson needed approximately $91,000 for the month of January in order to keep operations going. Instead, Caldwell told him to limit expenditures to $50,000. But what should he cut? In a review of the possibilities Robinson revealed the extent to which he comprehended the project he was overseeing. One is convinced after reading Robinson's review that there is a momentum involved in the construction of a railroad, which must be respected. The factors involved are so interdependent that to cut at one place will cause unwanted repercussions in other places and will lead to a loss of momentum and to a destruction of the organization essential to the project.

Behind the financial difficulties of Robinson during December was the approaching deadline for the payment of interest due on the first-mortgage and land-mortgage bonds of the Little Rock and Fort Smith Railroad Company. On January first, interest was due on $2,500,000 first-mortgage bonds and on $1,800,000 land-mortgage bonds. An examination of the dates of issuance of these bonds gives an estimated total of $145,230 due to the bondholders.[9] This interest payment was not honored, and from this date the bonds remained in arrears.[10] This fact would make future sale of mortgate bonds still more difficult.

Early in January, Robinson received $20,700 and paid out that amount toward their over-due debts, but he wrote Caldwell that $32,000 was still needed to pay up to December fifteenth and that another $50,000 would be required for present operations by January fifteenth. In addition to the Little Rock and Fort Smith needs there was now revealed another reason for the scarcity of money—expenditures on the Cairo and Fulton Railroad. Caldwell and Fisher were also interested in the construction of that road and had sent $25,300 toward over-due obligations related to the Cairo and Fulton, but they would have to send another $22,000 to pay up to December fifteenth. Another $30,000 would be needed for current operations.

Indeed, it appears that the decision to delay construction of the Little Rock and Fort Smith road was part of a larger decision to concentrate the Caldwell-Fisher resources on the construction of the Cairo and Fulton Railroad. January, 1871, may thus be considered a period during which the transition from the Little Rock and Fort Smith to the Cairo and Fulton was taking place. There continued to be efforts to keep the work going on the Little Rock and Fort Smith road, but the debts related to that road made the efforts increasingly difficult; in fact, those debts contributed to the failure of Caldwell and Fisher on the Cairo and Fulton.

Asa P. Robinson departed for New York and Boston about the twenty-third of January, carrying with him the $100,000 in state bonds which had been recently granted to the railroad by Governor Clayton. Robinson remained in the East and elsewhere until May third, adding his own testimony as chief engineer to the efforts of others then being made to raise funds for the continuation of the construction. During Robinson's absence, his son, Sanford, was in charge. As the pressure from unpaid workers and from anxious creditors mounted during February and March, it was Sanford who stood exposed to the rising tempers.

Laborers began quitting work on the Cairo and Fulton by the first of February. Sanford reported on February fifteenth that 262 men had not returned for two weeks. Economic pressures mounted in other ways as well; payment had to be made for the freight on the four boats, which were on their way from New Orleans with bolts and plates for the Cairo and Fulton. Furthermore, an inquiry for specific information about daily expenditures had been received from H.G. Marquand and Logan H. Roots. By March third, creditors had stopped supplies for the Cairo and Fulton, laborers were in town with payment-due notices, and the office was besieged. The bank had been instructed not to buy Cairo and Fulton claims. Sanford wired to his father: "Our difficulties are increasing hourly." Later the same day he reported that the laborers on the twelfth division of the Little Rock and Fort Smith road had gone on strike, had seized all of the property, and had threatened to destroy it.

During his father's absence, Sanford, as a means of pacifying the creditors, held out the promise of funds which would be forthcoming from Robinson's trip East. When conditions worsened during early March, he emphasized the urgency of the situation to his father: "Everybody relies upon you to fix up Railroad matters. It will not do for you to return here until after matters are all arranged and we have funds or there will be a big row." By the middle of March, Sanford felt matters were approaching a climax. Unless funds were available within the week, he could not answer for the consequences. Even now the boarding train hands were expected to strike on Wednesday. But he warned against sending funds enough for only Peirce, Steacy, and Yorston, for that action would bring the other creditors down upon the office.

By March twentieth, Sanford could no longer maintain his morale in the face of the circumstances. A report had been circulated by the bank that claims against Caldwell would no longer be honored. Sanford feared the consequences which a protest just then would bring and, out of his despair, sent a dispatch to his father. Sanford, on the strength of his father's dispatch, had given his word that certain bills would be paid. Unless that word could be honored, Sanford asked to be relieved from any further responsibility, for his use to the enterprise had been destroyed.

To relieve the pressure of the emergency situation, the Boston company sent $21,000 to Sanford Robinson. Following this action Josiah Caldwell suggested that Sanford attempt to buy at discounted prices some of the claims out against Warren Fisher, Jr., but this proposal came too late. Ironically, the $21,000 had restored confidence in the ultimate payment of these debts to the extent that creditors were now inclined to wait. Three weeks earlier creditors would have taken from forty-five to seventy cents on the dollar, but that opportunity had now passed. There seemed no easy way out for the company of Warren Fisher, Jr. Sanford described the situation in these terms to Josiah Caldwell: "The claims can only be depreciated by deceit on our part in giving false information and spread[ing] erroneous reports—and that would be a two edged sword cutting both ways—for it would stop supplies and credit of all kinds and of course the work would have to cease, and besides would be of course not a very reputable transaction."

All persons involved knew that these token payments, such as the $21,000, were stop-gap measures and that the work would not go smoothly again until the back payments were made. By April twelfth, Sanford reported to his father that no track had been laid since Robinson's departure in January and that none would be laid until financial matters had been settled. Indeed, Steacy had disbanded the track force and work had stopped entirely except for two crews. Funds, believed to be $38,000, were placed at Sanford's disposal on April fourteenth, and from these the February and March estimates were paid, but on April nineteenth, every man on the Cairo and Fulton struck for back pay, that is, for pre-February pay. Sanford reported that at least $10,000 would be necessary to start work again. By April twenty-fifth, however, Sanford's mood had brightened. Some arrangement had been made, and the men were all at work. He told his father not to hurry back.

An end to this brief period of optimism came the following day when Peirce, Steacy, and Yorston published a warning order against Warren Fisher, Jr. and attached all the property and rolling stock of the Little Rock and Fort Smith Railroad. The basis for this lawsuit was a claim for approximately $600,000 due to the sub-contractors by Warren Fisher, Jr. for work done on the road during the previous months. Sanford's untenable position was revealed in the letters which he wrote the next day to the assistant engineers, telling them of this development. He tried to be as optimistic as possible as he suggested a rapid settlement which would be followed by an early resumption of work, but he thought that "until we know more definitely the result of this move that you had better consider yourself as neither discharged nor yet permanently retained." This position could scarcely inspire confidence in the future.

The stockholders, in an attempt to settle with Peirce, Steacy, and Yorston, raised $100,000 to be paid on the account due to the sub-contractors if they would furnish fastenings and would lay the track to Clarksville. Peirce refused to accept the offer and inspired disgust among the stockholders, who expected the arrangement to give $30,000 to $40,000 toward the payment of old debts, to ensure completion of the road, and to provide a residue for the payment of claims.

After a brief return to Little Rock early in May, Robinson left again, this time for Chicago, where he remained until the middle of July. During his absence the demoralizing conditions continued to retard the work. The contractors who were working for Warren Fisher, Jr. were plagued with heavy debts, with the absence of credit, with insubordination among their men, with the inability to hire men, and with a constantly decreasing force of laborers. Law-

suits and attachments were constant threats. Under these circumstances Warren
Fisher, Jr. could not enforce orders which were vital to the continuation of the
work. Confidence in the company was so low that laborers were reluctant to
move from the Little Rock and Fort Smith road to work on the Cairo and
Fulton. It had become evident that unless the deficiencies could be made good,
the work would continue to drag until it finally stopped.

Upon his return in July, Robinson was met with protests upon protests which
"play the duce here and keep us in hot water all the time." These protests were
a great problem, but it was another matter which now brought forth Robinson's
harshest words to his employer. In early May, Robinson had expressed his
concern about the fate of men then at work on the Cairo and Fulton when their
function had been completed. The survey to the Texas border was expected to
be finished about the first of June. At that time the axmen and clearing men
likely would be paid off and discharged. But wages were so far in arrears for
these men that a special provision would be needed for their pay. Robinson's
estimate of the amount due to them read as follows:

| For work on Little Rock & Fort Smith | Dec. | $400 |
| For work on Little Rock & Fort Smith | Jan. | 100 |
| For work on Cairo & Fulton | Jan. | 325 |
| For work on Cairo & Fulton | May | 400 |
| For work on Cairo & Fulton | June | 100 |
| | | $1325 |

Robinson commented; "It is rather a hard matter to discharge men who have
worked faithfully during the whole winter, away from home without paying
them." His purpose in calling this matter to Caldwell's attention in May was to
avoid undue hardships for the men in June.

By July the welfare of other men was being disregarded when James A.
Morley, chief engineer for the Cairo and Fulton, discharged numerous old
employees of Robinson and replaced them with Morley's own workers. In
angry protest against this development Robinson wrote to Caldwell: "It is a
d——d shame to throw these men overboard with claims for wages long due and
put new men in employ who have no claims upon us—It is heartless.... I will
not stand tamely by and see these faithful men treated in this way. If they can
be paid so that they can get away I have no more to say but to bring in new men
and leave them in the helpless condition is a d———d outrage which I protest
against in the strongest terms."

The dismal experience of the railroad after November, when the "Boston
board" took over its control, was responsible for mounting opposition to that
board during August and during the following months. With six members from
the East and only three from Arkansas, the board had conducted its business

without informing members of the "old board" or any other interested parties in Arkansas. Now, impatience led to inquiry and then to a demand for action. One Clarksville stockholder wanted to know: "What has become of the old board of directors? Where is Scott, the president of the road; Haney, the engineer; Judge Rose, the attorney, and Gordon Peay, the secretary? What are they doing about it?"[11]

Some of the members of the "old board" were moving toward recapture of control as these inquiries were being made. Charles G. Scott informed Sanford Robinson, in the absence of his father, that Scott and his associates would await developments, but that nothing would satisfy them short of a new organization with Asa P. Robinson in charge of construction. Scott believed that an arrangement could then be made with Steacy to continue the road and that protection for the interests of the parties in the East could be given under the new organization.

In the meantime economic pressure was also increasing. On August second, Robinson informed Caldwell that Steacy had attached everything on the Cairo and Fulton and Caldwell's land interests as well. A second creditor had done the same. Steacy was asking for $220,000 toward his larger claim of more than $600,000 and for a strict adherence to their contract as the work progressed.[12] Prior to this attachment John C. Pratt, President of the Little Rock and Fort Smith Company, had answered Steacy's complaint by pointing to Fisher's responsibility rather than the company's, by stating that Fisher had been over-paid, and by claiming that negotiations which would have resumed the work, had been in progress at the time when Steacy originally attached the Little Rock and Fort Smith property. Creditors thus found no relief in a situation in which Warren Fisher, Jr., the contractor, was financially responsible to a company which was under the contractor's own control.[13] If the creditor turned to the contractor, he was referred to the company; if the creditor turned to the company, he was referred to the contractor.

By August twenty-second, Sanford reported difficulty in getting men to work and predicted that they would scatter soon. He believed that he could not hold out for more than three days. The contractors suspected that something was wrong, and this suspicion made the settlement of old matters even more difficult. Sanford expected Steacy to throw the company into bankruptcy and to have a receiver appointed, and Sanford noted that in this event the matter would come before Chancellor T.D.W. Yonley of the Pulaski Chancery Court.

Two days later members of the "old board" met and elected Charles G. Scott president. The election of the "Boston board" and all acts of that board were declared null and void. On August twenty-sixth, the *Gazette* carried a two-and-one-half column report of this meeting which included statements from Scott as president, from J.H. Haney, consulting engineer, and from Gordon N. Peay, secretary. This publication disclaimed knowledge of any actions of the

"Boston board" and defended the actions of Scott, Haney, Peay, and other members of the "old board." Charges that they had over-paid Warren Fisher, Jr. and that they "had been outwitted and swindled by the eastern parties" were denied.[14]

As the "old board" members were taking this action, Sanford stood helplessly by unable to counter with any practical action and, in his confusion, wondered what the trouble was in Boston. Men stopped work along the entire road and were expected to demand their wages. The "old board" took possession of the land office, and Sanford expected everything to fall into their hands momentarily. On August twenty-eighth, Sanford wired: "Steacy has taken possession of train and rolling stock and runs train tomorrow with his own Employees." It appeared to Sanford that Scott, Haney, and Steacy were working together to get control of the road. Two days later Steacy entered a new suit against Caldwell which placed a lien on twenty miles of the Cairo and Fulton.

The strategy of the "old board" was to reassert the legitimacy of their authority and to resume construction of the road under their leadership. This action had to be done without calling a stockholders' meeting, however, for the "Boston board" had command of the majority of the stockholders' votes. The response to this strategy in Boston was to call a stockholders' meeting for September twenty-eighth under the authority of the "Boston board" and thereby maintain their control.

As the date for the stockholders' meeting approached, maneuvers on both sides were executed in order to improve the position of interested parties. John C. Pratt resigned as president and was replaced by Charles W. Huntington, and the Boston parties advocated a reorganization of the board which would be more favorable to the Arkansas interests. Scott applied for a temporary injunction to restrain that meeting, and the injunction was granted.[15] On September twenty-ninth, the *Gazette* praised Scott for his action in preventing further swindle by the Boston capitalists.[16]

Asa P. Robinson, who had returned to Little Rock, was now reduced to his most ignoble action in the whole affair. On October second, there were indications that Scott and his associates were preparing for a raid on the land office in order to obtain possession of the papers and confidential records there. That evening Robinson and Huntington went to see U.M. Rose about the probability of such an event and about the proper way to meet it. Rose advised them that either a writ of replevin or an injunction followed by the appointment of a receiver would be the means used and that "in view of the facility with which injunctions are obtained here he thought the latter would be the case."

Robinson then went to his office and clandestinely prepared to remove the papers and documents. The next morning he sent one of the employees on the train to Memphis as a decoy. In the meantime, the papers had been packed during the night by other men in a manner unknown to Robinson, in order to protect him against future questioning, and these papers were sent to Memphis by an express wagon later that morning. Once in Memphis, the papers would be safely out of the jurisdiction of the local courts, and the secrets contained therein would be kept. With these documents safe, Robinson awaited the raid, which he expected to come that day. He was determined to deny Scott the satisfaction of even the slightest moral victory.

He wrote Caldwell: "You may rely that the only [end of these] difficulties is to do as I advised you on my departure viz, get rid of the d––d debts here." Robinson suggested that he could manage this feat quietly and economically. On the previous Saturday he could have settled $20,000 in claims for fifty cents on the dollar. But now a new eventuality was to be faced. Interest on the state bonds had not been paid, and State Treasurer Page could take possession under the law. The sequestration feature, which the capitalists had helped write into the law, took possession only of the income and receipts, however, and there was still hope of obtaining a receiver friendly to their interests. "It would be a great success if we could get such a receiver as we want, but you see the chance— As matters are situated now we are completely at the mercy of our opponents for Law is the last thing considered in their movements. There never was in the annals of History a more perfect reign of judicial tyranny rascality and lawlessness than now prevails in this state—Numerical strength & force is all that can resist it or else money."

October continued to be a miserable month for Robinson. As matters grew progressively worse, the loss of company credit involved Robinson in the loss of personal credit. By October nineteenth, Caldwell had made some move toward settling part of the debts, however, and five days later the *Gazette* happily reported the prospect of a settlement between the two boards which would end their troubles.[17] Resumption of work on the Cairo and Fulton was expected in a day or two.[18] Robinson also was happy that Caldwell had made a partial settlement and hoped that Caldwell would relieve him of his pecuniary troubles soon, for Robinson was utterly without funds.

On November sixth, Caldwell sent for Robinson to come to Boston, but Robinson did not have enough money to go. He wrote Candwell the next day: "My account at [the] Bank is overdrawn and my present bills for past two months are unpaid. I can't buy a Postage Stamp or pay my ferriage. You have so utterly discredited me here that I don't know where I could borrow a hundred dollars in any emergency, even if it were necessary to save my life—So long as I had any money I paid it out in your assurances of early return." Robinson continued: "It is impossible for me to be of any service to you in this way. I should be glad to come to Boston and render any aid in my power but I must pay my bills here and leave money behind me as well as have money to pay my expenses." Evidently Caldwell deposited the $1,000 Robinson considered necessary before he could depart, for Robinson left for Boston two days later.

Matters were rapidly coming to a close. Failure to pay interest on the state railroad-aid bonds resulted in the railroad's falling into the hands of the state treasurer before the end of November.[19] In December, Josiah Caldwell came to Little Rock to settle accounts and, during his stay in Arkansas, engaged J.H. Haney as chief engineer under Caldwell's contract for the completion of the Little Rock and Fort Smith Railroad.[20] Asa P. Robinson was thus relieved from that position, although he retained his connections with Caldwell.

On August 1, 1871, Asa P. Robinson had filed a plat for the town at Conway Station.[21] On January twelfth, and again on February 20, 1872, he filed applications for land with the Little Rock and Fort Smith land office. By September, Robinson was building a house in Conway, where he settled to become one of the town's founding fathers. Indeed, he may properly be considered as the founding father of this little town, for he secured a section of land where he, as engineer for the railroad, had located Conway Station. That section included most of the land which later became the town of Conway.[22] It is not surprising to learn, then, that he was the first mayor, that he donated the ground for the court house and for the railroad depot, that he served as president of the schoolboard, that he developed a fine plantation with some of the best cattle in the state, and that most of the deeds for property in early Conway bore his name.[23] Nor should it be surprising to find today that Colonel A.P. Robinson is a name vaguely revered as one of the town's founding fathers. Three adjacent streets running parallel to each other through the residential area of the town still bear the names of Caldwell, Robinson, and Scott, but the historic origin of their relationship has been lost to most citizens.

# CHAPTER FOURTEEN

# FINANCING A "STUMPTAIL" RAILROAD

J.H Haney commented in 1873 that after John C. Pratt and the "Boston board" took control of the company, in the fall of 1870, the history of the Little Rock and Fort Smith Railroad had been "simply a chaos of errors, blunders, frauds, and peculations, which, if unearthed, would doubtless astonish the simple-minded natives of Western Arkansas."[1] After a review of the available evidence, a person is convinced of the correctness of Haney's expectations concerning the astonishment of the people but is compelled to modify Haney's interpretation of the causes of the company's difficulties. Although the "Boston board" does appear to have disregarded the interests of the company, the troubles of the Little Rock and Fort Smith Railroad began long before November, 1870, the time when that board took charge of company affairs.

A series of factors contributed to the railroad's financial catastrophe, the first of which was the contract which the "old board" made with the capitalists. In October, 1869, Asa P. Robinson had written Josiah Caldwell that a careful examination of the contract as then perfected would show "that everything is entirely within our own control and that we can make any margin for laying the track that we choose."[2] The next month he telegraphed Caldwell that there would be at least $100,000 profit on eighty miles then under consideration—an estimate based on a construction cost of $9,000 per mile.[3] These comments somewhat prepared a person to expect a contract the specific terms of which would reveal a large profit going to the capitalists. The comments did not adequately prepare one, however, for the terms of this contract.

In obedience to a resolution passed at the board of directors' meeting held on February 8, 1870, Robinson was asked to prepare estimates of work completed and to be completed by the contractor.[4] A copy of Robinson's estimates of work done by July 1, 1870, which was sent to J.H. Haney for use in the board of directors' meeting on July eleventh, is perhaps the most revealing piece of available evidence concerning the history of the railroad.[5] Robinson's communication disclosed that Warren Fisher, Jr. had made a contract with the railroad company which called for a payment to Fisher of 5.142 times the estimated cost of construction![6]

Robinson's estimates of the totals for the entire road from Little Rock to Fort Smith are seen in Table 6.[7]

## TABLE 6

### ROBINSON'S COST ESTIMATE, SUBMITTED JULY, 1870

| Item | | | Ordinary Values | Pro Rat Values unde Contract (5.142 |
|---|---|---|---|---|
| Grading and Bridging | | | $ 880,500 | $ 4,527,707 |
| Track, Ties: 160½ miles @ $51,422 | | | 1,605,000 | 8,253,231 |
| Buildings, Right of Way and Depot Grounds | | | 55,000 | 282,811 |
| Equipment: | | | | |
| 15 Engines | $77,133 Each | $1,156,995 | | |
| 153 Cars | 5,142 Each | 786,726 | | |
| 8 Cars | 25,711 Each | 205,688 | 418,000 | 2,149,419 |
| Engineering: 153 miles @ $5,142 | | | 153,000 | 786,726 |
| | | Total | $3,111,500 | $15,999,894 |
| Undistributed balance in consequences of fractions | | | | 106 |
| | | Total | $3,111,500 | $16,000,000 |

The $16,000,000 costs of the construction were to be paid in the following manner:

| | | |
|---|---|---|
| First Mortgage Bonds | | $ 3,500,000 |
| State Aid Bonds | | 1,500,000 |
| Land Mortgage Bonds | | 5,000,000 |
| Stock | | 6,000,000 |
| | Total | $16,000,000 |

Robinson included in his estimates margins for contingencies which, when multiplied by the 5.142 factor, magnified their effect. For example, he added

10% to his estimate of the cost of grading and bridging for each of the fifteen divisions of the road. This totaled $88,050 at ordinary values, but when multiplied by the contract factor of 5.142, the margins amounted to $452,753. Costs skyrocketed again when Robinson's $10,000 per mile of track estimate was multiplied by 5.142 to arrive at the total of $51,420 per mile.[8] In comparison with cost estimates by others this estimate was unusually high. J.H. Haney estimated $23,000 per mile, and David Walker estimated $30,000 per mile for the Arkansas Western, which was to pass through much more rugged terrain than the Little Rock and Fort Smith route.[9] Peter A. Dey, chief engineer for the Union Pacific in 1864, estimated a cost of $30,000 per mile for the first one hundred and $27,000 per mile for the next two hundred before the estimate was raised to $50,000 per mile at the insistance of the vice president of that company.[10] There appears to be little doubt from the available evidence that the "old board" agreed to pay Warren Fisher, Jr. too high a price for the work to be done by the contractor.

If the contract itself may be considered the first factor in causing the financial catastrophe of the railroad, a second was the advance payments made to Warren Fisher, Jr. J. H. Haney looked back on this development with regret when he wrote Turner in 1873: "The first grave and mischievous error committed by the Board was in making advances of payments of bonds to Mr. Warren Fisher, Jr. in advance of the requirements of the contract, and to this must be attributed a large share of the misfortunes which overtook the road and now burden it with an inordinate debt."[11] This imbalance between work completed and securities issued to Fisher had already appeared in July, 1870, and the imbalance grew progressively worse as time passed.

When Robinson submitted his estimates in July, 1870, slightly more than twenty miles of track had been laid, grading had progressed in varying degrees along nine of the fifteen divisions, and two engines and thirty-seven cars had been purchased. According to the contract, Fisher was due $4,273,257 for work completed thus far.[12] The proportional sums to be paid in stocks and bonds are shown below, together with the payments authorized by the board on July eleventh and payments made by July twenty-eighth.

|  | Due Fisher[13] July 1, 1870 | Authorized[14] July 11, 1870 | Paid By[15] July 28, 1870 |
|---|---|---|---|
| First-Mortgage Bonds | $ 934,774.97 | $ 787,500.00 | $2,150,000.00 |
| State-Aid Bonds | 400,617.84 | 500,000.00 | 500,000.00 |
| Land-Mortgage Bonds | 1,335,392.82 | 1,125,000.00 | 1,300,000.00 |
| Common Stock | 801,235.69 | 675,000.00 | 1,500,000.00 |
| Preferred Stock | 801,235.69 | 675,000.00 | 1,500,000.00 |
|  | $4,273,257.00 | $3,762,500.00 | $6,950,000.00 |

At first glance these figures seem to deny the issuance of securities in advance of contract requirements, for on July eleventh the board authorized the issuance of only $3,762,500 in stocks and bonds. Before this date, however, other bonds had been hypothecated, and the board passed two resolutions at the July eleventh meeting which were to have unfortunate consequences for the future. One of these resolutions authorized the president to use his discretion in advancing stocks and bonds to Fisher, provided that the contractor gave "good and sufficient security."[16]  Another resolution authorized the president to take the company seal to Boston in order to be able to sign and to issue bonds in that city.[17]  The figures of July twenty-eighth reveal the growing imbalance between the issuance of securities and the performance of work done under the contract. By August eighth, Fisher had received $8,800,000 in company and state securities, and by September twenty-eighth, the figure had reached $9,400,000.[18]  If one divides this figure by the contract factor of 5.142, the work done at ordinary values should have represented the expenditure of $1,827,693 based on Robinson's estimates. In contrast to this figure, however, Robinson had informed Caldwell a few days earlier that his total checks by September first amounted to $577,602.49.[19]  It is only fair to be reminded that this situation had developed before the "Boston board" took over control on November fifteenth.[20]

Actions during the period of the "Boston board's" control are somewhat less known that those during the preceding months. Evidence is not as extensive, the constant presence of creditors blurs the transactions, and involvement with the Cairo and Fulton make comprehension of the evidence more difficult. Nevertheless, there is enough evidence to conclude that the imbalance between the issuance of securities and the completion of work grew impressively from November, 1870 to May, 1871.

It will be recalled that Robinson sent to Caldwell in late November and early December $2,200,000 worth of land-mortgage bonds and a package of blank first-mortgage bonds believed to have been worth $1,000,000.[21]  By June, 9, 1871, $1,586,000 in land-mortgage bonds and $785,000 in first-mortgage bonds had been transferred from the company to Fisher.[22]  When added to the $100,000 in state-aid bonds which the railroad received in January, 1871, these company bonds raised the total of securities transferred to Fisher to $11,871,000.[23]  When this sum is divided by the contract factor of 5.142, the quotient should represent work amounting to $2,301,050 calculated at ordinary values.

The question of how much Fisher actually spent toward the construction of the Little Rock and Fort Smith Railroad is impossible to answer precisely. There are four pieces of evidence, however, which help in arriving at an estimate of his expenditures.  There is hard evidence that Robinson wrote checks amounting to at least $623,802. In addition, there is hard evidence that Peirce,

## TABLE 7

### ESTIMATED COSTS OF THE LITTLE ROCK AND FORT SMITH RAILROAD TO AUGUST, 1871

| Item | Haney | | Robinson | |
| | Unit | Total | Unit | Total |
| --- | --- | --- | --- | --- |
| 120 miles of railroad (with deductions below) | $23,000 | $2,760,000 | $10,000 | $1,200,000 |
| 35 miles clearing | 800 | 28,000 | [a]800 | [a]28,000 |
| 25 miles ties | 960 | 24,000 | 840 | 21,000 |
| 2 miles siding | 8,000 | 16,000 | [a]8,000 | [a]16,000 |
| 7 locomotives | 14,000 | 98,000 | 15,000 | 105,000 |
| 2 passenger cars | 5,000 | 10,000 | 5,000 | 10,000 |
| 1 baggage car | 2,000 | 2,000 | [a]2,000 | [a]2,000 |
| 6 box cars | 1,000 | 6,000 | 1,000 | 6,000 |
| 55 flat cars | 600 | 33,000 | [a]600 | [a]33,000 |
| Depots, shops, water tanks, etc. | | 30,000 | | [a]30,000 |
| Depot grounds, right of way, etc. | | 10,000 | | [a]10,000 |
| Contingencies | | 43,000 | | [a]43,000 |
| | | $3,060,000 | | |
| Engineering and office | | | | 80,000 |
| | | | | $1,584,000 |
| Deduct to complete the above 120 miles | | | | |
| 30 miles iron rails and fastenings | 8,000 | 240,000 | 7,280 | 218,000 |
| 70 miles track laying and surfacing | 1,000 | 70,000 | | |
| 50 miles track laying and surfacing | | | 650 | 32,500 |
| Masonry and bridging 25 miles | | 50,000 | | 137,731 |
| | | $ 360,000 | | $ 388,231 |
| Total value of work | | $2,700,000 | | $1,195,769 |

Source: Report from J.H. Haney to Charles G. Scott, Little Rock, August, [1871]. *Gazette*, August 26, 1871, p. 1, c. 2; report from Asa P. Robinson to J.H. Haney, July, 1871. Arkansas History Commission, Asa P. Robinson Papers. Haney's figures are designated with an "a."

Steacy, and Yorston held Fisher in their debt for some $600,000, on the basis of which they attached the railroad property.[24]   These figures added together would give a total of $1,223,802 which was spent before the cessation of work. A third piece of hard evidence is the citation from the contractor's books that the total expenditures on the Little Rock and Fort Smith Railroad by March fourteenth, according to those books, were $1,172,000, of which Peirce, Steacy, and Yorston had $901,000.[25]   A final piece of acceptable evidence is a calculation based on J.H. Haney's inventory, made in August, 1871, of work actually completed.[26]   By accepting Haney's inventory and applying Robinson's estimates of that inventory, one reaches the total of $1,195,769 for Fisher's expenditures.[27] This total is very close to the former one given above and is perhaps as close to the actual figures as one can get.

If $1,195,769 is accepted as an estimate of the actual expenditures made by Fisher, and when the $600,000 owed by Fisher to Peirce, Steacy, and Yorston has been subtracted, the total estimation of money spent by Fisher toward the fulfillment of the contract would be $595,769. This total was close to the amount which had been received from the state in railroad-aid bonds, for it has been roughly estimated that approximately $589,000 was received from the sale of the $900,000 issued by the state.[28]   The economic collapse left the company and the state liable for securities amounting to $11,871,000. Annual interest due on the $900,000 state railroad-aid bonds would be $54,000. And interest on the first-mortgage and land-mortgage bonds, amounting to $498,120 annually, was enough to threaten the company's existence at any moment. For this catastrophe the company could show $1,195,769 worth of railroad for which the company had paid $2,301,050 calculated in ordinary values.

A third factor in causing this financial catastrophe, in addition to the nature of the contract and the advance payments to the contractor, was the dominance of the company by the contractor. The inequality in the economic position of the board in relation to the contractor allowed the latter to dominate the former to an increasing extent, a situation which finally resulted in the capitulation of the "old board" in November, 1870.  This dominance had progressed sufficiently by July 11, 1870, to secure the two resolutions mentioned above which authorized the president to use his discretion in advancing bonds to Fisher and to take the company seal to Boston to execute and to deliver the bonds according to the board's resolutions. The growth of the contractor's dominance was indicated by the following resolution which was unanimously adopted at the director's meeting held on November fifteenth: "Resolved, that the executive committee shall have full power to deliver to Warren Fisher, Jr., the contractor, or his assigns, the stock and bonds of this road in such amounts and at such times as they may deem expedient."[29]   It will be recalled that this meeting marked the beginning of the "Boston board's" control of the company. The transfer of power appears to have been almost total. In fairness to the participants in the unanimous vote, however, the context in which this action was taken should be remembered. Conditions in the company had never been better according to the public view of things. Josiah Caldwell, Warren Fisher, Jr., and their party were in Arkansas at that time, and everyone was eagerly anticipating the opening of regular train service to Lewisburg which was to begin on November twenty-first.

One cannot abandon the belief that the Pennywit account served to advance the contractor's domination of the company, although evidence relating to the account is not sufficiently complete to allow one to draw firm conclusions. There was about the matter, however, enough irregularity to make the threat of its exposure a perpetual embarrassment to members of the "old board." Perhaps this vulnerability was utilized by Josiah Caldwell and his Boston associates to gain additional concessions from the Arkansas members of the board. Certainly the president in the use of his discretion in advancing bonds to Warren Fisher, Jr. was in a questionable position and would have a difficult time, indeed, in acting as an independent agent in relation to the contractor.

Circumstances made Charles G. Scott more vulnerable than he normally would have been. On March 29, 1870, Asa P. Robinson wrote to Caldwell about the financial condition of the Little Rock and Fort Smith Railroad Company.[30] Robinson had become curious about that condition because he had been repeatedly asked to approve bills for company expenses which he thought should have been paid out of company funds. But there appeared to be no funds. When he looked into the company's records, he found information concerning the Pennywit account, which he transmitted to Caldwell with the comment: "Whether you and your associates have any interest in the following matter is for you to determine."[31]

Robinson found that the Pennywit account, which had been signed in December, 1867, a few days prior to Pennywit's death, had been prepared by Pennywit's friend and executor, Charles G. Scott, whose children were made the heirs of the Pennywit estate.[32] Robinson's audit of the company's records convinced him that from the $2,010 in gold lost by theft, the $7,800 claim of Pennywit against the company, and the $4,038.92 difference between gold and currency exchange on money spent by the company, and from other sources, the Pennywit estate, and hence Charles G. Scott, had received some $13,663.91 in gold.[33] This was Robinson's explanation for the empty treasury of the company.

A claim for this amount was presented against the Pennywit estate to Scott and to the other executors, but they refused to endorse it. The matter then remained dormant because no person on the board wanted to raise the issue. Robinson believed, however, that all members of the board wanted Scott to surrender the money.[34] Evidence to validate Robinson's report is not available, although hints contained in Haney's correspondence indicate that greater irregularities existed than the $2,010 theft included in the Pennywit account.

Robinson's motives in placing this information in the hands of Josiah Caldwell, however, are more definite. Robinson indicated to Caldwell that the two years' time limitation for filing claims against the Pennywit estate would expire on May fifteenth. If Caldwell wanted the board to take action, the vote to do so would have to be taken before that date. In conclusion Robinson added: "I thought it best to post you on this matter of gobble. If you don't care about it, no harm done."[35]

Caldwell's reception and use of this information is not known. The company did file suit against the Pennywit estate, however, and that suit was dropped under unusual circumstances early in 1873.[36] The point in mentioning a situation for which the evidence is incomplete is to stress the probability that Scott and other Arkansas members of the board were in a highly vulnerable position in relation to Josiah Caldwell. This vulnerability permitted duress to be applied if needed to gain concessions and to increase the dominance of the company by the contractor.

A fourth factor in the financial catastrophe was the failure to obtain for the company's benefit the economic resources promised by the financing of the venture. Josiah Caldwell and his associates had been told that $500,000 could be expected from each of the five counties through which the road passed, but in the early stages of the venture the capitalists were indifferent to this source of capital.[37] Nevertheless, Crawford County voted to subscribe $100,000 early in 1870.[38] A change in attitude had occurred by May sixteenth when Robinson wrote Charles G. Scott urging the promotion of county elections in the other counties.[39] Ironically, because of the progress made on the railroad by that time, the counties were reluctant to subscribe, for the people had come to believe that the road would be completed without their financial assistance.[40] Efforts by Scott, who received $1,000, and John N. Sarber, who received $450, from Robinson to be used in promoting victory in the county-bond elections were not successful, and the county elections held in August voted down the bond issues in the four remaining counties.[41] The available evidence does not indicate that Crawford County actually issued the bonds which had been authorized; therefore, as far as is known the counties did not contribute capital to the road.

State railroad-aid bonds totaling $900,000 were granted to the road. Because of the credit reputation of the state, the amount of capital derived from the sale of these bonds is estimated to have been approximately $589,000.[42] The greatest loss in financial potential, however, came from the failure of the company's own stocks and bonds to make their proper contribution toward the construction of the road.

Why these securities did not supply the necessary means for completing the road under the Fisher contract cannot be fully explained, but two qualifications concerning their sale will make some contribution toward an answer. James Ford Rhodes in commenting about James G. Blaine's involvement in the sale of Little Rock and Fort Smith bonds, revealed that the usual condition of sale by Fisher was "to give four dollars in securities for one in money."[43] Thus, had all of the securities issued by the company to Warren Fisher, Jr. been sold under these usual conditions of sale, the financial return would have been $2,767,750 instead of the misleading total of $10,971,000. A second qualification on the amount received by Fisher was related to the prices at which these bonds could be sold in the New York market. From July 1, 1870 until November 11, 1871, a rough sampling of the prices bid for these bonds in the New York market revealed that the bids ranged from seventy-five cents on July first to forty-three cents on November eleventh for the 7% land-mortgage bonds.[44] The weakness of these bids is mentioned to suggest that Fisher probably received considerably less than the $2,767,750 which would have been forthcoming had the demand for these securities been greater.

There were various contingencies which Robinson, Caldwell, and Fisher had to face that may be collectively considered as a final factor contributing to the financial catastrophe which happened to the railroad. Without the delay in track-laying caused by the heat during the summer of 1870, perhaps Robinson could have completed enough road to secure better prices for the company's securities and thereby could have raised enough money to keep the momentum going.

Caldwell's involvement in financial matters was too widespread to keep a very accurate conception of what was being done on the Little Rock and Fort Smith road at any given time. Perhaps matters were beyond his comprehension for too long a period to be corrected. Certainly Caldwell experienced some confusion about the Arkansas situation on several occasions. Also administrative difficulties were multiplied for everyone because construction was being carried out on two roads simultaneously—a fact which added to the confusion. The failure was definitely a financial failure rather than a professional failure, for Asa P. Robinson must be considered a competent engineer, and he considered Peirce, Steacy, and Yorston as the best contractors with whom he had worked.

One temptation which the student of history needs to resist after witnessing such a miserable financial failure is the temptation to label Josiah Caldwell and Warren Fisher, Jr. unadulterated "robber barons." The historian would more properly remember that all of the financial mistakes were not made by them. And it would be more to the point to ask whether Caldwell would have purposely discredited Robinson and himself if matters were within his control, or whether these men were discredited because financial circumstances had gone beyond their control.

These comments are certainly not intended to exonerate Josiah Caldwell,

Warren Fisher, Jr., and company, but are intended to suggest that the financial catastrophe was caused not by the actions of a single man but by the interplay of several factors. The contract, the advance payments without proper security, the domination of the company by the contractor, the credit reputation of the state, as well as various contingencies, all contributed to that catastrophe.

Josiah Caldwell, according to J.H. Haney, led Haney to understand that money would be made available for the completion of the road and that Haney, as chief engineer, would be in charge of construction if the men Caldwell wanted on the board of directors were chosen at the meeting to be held on the third Monday in December, 1871. These men were chosen, and on December twenty-first Haney was appointed chief engineer to replace Asa P. Robinson.[45] At that time negotiations were pending for a consolidation of the Little Rock and Fort Smith and the Memphis and Little Rock companies. This new company was then to be leased by the Southern Railway Security Company. A previous agreement to lease had required that the Little Rock and Fort Smith road first be completed to Fort Smith. Now a new contract between Caldwell and the Little Rock and Fort Smith company to complete the road had been made contingent upon the acceptance of the lease by the Southern Railway Security Company. When the latter company refused to accept the lease, the consolidation failed, and Caldwell's contract expired.[46] Haney found himself chief engineer for a company without a construction contract.

By August, 1872, Haney was determined to rescue the company from any control or influence of the Boston capitalists. He secured from Charles G. Scott a promise that Scott would not act without Haney's cooperation or consent. In December, however, Josiah Caldwell appeared with the Boston proxies and "by threatening or coaxing—or perhaps other means—he cajoled Mr. Scott into a postponement of the election for Directors."[47]

After one or two postponements the election was held in February, and Scott revealed to Haney that he had arranged with Caldwell for a mixed board. Haney protested vigorously to Scott against the broken promise, but Scott had now pledged his word to Caldwell and would not retreat. Scott was elected president of the new board, but shortly thereafter resigned in favor of a Boston party. As if to represent the second half of a bargain, the board passed an order "directing the Company's Attorney to dismiss the suit pending against the Estate of Pennywit & enter satisfaction in full of said claim—which was done."[48]

In disgust, J.H. Haney resigned his position as chief engineer in January, 1873, and sued Josiah Caldwell for his unpaid salary amounting to $25,000.[49] The position of chief engineer was then filled again by a Conway resident, Asa P. Robinson. On February twenty-first, Governor Baxter issued $100,000 in railroad-aid bonds to the road, and action slowly moved toward the completion of the road to Clarksville by the middle of June.[50]

The ten-year land grant authorized by Congress would expire July 28, 1876 unless the road was completed by that date. If bondholders' interests were to be protected, the land grant had to be saved. With these considerations in mind, the bondholders took legal action.[51] On October 3, 1874, an amendment to the bill for foreclosure was made which anticipated the appointment of a receiver for the road. By raising money on receiver's certificates, the bondholders hoped to raise enough money for the construction of the road.[52]

On November 6, 1874, a judgment in behalf of the bondholders ordered the mortgaged property sold unless the principal and interest were paid by December tenth. At the sale which followed on December nineteenth, parties were present who represented $6,097,000 of the $8,500,000 first-mortgage and land-mortgage bonds issued. In behalf of the bondholders these parties purchased the railroad for $50,000 and purchased the land grant for another $50,000.[53]

They then declared their intention to organize a corporation to manage the property and to complete the construction of the railroad. It was announced that any bondholder possessing either kind of these bonds could convert those bonds into proportionate shares of stock in the new company.[54] By these means the land grant was to be saved and the bondholders' equity preserved.

On November twenty-first, in the United States Circuit Court for the Eastern District of Arkansas, an exhibit of an affidavit used during that day's argument revealed the names and holdings of those parties who were bondholders or who were representing bondholders at the time of the reorganization. Collectively these parties represented $3,585,000 first-mortgage bonds and $2,580,000 land-mortgage bonds.[55] Table 8 lists a few of the names included in the exhibit and their holdings.[56]

## TABLE 8

### BONDHOLDERS AT TIME OF REORGANIZATION

|  |  | First Mortgage | Land Mortgage |
|---|---|---|---|
| J. G. Blaine | Augusta, Me. | 19 | 48 |
| L. Saltenstall | Boston | 15 | 15 |
| J. S. Robinson | Boston | 6 | 6 |
| J. P. Robinson | New York | 60 | 220 |
| D. D. Stackpole | Boston | 55 | 12 |
| E. Atkins | Boston | 282 | 476 |
| W. P. Denkla | New York | 43 | 28 |
| J. C. Pratt | Boston | — | 8 |
| H. Saltenstall | Boston | — | 23 |
| H. Saltenstall | — | 50 | 20 |
| G. C. Richardson | Boston | 20 | 20 |
| Mo. Kansas T. R. Co. | — | 50 | — |
| E. Atkins | — | 484 | — |

Two names on the list are of particular interest—James G. Blaine and Elisha Atkins. Blaine is of interest, of course, because of his association with Warren Fisher, Jr. and the "Mulligan letters." And Elisha Atkins, representing the largest holdings of bonds, is of interest because he, too, was closely associated with Fisher. The obvious question one would like to have answered is whether any of the bonds under Atkins' name actually belonged to Caldwell and Fisher, for their names are conspicuously absent from the list. Unfortunately, the answer is not available.[57]

With the reorganization of the company, the old friends of the railroad took heart. On February 1, 1875, Jesse Turner happily added a postscript to a letter he had written to his son, Jesse, who was then attending Kenmore University High School at Amherst Court House, Virginia, in which he remarked: "I think the L.R. & F.S.R.R. will now be built without delay. Probably completed to Van Buren by next Christmas."[58] Four weeks later Turner was even more optimistic and expected the road to reach Van Buren by fall.[59]

These expectations had to be modified, but by October twenty-fourth the contracts had been let along the entire distance, and Turner expected the road's completion by the first of July.[60] No doubt it was true, as Oberholtzer remarked, that this was "a little 'stumptail' railroad in a Southern state, which came from nowhere and led no whither,"[61] and yet there was a certain excitement in Jesse Turner's heart when he wrote to his son in June that "the iron on the R. R. is laid down to a point within four miles of this place, and will be here by the 10th."[62]

# CHAPTER FIFTEEN

# THE LOSS OF STATE CREDIT

Reconstruction in Arkansas can best be understood when it is considered as part of a continuing development of the state rather than as a separate time period. The continuing influence of geography, social attitudes, and leadership has been illustrated in previous divisions of this work. The persistent difficulty in financing the development of natural resources is the concern of the present division.

In 1868, Powell Clayton and the Republican party had to find some means of restoring the credit of the state, for the broken dreams of ante-bellum days had left the state with a public debt of some $3,363,509.19[1] This legacy had also brought with it the belief that part of the debt was unjust. On this belief had been constructed a theme in Arkansas politics, dating from the time of Governor Yell, that the illegitimate portion of the Holford bond debt must not be paid.[2] When the McCullough Funding Bill, which included provision for funding the entire Holford debt, was approved by Governor Clayton on April 6, 1869, a storm of protest was raised.[3]   In words which could have been transcribed directly from Governor Yell's letterbook, the *Fayetteville Democrat* commented that the correct policy should have been "to pay the State's honest debts and not one cent more."[4]

Anxious though he was to reestablish the state's credit, Governor Clayton held back those bonds intended to fund the Holford debt until he could inform himself more fully about the history of this debt and could investigate charges of legislative corruption in the passage of the Act. For this action the Governor was severely criticized, and he finally decided to release the bonds. To have amended the Funding Act would have required reassembling the legislature, an action which might have jeopardized the entire Funding Act.[5]   From the point of view of New York investors the funding of the entire debt was important, if good credit were to be established. These actions of the legislature and of Governor Clayton were far more understandable than one observer has made them appear to be.[6]

Bonds for $3,000,000 were authorized under the Funding Act.[7]  Clayton appears to have exercised appropriate care in the issuance of those bonds. When, in January, 1870, funds were not available to pay the interest which would come due on any additional bonds, Clayton stopped the funding until taxes could produce the money needed.   He did not want "bonds thrown on the market that will not be paid."[8]  By May new money had been provided, and Clayton wanted additional bond exchanges.[9]

Clayton was anxious, as any governor would have been, to establish the credit of the state as a means of developing resources. Refunding was less effective in establishing this credit than Clayton had hoped, however, and future bond issues continued to sell at low figures.[10]  The cumulative effects of the state's financial history and the Civil War continued to hinder economic development. Ironically, the louder Arkansas protested against the *de facto* nature of the government, the more likely were bond prices in New York to decline.

The unfortunate failure of the state banks made the authors of the Constitution of 1868 very careful about any future use of the faith and credit of the state.[11]    As a precaution, they had written into the Constitution that: "the credit of the State or counties, shall never be loaned for any purpose without the consent of the people thereof, expressed through the ballot box."[12]  The passion for railroads was no weaker under Governor Clayton than it had been under Governor Murphy, however, and an Act providing for the issuance of state bonds to promote railroad construction was passed by the legislature on July 21, 1868.[13]  In compliance with the constitutional provision mentioned above, this Act required that the people vote "for" or "against" railroads in the forthcoming general election in November.[14]

But perhaps because of either legislative oversight or eagerness to rush the construction of railroads, there was a flaw in the bill which would have repercussions in the future. Without specific instructions to the contrary, an act could not become effective until ninety days after the adjournment of the legislative session during which the act had been passed. How could this Act passed in July become immediately effective in order to authorize the election in November without the required statutory specification? Anticipation of the construction of railroads was too strong for this flaw to be noticed in that day, and on November third the people voted in favor of railroads by a vote of 25,984 to 5,210.[15]

Available evidence indicates that Clayton took rather seriously his responsibility to see that railroad companies used the aid properly.[16]  Aid was extended only to the main arteries for the most part, and a comparison between the roads proposed before the Civil War and those roads which received assistance under the Republicans shows a strong similarity.[17] For the number of railroads which received aid to be limited to five—at a time when there were forty railroad corporations, and a bit later, eighty-six—was no small accomplishment.[18] To frustrate the over-optimistic expectations of so many railroad enthusiasts, however, was bound to promote animosity toward Governor Clayton himself because he possessed so much power over these expectations by virtue of his office as Chairman of the Board of Railroad Commissioners.

Especially bitter toward Clayton for his railroad administration were the people of the northwest, who were envious of the delta region, which was getting railroads to supplement the existing river system at a time when the northwest had neither of these transportation methods to provide a reliable escape from geographic isolation. From the point of view of the northwest the Governor had distributed aid to eastern, southeastern, and southern roads and was ignoring northwestern interests.[19]

In a comparative study of state aid to Southern railroads Professor Carter Goodrich found Arkansas to be a case in which "the mileage actually constructed under state aid approached very closely the mileage for which the assistance was intended."[20] The $5,350,000 in bonds which were actually issued were intended to encourage the construction of 420 miles of railroad.[21]

In terms of state aid to railroads authorized and actually awarded, the record under the Republicans appears in Table 9.[22]

## TABLE 9

### STATE BONDS ISSUED

|  | Authorized | Issued |
|---|---|---|
| Memphis and Little Rock | $1,200,000 | $1,200,000 |
| Little Rock, Pine Bluff, and New Orleans | 1,800,000 | 1,200,000 |
| Mississippi, Ouachita, and Red River | 1,950,000 | 600,000 |
| Little Rock and Fort Smith | 1,500,000 | 1,000,000 |
| Little Rock and Helena | 450,000 | —— |
| Cairo and Fulton | 3,000,000 | —— |
| Arkansas Central | —— | 1,350,000 |
|  | $9,900,000 | $5,350,000 |

According to *Poor's Railroad Manual*, track mileage had increased 662 miles during the years of Republican rule, although approximately 249 miles included in this total were on the Cairo and Fulton, which had been built without state aid.[23] But all of the roads were in default on their interest after 1873.[24]

In addition to the $1,370,000 issued to fund the Holford claim and the $5,350,000 in railroad-aid bonds, by 1874 the Republican administrations had issued $3,000,000 in levee bonds under authority of an act passed on March 16, 1869.[25] The depreciation on these bonds was severe, and a major financial mistake was committed when the bonds were made receivable for internal improvement lands in 1871.[26] These lands were sold for $1.25 per acre for cash or credit. The credit system resulted in hundreds of suits to collect the purchase money, with each suit costing the state from $65 to $110. The average acreage in these suits amounted to eighty acres, but if one assumed 160 acres in a forfeiture, the state would have to pay fifty cents per acre to repossess the land. The 160 acres could then be sold for $1.25 per acre, but when the state received levee bonds in payment, as by law it had to, the value received by the state was worth less than one-tenth of that amount, for the levee bonds were selling for ten cents. Thus in a contract for the 160 acres the state would have paid out $80 in court costs and received $20 in the sale price—a loss of $60![27] It is no wonder that the state land commissioner pleaded for a change in the system in his biennial report in 1874.

In addition to the Holford funding bonds, the railroad-aid bonds, and the levee bonds, the state had $3,000,000 in its own scrip outstanding by 1874. A depreciation similar to that experienced with the levee bonds occurred in this form of currency. Prices in scrip had declined to eighteen to twenty-five cents on the dollar by the end of Republican rule. County and municipal scrip was also issued and had suffered the same experience of depreciation, in some counties the value being not more than ten cents.[28]

Enough has been said to illustrate the miserable experiences associated with a second failure in the attempt to use the state's credit to finance the development of natural resources. When one compares these experiences with the exaggerated expectations of an era in which railroads offered the promise of utopian development of resources, it is easier to understand why the politics of the day took on such an atmosphere of conspiracy. Before the end of Reconstruction the theme of a "just" and an "unjust" debt had been extended beyond the Holford claim to include the railroad-aid bonds and the levee bonds.

When interest on this enlarged "unjust" debt—a debt which had failed to accomplish its purposes and one which had been sponsored by a *de facto* government—appeared annually as a part of the public debt, the stage was set for repudiation if some political leader chose to exploit the issue.

Table 10 shows the categories of undisputed and disputed indebtedness on July 1, 1874.[29]

The annual interest on this debt from July first forward amounted to $251,540 on the undisputed part of the debt and $596,700 on the disputed part.[30] Some measure of what this meant is gained from noting that in 1873 the taxable property in the state amounted to $104,560,292, on which was levied

$1,014,682.88 in taxes.[31] The total interest on the debt mentioned above would require $848,240 annually. By 1876 the situation was still worse, for under the conservatives a policy of retrenchment had reduced property evaluation to $95,000,000. A 1% tax on this amount would net $950,000, but by 1876 the interest on the public debt had become $970,000 a year.[32] Some adjustment of the debt obviously had to be made.

## TABLE 10

## DEBT CATEGORIES

|  | Total State Indebtedness July 1, 1874 and Interest on Same to that Date |
| --- | --- |
| Undisputed |  |
| State Bank Bonds | $   744,120.00 |
| Real Estate Bank Bonds | 1,486,230.00 |
| Arkansas Funding Bonds | 1,925,500.00 |
| State Deficit Bonds | 65,000.00 |
| 1874 War Bonds | 200,000.00 |
| State Scrip Outstanding | 1,750,000.00 |
| Total Undisputed Debt | $6,170,850.00 |
|  |  |
| Disputed |  |
| Holford Bonds | $1,534,400.00 |
| Memphis and Little Rock Rail Road Bonds | 1,389,000.00 |
| Mississippi, Ouachita, and Red River Railroad Bonds | 684,315.00 |
| Little Rock, Pine Bluff, and New Orleans Railroad Bonds | 1,365,515.00 |
| Little Rock and Fort Smith Railroad Bonds | 1,154,000.00 |
| Arkansas Central Railroad Bonds | 1,524,335.00 |
| Arkansas Levee Bonds | 2,343,658.55 |
| Total Disputed Debt | $9,995,223.55 |
| Total State Indebtedness | $16,166,073.55 |

The first major development occurred in the Arkansas Supreme Court, where in June, 1877, a decision was handed down which declared the railroad-aid bonds unconstitutional. The provision of the Constitution which required ninety days from the expiration of the legislative session in which an act was passed had not been observed. The session in which the Railroad-aid Act was passed had not expired until April 10, 1869; therefore, the Act itself could not have been in effect before July 10, 1869. In violation of this constitutional requirement the election, which authorized the pledge of the faith and credit of the state, had been held on November 3, 1868. That election was now declared to have been a nullity, and, therefore, the bonds which had been issued following that election had been issued without authority of law. These bonds, therefore, created no liability on the state and were void in the hands of innocent holders.[33]

The decision involved two persons in a most ironic way. The author of the decision was David Walker, who had been opposed to the use of state bonds since the unfortunate experience with the banks during the days of Governor Yell. Walker had shared the belief of other citizens in his section that Governor Clayton had been unfair to the northwest in distributing railroad aid. In addition to this, Walker had temporarily thought of using railroad-aid bonds to finance construction of the Arkansas Western Railroad and had been roughly handled by Asa P. Robinson and his associates during the struggle for control of that road. These statements are not to suggest a cause and effect relationship between Walker's experience and his judicial decision, but are merely to point out the irony in his position, especially in relation to the second person, Powell Clayton.

The decision concerned bonds granted to the Little Rock, Mississippi River and Texas Railway Company, the president of which was Powell Clayton. Before he became president and while he was governor, Clayton, acting as Chairman of the Board of Railroad Commissioners, had granted most of the bonds now under consideration to the road, then known as the Little Rock, Pine Bluff and New Orleans Railroad. Clayton had a personal interest in the development of the road, for one of its important stations was "Linwood," located on Clayton's plantation downriver from Pine Bluff. He had donated the land in order to secure reliable transportation to New Orleans and had established there a store and a sawmill to aid in the development of his cypress lumber interests.[34] These matters are noted not to condemn Clayton, but rather to point out the identification of Clayton with this particular railroad and with this particular decision, an identification which was no doubt made by the people of that day.

Walker's decision eliminated $5,350,000 in state railroad-aid bonds from the state public debt. He was anxious, however, that his decision not be interpreted as repudiation and was careful to say in his text that "it is no repudiation of a contract to deny its payment, because, not being a contract, there can be no repudiation of it."[35] The *Gazette* echoed this sentiment and praised Walker for his decision.[36]

As might be expected, the *New York Times*, echoing the bondholders' sentiments, saw the decision quite differently. The grounds upon which Walker had based his decision, the New York writer thought, were "technical and trumpery as against the equitable rights of the bondholders, who advanced their money on the credit of the state, pledged—so far as they could see—with all the sanction which a State could confer in dealing with investors. Having thus cast off its railroad liabilities, of course Arkansas will by and by relieve itself still further."[37]

Two months after Walker's decision, John D. Adams wrote Walker about Arkansas' credit situation. The state had just tried to borrow money, only to be refused. Adams did not feel that either the bondholders' influence or Walker's decision was responsible for this refusal, but rather the action of the legislature, which had recently reduced taxes. Adams commented to Walker: "We must admit after disinterested reflection, that it could not be very encouraging to lenders, to see a State reduce her taxes, & borrow money to pay current expenses, then collect just enough taxes, to pay that money back at the end of the year, & leave the State in just the same financial condition as when she borrowed the year before." Adams continued: "The truth is, my good friend, we in Arkansas, must show the world that we are, at least, willing to pay the *just* debt of the State, and you & I know the best people are in favour of a compromise with our creditors."[38]

John D. Adams deserves a good place in the history of Arkansas for his valiant efforts to obtain a compromise with the creditors for settling the public debt of the state. Governor Miller had suggested a plan early in 1877, and the state board of finance had a second plan in mind, but the efforts of John D. Adams surpassed these previous attempts as he tried to restore the state's financial reputation by means of a compromise with the creditors.[39]

In the fall of 1877, Adams went to New York to meet with creditors and was successful in getting agreement with all except those holding the Holford bonds. He then departed for Liverpool on December twenty-seventh to pursue the possibilities in England.[40] His trip there was evidently unsuccessful, for the compromise did not develop.

The theme of paying only the "just" debt of the state had always contained in it the latent threat of repudiation. If repudiation were ever combined with the resentments felt toward the *de facto* government during Reconstruction, the political potential would be great. The man who took the lead in making that association was William M. Fishback.

Fishback sponsored an amendment to the Constitution which would prohibit the legislature from levying any tax or from making any appropriation to pay the principal or interest of either the Holford bonds, the railroad-aid bonds, or the levee bonds.[41] The legislature approved the amendment on April 2, 1879, and the proposal was submitted to the people in general election in 1880. U.M. Rose and Augustus H. Garland were prominent leaders in the opposition to that amendment. Despite their best efforts, however, the amendment was defeated by only a 3,321 majority.[42] Such a vote would not allow the proposal to fade away—nor would William M. Fishback permit such a demise.

Four years later the amendment was again sponsored by the legislature; and in an election held on September 2, 1884, the First Amendment, the "Fishback

Figure 23.    William M. Fishback
              John D. Adams

Amendment," was overwhelmingly passed by a vote of 119,000 to 15,500.[43] And Fishback himself was elected governor in 1892.[44]

Now the state had joined those other Southern states which had openly repudiated their public debt. The second failure to use state credit successfully had indeed been a costly failure, and the effects would continue through the decades. As Professor Evans commented: "It is significant that even as late as 1917 New York banks were not allowed to handle any State securities of Arkansas. New York still looked askance at securities issued by a state that had once gone on record in favor of repudiation and that would not levy a tax to liquidate a fiscal deficit."[45]

# PART FOUR

## CONCLUSION

# CHAPTER SIXTEEN

# CONCLUSION

The continuation of certain influences throughout Arkansas history needs to be recognized in the study of Reconstruction. The importance of these influences becomes evident when Reconstruction is considered as part of a continuous development of the social and economic forces in the state rather than as a separate and unique period. Among the influences that must be included are geography, patriotism, personality of leadership, and failure to successfully finance the development of natural resources.

The social contrasts created by geographical influences were important in Arkansas. The three sections of the state encouraged the development of three societies which continually affected politics and made Arkansas a border state politically as well as geographically. Although geography has been important throughout the state's history, its importance during Reconstruction took on new meaning. The distribution of the plantation system, and therefore the concentration of the Negro population, had been related to soil conditions. When, during Reconstruction, social reforms were advocated which pertained to the Negro's place in the society of the state at large, those reforms could not fail to assume geographic importance.

Patriotism provided a second continuing influence in the state's development. There was a Unionist majority in the state at the time of the secession crisis just as there was a Unionist majority in the state under Governor Murphy after the Civil War. But it would be a fundamental mistake to identify this Unionist sentiment as being nationalist. Perhaps most men did not go as far as George C. Watkins did when he said that "the best Government the world ever saw is in danger of being wrecked on this idea of nationality." But many Unionists shared his apprehension that "We would be no longer a Union of States but a *Nation.*"[1]

Free government was identified with local self-government, and the regime

(243)

established under Congressional Reconstruction policies appeared to these conservatives to be an alien, *de facto* government. Their attitude was the same during Reconstruction as it had been during secession: "No man can renounce his allegiance to any government by proxy—no man can acknowledge allegiance to any government by proxy."[2] Each man, therefore, had to make his own patriotic adjustment to post-war conditions.

David Walker and Augustus H. Garland illustrate the problems of adjustment related to *de facto* v. *de jure* government in Arkansas during Reconstruction. They also illustrate the importance of personality in leadership as they expressed their patriotic commitments. The legalistic nature of Walker made him less willing to grant *de facto* recognition to the Reconstruction government and more reluctant to abandon his Whig background in order to join the Democrats. The political nature of Garland allowed him more flexibility as he moved with relative ease from his ante-bellum Whig background into a leading position among the Democrats. Walker was motivated by principle; Garland was motivated by results. Both men were Whig Unionists before the Civil War, but they reacted so differently when faced with a *de facto* government during Reconstruction that their behavior seems to have been determined more by personality and character than by political affiliation.

Political opposition to the Republican regime in Arkansas might have consolidated under the leadership of either David Walker, Harris Flanagin, or Augustus H. Garland. Both Walker and Flanagin, however, suffered disadvantages which made them essentially sectional leaders. Walker's loyalty to Brooks' claim to the governor's office and Walker's own Whig reserve limited his effectiveness as a statewide leader. Flanagin's advocacy of secession limited his statewide acceptance, and his death in 1874 removed him from the scene. Augustus H. Garland enjoyed a happy combination of factors which included his reputation for successful relations with the Federal government, his essentially political personality, and his place of residence. The elements of this combination served to elevate Garland to a position of statewide prominence and to assure that the consolidation of political forces would occur under his leadership.

Inability to successfully finance development of natural resources persisted. In infancy the faith and credit of the state were pledged in creating state banks to promote plantation development and to create a fiscal agent for the state. The exaggerated expectations from this enterprise were destroyed by the panic of 1837. Mismanagement, plus the dishonorable action of a New York banking house, created a part of the emerging state debt which was unjust. The fraudulence associated with the debt and the disillusionment felt from the failure of the banks combined to create a resentment which constituted a theme throughout Arkansas history; the people were willing to pay whatever was necessary to uphold the faith and credit of the state, but they were unwilling to pay one cent toward any "unjust" debt.

Reconstruction was a second period of exaggerated expectations arising from the use of state credit to finance the development of natural resources. This time railroads instead of banks offered the promise of rapid economic development. But before the faith and credit of the state could be utilized, that credit had to be reestablished through a funding of the state debt. In order to strengthen that credit, the legislature included all of the ante-bellum debt in the funding. This action revitalized the old issue relating to the justice or injustice of the Holford claim, for that claim had been funded along with the rest of the debt.

By 1874, the credit had been lost through depreciation, the railroads had defaulted on the interest payments, and the state debt had appeared as an annual curse. Consequently, after this time the resentment felt against funding the Holford claim was enlarged to include the railroad-aid and levee bonds. When the hostility felt toward a *de facto* government was added, the new expression of the old political theme led to repudiation.

If the Little Rock and Fort Smith Railroad is a fair example, Governor Clayton acted much more responsibly in caring for the public securities than the capitalists acted in caring for the corporation's securities. The reputation of one type of security affected the reputation of the other, however, and the resulting depreciation added debt without producing comparable value. In 1873, one bond promoter irresponsibly argued the merits of investment in Arkansas state bonds.[3]   The investor was told that he could make 20% interest on a one-hundred-dollar thirty-year bond which could be purchased for $38.75. One might add facetiously that if the investor were lucky, he might do even better than that, for the average price for Arkansas securities that year was only $30.[4]

Some measure of the cumulative effect of the loss of credit suffered by Arkansas can be perceived by the figures in Table 10, which show fluctuations in state securities from 1872 to 1879. The figures shown represent the average price for the specified time.[5] Of the twenty-five states for which figures of this type are known, Arkansas' average price of nineteen stands lowest on the list. It is reasonable to conclude, therefore, that the failure of the state's credit continued to be a retarding factor in the development of the state's resources.

One is prompted to ask whether the views of Reconstruction in the decades since that era have not over-estimated the political villainy and under-estimated the credit failure of the period. Or the question might be put in another way: If the establishment of credit had been successful, would the deeds of the political villains appear so dark?

# TABLE 11

## VALUES OF STATE SECURITIES

| State | 1872 | 1873 | 1874 | 1875 | 1876 | 1877 | 1878 | 1879 | Average |
|-------|------|------|------|------|------|------|------|------|---------|
| Massachusetts | 103 | 103 | 103 | 103 | 103 | 103 | 103 | 103 | 103 |
| New York | 104 | 105 | 106 | 109 | 110 | 113 | 115 | 114 | 110 |
| Virginia | 50 | 42 | 35 | 35 | 44 | 39 | 36 | 36 | 38 |
| So. Carolina | 34 | 27 | 15 | 28 | 31 | 32 | 31 | 11 | 26 |
| Louisiana | 68 | 50 | 19 | 25 | 35 | 39 | 61 | 67 | 46 |
| Arkansas | 50 | 30 | 19 | 12 | 15 | 11 | 8 | 7 | 19 |
| Michigan | 98 | 97 | 94 | 102 | 105 | 104 | 104 | 107 | 101 |
| Illinois | 99 | 95 | 95 | 99 | 101 | 100 | 102 | 103 | 99 |

# BIBLIOGRAPHY

## SOURCE MATERIALS

*Manuscript Collections*

Arkansas and Ohio Granger's Correspondence, 1874, MSS., University of Arkansas Library, Fayetteville, Arkansas.

Arkansas Manuscripts selected by Walter L. Brown, in the Manuscripts Division, Library of Chicago Historical Society, University of Arkansas Library, Microfilm 109.

Bliss, Calvin C., MSS., Arkansas History Commission, Little Rock

Bliss, James M., MSS., University of Arkansas Library.

Camden, Johnson Newton, MSS., West Virginia University Library, Morgantown.

Clayton, Powell, Letterbook 1870, MSS., Arkansas History Commission.

Cook, Gertrude Fallin, MSS., University of Arkansas Library.

Davies, Mary Lou, MSS., University of Arkansas Library.

Eno, Clara Bertha, Collection, MSS., Arkansas History Commission.

Eno, Clara Bertha, Collection, MSS., University of Arkansas Library.

Flanagin, Harris, MSS., Arkansas History Commission.

Fuller, Melville Weston, MSS., Chicago Historical Society Library.

Gulley, L. C., Collection of State Papers, MSS., Arkansas History Commission.

Hayes, Rutherford B., MSS., Rutherford B. Hayes Library, Freemont, Ohio.

Jennings, Roscoe J., MSS., Arkansas History Commission.

Johnson, President Andrew. Letter of Pardon to Charles Cane, Washington, D. C., August 3, 1868, MS., University of Arkansas Library.

Letters Illustrative of Arkansas History, 1838–1865, MSS., University of Arkansas Library. Originals in Illinois State Historical Library, Springfield, Illinois.

Mansfield, William W., MSS., Arkansas History Commission.

Miller, Minos, MSS., University of Arkansas Library.

Quesenbury, William Q., MSS., University of Arkansas Library.

Rector, Henry M., MSS., Arkansas History Commission.

Remmel, Harmon L., MSS., University of Arkansas Library.
Reynolds, Daniel Harris, MSS., University of Arkansas Library.
Reynolds, John Hugh, MSS., Arkansas History Commission.
Robinson, Asa P., MSS., Arkansas History Commission.
Scott, Christopher C., MSS., Arkansas History Commission.
Single Letters, MSS., University of Arkansas Library.
Stebbins, A. Howard, Jr., Collection, MSS., Arkansas History Commission.
Stebbins, A. Howard, Jr., Documents and Currency, University of Arkansas Library.
Stephens, Alexander H., MSS., Library of Congress, Washington, D. C.
Telegram manuscripts relating to the Brooks-Baxter War. Subject File, Arkansas History Commission.
Trimble, Robert W., Collection, MSS., Arkansas History Commission.
Tufts, A. A., MSS., Arkansas History Commission.
Turner, Jesse, MSS., Arkansas History Commission.
Turner, Jesse, MSS., Duke University Library, Durham, North Carolina.
Turner, Jesse, MSS., University of Arkansas Library.
U. S. National Archives. Records of the War Department, the Adjutant General's Office. Record Group 94. *Amnesty Papers Arkansas.* Washington D. C.: National Archives and Records Service, 1959. University of Arkansas Library, Microfilm 375.
Walker, David, MSS., University of Arkansas Library.
Walker, Sue, MSS., University of Arkansas Library.
Williams, David C., MSS., Arkansas History Commission.
Williams, J. Edwin, MSS., Arkansas History Commission.
Williams, Samuel W., MSS., Arkansas History Commission.
Wright, Weldon E., MSS., Arkansas History Commission.
Yell, Archibald, Letterbook 1841, MSS., Arkansas History Commission.


*Federal and State Government Publications*

Arkansas. Auditor of the State. *Biennial Report, 1872-1874.*
———. *Charter of the Branch Bank of the State of Arkansas, at Arkansas* (1837).
———. *Charter of the Real Estate Bank of the State of Arkansas* (1836).
———. Commissioner of Common Schools. *Biennial Report, 1854-1856.*
———. Commissioner of Common Schools. *Biennial Report, 1856-1858.*
———. Commissioner of State Lands. *Biennial Report, 1872-1874.*
———. Constitutional Convention, 1868. *Debates and Proceedings.* Little Rock Ark.: J. G. Price, 1868.
———. Constitutional Convention, 1836. *Journal.*
———. Constitutional Convention, 1874. *Journal.*
———. General Assembly. *Acts of Arkansas* (1860-1861).
———. General Assembly. *Acts of Arkansas* (1866-1867).
———. General Assembly. *Acts of Arkansas* (1868-1869).
———. Governor Powell Clayton. *Biennial Message.* January 2, 1871.
———. Governor William R. Miller. *Special Message to the Senate and House of Representatives, Respecting the Bonded and Floating Indebtedness of the State.* February 13, 1877. Little Rock, Ark.: *Arkansas Gazette* Book and Job Printing House, 1877.

——. House of Representatives. *Journal* (1866–1867).

——. Senate. *Report of the Senate Bank Committee in Relation to the Real Estate Bank,* George W. Lemoyne, Chairman (1852).

——. State Board of Finance. Letter of the State Board of Finance to the People of Arkansas, on the Proposition Submitted to the Board for the Settlement of the Public Debt, October 8, 1877.

——. Superintendent of Common Schools. *Biennial Report, 1858–1860.*

Hall, C. G. "Crip." *Historical Report of the Secretary of State.* Little Rock, Ark.: State of Arkansas, 1958.

U. S. Bureau of the Census. *Eighth Census of the United States: 1860. Population,* I.

——. *Eighth Census of the United States: 1860. Social Statistics,* IV.

——. *Historical Statistics of the United States Colonial Times to 1957.* Washington, D. C.: Government Printing Office, 1960.

——. *Ninth Census of the United States: 1870. Population,* I.

——. *Ninth Census of the United States: 1870. Wealth and Industry,* III.

——. *Tenth Census of the United States: 1880. Population,* I.

U. S. *Congressional Globe.* 39th Cong., 1st Sess., 1866, Part 5, Appendix.

——. 40th Cong., 3d Sess., 1869, Part 3.

U. S. House of Representatives. *Select Committee to Inquire Into the Condition of Affairs in Arkansas.* Report No. 771. 43rd Cong., 1st Sess., 1874.

U. S. *Statutes at Large,* Vol. XIII.


*Legal Decisions*


*Baxter* v. *Brooks,* 29 Ark. 174 (1874).

*Borden et al.* v. *State, use etc.,* 11 Ark. 519 (1851).

*Ex parte Garland,* 71 U. S. 333 (1867).

*Ex parte McCardle,* 73 U. S. 318 (1867).

*Hawkins* v. *Filkins,* 24 Ark. 286 (1866).

*Haney* v. *Caldwell,* 35 Ark. 156 (1879).

*Haney* v. *Caldwell,* 43 Ark. 184 (1884).

*Hot Springs Cases,* 92 U. S. 698 (1876).

*Huntington et al., Trustees,* v. *Little Rock & Ft. S. R. Co. et. al.,* 100 U. S. 605 (1882).

*Little Rock & Ft. S. Ry.* v. *Huntington,* 120 U. S. 160 (1887).

*Meux* v. *Anthony et al.,* 11 Ark. 411 (1850).

*Osborn* v. *Nicholson,* 80 U. S. 654 (1872).

*Shaw et al.* v. *Little Rock & Ft. S. Ry.,* 100 U. S. 605 (1880).

*State of Arkansas* v. *Little Rock, Mississippi River and Texas Railway Company,* 31 Ark. 701 (1877).

*Steacy* v. *Little Rock & Ft. S. R. Co. et al.,* 22 Fed. Cas. 1142, No. 13,329 (1879–1880).

*St. Louis, Iron Mountain & Southern Ry.* v. *Loftin Collector,* 30 Ark. 693 (1875).

*William H. Tompkins, Appt.,* v. *Little Rock and Fort Smith Railway et al.,* 125 U. S. 109 (1888).

*Published Letters, Diaries, Speeches, and Reports*

*Baxter Sustained* (Published, 1874). University of Arkansas Library, Sue Walker Papers.

Beebe, Roswell, et al. *Memorial to the Legislature.* Little Rock, Ark.: *True Democrat,* 1852. University of Arkansas Library, Microfilm 27.

Cairo and Fulton Railroad Company. *Proceedings of the Second Annual Meeting of the Stockholders.* Little Rock, Ark.: *True Democrat* Office, May 7, 1855. University of Arkansas Library, Microfilm 27.

Clayton, Powell. *Inaugural Address and Message of Powell Clayton, usurping governor of Arkansas. Gazette* Supplement. Little Rock, Ark.: *Arkansas Gazette,* 1868.

Fayetteville Railroad Convention. *Proceedings of the Railroad Convention.* Fayetteville, Arkansas, August 15, 1870. University of Arkansas Library, Sue Walker Papers.

Hallum, John. *The Diary of an Old Laywer: or Scenes Behind the Curtain.* Nashville, Tenn.: Southwestern Publishing House, 1895.

Hindman, Thomas C. Speech of Hon. Thomas C. Hindman delivered at Helena, Arkansas, November 28, 1859. University of Arkansas Library, Sue Walker Papers.

Johnson, Richard H. *Address to the People of Arkansas.* Little Rock, Arkansas, May 31, 1860. University of Arkansas Library, Microfilm 27. Original in the University of Texas Library.

Lemke, Walker J., comp. and ed. *The Life and Letters of Judge David Walker.* Fayetteville, Ark.: Washington County Historical Society, 1957.

Little Rock and Fort Smith Railroad Company. *Report of the President to His Excellency, Henry M. Rector.* November 26, 1860. University of Arkansas Library, Jesse Turner Papers.

Memphis and Little Rock Rail Road Company. *Report of the President to His Excellency, Elias N. Conway.* Octoer 22, 1860. University of Arkansas Library.

New Orleans, Little Rock and St. Louis Railroad Company. *Proceedings of the First Regular Annual Meeting of the Stockholders* (1873). University of Arkansas Library, Microfilm 27.

Pike, Albert, and Johnson, Robert W. *The True Merits of the Controversy in Arkansas, for the Consideration of Honest Men.* Washington, D. C.: Privately printed, 1874.

Rose, Uriah M. *Addresses; with a Brief Memoir by George B. Rose.* Chicago, Ill.: George I. Jones, 1914.

Wilshire, W. W. Speech of W. W. Wilshire delivered in the Hall of the House of Representatives, Little Rock, Arkansas, May 28, 1874. University of Arkansas Library, Sue Walker Papers.


*Memoirs, Reminiscences*

Carrigan, Alfred Holt. "Reminiscences of the Secession Convention," Part I, *Publications of the Arkansas Historical Association.* Edited by John Hugh Reynolds. Fayetteville, Ark.: Arkansas Historical Association, 1906. Vol. 1, pp. 305–13.

Cypert, Jesse N. "Secession Convention," Part II, *Publications of the Arkansas Historical Association*. Edited by John Hugh Reynolds. Fayetteville, Ark.: Arkansas Historical Association, 1906. Vol. I, pp. 314–23.

Garland, Augustus Hill. *Experience in the Supreme Court of the United States, with some Reflections and Suggestions as to that Tribunal.* Washington, D. C.: J. Byrne & Company, 1898.

House, Joseph W. "The Constitutional Convention of 1874–Reminiscences," *Publications of the Arkansas Historical Association*. Edited by John Hugh Reynolds. Conway, Ark.: Arkansas Historical Association, 1917. Vol. IV, pp. 210–68.

Walker, Sue H. Personal Reminiscences (1935). University of Arkansas Library, Sue Walker Papers.


*Newspapers*

*Arkansas Gazette*, 1841–1843, 1860–1877.

*Fayetteville Democrat*, 1868–1874, April 25, 1928.

*Frank Leslie's Illustrated Newspaper*, March 20, 1875.

*New York Times*, 1870–1871.

*True Democrat*, 1852.

Vaughan, Jeanette R. Scrapbook of mounted newspaper clippings relating to Reconstruction in Arkansas, 1869–1879. University of Arkansas Library.

*Washington Telegraph*, July 18, 1866.


*Maps*

Branner, George C. *Geology of Arkansas: Surface and Below Surface.* Revised. Little Rock, Ark.: Arkansas Geological and Conservation Commission, 1959.

Cram, George Franklin. *Cram's Railroad & Township Map of Arkansas.* Chicago, Ill.: G. F. Cram, 1875.

*Roads, Old Trails, Traces and Historical Places of Arkansas.* Results of a survey conducted by George F. Metzler, Extension Recreation Specialist, Agricultural Extension Service, University of Arkansas. Prepared by the Arkansas State Highway Department in cooperation with the U. S. Department of Commerce, 1965.

*Township Map of the State of Arkansas.* Little Rock, Ark.: T. B. Mills & Co., 1875.

U. S. Department of Agriculture, Soil Conservation Service. *Soil Association Map: State of Arkansas.* N.p.: Agricultural Extension Service, University of Arkansas, 1959.

## SECONDARY ACCOUNTS

*General Works*

*Appleton's Annual Cyclopedia and Register of Important Events of the Year 1875.* Vol. XV. New York: D. Appleton and Co., 1895.

*Biographical and Historical Memoirs of Central Arkansas.* Chicago, Ill.: Goodspeed Publishing Co., 1889.

Commager, Henry Steele (ed.) *Documents of American History.* 7th ed. New York: Appleton Century Crofts, 1963.

Coulter, E. Merton. *The South During Reconstruction, 1865–1877.* Vol. VIII of *A History of the South.* Edited by Wendell Holmes Stephenson and E. Merton Coulter. Baton Rouge, La.: Louisiana State University Press, 1947.

Eisenstadt, Abraham S. (ed.) *American History: Recent Interpretations.* Vol. I. New York: Thomas Y. Crowell Co., 1962.

Ferguson, John L., and Atkinson, James H. *Historic Arkansas.* Little Rock, Ark.: Arkansas History Commission, 1966.

Hallum, John. *Biographical and Pictorial History of Arkansas.* Vol. I. Albany, N. Y.: Weed, Parsons and Co., 1887.

Hempstead, Fay. *Historical Review of Arkansas: Its Commerce, Industry and Modern Affairs.* Vol. I. Chicago, Ill: Lewis Publishing Co., 1911.

Henry, James P. *The Arkansas Gazetteer for 1873 and Emigrant's Guide to Arkansas, Showing Little Rock for 1872.* Little Rock, Ark.: Price & McClure, State Printers, 1873.

——. *Resources of the State of Arkansas, with a Description of Counties, Railroads, Mines, and the City of Little Rock.* 3rd ed. Little Rock, Ark.: Price & McClure, State Printers, 1873.

Herndon, Dallas T. *Centennial History of Arkansas.* 4 vols. Chicago, Ill.: S. J. Clarke Publishing Co., 1922.

Hopkins, Joseph G. E., *et al.* (eds.) *Concise Dictionary of American Biography.* New York: Charles Scribner's Sons, 1964.

Johnson, Allen, and Malone, Dumas (eds.) *Dictionary of American Biography.* Vol. X. New York: Charles Scribner's Sons, 1933.

Josephson, Matthew. *The Politicos, 1865–1896.* New York: Harcourt, Brace & World, Inc., 1938.

——. *The Robber Barons: The Great American Capitalists, 1861–1901.* New York: Harcourt, Brace & World, Inc., 1934.

Morris, Richard B. (ed.) *Encyclopedia of American History.* Updated and revised. New York: Harper & Row, Publishers, 1965.

Oberholtzer, Ellis Paxon. *A History of the United States Since the Civil War.* Vol. II. New York: Macmillan Company, 1922.

Reynolds, John Hugh (ed.) *Publications of the Arkansas Historical Association.* 4 vols. Fayetteville and Conway, Ark.: Arkansas Historical Association, 1906–1917.

Rhodes, James Ford. *History of the United States from the Compromise of 1850.* Vol. VII. New York: Macmillan Company, 1906.

Shinn, Josiah Hazen. *Pioneers and Makers of Arkansas.* N. p.: Geneological and Historical Publishing Co., 1908.

Thomas, David Y. (ed.) *Arkansas and Its People: A History, 1541–1930.* 4 vols. New York: American Historical Society, 1930.

*Monographs*

Blocher, W. D. *Arkansas Finances.* Little Rock, Ark.: *The Evening Star,* 1876.

Bishop, Albert Webb. *Loyalty on the Frontier or Sketches of Union Men of the South-West.* St. Louis, Mo.: R. P. Studley & Co., 1863.

Clayton, Powell. *Aftermath of the Civil War in Arkansas.* New York: Neale Publishing Co., 1915.

Eno, Clara Bertha. *History of Crawford County, Arkansas.* Van Buren, Ark.: The Press Argus, n.d.

Gatewood, Robert L. *Faulkner County, Arkansas, 1778-1964: A History.* Revised and enlarged. Conway, Ark.: Published by the author, 1964.

Gibbs, Mifflin Wistar. *Shadow and Light: An Autobiography.* Washington, D. C.: N.p., 1902.

Harrell, John M. *The Brooks and Baxter War: A History of the Reconstruction Period in Arkansas.* St. Louis, Mo.: Slawson Printing Co., 1893.

*History of the North-Western Editorial Excursion to Arkansas.* Little Rock, Ark.: T. B. Mills & Co., Publishers, 1876.

McGrane, Reginald Charles. *Foreign Bondholders and American State Debts.* New York: Macmillan Company, 1935.

Mills, Theodore B. *Financial Resources of the State of Arkansas, with the State and Municipal Debt of Each State in the Union.* Little Rock, Ark.: Little Rock Printing and Publishing Co., 1873.

Morgan, W. Scott. *History of the Wheel and Alliance and the Impending Revolution.* St. Louis, Mo.: Woodward Co., 1891.

Muzzey, David Saville. *James G. Blaine: A Political Idol of Other Days.* New York: Dodd, Mead & Co., 1935.

Myrdal, Gunnar. *Rich Lands and Poor: The Road to World Prosperity.* Vol. XVI of *World Perspectives.* Edited by Ruth Nanda Anshen. New York: Harper & Brothers, 1957.

Newberry, Farrar. *A Life of Mr. Garland of Arkansas.* N.p.; Published by the author, 1908.

Russell, Charles Edward. *Blaine of Maine: His Life and Times.* New York: Cosmopolitan Book Corp., 1931.

Scott, William A. *The Repudiation of State Debts.* (Vol. II of University of Wisconsin, *Library of Economics and Politics,* ed. Richard. T. Ely). New York: Thomas Y. Crowell, 1893.

Stampp, Kenneth M. *The Era of Reconstruction: 1865-1877.* New York: Alfred A. Knopf, 1965.

Staples, Thomas S. *Reconstruction in Arkansas, 1862-1874.* New York: Longmans, Green & Co., 1923.

Stover, John F. *The Railroads of the South, 1865-1900.* Chapel Hill, N. C.: University of North Carolina Press, 1955.

Van Horne, John Douglass. *Jefferson Davis and Repudiation in Mississippi.* Baltimore, Md.: The Sun Book and Job Printing Office, 1915.


*Articles in Periodicals*

Atkinson, James H. "The Adoption of the Constitution of 1874 and the Passing of the Reconstruction Regime," *Arkansas Historical Quarterly,* V, No. 3 (Fall, 1946), pp. 288-96.

———. "The Brooks-Baxter Contest," *Arkansas Historical Quarterly,* IV, No. 2 (Summer, 1945), pp. 124-49.

Bayliss, Garland E. "Post-Reconstruction Repudiation: Evil Blot Or Financial Necessity?" *Arkansas Historical Quarterly*, XXIII, No. 3 (Autumn, 1964), pp. 243–59.

Brough, Charles Hillman. "The Industrial History of Arkansas," *Publications of the Arkansas Historical Association.* Edited by John Hugh Reynolds. Fayetteville, Ark.: Arkansas Historical Association, 1906. Vol. I pp. 191–229.

Brown, Walter L. "The Henry M. Rector Claim to the Hot Springs of Arkansas," *Arkansas Historical Quarterly*, XV, No. 4 (Winter, 1956), pp. 281–92.

Cypert, Eugene. "Constitutional Convention of 1868," *Publications of the Arkansas Historical Association.* Edited by John Hugh Reynolds. Conway, Ark.: Arkansas Historical Association, 1917. Vol. IV, pp. 7–56.

Driggs, Orval Truman, Jr. "The Issues of the Powell Clayton Regime. 1868–1871," *Arkansas Historical Quarterly*, VIII, No. 1 (Spring, 1949), pp. 1–75.

Evans, W. C. "The Public Debt," Chapters XXXII and XXXIII of *Arkansas and Its People: A History, 1541–1930.* Edited by David Y. Thomas. New York: The American Historical Society, Inc., 1930. Vol. I, pp. 355–77.

Ewing, Cortez A. M. "Arkansas Reconstruction Impeachments," *Arkansas Historical Quarterly*, XIII, No. 2 (Summer, 1954), pp. 131–53.

Goodrich, Carter, "American Development Policy: The Case of Internal Improvements," *The Journal of Economic History*, XVI (December, 1956), pp. 449–60.

——. "Public Aid to Railroads in the Reconstruction South," *Political Science Quarterly*, LXXI, No. 3 (September, 1956), pp. 407–42.

Hesseltine, William B., and Gara, Larry. "Arkansas' Confederate Leaders after the War," *Arkansas Historical Quarterly*, IX, No. 4 (Winter, 1950), pp. 259–69.

Jones, Virgil L. "Arkansas Literature," Chapter XLIX of *Arkansas and Its People: A History, 1541–1930.* Edited by David Y. Thomas. New York: The American Historical Society, Inc., 1930. Vol. II, pp. 574–83.

Lewis, Elsie M. "Robert Ward Johnson: Militant Spokesman of the Old South-West," *Arkansas Historical Quarterly*, XIII, No. 1 (Spring, 1954), pp. 16–30.

Lucy, J. M. "History of Immigration to Arkansas," *Publications of the Arkansas Historical Association.* Edited by John Hugh Reynolds. Fayetteville, Ark.: Arkansas Historical Association, 1911. Vol. III, pp. 201–19.

Moore, Samuel W. "State Supervision of Railroad Transportation in Arkansas," *Publications of the Arkansas Historical Association.* Edited by John Hugh Reynolds. Fayetteville, Ark.: Arkansas Historical Association, 1911. Vol. III, pp. 267–309.

Nolte, Eugene A. "Four Unpublished Letters from Augustus Garland," *Arkansas Historical Quarterly*, XVIII, No. 2 (Summer, 1959), pp. 78–89.

Peterson, Svend. "Arkansas in Presidential Elections," *Arkansas Historical Quarterly*, VII, No. 3 (Autumn, 1948), pp. 194–209.

Randolph, Bessie Carter. "Foreign Bondholders and the Repudiated Debts of the Southern States," *American Journal of International Law*, XXV, No. 1 (January, 1931), pp. 63–82.

Rector, W. Henry. "A Reconstruction Episode: Bishop Lay and Episcopal Church Reunion, 1865," *Arkansas Historical Quarterly*, II, No. 3 (September, 1943), pp. 193–201.

Reynolds, John Hugh. "Presidential Reconstruction in Arkansas," *Publications of the Arkansas Historical Association*. Edited by John Hugh Reynolds. Fayetteville, Ark.: Arkansas Historical Association, 1906. Vol. I, pp. 352–61.

Richards, Ira Don. "Little Rock on the Road to Reunion, 1865–1880," *Arkansas Historical Quarterly*, XXV, No. 4 (Winter, 1966), pp. 312–35.

Rose, F. P. "Butterfield Overland Mail Company," *Arkansas Historical Quarterly*, XV, No. 1 (Spring, 1956), pp. 62–75.

Ross, Margaret Smith. "Augustus H. Garland–Arkansas's Biggest Man: Leader in Law, in State and National Politics," *Arkansas Gazette*, January 22, 1956, pp. 2–3F.

——. "Governor Elisha Baxter Was a Unionist–And He Suffered for It in the Civil War," *Arkansas Gazette*, December 4, 1966, p. 6E, cc. 4–6.

Russ, William A., Jr. "The Attempt to Create a Republican Party in Arkansas During Reconstruction," *Arkansas Historical Quarterly*, I, No. 3 (September, 1942), pp. 206–22.

Scroggs, Jack B. "Arkansas in the Secession Crisis," *Arkansas Historical Quarterly*, XII, No. 3 (Autumn, 1953), pp. 179–224.

Shinn, Josiah H. "Augustus Hill Garland Was Born Seventy-Six Years Ago: His Life and Services to Arkansas, the Confederacy and the Nation," *Arkansas Gazette*, June 11, 1908, pp. 3, 10.

Singletary, Otis A. "Militia Disturbances in Arkansas during Reconstruction," *Arkansas Historical Quarterly*, XV, No. 2 (Summer, 1956), pp. 140–50.

Turner, Jesse, Jr. "The Convention of 1836," *Publications of the Arkansas Historical Association*. Edited by John Hugh Reynolds. Fayetteville, Ark.: Arkansas Historical Association, 1911. Vol. III, pp. 74–166.

Walz, Robert B. "Arkansas Slaveholdings and Slaveholders in 1850," *Arkansas Historical Quarterly*, XII, No. 1 (Spring, 1953), pp. 38–74.

Wood, Stephen E. "The Development of Arkansas Railroads Part I: Early Interest and Activities," *Arkansas Historical Quarterly*, VII, No. 2 (Summer, 1948), pp. 103–40.

——. "The Development of Arkansas Railroads Part II: The Great Railroad Boom," *Arkansas Historical Quarterly*, VII, No. 3 (Autumn, 1948), pp. 155–93.

Wooster, Ralph. "The Arkansas Secession Convention," *Arkansas Historical Quarterly*, XIII, No. 2 (Summer, 1954), pp. 172–95.

Worley, Ted R. "The Arkansas State Bank: Ante-Bellum Period," *Arkansas Historical Quarterly*, XXIII, No. 1 (Spring, 1964), pp. 65–73.

——. "The Control of the Real Estate Bank of the State of Arkansas, 1836–1855," *Mississippi Valley Historical Review*, XXXVII (December, 1950), pp. 403–26.

——. "Letters to David Walker Relating to Reconstruction in Arkansas, 1866–1874," *Arkansas Historical Quarterly*, XVI, No. 3 (Autumn, 1957), pp. 319–26.

*Unpublished Materials*

Arkansas. Historical Records Survey. "The Arkansas State Legislature: A List of Members, Officers and Employees of the Senate and House of Representatives from the formation of Arkansas as a Territory 1819 to 1840." Compiled by O'Neall Petre. Little Rock, Ark., 1940. (Mimeographed) University of Arkansas Library.

Brown, Mattie.    "A History of River Transportation in Arkansas from
    1819–1880."    Unpublished Master's thesis, Department of History,
    University of Arkansas, 1933.
Brown, Walter L.    "Albert Pike."    Unpublished Ph.D. dissertation, Department
    of History, University of Texas, 1955.  University of Arkansas Library, Micro-
    film 80.
Carmichael, Maude.  "The Plantation System in Arkansas, 1850–1876."  Unpub-
    lished Ph.D. dissertation, Department of Economics, Radcliffe College, 1935.
    University of Arkansas Library, microfilm 201.
Harper, Clio (comp.).  "Early Arkansas Bar."  Typescript arranged and bound by
    the Work Projects Administration, 1940.  Sponsored by the Arkansas History
    Commission.
Kane, John Ewing.  "Business Fluctuations in Arkansas since 1866."  Unpub-
    lished Master's thesis, School of Business Administration, University of
    Arkansas, 1939.
Mapes, Evert Eugene.  "Business Cycles in Arkansas."  Unpublished Master's
    thesis, School of Business Administration, University of Arkansas, 1938.
Mulhollen, Paige E.    "The Public Career of James H. Berry."  Unpublished
    Master's thesis, Department of History, University of Arkansas, 1962.
Walz, Robert B.    "Migration Into Arkansas, 1834–1880."  Unpublished Ph.D.
    dissertation, Department of History, University of Texas, 1958.  University
    of Arkansas Library, Microfilm 271.

# NOTES

## CHAPTER 1: THE THREE SOCIETIES

    1.  George C. Branner, *Geology of Arkansas: Surface and Below Surface.* Map. (Revised, Little Rock, Ark.: Arkansas Geological and Conservation Commission, 1959).

    2.  Discussions of this conflict can be found in the following: Jesse Turner, [Jr.], "The Convention of 1836," *Publications of the Arkansas Historical Association,* ed. John Hugh Reynolds (4 vols.; Fayetteville, Ark.: Arkansas Historical Association, 1906-1917), III, pp. 74-166; Dallas T. Herndon, *Centennial History of Arkansas* (4 vols.; Chicago, Ill.: S. J. Clarke Publishing Co., 1922), I, pp. 228-30; Maude Carmichael, "The Plantation System in Arkansas, 1850-1876" (unpublished Ph.D. dissertation, Dept. of Economics, Radcliffe College, 1935), pp. 42-44. University of Arkansas, Microfilm, 201.

    3.  Mattie Brown, "A History of River Tranportation in Arkansas from 1819-1880" (unpublished Master's thesis, Dept. of History, University of Arkansas, 1933), p. 4.

    4.  *Ibid.,* p. 7. Carmichael names Clarendon or Augusta as good low-water inland ports most of the year. Carmichael, *op. cit.*, pp. 161-62.

    5.  Brown, *op. cit.*, p. 43.

    6.  Carmichael, *loc. cit.*

    7.  *Ibid.*

    8.  Brown, *op. cit.,* p. 44.

    9.  From an article in *Niles Register*, 1840's, quoted by Brown, *ibid.*, p. 34.

  10.  *Ibid.*, p. 17.

  11.  F. P. Rose, "Butterfield Overland Mail Company," *Arkansas Historical Quarterly,* XV, No. 1 (Spring, 1956), pp. 68-69.

  12.  Letter from Grace J. Clark to Jesse Turner, Van Buren, Ark.; Little Rock, November 29, 1860. University of Arkansas, Jesse Turner Papers, MST 85, fol. 2.

  13.  Carmichael, *loc. cit.*

  14.  *Ibid.*, p. 160.

  15.  Cairo and Fulton Railroad Company, *Proceedings of the Second Annual Meeting of the Stockholders*, May 7, 1855. (Little Rock, Ark.: *True Democrat* Office, 1855), p. 14.

  16.  Carmichael, *op. cit.,* pp. 115-16. Miss Carmichael's study divides the state into six areas based on county boundaries of 1828. These are:

     I  Delta—Arkansas, Crittenden, St. Francis, Phillips, Chicot, and counties carved from these.

II   Hempstead—Hempstead, Sevier, Lafayette, Miller, and daughter counties.
III  Clark—counties lying partly in the Ouachita basin.
IV   Pulaski—Pulaski and Conway.
V    Crawford and Washington—mountainous areas on both sides of river above the
     center of the state.
VI   Lawrence, Izard, and Independence—the northern table lands. (p. 68)

Part of her description of the Hempstead area follows:

... first settlers who made up its population were in the migration that made the entire circuit chiefly from Virginia and North Carolina through Kentucky, Tennessee and Missouri into the State principally by way of the National Road. They were members of cultured and prominent slaveholding families in the old home states. They formed settlements at Washington, Columbus, Spring Hill and other towns to which their kinsmen and friends migrated. The population was thus united by ties of blood, friendship and a common culture. This unity was strengthened, on the one hand, by their relative isolation from the easier and more frequent contacts with the outside world enjoyed by the delta population, and on the other, by the contact made possible by the National Road which traversed the county. This road tended not only to equalize the advantages of transportation between the river and the upland planters, but to draw them closer together in their common desire to remove the Raft and establish better means of transportation. It aided also in developing a closer relationship between the entire planter society in all interests. While they lacked the stimulus of intellectual and social intercourse enjoyed by their delta neighbors, they had the distinction of developing their "old South" culture on new soils. They built schools and trained their sons in the arts of statesmanship. They were strongly national in their patriotism, and for the most part, Whig in politics. When the State seceded, however, they became defenders of the slave order, and assumed a leadership which was retained throughout the nineteenth century.

17.   U. S. Department of Agriculture, Soil Conservation Service, *Soil Association Map: State of Arkansas* (n.p.: Agricultural Extension Service, University of Arkansas, 1959).

18.   Derived by comparing the portion of bottomlands in a county with the percentage of slave population and per capita income in that county (1860) as shown by Ralph Wooster, "The Arkansas Secession Convention," *Arkansas Historical Quarterly,* XIII, No. 2 (Summer, 1954), pp. 189, 191.

19.   U. S. Bureau of the Census, *Tenth Census of the United States: 1880. Population,* I, maps opposite pp. 353, 369, 449. These indicate the population density of the residence in 1880 of the natives of the states of Alabama, Georgia, and Mississippi.

20.   *Roads, Old Trails, Traces and Historical Places of Arkansas.* Map. Results of a survey conducted by George F. Metzler, Extension Recreation Specialist, Agricultural Extension Service, University of Arkansas. Prepared by the Arkansas State Highway Department in cooperation with the U. S. Department of Commerce, 1965.

21.   The four counties on the Southwest Trail were Lawrence (1815), Pulaski (1818), Clark (1818), and Hempstead (1818). Arkansas (1813), the fifth county, was located in eastern Arkansas.

22.   Carmichael, *op. cit.* p. 208.

23.   There were five delta counties showing a per capita income of over $2,000 in 1860. Four of these had a slave population of over 50%; the fifth counted from 25% to 50%. In the southwest two counties had a slave population of over 50%, but their income was from $1,000 to $2,000 per capita. Wooster, *loc. cit.*

24.   Letter from David Walker to D. C. Williams, Van Buren, Ark.; Fayetteville, January 28, 1861. W. J. Lemke (comp. and ed.), *The Life and Letters of Judge David Walker.* (Fayetteville, Ark.: Washington County Historical Society, 1957), p. 43.

25.   David Walker reminded his people of this in his "Address to the People of Washington County," April 26, 1861. *Ibid.,* p. 101.

26.   Population statistics from U. S. Bureau of the Census, *Ninth Census of the United States: 1870. Population,* I, pp. 84, 85, 87, 89.

27.   Letter from David Walker to C. C. Scott, [Camden, Ark.]; Fayetteville, July 14, 1857. Lemke, *op. cit.,* pp. 39-40.

CHAPTER 2: PATRIOTISM: SECESSION

1.  D. C. Williams, Broadside "To the People of Arkansas," Van Buren, Ark., January 29, 1861. Photostat. A. Howard Stebbins, Jr., Documents and Currency, University of Arkansas Library.
2.  Ted R. Worley, "The Control of the Real Estate Bank of the State of Arkansas 1836-1855," *Mississippi Valley Historical Review*, XXXVII (December, 1950), p. 413.
3.  Carmichael, *op. cit.*, p. 34.
4.  Worley, *op. cit.*, p. 413n.
5.  John Hallum, *Biographical and Pictorial History of Arkansas* (Albany, N.Y.: Weed, Parsons and Co., 1887), I, p. 408; Jack B. Scroggs, "Arkansas in the Secession Crisis," *Arkansas Historical Quarterly*, XII, No. 3 (Autumn, 1953), p. 184.
6.  Herndon, *op. cit.*, p. 276; quoting Josiah Hazen Shinn, *Pioneers and Makers of Arkansas* (n.p.:Genealogical and Historical Publishing Co., 1908).
7.  Svend Peterson, "Arkansas in Presidential Elections," *Arkansas Historical Quarterly*, VII, No. 3 (Autumn, 1948), pp. 207-208.
8.  *Gazette*, August 11, 1860, p. 2, c. 2. The *Arkansas Gazette*, important Little Rock newspaper, was published under various titles during its history. For the purposes of this study, references to it will be made in the abbreviated form, the *Gazette*.
9.  *Ibid.*, August 25, 1860, p. 3, c. 1; *ibid.*, September 1, 1860, p. 2, c. 1.
10.  *Ibid.*, October 20, 1860, p. 2, c. 6.
11.  Walter L. Brown, "Albert Pike" (unpublished Ph.D. dissertation, Dept. of History, University of Texas, 1955), p. 522. University of Arkansas, Microfilm 80.
12.  Albert Webb Bishop, *Loyalty on the Frontier* (St. Louis, Mo.: R. P. Studley & Co., 1863), pp. 19-20.
13.  Carmichael, *op. cit.*, p. 273.
14.  *Gazette*, November 17, 1860, p. 2, cc. 2-3.
15.  *Ibid.*, December 22, 1860, p. 2, c. 2.
16.  *Ibid.*, December 8, 1860, p. 2, cc. 2-3.
17.  Clio Harper (comp.), "Early Arkansas Bar," ( n.p.:typescript arranged and bound by the Work Projects Administration for the Arkansas History Commission, 1940), p. 371.
18.  Letter from Jesse Turner to the Editor of the *New York Express*, New York, N. Y.; Van Buren, Ark., December 10, 1860. Duke University, Jesse Turner Papers. Hereafter these will be referred to as the Turner Papers.
19.  *Gazette*, December 22, 1860, p. 1, cc. 5-6.
20.  *Ibid.*, p. 1, c. 7.
21.  *Ibid.*, p. 1, c. 8.
22.  "In reply to your inquiry, I have to say that I think there is not a rational hope of preserving the Union. Don't despair of the republic." Telegram from J. J. Crittenden to Jesse Turner, Van Buren, Ark.; Washington, D. C., December 29, 1860. Duke University, Turner Papers.
23.  Fay Hempstead, *Historical Review of Arkansas: Its Commerce, Industry, and Modern Affairs* (Chicago, Ill.: The Lewis Publishing Co., 1911), I., p. 209.
24.  *Gazette*, January 19, 1861, p. 2, c. 2.
25.  Letter to the Editor of the *Gazette* from W[illiam] Q[uesenberry], Fayetteville, Ark.; February 18, 1861. *Ibid.*, March 2, 1861, p. 2, c. 4.
26.  Behind this strong emphasis on letting the people decide was a dissatisfaction with the convention bill, which did not require referral to the people of the action taken by the Convention. David Walker, Jesse Turner, D. C. Williams, and others campaigned for the election of delegates pledged to return the matter to the people. In this way they hoped to correct what they considered to be an error in the convention bill. Letter from David Walker to D. C. Williams, Van Buren, Ark.; Underwood, January 29, 1861. Lemke, *op. cit.*, pp. 44-45.
27.  The following letters reflect the influence of Williams' work during this period: William Fishback to Williams, Greenwood, Ark., January 29, 1861; J. M. Tebbetts to Williams (telegram), Fayetteville, Ark., February 2, 1861; J. W. Talkington to Williams,

260NOTES

Hebron, Ark., February 4, 1861; Samuel L. Griffith to Williams, Fort Smith, Ark., February 4, 1861; John Smith to Williams, Osage Mill, Ark., February 7, 1861; James Grieg to Williams, [n.p.], February 9, 1861; W. F. Holtzman to Williams, Little Rock, Ark., February 10, 1861; Benjamin Callender to Williams, Boston, Mass., February 13, 1861; S. J. Howell to Williams, Oxford, Ohio, February 16, 1861; B. M. Colman to Williams, St. Louis, Mo., February 16, 1861. Arkansas History Commission, D. C. Williams Papers.

28.    Influential speakers in the canvass included the following:

| Union Speakers | | Secessionist Speakers |
|---|---|---|
| David Walker | Washington County | U. S. Senator Robert W. Johnson |
| Thomas M. Gunter | Washington County | Governor Henry M. Rector |
| Hugh F. Thomason | Crawford County | Richard H. Johnson |
| Jesse Turner | Crawford County | Thomas C. Hindman |
| Isaac Murphy | Madison County | None of these men |
| William M. Fishback | Sebastian County | were candidates for |
| Jesse Cypert | White County | the Convention. |
| All of these men became | | |
| members of the Convention. | | |

Carmichael, *op. cit.,* p. 273.

29.    David Y. Thomas (ed.), *Arkansas and Its People: A History, 1541-1930.* 4 vols. (New York: American Historical Society, 1930), I, p. 121.

30.    Carmichael, *op. cit.,* p. 274.

31.    *Gazette,* February 23, 1861, p. 2, c. 4; *ibid.,* March 2, 1861, p. 2, c. 4.

32.    *Ibid.,* March 9, 1861, p. 2, c. 5.

33.    Only two men who had voted for Walker for president of the Convention voted in favor of the Hanly resolution to secede. One of these was B. C. Totten, Walker's opponent for the office, who had given him a courtesy vote. Of those voting for Totten for president, only David Walker voted against the Hanly motion. Jesse Cypert, "Secession," *Publications, op. cit.,* I, p. 315; Wooster, *op. cit.,* Appendix I.

34.    Letter from Jesse Turner to his wife, Rebecca, Van Buren, Ark.; Little Rock, March 7, 1861. Duke University, Turner Papers.

35.    *Ibid.*

36.    A. H. Carrigan, "Reminiscences of the Secession Convention," Part I, *Publications, op. cit.,* I, p. 306.

37.    Letter from Jesse Turner to his wife, Rebecca, Van Buren, Ark.; Little Rock, March 9, 1861. Duke University, Turner Papers.

38.    Letter from D. C. Williams to Jesse Turner, Little Rock, Ark.; Van Buren, March 11, 1861; Letter from Williams to Turner, Little Rock, Ark.; Van Buren, March 15, 1861. Duke University, Turner Papers.

39.    Letter from Jesse Turner to his wife, Rebecca, Van Buren, Ark.; Little Rock, March 19, 1861. Duke University, Turner Papers. Ralph Wooster gives the vote as being forty to thirty-four. Wooster, *loc. cit.*

40.    Turner to Rebecca, *op. cit.*

41.    Letter from E. P. Lane to D. C. Williams, Van Buren, Ark.; Little Rock, March 19, 1861. Arkansas History Commission, D. C. Williams Papers.

42.    Letter from William M. Fishback to D. C. Williams, Van Buren, Ark.; Greenwood, April 10, 1861. Duke University, Turner Papers.

43.    Letter from William Stout to Jesse Turner, Van Buren, Ark.; Dover, April 14, 1861. Duke University, Turner Papers.

44.    Lemke, *op. cit.,* p. 102.

45.    Letter from W. W. Mansfield to Jesse Turner, Van Buren, Ark.; Ozark, April 15, 1861. Duke University, Turner Papers.

46.    Letter from A. W. Hobson to Jesse Turner, Van Buren, Ark.; Camden, April 16, 1861. Duke University, Turner Papers.

47.    Letter from G. W. Lemoyne to Jesse Turner, Van Buren, Ark.; Dardanelle, April 17, 1861. Duke University, Turner Papers.

48. Letter from S. J. Stallings to Jesse Turner, Van Buren, Ark.; Lewisburg, April 19, 1861. Duke University, Turner Papers.

49. Letter from Thomas B. Hanly to David Walker, Fayetteville, Ark.; Helena, April 17, 1861. University of Arkansas, David Walker Letters, MS W 15, fol. 1. Hereafter these will be referred to as the Walker Letters.

50. Letter from L. R. Cockrill to Governor Henry M. Rector, Little Rock, Ark.; Memphis, Tenn., April 18, 1861. University of Arkansas, Microfilm, 109. Arkansas Manuscripts selected by Walter L. Brown, in the Manuscripts Division, Library of Chicago Historical Society.

51. *Gazette,* April 20, 1861, p. 2, c. 3. A. H. Garland and J. Stillwell, Union delegates from Little Rock, were out of town when the address was signed. A week later they explained their absence and strongly endorsed the address. *Ibid.*, April 27, 1861, p. 2, c. 3.

52. Hempstead, *op. cit.*, p. 213.

53. "Thus situated it seems to me, that we should make the issue broadly at the polls, in the approaching election, and to exact of every candidate who runs *a positive unequivocal pledge* that in no event will he take any step to disturb our present federal relations or to inaugerate [*sic*] any new Government that is to bind the people before it is referred back to them [to] be voted upon and approved." Letter from David Walker to D. C. Williams, Van Buren, Ark.; Underwood, January 29, 1861. Arkansas History Commission, D. C. Williams Papers.

54. Lemke, *op. cit.*, pp. 101-102.

55. Bishop, *op. cit.*, p. 180.

56. *Ibid.*, p. 25.

57. *Ibid.*, p. 22.

58. *Ibid.*, p. 92. Members of Bishop's triumverate included: Thomas M. Gunter, David Walker, and John Parks. All were delegates to the Convention from Washington County.

59. *Ibid.*, pp. 178-79.

60. *Gazette,* April 20, 1861. p. 2, c. 2.; *ibid.,* March 30, 1861, p. 2, c. 4.

61. *Ibid.*, April 20, 1861, p. 2, c. 2.

62. Letter from George C. Watkins to David Walker, Fayetteville, Ark.; Little Rock, April 19, 1861. Arkansas History Commission, Robert W. Trimble Collection.

63. Letter from C. C. Danley to W. W. Mansfield, Ozark, Ark.; Steam Boat *Tahlequah*, April 23, 1861. Arkansas History Commission, W. W. Mansfield Papers.

64. Letter from Jesse Turner to his wife, Rebecca, [Pennsylvania] ; Van Buren, May 2, 1861. Duke University, Turner Papers.

65. Letter from D. C. Williams to Jesse Turner, Little Rock, Ark.; Van Buren, May 7, 1861. Duke University, Turner Papers.

66. Hempstead, *op. cit.*, p. 213.

67. Cypert, *op. cit.*, p. 318; Walker quoted by Cypert from memory, *ibid.*, p. 319. The five negative votes were cast by:

> H. H. Bolinger, Madison County
> Isaac Murphy, Madison County
> John Campbell, Searcy County
> Samuel Kelley, Pike County
> T. M. Gunter, Washington County

68. Carrigan, *op. cit.,* pp. 312-13; Cypert, *loc. cit.*

69. Hempstead, *op. cit.*, p. 213.

70. Letter from James Grieg to D. C. Williams, Van Buren, Ark.; n.p., May 9, 1861. Arkansas History Commission, D. C. Williams Papers.

71. Letter from Jesse Turner to his wife, Rebecca, Pittsburgh, Penn.; Little Rock, May 8, 1861. Duke University, Turner Papers.

72. *Ibid.*

CHAPTER 3: PATRIOTISM: AMNESTY

1.  Letter from John MacLean to General D. H. Reynolds, n.p.; Bayou Mason, Chicot County Ark., October 16, 1864. University of Arkansas, David Harris Reynolds Papers, MS R 32, fol. 4. Hereafter these will be referred to as the Reynolds Papers.
2.  Letter from George C. Watkins to David Walker, Fayetteville, Ark.; Little Rock, August 22, 1868. University of Arkansas, Walker Letters, fol. 3.
3.  Letter from J. J. Walker to W. W. Mansfield, Ozark, Ark.; Camp near Cassville, Mo., July 31, 1861. Arkansas History Commission, W. W. Mansfield Papers.
4.  Letter from Brigadier General Ben McCulloch to Governor Henry M. Rector, Little Rock, Ark.; Headquarters, Camp Jackson, Ark.; September 25, 1861. University of Arkansas, Single Letters, MS L 34.
5.  Letter from Henry M. Rector [Governor of Arkansas] to W. F. Pickens [Governor of South Carolina], n.p.; Little Rock, April 11, 1862. University of Arkansas, Letters Illustrative of Arkansas History, 1838 – 1865, box 1. Photostat. Original in the Illinois State Historical Library.
6.  Letter from P. B. Cox to Governor Henry M. Rector, Little Rock, Ark.; Perry County at Brown's Landing, July 15, 1861. University of Arkansas, Microfilm, 109. Original in the Library of Chicago Historical Society.
7.  Bishop, *op. cit.*, p. 11.
8.  *Ibid.*, p. 7.
9.  Copy of letter from D. H. Reynolds to the Editor of the *Advertiser*, Montgomery, Ala., September 7, 1863. University of Arkansas, Reynolds Papers, fol. 1.
10. Carmichael,, *op. cit.*, p. 294.
11. *Ibid.*, pp. 300 – 301.
12. John MacLean to D. H. Reynolds, *op. cit.* -
13. Letter from D. H. Reynolds to President Andrew Johnson, Washington, D. C.; Lake Village, Ark., August 22, 1865. U. S. National Archives, Records of the War Department, the Adjutant General's Office. Record Group No. 94. *Amnesty Papers Arkansas* (Washington, D. C.: National Archives and Records Service, 1959). University of Arkansas, Microfilm, 375. Hereafter these will be referred to as *Amnesty Papers*.
14. Letter from D. H. Reynolds to Major D. W. Sanders, Headquarters 1st Ark. Mounted Riflemen, McNair's Brigade, January 18, 1864. University of Arkansas, Reynolds Papers, fol. 2.
15  *Ibid.*, endorsement of Reynolds' letter by Maj. D. W. Landers by command of Ma, General French, January 18, 1864.
16. Letter from Robert W. Johnson to D. H. Reynolds, n.p.; [Richmond, Va.], March 14, 1864. University of Arkansas, Reynolds Papers, fol. 2.
17. Letter from A. H. Garland to D. H. Reynolds, n.p., Richmond, Va., April 18, 1864. University of Arkansas, Reynolds Papers, fol. 2.
18. Reynolds to President Johnson, *op. cit.*
19. Letter from D. H. Reynolds to Hon. Henry Stansberry [*sic*] [U. S. Attorney General], [Washington, D. C.]; Lake Village, Ark., September 29, 1866. *Amnesty Papers.*
20. Letter from E. C. Walthall to General D. H. Reynolds, [Lake Village, Ark.]; Holly Springs, Miss., August 1, 1865. University of Arkansas, Reynolds Papers, fol. 5.
21. Letter from D. H. Reynolds to President Andrew Johnson, [Washington, D. C.]; Lake Village, Ark., October 25, 1866. *Amnesty Papers.*
22. Executive order of the President, November 13, 1866. *Amnesty Papers.*
23. Herndon, *op. cit.*, p. 606.
24. *Ibid.*, p. 607.
25. Virgil L. Jones, "Arkansas Literature," Thomas, *op. cit.*, II, p. 577.
26. Herndon, *loc. cit.*
27. Worley, *op. cit.*, p. 423.
28. Herndon, *op. cit.*, p. 607.
29. Letter from Albert Pike to President Andrew Johnson, Washington, D. C., Memphis, Tenn, June 24, 1865. *Amnesty Papers.* ·

30. *Ibid.*, letter from B. B. French to James Speed [U. S. Attorney General], Washington, D. C.; Washington, January 5, 1865 [6]. *Amnesty Papers.*

31. Pike to President Johnson, *op. cit.*

32. Henry Steele Commager (ed.), *Documents of American History* (7th ed.; New York: Appleton Century Crofts, 1963), I, p. 457.

33. Letter from B. B. French to President Andrew Johnson, Washington, D. C.; Washington, July 1, 1865. *Amnesty Papers.*

34. Affidavit by Albert Pike, August 4, 1865. *Amnesty Papers.*

35. Petition signed by fourteen Masonic Brothers to President Andrew Johnson, Washington, D. C.; Memphis, Tenn., June 26, 1865. *Amnesty Papers.*

36. Letter from B. B. French to President Andrew Johnson, Washington, D. C.; Washington, July 1, 1865; letter from B. B. French to President Andrew Johnson, Washington, D. C.; Washington, July 6, 1865; letter from B. B. French to Attorney General James Speed, Washington, D. C.; Washington, January 5, 1865 [6]. *Amnesty Papers.*

37. Letter from A. T. C. Pierson *et al.* to President Andrew Johnson, Washington, D. C.; New York, N. Y., July [n.d.], 1865. *Amnesty Papers.*

38. Letter from Albert Pike to B. B. French, [Washington, D. C.]; Little Rock, December 13, 1865. *Amnesty Papers.*

39. Letter from Tal P. Shaffner to Attorney General James Speed, Washington, D. C.; n.p., April 20, 1866. *Amnesty Papers.*

40. Executive order from the President to the Attorney General, Executive Mansion, April 22, 1866. *Amnesty Papers.*

41. Brown, "Albert Pike," pp. 780–81.

42. *Ibid.*, p. 796.

43. *Ibid.*, p. 835.

44. Walter L. Brown, "The Henry M. Rector Claim to the Hot Springs of Arkansas," *Arkansas Historical Quarterly,* XV, No. 4 (Winter, 1956), pp. 283, 292.

45. *Ibid.*, pp. 285–86.

46. *Ibid.*, pp. 289–90; *Hot Springs Cases,* 92 U. S. 698 (1876).

47. Brown, *op. cit.*, p. 291.

48. Elsie M. Lewis, "Robert Ward Johnson: Militant Spokesman of the Old South-West," *Arkansas Historical Quarterly,* XIII, No. 1 (Spring, 1954), p. 30.

49. Robert B. Walz, "Arkansas Slaveholdings and Slaveholders in 1850," *Arkansas Historical Quarterly,* XII, No. 1 (Spring, 1953), p. 62; letter from Robert W. Johnson to Hon. Preston King [Senator from New York], n.p.; Marlin Falls County, Texas, August 16, 1865. *Amnesty Papers.*

50. Lewis, *loc. cit.*

51. Carrigan, *op. cit.*, p. 308. The delegates to the Provisional Congress were: Robert W. Johnson, Augustus H. Garland, Hugh F. Thomason, W. W. Watkins, and Albert Rust. Except for Johnson, these men had been Union men prior to April 15, 1861.

52. Letter from Robert W. Johnson to President Andrew Johnson, [Washington, D. C.]; Galveston, Texas, June 27, 1865. *Amnesty Papers.*

53. Letter from Robert W. Johnson to Maj. General Gordon Granger, Commanding District of Texas, [Galveston, Texas]; n.p., June 19, 1865. *Amnesty Papers.*

54. Robert W. Johnson to President Johnson, *op. cit.*

55. Endorsement of Robert W. Johnson's letter to President Andrew Johnson, June 27, 1865, by Maj. General Gordon Granger, Galveston, Texas, July 1, 1865. *Amnesty Papers.*

56. Letter from Robert W. Johnson to Preston King, n.p.; Marlin Falls County, Texas, August 16, 1865. *Amnesty Papers.*

57. *Dictionary of American Biography,* eds. Allen Johnson and Dumas Malone (21 vols., including index col.; New York, Charles Scribner's Son, 1928-37), X, p. 397.

58. Robert W. Johnson to Preston King, *op. cit.*

59. Letter from Robert W. Johnson to Preston King, n.p.; Marlin [Falls], Texas, August 19, 1865. *Amnesty Papers.*

60. Letter from Preston King to President Johnson, Washington, D. C.; New York, September 25, 1865; Executive Order from President Johnson to Attorney General [Speed],

September 28, 1865; letter from Preston King to President Andrew Johnson, Washington, D. C.; New York, October 2, 1865. *Amnesty Papers.*

61.  Endorsement of [Robert W. Johnson] by Isaac Murphy, Little Rock, Ark., October 28, 1865. *Amnesty Papers.*

62.  Letter from Robert W. Johnson to Colonel Wright Rives, n.p.; Pine Bluff, Ark., April 6, 1866. *Amnesty Papers.*

63.  *Amnesty Papers.*

64.  Lewis, *op. cit.*, p. 30.

65.  Garland became Attorney General in President Cleveland's Cabinet, 1885–1889.

66.  Hallum, *op. cit.*, p. 382.

67.  Hempstead, *op. cit.*, p. 281.

68.  Hallum, *op. cit.*, p. 381.

69.  *Ex parte Garland,* 71 U. S. 333 (1867); Hallum, *loc cit.*

70.  *Ibid.,* pp. 381–82.

71.  Letter from Augustus H. Garland to President Andrew Johnson, Washington, D. C.; Little Rock, June 28, 1865. *Amnesty Papers.*

72.  Carrigan, *op. cit.*, p. 307.

73.  Hempstead, *op. cit.*, p. 283.

74.  Augustus H. Garland to President Johnson, *op. cit.*

75.  *Ibid.;* Thomas S. Staples, *Reconstruction in Arkansas, 1862-1874* (New York: Longmans, Green & Co., 1923), p. 59, p. 59n. A. H. Garland and Judge J. J. Clendenin were commissioners appointed by Governor Flanagin on May 22, 1865. But Garland would have the President believe his mission was more successful than it was. General Reynolds refused to meet them as commissioners. Garland and others were allowed to see him as private citizens, but he rejected almost totally the terms of a plan of adjustment submitted by them.

76.  Augustus H. Garland to President Johnson, *op. cit.*

77.  Endorsement by Elisha Baxter of Garland's letter to the President, Little Rock, June 28, 1865. *Amnesty Papers.* [endorsement of William M. Fishback recorded, but the document is missing.]

78.  Endorsement of Powell Clayton recorded, but the document is missing. *Amnesty Papers.*

79.  Endorsement of Major General J. J. Reynolds, Headquarters, Department of Arkansas, Little Rock, June 30, 1865. *Amnesty Papers.*

80.  Endorsement of C. V. Meador; endorsement of Robert J. T. White, Secretary of State of Arkansas, *Amnesty Papers.*

81.  Staples, *op. cit.*, p. 12.

82.  Letter from E. W. Gantt to Secretary of State William H. Seward, [Washington, D. C.]; Little Rock, June 29, 1865. *Amnesty Papers.*

83.  Endorsement of Governor Isaac Murphy, n.p.; n.d. *Amnesty Papers.*

84.  Letter from Secretary of Interior James Harlan to President Andrew Johnson, [Washington, D. C.]. Washington, July 10, 1865. *Amnesty Papers.*

85.  Special Order of the President, July 15, 1865. *Amnesty Papers.*

86.  Letter from David Walker to President Andrew Johnson, Washington, D. C.; Little Rock, September 14, 1865. *Amnesty Papers.*

87.  Letter from Lt. Colonel Frederick William Lewis, Commanding 1st Missouri Cavalry, to David Walker, Fayetteville, Ark.; Camp at White River, March 30, 1862. *Amnesty Papers.* Walker's dislocation probably resulted from the aftermath of the Battle of Pea Ridge fought March 7, 1862, about forty miles north of Fayetteville.

88.  Letter from David Walker to his daughter, Mary (Mrs. J. D. Walker), n.p.; Washington, Ark., January 22, 1865. Lemke, *op. cit.*, p. 17.

89.  Harper, *op. cit.*, p. 378.

90.  Letter from David Walker to "Dear Sir," n.p.; Underwood, April 3, 1860. University of Arkansas, Walker Letters, fol. 1; Bishop, *op. cit.*, p. 180.

91.  Letter from David Walker to Christopher C. Scott, [Camden, Ark.]; Fayetteville, May 28, 1855. Lemke, *op. cit.*, p. 31.

92.  Wooster, *op. cit.*, Appendix I.
93.  Letter from David Walker to "Dear Sir," n.p.; Underwood, April 3, 1860. University of Arkansas, Walker Letters, fol. 1.
94.  Letter from David Walker to "Dear Sir," n.p.; Underwood, May 9, 1860. University of Arkansas, Walker Letters, fol. 1.
95.  The last letter known to be written from Fayetteville was dated October 8, 1862. The first letter received by Walker sent to Lewisburg was April 30, 1863. Letter from David Walker to D. C. Williams, [Van Buren, Ark.]; [Fayetteville], October 8, 1862. Arkansas History Commission, D. C. Williams Papers; letter from George C. Watkins to David Walker, Lewisburg, Ark.; Little Rock, April 30, 1863. Arkansas History Commission, A. Howard Stebbins, Jr. Collection, lot D.
96.  Hempstead *op. cit.*, p. 227.
97.  *Ibid.*, p. 230.
98.  Lemke, *op. cit.*, p. 27. Walker's colleagues on the military tribunal were George C. Watkins of Little Rock and Trusten Polk of St. Louis.
99.  *Ibid.*, p. 53.
100.  *Ibid.*, p. 50.
101.  *Ibid.*, p. 53.
102.  Letter from David Walker to Judge Hiram Davis, [Ft. Worth, Texas]; Lewisville, Ark., April 27, 1864. *Ibid.*, p. 72.
103.  Letter from David Walker to his daughter, Mary (Mrs. J. D. Walker), n.p.; Washington, Ark., January 22, 1865. *Ibid.*, pp. 9–18; letter from David Walker to his daughter, Mary, n.p.; Washington, Ark., February 10, 1865. *Ibid.*, pp. 18–22.
104.  Unfinished letter from David Walker to "Dear Sir," n.p.; Lewisville, Ark., May 6, 1865. *Ibid.*, p. 52.
105.  Letter from George C. Watkins to David Walker, Corsicana, Texas; Little Rock, July 12, 1865. University of Arkansas, Walker Letters, fol. 2.
106.  Letter from David Walker to President Andrew Johnson, [Washington, D. C.], Little Rock, September 14, 1865. *Amnesty Papers.*
107.  John M. Harrell, *The Brooks and Baxter War: A History of the Reconstruction Period in Arkansas* (St. Louis, Mo.: Slawson Printing Co., 1893), p. 11.
108.  Endorsement by Governor Isaac Murphy, Little Rock, Ark., September 14, 1865. *Amnesty Papers.*
109.  *Amnesty Papers.*
110.  Letter from Isaac Murphy to David Walker, [Fayetteville, Ark.]; Little Rock, May 16, 1866. Arkansas History Commission, A. Howard Stebbins, Jr. Collection, lot D.
111.  *Washington Telegraph*, July 18, 1866, p. 2, c. 1.

## CHAPTER 4: THE PROBLEM STATED

1.  *Hawkins v. Filkins*, 24 Ark. 310–11 (1866).
2.  *Ibid.*, pp. 294–95.
3.  *Ibid.*, 288, 292. Lawyers for Hawkins were Rose, Gallagher and Newton with Garland and Nash, while Filkins was defended by B. F. Rice.
4.  Letter from David Walker to Robert W. Trimble, Pine Bluff, Ark.; Fayetteville, July 5, 1876. Arkansas History Commission, Robert W. Trimble Collection; also in Lemke, *op. cit.*, pp. 90–91. A. H. Garland considered the decision important enough to send a copy to Alexander H. Stephens. Letter from A. H. Garland to Alexander H. Stephens, n.p.; Little Rock, February 26, 1876. Library of Congress, Alexander H. Stephens Papers.
5.  *Hawkins v. Filkins, op. cit.*, pp. 310–11.
6.  *Ibid.*, p. 326.
7.  Hiram Davis, "Biographical Sketch of David Walker." Arkansas History Commission, Robert W. Trimble Collection. This manuscript was written in 1876 by Walker's friend, Judge Hiram Davis. As Davis expressed it, "Refusing to take the test oath imposed by the reconstruction acts of Congress, he retired from public life, and passed his time in the

management of his private affairs, and improvements of his farm, in which he took great delight, until the sudden and complete collapse of the Clayton despotism in the year 1874, when he was called by the voice of the people again to the bench of the Supreme Court, . . ."

8. Walter J. Lemke in Lemke, *op. cit.*, p. 3.

9. Staples, *op. cit.*, p. 130.

10. Letter from F. W. Compton to David Walker, Fayetteville, Ark.; Princeton, [Ark.], May 4, 1867. University of Arkansas, Walker Letters, fol. 3.

11. Letter from John R. Eakin to David Walker [Little Rock, Ark.] ; Washington, Ark., June 18, 1867. University of Arkansas, Walker Letters, fol. 3.

12. Letter from J. J. Clendenin to David Walker, Fayetteville, Ark.; Little Rock, July 31, 1867. University of Arkansas, Walker Letters, fol. 3.

13. Staples, *op. cit.*, p. 135.

14. Copy of letter from J. J. Clendenin to Major General E. O. C. Ord, Vicksburg, Miss.; Little Rock, August 16, 1867. University of Arkansas, Walker Letters, fol. 3.

15. Staples, *op. cit.*, pp. 137–40, *passim.*

16. *Ibid.*, pp. 132–33.

17. *Ibid.*, pp. 154, 175.

18. Letter from John R. Eakin to David Walker, Fayetteville, Ark.; Washington, August 27, 1867. University of Arkansas, Walker Letters, fol. 3.

19. *Debates and Proceedings of the Constitution Convention, 1868* (Little Rock: J. G. Price, 1868), pp. 27–31.

20. Carmichael, *op. cit.*, p. 42.

21. *Ibid.*, pp. 43–44.

22. Herndon, *op. cit.*, pp. 229–30.

23. C. G. "Crip" Hall, *Historical Report of the Secretary of State* (Little Rock, Ark.: State of Arkansas, 1958), pp. 267–69.

24. *Debates and Proceedings, op. cit.*, p. 769.

25. *Ibid.*; U. S. Bureau of the Census, *Ninth Census: 1870. Population,* I, p. 623. Calculated from material derived from these sources.

26. The basis for this estimate is shown below:

| | | | Estimated adult male population, 1867 | | | 92,972[a] |
| Less estimated adult male population of Pulaski County | | | | | | 7,470[b] |
| | | | Estimated adult male population of the three societies | | | 85,502 |
| | *Estimated Adult*[c] *Male Population, 1867 (estimated)* | | *Registered*[d] *Voters* | *Unregistered (estimated)* | *Voting* | *Registered Not Voting* |
|---|---|---|---|---|---|---|
| NW | (40%) | (34,201) | 18,902 | (15,299) | 9,864 | 9,038 |
| D | (34%) | (29,071) | 23,893 | ( 5,178) | 13,816 | 10,077 |
| SW | (26%) | (22,230) | 20,727 | ( 1,503) | 10,941 | 9,786 |
| | | (85,502) | 63,522 | (21,980) | 34,621 | 28,901 |

a. This figure was calculated at 20% of the estimated total population for 1867. Total population in 1867 was estimated at the 1860 total population plus 60% of the difference between 1860 and 1870 totals.

b. The figure 92,972 is 89% of the adult male count in 1870; 7,740 is 88% of the Pulaski adult male count in 1870.

c. The estimated percentage in each area was based on the percentage in that area of the adult male population in 1870.

d. *Debates and Proceedings, op. cit.*, p. 769.

e. *Ibid.*, p. 770.

27. Hall, *loc. cit.; Debates and Proceedings, op. cit.*, p. 31. Calculations have been based on these sources. The other areas had representation as follows:

|           | *1860* | *1867* |
|-----------|--------|--------|
| Delta     | 27.9%  | 38%    |
| Southwest | 25%    | 30.3%  |

28.  *Ibid.*, p. 770. Note: a large part of the difference in the number of registered voters not voting reported here and those reported in footnote twenty-six is due to differences appearing in the unofficial sources, which had to be used there, and the official totals used here. Official totals reported 41,134 voting; unofficial totals reported 39,130.

29.  *Ibid.*, pp. 769-70. Calculations have been based on this source, i.e., the unofficial returns.

30.  Herndon, *op. cit.*, p. 1010.

31.  Carmichael, *op. cit.*, pp. 356-57.

32.  Constitution of the State of Arkansas, 1868, Article XIV, *Debates and Proceedings, op. cit.*, pp. 888-89. It is ironic to note that David Walker's successor as Chief Justice of the Arkansas Supreme Court, John McClure, was on the Apportionment Committee. *Ibid.*, p. 61.

33.  Constitution of the State of Arkansas, 1868, Article V, sect. 8, *ibid.*, p. 862.

34.  Roster of the seventeenth General Assembly (November 17, 1868 to April 10, 1869), Hall, *op. cit.*, pp. 275-77. Calculations have been based on this source.

35.  *Gazette*, February 25, 1868, p. 1, cc. 1-2. Also see map p. 70.

36.  *Ninth Census, op. cit.*, pp. 13-14. Calculations have been based on this source.

37.  *Ibid.*; also Hall, *op. cit.*, pp. 267-69, 275-77. Calculations have been based on this source.

38.  Staples, *op. cit.*, p. 252n.

39.  *Ibid.*, p. 249.

40.  *Ibid.*, p. 250.

41.  *Ibid.*, p. 257.

42.  Letter from George C. Watkins to David Walker, Fayetteville, Ark.; Little Rock, March 6, 1868. University of Arkansas, Walker Letters, fol. 3.

43.  Letter from William E. Woodruff, Jr. to David Walker, Fayetteville, Ark.; Little Rock, March 3, 1868. Arkansas History Commission, A. Howard Stebbins, Jr. Collection, lot D; letter from George C. Watkins to David Walker, Fayetteville, Ark.; Little Rock, March 13, 1868. University of Arkansas, Walker Letters, fol. 3. *Ex parte McCardle, 73 U. S. 318 (1867)*.

44.  Watkins to Walker, March 13, 1868, *op. cit.*

45.  Staples, *op. cit.*, pp. 260-61.

46.  Letter from George C. Watkins to David Walker, Fayetteville, Ark.; Little Rock March 29, 1868. Arkansas History Commission, A. Howard Stebbins, Jr. Collection, lot D.

47.  Staples, *op. cit.*, p. 262.

48.  *Ibid.*, p. 261; *Debates and Proceedings, op. cit.*, p. 795.

49.  *Ibid.*, p. 806.

50.  *Ibid.*, p. 807. Calculations have been based on these figures.

51.  *Ibid.*

52.  *Ibid.*

53.  *Ibid.*, p. 809.

54.  Staples, *op. cit.*, pp. 264-67, *passim.*

55.  Watkins to Walker, March 6, 1868, *op. cit.*; letter from J. J. Clendenin to David Walker, Fayetteville, Ark.; Little Rock, April 15, 1868. University of Arkansas, Walker Letters, fol. 3.

56.  Letter from George C. Watkins to David Walker, Fayetteville, Ark.; Little Rock, March 13, 1868; letter from George C. Watkins to David Walker, Fayetteville, Ark.; Little Rock, June 9, 1868. University of Arkansas, Walker Letters, fol. 3.

57.  Staples, *op. cit.*, p. 262.

58.  Clendenin to Walker, April 15, 1868, *op. cit.*

59.  *Debates and Proceedings, loc. cit.*

60.  Staples, *op. cit.*, p. 288.

61. *Ibid.*, p. 333.
62. Letter from F. W. Compton to David Walker, Fayetteville, Ark.; Little Rock, June 25, 1868. University of Arkansas, Walker Letters, fol. 3.
63. *Ibid.*

## CHAPTER 5: A DIFFERENCE REGARDING MEANS

1. Value of real and personal estate:

|       | 1860 *Aggregate Value*[a] | 1870 *Total Valuation*[b] |
|-------|---------------------------|---------------------------|
| NW    | $ 57,819,944              | $ 51,408,006              |
| D     | 113,998,956               | 56,398,553                |
| SW    | 70,628,870                | 26,148,456                |
|       | $242,447,770              | $133,954,995              |

a.   U. S. Bureau of the Census, *Eighth Census of the United States: 1860. Social Statistics,* IV, p. 296. Calculations have been based on this source.
b.   U. S. Bureau of the Census, *Ninth Census of the United States: 1870. Wealth and Industry,* III, pp. 16–17. Calculations have been based on this source.

2. Letter from John R. Eakin to David Walker, Fayetteville, Ark.; Washington, Ark.; June 28, 1868. University of Arkansas, Walker Letters, fol. 3.
3. Letter by the wife of the owner of Grassmede Plantation, Phillips County, June 20, 1865, quoted by Carmichael, *op. cit.*, p. 429.
4. From an unpublished "Journal of a Southern Woman Living on a Plantation in Phillips County" (1863–1864), quoted by Carmichael, *ibid.*, p. 298.
5. *Ninth Census, op. cit.,* pp. 13–14. Calculations have been based on these figures.
6. *Fayetteville Democrat*, January 30, 1869, p. 2, c. 1.
7. *Ibid.*, October 9, 1869, p. 2, c. 4.
8. *Ibid.*, November 12, 1860, p. 2, c. 2.
9. Evert Eugene Mapes, "Business Cycles in Arkansas" (Unpublished Master's thesis, School of Business Administration, University of Arkansas, 1938), p. 37.
10. *Ibid.*, p. 137.
11. John Ewing Kane, "Business Fluctuations in Arkansas since 1866" (unpublished Master's thesis, School of Business Administration, University of Arkansas, 1939).
12. Carmichael, *op. cit.*, p. 483.
13. *Ibid.*, p. 548.
14. *Ibid., passim,* especially pp. 319–30 and pp. 483–550.
15. *Ibid.*, p. 532.
16. *Gazette*, December 4, 1868, p. 4, c. 2. Staples' estimate is 93,500, the difference being his estimate of 500 carpetbaggers instead of the *Gazette's* estimate of 1,500. Staples, *op. cit.*, p. 278.
17. *Gazette, loc. cit.*
18. Staples, *op. cit.*, p. 278n.
19. *Ibid.*, pp. 277–78.
20. Letter from Governor Powell Clayton [J. H. Burton, Private Secretary] to all Assessors, Little Rock, January 24, 1870. Arkansas History Commission, Clayton Letterbook, pp. 40–41.
21. Staples, *loc cit.*
22. Clayton Letterbook, *op. cit., passim.*
23. Letter from Powell Clayton to E. P. Jones, Knowlton, Desha County, Ark.; Little Rock, May 26, 1870. *Ibid.*, pp. 244–45.

24.   Letter from Powell Clayton to Harmon L. Remmel, Little Rock, Ark.; Mexico City, Mexico, October 23, 1899. University of Arkansas, Harmon L. Remmel Papers, R 23, box 1, fol. 2.

25.   Letter from Powell Clayton to F. P. Walker, Lake Village, Ark.; Little Rock, June 28, 1870. Arkansas History Commission, Clayton Letterbook, *op. cit.*, p. 354.

26.   Staples, *op. cit.*, p. 333.

27.   *Ibid.*, p. 332.

28.   Constitution of the State of Arkansas, 1868, Article V, sect. 2, *Debates and Proceedings, op. cit.*, p. 861.

29.   Staples, *op. cit.*, p. 272.

30.   *Ibid.*, pp. 350-51.

31.   *Ibid.*, p. 281.

32.   *Ibid.*, p. 283.

33.   Letter from Augustus H. Garland to David Walker, Fayetteville, Ark.; Little Rock, July 30, 1868. University of Arkansas, Walker Letters, fol. 3.

34.   Above p. 52.

35.   Letter from George C. Watkins to David Walker, Fayetteville, Ark.; Little Rock, August 22, 1868. University of Arkansas, Walker Letters, fol. 3.

36.   *Ibid.*

37.   Letter from W. E. Woodruff, Jr. to David Walker, Fayetteville, Ark.; Little Rock, September 11, 1868. Arkansas History Commission, A. Howard Stebbins, Jr. Collection, lot D; letter from David Walker to W. E. Woodruff, Jr., Little Rock, Ark.; Fayetteville, September 24, 1868. University of Arkansas, Walker Letters, fol. 3.

38.   Woodruff to Walker, September 11, 1868, *op. cit.*

39.   Walker to Woodruff, September 24, 1868, *op. cit.* Woodruff responded to Walker's position with a *de facto* argument in favor of taking the voter's oath. Reminding him that they had sworn allegiance to other constitutions in 1836, 1861, and 1864, which oaths were binding only during the life of those governments, he found no scruples against taking this one, especially since he believed the oath was "not binding in conscience or law." Continuing his argument, Woodruff wrote, "I endanger my soul no more by taking this elector's oath than I did during the war when I killed a man in battle.—False swearing (if you will) and the taking of human life are alike prohibited by religion and law.—As we are circumstanced the one act is no worse than the other." Letter from W. E. Woodruff, Jr. to David Walker, Fayetteville, Ark.; Little Rock, October 16, 1868. Arkansas History Commission, A. Howard Stebbins, Jr. Collection, lot D.

40.   Staples, *op. cit.*, p. 286. These counties were Ashley, Bradley, Columbia, Craighead, Greene, Hot Spring, Lafayette, Mississippi, Sevier, Sharp, and Woodruff. On November first Randolph County's registration was set aside.

      The *Hesper*, en route from Memphis to Little Rock with 4,000 stands of arms, was boarded on October fifteenth by unknown individuals who threw the arms overboard and then retired. Governor Clayton had arranged for these arms through an agent of the state, James L. Hodges, who obtained them in the North. They had been intended for use by the militia. *Ibid.*, p. 293.

41.   Letter from B. T. DuVal [Chairman of the Democratic Committee] to Messrs. J. R. Pettigrew and T. M. Gunter, Fayetteville, Ark.; Fort Smith, September 16, 1868. Published in the *Gazette*, October 7, 1868, p. 1, c. 2.

42.   *Fayetteville Democrat*, October 31, 1868, p. 2, c. 2.

43.   *Gazette*, November 17, 1868, p. 2, c. 2; *Fayetteville Democrat,* June 12, 1869, p. 2, c. 1.

44.   Herndon, *op. cit.*, p. 297. Staples agrees with Herndon's figures (Staples, *op. cit.*, p. 287), but the *Gazette*, reporting official returns received from the governor's private secretary, published slightly different results:

|                |        |
|----------------|--------|
| Republicans    | 22,153 |
| Democrats      | 19,945 |
|                | 42,098 |

*Gazette*, December 15, 1868, p. 2, c. 2.

45. Staples, *loc. cit.*

46. Letter from Trusten Polk to David Walker, Fayetteville, Ark.; St. Louis, July 2, 1870. University of Arkansas, Walker Letters, fol. 3. Trusten Polk, former governor and United States Senator from Missouri and spokesman for the Confederate cause, was associated with David Walker during the closing months of the Civil War. For a short time after the war both men were refugees together in Corsicana, Texas.

47. Letter from David Walker to W. W. Mansfield, Little Rock, Ark.; Fayetteville, July 26, 1874. Arkansas History Commission, W. W. Mansfield Papers.

48. Letter from David Walker to John R. Eakin, Washington, Ark.; Fayetteville, August 6, 1869. University of Arkansas, Walker Letters, fol. 3.

49. *Ibid.*

50. *Fayetteville Democrat*, April 2, 1870, p. 2, c. 2; *ibid.*, May 21, 1870, p. 2, c. 1; *ibid.*, July 30, 1870, p. 2, c. 1.

51. Letter from David Walker to Sol F. Clark, Little Rock, Ark.; Fayetteville, August 21, 1870. University of Arkansas, Walker Letters, fol. 3.

52. Hall, *op. cit.*, p. 184.

53. Walker to Clark, August 21, 1870, *op. cit.*

54. Letter from John M. Harrel to David Walker, Fayetteville, Ark.; Little Rock, July 12, 1870. University of Arkansas, Walker Letters, fol. 3.

55. Walker to Clark, August 21, 1870, *op. cit.*

56. Hall, *op. cit.*

57. *Fayetteville Democrat*, November 12, 1870, p. 2, c. 2.

58. *Ibid.*, November 27, 1870, p. 2, c. 2.

59. *Ibid.*, May 13, 1871, p. 2, c. 1, quoting the Arkadelphia *Southern Standard*.

60. *Ibid.*, October 7, 1871, p. 2, c. 1.

61. The label "minstrel" refers to the regular Republicans who were in sympathy with the leadership of Senator Clayton. These were "followers of a Republican leader who had been a member of a minstrel company." Staples, *op. cit.*, p. 389n.

62. The flamboyant behavior of Joseph Brooks on a political platform prompted an opponent to compare him to a "brindletail bull." Consequently, followers of Brooks came to be known as "brindletails." *Ibid.*

63. *Ibid.*, p. 389.

64. *Gazette*, June 15, 1872, p. 2, c. 2.

65. See apportionment table above, p. 68.

66. Arkansas History Commission, Harris Flanagin Papers, *passim.*

67. Letter from B. F. Askew to Harris Flanagin, Arkadelphia, Ark.; Magnolia, March 25, 1872. Arkansas History Commission, Harris Flanagin Papers.

68. Letter from Augustus H. Garland to Harris Flanagin, Arkadelphia, Ark.; Little Rock, June 6, 1872. Arkansas History Commission, Harris Flanagin Papers.

69. Letter from Augustus H. Garland to Harris Flanagin, Arkadelphia, Ark.; Little Rock, June 13, 1872. Arkansas History Commission, Harris Flanagin Papers.

70. Staples, *op. cit.*, p. 392.

71. *Fayetteville Democrat*, June 29, 1872, p. 4, c. 1.

72. Letter from W. E. Woodruff, Jr. to David Walker, Fayetteville, Ark.; Little Rock, July 2, 1872. Arkansas History Commission, A. Howard Stebbins, Jr. Collection, lot D.

73. Letter from Augustus H. Garland to Henry M. Rector, n.p.; Little Rock, July 3, 1872. Arkansas History Commission, A. Howard Stebbins, Jr. Collection, lot E.

74. *Ibid.*

75. *Fayetteville Democrat*, June 29, 1872, p. 1, c. 5.

76. *Ibid.*

77. Letter from David Walker to Harris Flanagin, Arkadelphia, Ark.; Fayetteville, July 25, 1872. Arkansas History Commission, Harris Flanagin Papers.

78. Staples, *loc. cit.*

79. *Ibid.*, p. 394.

80. *Ibid.*, pp. 394-95.

81. *Ibid.*, pp. 393-94.

## CHAPTER 6: JOSEPH BROOKS WINS THE ELECTION

1. Commager, *op. cit.*, p. 521.
2. Richard B. Morris, ed. *Encyclopedia of American History* (updated and rev. ed.; New York: Harper & Row, Publishers, 1965), p. 250.
3. Staples, *op. cit.*, p. 391.
4. *Ibid.*, pp. 396, 393.
5. Letter from A. H. Garland to Harris Flanagin, Arkadelphia, Ark.; Little Rock, September 4, 1872. Arkansas History Commission, Harris Flanagin Papers.
6. Letter from David Walker to J. M. Pittman, Elijah Davidson, *et al.*, n.p.; Fayetteville, August 29, 1872. *Fayetteville Democrat,* September 7, 1872, p. 4, c. 5.
7. Staples, *op. cit.*, p. 221.
8. Eugene Cypert, "Constitutional Convention of 1868," *Publications of the Arkansas Historical Association,* IV, p. 55.
9. Letters from B. F. Rice to Harris Flanagin, Arkadelphia, Ark.; Little Rock, September 7, September 14, October 7, 1872. Arkansas History Commission, Harris Flanagin Papers.
10. Letter from C. B. Moore to Harris Flanagin, Arkadelphia, Ark.; Little Rock, October 4, 1872. Arkansas History Commission, Harris Flanagin Papers.
11. Staples, *op. cit.*, p. 394.
12. Garland to Flanagin, June 6, 1872, *op. cit.*
13. Staples, *op. cit.*, p. 395.
14. Telegram from B. F. Rice to Harris Flanagin, Arkadelphia, Ark.; Little Rock, October 8, 1872. Arkansas History Commission, Harris Flanagin Papers.
15. Letter from James Mitchell to David Walker, Fayetteville, Ark.; Cane Hill, October 8, 1872. University of Arkansas, Walker Letters, fol. 3.
16. *Fayetteville Democrat*, October 19, 1872, p. 1, c. 2.
17. *Gazette*, October 11, 1872, p. 2, c. 4.
18. Letter from H. F. Thomason to David Walker, Fayetteville, Ark., Van Buren, November 22, 1872. University of Arkansas, Walker Letters, fol. 3.
19. *Fayetteville Democrat*, November 30, 1872, p. 4, c. 1.
20. *Ibid.*, p. 4, c. 2.
21. *Gazette*, December 13, 1872, p. 4, cc. 4–5.
22. Validity for this statement can be found in the following correspondence: letter from David Walker to William E. Woodruff, Jr., editor of the *Gazette*, [Little Rock, Ark.], Fayetteville, November 18, 1873. *Gazette*, December 10, 1873, p. 2, cc. 2–5; letter from H. F. Thomason to David Walker, Fayetteville, Ark., Van Buren, November 22, 1872. University of Arkansas, Walker Letters, fol. 3; letter from Isaac Murphy to gentleman [*sic*] at Little Rock, Huntsville, June 5, 1873. *Fayetteville Democrat*, July 5, 1873, p. 2, c. 3, quoting the *Republican*; letter from James Mitchell to David Walker, Fayetteville, Ark., Boonsboro, July 1, 1873. University of Arkansas, Walker Letters, fol. 3; letter from U. M. Rose to Harris Flanagin, Arkadelphia, Ark., Little Rock, July 1, 1873. Arkansas History Commission, Harris Flanagin Papers; letter from William E. Woodruff, Jr. to Harris Flanagin, Arkadelphia, Ark., Little Rock, September 30, 1873. Arkansas History Commission, Harris Flanagin Papers; letter from John R. Eakin to David Walker, Fayetteville, Ark., Washington, December 12, 1873. University of Arkansas, Walker Letters, fol. 3.
23. See map p. 102.
24. Cypert, *loc. cit.*
25. *Gazette*, December 13, 1872, p. 4, cc. 4–5. Calculations have been based on this source.
26. Letter from Gordon W. Peay to Harris Flanagin, Arkadelphia, Ark.; Little Rock, October 11, 1872. Arkansas History Commission, Harris Flanagin Papers.
27. Staples, *op. cit.*, p. 397.
28. *Ibid.*, p. 398.
29. *Fayetteville Democrat*, December 21, 1872, p. 4, c. 1.
30. Staples, *op. cit.*, p. 400.

31. Reform Convention's "Address to the People," *Gazette,* January 23, 1873, p. 2, c. 3.
32. *Fayetteville Democrat,* January 18, 1872[3], p. 4, c. 1.
33. *Gazette,* January 23, 1873, p. 2, c. 4.
34. *Ibid.,* p. 2, c. 3.
35. *Ibid.* Calculations have been based on this source. See map p. 103.
36. *Ibid.,* p. 2, c. 4.

## CHAPTER 7: ELISHA BAXTER WINS THE OFFICE

1. Hempstead, *op. cit.,* p. 273.
2. Staples, *op. cit.,* p. 62.
3. *Gazette,* January 8, 1873, p. 2, c. 2.
4. Garland to Flanagin, June 6, 1872, *op. cit.*
5. Harrell, *op. cit.,* p. 171. It is interesting to recall that Augustus H. Garland had been elected United States Senator in February, 1867, but had never taken office due to Congressional Reconstruction. B. F. Rice became Senator to fill that vacancy.
6. *Ibid.* Two other minor candidates, McDonald and Wilshire, received six votes between them.
7. *Gazette,* January 19, 1873, p. 2, c. 2.
8. Harrell, *loc. cit.* This is not David Walker.
9. *Gazette, loc. cit.*
10. *Ibid.,* January 8, 1873, p. 4, c. 4.
11. *Ibid.,* March 27, 1873, p. [2], c. 2. It is suggested here that the Dorsey men promised to join the Democrats in securing all the legislation they desired if the Democrats would support Dorsey.
12. *Ibid.,* February 9, 1873, p. 1, c. 1.
13. *Ibid.,* April 11, 1873, p. 2, c. 2.
14. *Ibid.,* January 8, 1873, p. 2, c. 2.
15. *Ibid.,* January 23, 1873, p. 1, c. 1.
16. *Ibid.,* February 5, 1873, p. 1, c. 1.
17. *Ibid.,* February 7, 1873, p. 2, c. 2.
18. *Ibid.,* February 22, 1873, p. 2, c. 3.
19. *Ibid.,* March 22, 1873, p. 2, c. 2.
20. *Ibid.,* February 28, 1873, p. 2, c. 2.
21. *Ibid.,* May 21, 1873, p. 1, c. 1.
22. *Ibid.,* April 1, 1873, p. 2, c. 2.
23. *Ibid.,* April 4, 1873, p. 1, c. 1.
24. Letter from E. H. English to Governor Elisha Baxter, Little Rock, Ark.; Little Rock, January 28, 1873. Arkansas History Commission, L. C. Gulley Collection of State Papers.
25. *Ibid.*
26. Letter from U. M. Rose to Harris Flanagin, Arkadelphia, Ark.; Little Rock, March 31, 1873. Arkansas History Commission, Harris Flanagin Papers.
27. *Ibid.*
28. *Gazette,* April 11, 1873, p. 2, c. 3.
29. *Ibid.,* quoted from the *Republican.*
30. *Ibid.,* April 11, 1873, p. 2, c. 2.
31. *Ibid.,* April 15, 1873, p. 2, c. 2.
32. *Ibid.,* April 18, 1873, p. 2, c. 2.
33. *Ibid.,* April 19, 1873, p. 4, c. 2.
34. *Ibid.,* p. 4, cc. 2–3.
35. Speech of Representative H. M. McVeigh of Mississippi County, *ibid.,* April 22, 1873, p. 1, c. 2.
36. Speech of Representative J. F. Cunningham of Fulton County, *ibid.,* p. 1, cc. 2–4.
37. *Ibid.,* April 23, 1873, p. 1, c. 1.

38. Letter from James L. Witherspoon to Harris Flanagin, Arkadelphia, Ark.; Little Rock, April 21, 1873. Arkansas History Commission, Harris Flanagin Papers.

39. *Gazette*, April 22, 1873, p. 2, c. 2.

40. *Ibid.*, April 19, 1873, p. 4, c. 3; *ibid.*, April 26, 1873, p. 4, c. 3. Representative Thrower, who introduced Brooks' petition, voted against the Railroad-aid Bond Bill.

41. This road was to go westward from the Mississippi beginning at Eunice (Chicot County) and was to pass through Camden (Ouachita) on its way to Lewisville and Texarkana (Lafayette). A connecting link from Arkadelphia to Camden was to tie Clark and the adjacent counties to the Mississippi River system.

42. Herndon, *op. cit.*, p. 1010.

43. *Gazette*, April 25, 1873, p. 4, c. 6.

44. *Ibid.*, April 26, 1873, p. 2, c. 3.

45. *Ibid.*, April 29, 1873, p. 2, c. 2.

## CHAPTER 8: DAVID WALKER WRITES A LETTER

1. *Gazette,* May 16, 1873, p. 1, c. 1.

2. *Ibid.,* May 18, 1873, p. 2, c. 2.

3. *Ibid.,* May 16, 1873, p. 1, c. 1.

4. Letter from R. C. Newton to Harris Flanagin, Arkadelphia, Ark.; Washington, May 16, 1873. Arkansas History Commission, Harris Flanagin Papers.

5. Margaret Smith Ross, "Governor Elisha Baxter Was a Unionist—And He Suffered for It in the Civil War," *Gazette*, December 4, 1966, p. 6E, c. 6.

6. Letter from George A. Gallagher to Harris Flanagin, Arkadelphia, Ark.; Little Rock, May 19, 1873. Arkansas History Commission, Harris Flanagin Papers.

7. *Gazette*, May 22, 1873, p. 2, c. 2.

8. *Ibid.*, May 25, 1873, p. 2, c. 3, quoting the *Washington Telegraph; Fayetteville Democrat*, May 29, 1873, p. 1, c. 1.

9. *Gazette*, May 31, 1873, p. 1, c. 1.

10. *Ibid.*, June 3, 1873, p. 4, c. 3.

11. *Ibid.*, June 4, 1873, p. 2, c. 2.

12. *Ibid.*, p. 1, c. 1.

13. *Ibid.*, June 5, 1873, p. 4, c. 4.

14. *Ibid.*, p. 1, c. 1.

15. *Ibid.*, June 10, 1873, p. 4, c. 4.

16. *Ibid.*, p. 1, c. 1, quoting the *Augusta Bulletin.*

17. *Ibid.*, June 24, 1873, p. 2. c. 2, quoting the Fort Smith *Independent.*

18. Staples, *op. cit.*, p. 403.

19. *Fayetteville Democrat*, August 2, 1873, p. 2, c. 2.

20. *Gazette*, August 27, 1873, p. 2, c. 2. The ten anti-Baxter papers were: *Republican* (Little Rock) Republican; *Monticellonian* (Monticello) Democrat; *Chronicle* (Little Rock) Independent; *Democrat* (Fayetteville) Democrat; *Herald* (Fort Smith) Democrat; *Courier* (Hot Springs) Republican; *Independent* (Fort Smith) Democrat; *Statesman* (Jacksonport) Republican; *Tribune* (Camden) Democrat; *Laborer* (Dardanelle) Democrat.

21. Staples, *op. cit.*, p. 404.

22. *Gazette*, July 1, 1873, p. 2, c. 2.

23. *Ibid.*, June 29, 1873, p. 2, c. 2.

24. Letter from James Mitchell to David Walker, Fayetteville, Ark.; Boonsboro, July 1, 1873. University of Arkansas, Walker Letters, fol. 3.

25. *Fayetteville Democrat*, July 12, 1873, p. 2, c. 1; July 19, 1873, p. 2, c. 1; July 26, 1873, p. 2, c. 2.

26. Letter from U. M. Rose to Harris Flanagin, Arkadelphia, Ark.; Little Rock, July 1, 1873. Arkansas History Commission, Harris Flanagin Papers.

27. *Gazette*, November 4, 1873, p. 2, c. 3.

28. *Ibid.*, July 12, 1873, p. 2, c. 3; *ibid.*, July 15, 1873, p. 1, c. 1; *ibid.*, July 16, 1873, p.

2, c. 2; *ibid.*, July 17, 1873, p. 2, c. 3; *ibid.*, July 23, 1873, p. 2, c. 2; *ibid.*, p. 1, c. 2; *ibid.*, August 27, 1873, p. 2, c. 3; *Fayetteville Democrat*, August 22, 1873, p. 2, c. 1.

29.  *Gazette*, July 31, 1873, p. 2, c. 3.

30.  *Ibid.*, July 27, 1873, p. 2, c. 2.

31.  *Ibid.*, August 21, 1873, p. 3, c. 2.

32.  Letter from Attorney General George H. Williams to Governor Elisha Baxter, Little Rock, Ark.; Washington, D. C., September 15, 1873. Arkansas History Commission, Robert W. Trimble Collection.

33.  *Gazette*, October 1, 1873, p. 2, c. 2.

34.  Mitchell to Walker, July 1, 1873, *op. cit.*

35.  *Gazette*, August 3, 1873, p. 2, c. 2; *ibid*, August 27, 1873, p. 2, c. 2; *ibid.*, September 10, 1873, p. 2, c. 2; *Fayetteville Democrat*, November 29, 1873, p. 2, c. 2.

36.  Letter from William E. Woodruff, Jr. to Harris Flanagin, Arkadelphia, Ark.; Little Rock, September 30, 1873. Arkansas History Commission, Harris Flanagin Papers.

37.  *Gazette*, August 3, 1873, p. 2, c. 2.

38.  *Ibid.*, August 27, 1873, p. 2, c. 2.

39.  Letter from David Walker to William E. Woodruff, Jr., Editor of the *Daily Arkansas Gazette*, Little Rock, Ark.; Fayetteville, November 18, 1873. *Gazette*, December 10, 1873, p.2, cc. 2–5.

40.  Bishop, *op. cit.*, p. 25. A. W. Bishop accused Walker of having "an over-weening love of applause."

41.  Walker to Woodruff, November 18, 1873, *op. cit.*

42.  *Ibid.*

43.  Letter from John R. Eakin to David Walker, Fayetteville, Ark.; Washington, December 12, 1873. University of Arkansas, Walker Letters, fol. 3.

## CHAPTER 9: AUGUSTUS H. GARLAND

1.  Harrell, *op. cit.*, p. 12, quoting from Isaac Murphy.

2.  Hallum, *op. cit.*, p. 410.

3.  Garland to Rector, July 3, 1873, *op. cit.*

4.  Letter from A. H. Garland to Harris Flanagin, Arkadelphia, Ark.; Little Rock, April 30, 1874. Arkansas History Commission, Harris Flanagin Papers.

5.  Harper, *op. cit.*, p. 133; Margaret Smith Ross, "Augustus H. Garland—Arkansas's Biggest Man: Leader in Law, in State and National Politics," *Gazette,* January 22, 1956, p. 2F, c. 1.

6.  Farrar Newberry, *A Life of Mr. Garland of Arkansas* (n.p.: Published by author, 1908), pp. 4–5.

7.  Ross, *loc. cit.*

8.  Harper, *loc. cit.*

9.  Ross, *loc cit.*

10.  *Ibid.*, p. 2F, cc. 1–2.

11.  *Ibid.*, p. 2F, c. 2.

12.  Eugene A. Nolte, "Four Unpublished Letters from Augustus Garland," *Arkansas Historical Quarterly,* XVIII, No. 2 (Summer, 1959), p. 78.

13.  Letter from Augustus H. Garland to [Dr. Roscoe J.] Jennings, n.p.; Little Rock, July 2, 1857. Published in Nolte, *op. cit.*, pp. 81–82. The four letters included in Nolte's article were written during July, 1857. They indicate that Garland was doing battle with a drinking problem, which might have endangered his otherwise promising future. He evidently mastered his problem during this period. See pp. 82–84, 85–86, 87, 88–89.

14.  Ross, *loc. cit.*

15.  *Gazette*, April 20, 1861, p. 2, c. 3.

16.  *Ibid.*, April 27, 1861, p. 2, c. 3.

17.  Ross, *op. cit.*, p. 2F, c. 3.

18.  *Ibid.* John P. Johnson, Garland's opponent, contested this election and continued to

believe he had won. The committee on contested elections, however, reported in favor of Garland.

19. *Ibid.* In the light of later developments it is interesting to notice that several members of the Confederate Congress in February, 1864, tired to secure for Garland the appointment as Attorney General of the Confederate government. Before Jefferson Davis knew of this movement he had appointed Senator Davis of North Carolina to the post.

20. Staples, *op.cit.,* p. 59.

21. Garland to President Johnson, June 28, 1865, *op. cit.*

22. U. S., *Statutes at Large,* XIII, 424.

23. Ross, *op. cit.,* p. 2F, c. 4.

24. *Ex parte Garland,* 71 U. S. 333 (1867) 18 LEd., 367.

25. *Ibid.,* Commager, *loc. cit.*

26. Ross, *loc. cit.*

27. Letter from Augustus H. Garland to Alexander H. Stephens, n.p.; Little Rock, February 25, 1867. Library of Congress, Alexander H. Stephens Papers.

28. Letter from Augustus H. Garland to Alexander H. Stephens, n.p.; Washington, D. C., March 22, 1867. Library of Congress, Alexander H. Stephens Papers.

29. Letter from Augustus H. Garland to Alexander H. Stephens, n.p.; Washington, D. C., March 31, 1867. Library of Congress, Alexander H. Stephens Papers.

30. *Osborn* v. *Nicholson,* 80 U. S. 654 (1872); 20 LEd., 689.

31. *Ibid.,* 693.

32. *Ibid.,* 691.

33. *Ibid.,* 689.

34. *Ibid.,* 689–90.

35. *Ibid.,* 690.

36. *Ibid.*

37. *Ibid.,* 690–91.

38. *Ibid.,* 691.

39. *Ibid.*

40. *Ibid.,* 689, 693.

41. Letter from Augustus H. Garland to Henry M. Rector, n.p.; Little Rock, November 12, 1871. Arkansas History Commission, A. Howard Stebbins, Jr. Collection, lot E. Garland considered his argument important enough to send a copy of it to Alexander H. Stephens for his consideration. Letter from Augustus H. Garland to Alexander H. Stephens, n.p.; Little Rock, November 13, 1871. Library of Congress, Alexander H. Stephens Papers. Garland's family had owned slaves before the Civil War. His father brought eleven slaves with the family from Tennessee, and six more had been added by 1841, thus making a total of seventeen owned by the Hubbard family. In 1860 Garland personally owned three slaves. Ross, *op. cit.,* p. 2F, c. 1; Wooster, *op. cit.,* Appendix I.

42. Hallum, *op. cit.,* p. 410.

43. Garland to Rector, July 3, 1872, *op. cit.*

44. Ross, *op. cit.,* p. 2F, c. 4.

45. Letter from Augustus H. Garland to Alexander H. Stephens, n.p.; Washington, D. C., March 27, 1867. Library of Congress, Alexander H. Stephens Papers.

46. Hallum, *loc. cit.*

47. Staples, *op. cit.,* p. 255.

48. Garland to Walker, July 30, 1868, *op. cit.*

49. Letter from Augustus H. Garland to Alexander H. Stephens, n.p.; Little Rock, November 9, 1868. Library of Congress, Alexander H. Stephens Papers.

50. *Ibid.*

51. *Ibid.* William Alexander Graham had served North Carolina as state legislator from 1833 to 1840, as United States Senator (Whig) from 1840 to 1843, and as Governor from 1845 to 1849. He had been Secretary of the Navy from 1850 to 1852 and was Vice Presidential candidate on General Winfield Scott's ticket in 1852. Although against secession, he became a Confederate Senator. He was a leader of the moderate forces of his state after the Civil War.

James L. Orr was a Democratic Congressman from South Carolina from 1849 to 1859 and was Speaker of the House from 1857 to 1859. He was against secession and supported the policies of Stephen A. Douglas. In 1860 Orr became an advocate of secession and later served as a Confederate Senator. Supporting President Johnson's policies, he was elected governor in 1866. After losing the confidence of his people he joined the radical party and supported the re-election of President Grant in 1872. Following Grant's election he was appointed United States Minister to Russia. Joseph G. E. Hopkins, *et al,* eds. *Concise Dictionary of American Biography* (New York: Charles Scribner's Sons, 1964), pp. 360, 751.

52.   Garland to Stephens, November 9, 1868, *op. cit.*
53.   Garland to Rector, July 3, 1872, *op. cit.*
54.   Staples, *op. cit.*, pp. 407–408.
55.   Charles Hillman Brough, "The Industrial History of Arkansas," *Publications, op. cit.,* I, p. 207.
56.   Letter from Stephen W. Dorsey to Governor O. A. Hadley, Little Rock, Ark.; New York, September 26, 1871. Arkansas History Commission, L. C. Gulley Collection of State Papers.
57.   Arkansas, Auditor of the State, *Biennial Report, 1872-1874,* pp. 35-36. University of Arkansas, Microfilm 24, reel 3.
58.   Letter from Governor Elisha Baxter to A. H. Johnson, President of the Arkansas Central Railway, n.p.; Executive Office, Little Rock, Ark,. March 16, 1874. *Gazette,* March 20, 1874, p. 1, cc. 1-3.
59.   *Ibid.*, p. 1, c. 2. The Constitution of 1868 had stated in no uncertain terms that: "The credit of the State or counties, shall never be loaned for any purpose without the consent of the people thereof, expressed through the ballot box." Constitution of the State of Arkansas, 1868, Article X, section six, *Debates and Proceedings, op. cit.,* p. 883. The question which Baxter asked and which would be asked in years to follow was whether voting "FOR" or "AGAINST" railroads satisfied the constitutional limitation referred to above.
60.   *Gazette, loc cit.*
61.   *Ibid.*, p. 1, c. 3.
62.   *Ibid.;* Carmichael, *op. cit.,* p. 396.
63.   *Fayetteville Democrat,* March 28, 1874, p. 1, c. 3.
64.   *Gazette,* March 20, 1874, p. 4, c. 3.
65.   *Ibid.*, March 26, 1874, p. 2, c. 2.
66.   *Fayetteville Democrat,* March 28, 1874, *loc. cit.*
67.   Herndon, *op. cit.*, p. 309, quoting Baxter in the *New York Herald.*
68.   See above p. 127.
69.   Herdnon, *loc. cit.;* (Staples, *op. cit.,* pp. 408-409.
70.   Herndon, *loc. cit.;* U. M. Rose, "Brief for Baxter," p. 5. Brief presented in *Brooks v. Baxter,* Washington, D. C., May 1, 1874. Arkansas History Commission, Robert W. Trimble Collection.
71.   For a more complete consideration of the events of the Brooks-Baxter War see the following articles: James H. Atkinson, "The Brooks-Baxter Contest," *Arkansas Historical Quarterly,* IV, No. 2 (Summer, 1945), pp. 124-49; "The Adoption of the Constitution of 1874 and the Passing of the Reconstruction Regime," *ibid.,* V, No. 3 (Fall, 1946), pp. 288-96.
72.   Atkinson, "The Brooks-Baxter Contest," *op. cit.,* p. 129.
73.   *Ibid.*, p. 133.
74.   *Ibid.*, pp. 133-34.
75.   *Ibid:*, p. 137.
76.   *Ibid,* pp. 138-39.
77.   *Ibid.*, pp. 141-42
78.   Josiah H. Shinn, "Augustus Hill Garland Was Born Seventy-Six Years Ago," *Gazette,* June 11, 1908, p. 10, c. 1; Ross, *op. cit.,* p. 2F, cc. 4-5.
79.   Shinn, *loc. cit.*

80. Herndon, *loc. cit.*

81. Harrell, *op. cit.*, p. 217.

82. *Ibid.* Among the signers of this address were: R. C. Newton, William E. Woodruff, John C. Peay, Thomas W. Newton, Thomas Fletcher, Sol F. Clark, U. M. Rose, F. W. Compton, Dick Gantt, E. H. English, A. H. Garland, John Fletcher, James Pomeroy, John D. Adams, Gordon N. Peay, and S. R. Cockrill.

83. United States Attorney General George H. William's opinion in *Brooks* v. *Baxter*, p. 15, *Baxter Sustained.* University of Arkansas, Sue Walker Papers.

84. *Ibid.* The dispute referred to was an artificial case, *Brooks* v. *Page*, which had been created to provide an opportunity for the Arkansas Supreme Court to uphold Judge Whytock's decision.

85. Proclamation by the Governor to the Members of the Senate and House of Representatives of the General Assembly of the State of Arkansas, April 22, 1874. Arkansas History Commission, Robert W. Trimble Collection.

86. Garland to Flanagin, April 30, 1874, *op. cit.*

87. *Ibid.*

88. Rose, *op. cit.*, p. 8. Also assisting Rose was W. W. Wilshire, but his stature did not equal that of his associates.

89. Speech by W. W. Wilshire, May 28, 1874, p. 4. University of Arkansas, Sue Walker Papers.

90. Letter from T. M. Gunter to David Walker, Fayetteville, Ark.; Washington, D. C., April 16, 1874. Arkansas History Commission, A. Howard Stebbins, Jr. Collection, lot D.

91. Copy of a letter from David Walker to S. W. Williams, Little Rock, Ark., Fayetteville, April 22, 1874. University of Arkansas, Walker Letters, fol. 3.

92. *Ibid.; Fayetteville Democrat*, May 9, 1874, p. 1, c. 2.

93. *Fayetteville Democrat*, May 2, 1874, p. 1, c. 4. The list of papers supporting Governor Brooks included the following: *Little Rock Republican, Ouachita Commercial, Pine Bluff Republican, Fort Smith Herald, Fort Smith Independent, White River Journal, Fort Smith New Era, Fayetteville Democrat, Monticellonian, Star of Hope, Dardanelle Laborer, Helena Shield, Arkansas Statesman, Augusta Advocate, Hot Springs Courier, Mound City Press, Arkansas County Enterprise, Forrest City Times,* and *Boone County Highlander.*

94. *Fayetteville Democrat*, April 25, 1874, p. 1, c. 1. See above pp. 130–31.

95. *Gazette*, May 3, 1874, p. 1, c. 3.

96. Staples, *op. cit.*, p. 420.

97. Letter from T. M. Gunter (House of Representatives) to Harris Flanagin, Arkadelphia, Ark.; Washington, D. C., May 2, 1874. Arkansas History Commission, Harris Flanagin Papers.

98. See above p. 154.

99. *Gazette*, May 3, 1874, p. 1, c. 5.

100. Letter from Attorney General George H. Williams to Hon. Joseph Brooks, Little Rock, Ark.; Washington, D. C., May 9, 1874. Published as a part of a proclamation by Governor Joseph Brooks, May 11, 1874. Arkansas History Commission, Robert W. Trimble Collection.

101. Proclamation by Governor Joseph Brooks, May 11, 1874. Arkansas History Commission, Robert W. Trimble Collection.

102. *Ibid.* In a note added at the bottom of this proclamation Governor Baxter wrote this comment.

103. Telegram from A. H. Garland to W. M. Harrison, Pine Bluff, Ark.; Little Rock, May 11, 1874. Arkansas History Commission, Subject File, telegram manuscripts relating to the Brooks-Baxter War.

104. Telegram from [Brigadier General] H. King White to Colonel T. C. Flournoy, Pine Bluff, Ark.; Little Rock, May 11, 1874. Arkansas History Commission, Subject File, telegram manuscripts relating to the Brooks-Baxter War. Staples notes that Brooks hurt his cause by sending two telegrams to President Grant (May eleventh and fourteenth) in which were conveyed an obstinate and a demanding attitude. It is thought that these messages damaged Brooks' position in Washington. Staples, *op. cit.*, pp. 418–20.

105.   Atkinson, "The Brooks-Baxter Contest," *op. cit.*, pp. 141–42.

106.   *Ibid.*, p. 143; telegram from A. J. Wheat to Colonels [T. C.] Flournoy and Haris [*sic*], Pine Bluff, Ark.; Little Rock, May 14, 1874. Arkansas History Commission, Subject File, telegram manuscripts relating to the Brooks-Baxter War.

107.   Telegram from [Brigadier General] H. King White to Colonel T. C. Flournoy, Pine Bluff, Ark.; Little Rock, May 14, 1874. Arkansas History Commission, Subject File, telegram manuscripts relating to Brooks-Baxter War.

108.   Staples, *op. cit.*, p. 421; Hempstead, *op cit.*, p. 277.

109.   *Ibid.* Staples makes note that the presiding officers of both houses of the legislature received the President's proclamation. Staples, *loc. cit.*

110.   Hempstead, *op. cit.*, p. 277–78.

111.   *Ibid.*, p. 278.

112.   *Baxter* v. *Brooks,* 29 Ark., 198 (1874).  In his opinion Attorney General Williams made the comment that "Unconstitutional methods of filling offices cannot be resorted to because there is some real or imagined unfairness about the election."

113.   *Fayetteville Democrat*, May 23, 1874, p. 1, c. 1.

114.   Staples, *op. cit.*, pp. 421–22.

115.   Letter from B. F. Askew to Harris Flanagin, Arkadelphia, Ark.; Little Rock, May 17, 1874. Arkansas History Commission, Harris Flanagin Papers.

116.   Hempstead, *loc. cit.*

117.   Hall, *op. cit.*, pp. 206–207.

118.   See above p. 95.

119.   Thomas, I, *op. cit.*, pp. 91, 125, 129, 160.

120.   Letter from S. H. Tucker to Jesse Turner, Van Buren, Ark.; Little Rock, May 29, 1874. Duke University, Turner Papers.

## CHAPTER 10: THE PROBLEM RESOLVED

1.   Staples, *op. cit.*, p. 434.

2.   U. S. Congress, House, *Select Committee to Inquire Into the Condition of Affairs in Arkansas*, 43d Cong., 1st Sess., 1874, House Rept. 771, p. 143.

3.   Staples, *op. cit.*, p. 435.

4.   Arkansas, Constitutional Convention, 1874. *Journal*, p. 27. Arkansas History Commission, Microfilm.  Other members were: Dudley E. Jones and Gordon N. Peay.

5.   *Ibid.*, p. 31.

6.   Staples, *op. cit.* p. 424.

7.   Atkinson, "The Adoption of the Constitution of 1874 . . . ," *op. cit.*, p. 291.

8.   *Fayetteville Democrat*, May 30, 1874, p. 1, c. 1.

9.   The results of the election in Washington County were as follows:

| | |
|---|---:|
| B. F. Walker | 2389 |
| T. N. Thomason | 2038 |
| M. F. Lake | 2240 |
| David Walker | 760 |
| A. M. Wilson | 431 |
| E. W. McClure | 306 |
| For Convention | 2776 |
| Against Convention | 25 |

*Fayetteville Democrat,* July 4, 1874, p. 1, c. 2.

10.   Walker to Mansfield, July 26, 1874, *op. cit.*

11.   Carmichael, *op. cit.*, p. 369; Staples, *op. cit.*, pp. 426–27.

12.   Carmichael, *loc cit.*

13.   See Table 1, pp. 68–69.

14.   See Figure 12, p. 74.

15.   Article two of the Constitution contained a liberal statement of individual rights and

guaranteed the equality of those rights to all men. *Constitution of the State of Arkansas,* 1874, Article II, Hall, *op. cit.*, pp. 109–12.

16. Letter from Hugh F. Thomason to David Walker, Fayetteville, Ark.; Van Buren, June 3, 1874. University of Arkansas, Walker Letters, fol. 3.

17. Letter from L. C. Gause to David Walker, Fayetteville, Ark.; Jacksonport, July 11, 1874. University of Arkansas, Walker Letters, fol. 3. Gause wanted Walker to join him and other friends from the northwest for a strategy conference in Little Rock, but, as far as is known, Walker did not go to Little Rock until September.

18. Letter from Jesse Turner to Harris Flanagin, Arkadelphia, Ark.; Van Buren, August 1, 1874. Arkansas History Commission, Harris Flanagin Papers.

19. Fragment of a letter from John R. Eakin to David Walker, [Fayetteville, Ark.]; n.p., n.d. University of Arkansas, Walker Letters, fol. 5.

20. Walker to Mansfield, July 26, 1874, *op. cit.*

21. Atkinson, "The Adoption of the Constitution of 1874 . . .," *loc. cit.*

22. *Gazette*, September 10, 1874, p. 1, cc. 3–7.

23. *Ibid.*, p. 1, c. 7. Baxter received fifty-two votes, Garland received ten, and the remaining votes were scattered.

24. *Ibid.*, p. 1, c. 8.

25. *Ibid.*, p. 4, c. 1.

26. *Gazette*, September 11, 1874, p. 1, c. 4. Nominations for governor included:

> Augustus H. Garland (Pulaski)
> R. C. Newton (Pulaski and Jefferson)
> Gen. D. H. Reynolds (Chicot)
> J. E. Cravens (Johnson)
> Grandison D. Royston (Hempstead)

27. The absence of Harris Flanagin's name as being among the active leaders is explained by his declining health, which resulted in his death on October twenty-third. Herndon, *op. cit.*, p. 285.

28. *Ibid.* The vote for Supreme Court justices was as follows:

> | David Walker | 50½ Washington |
> |---|---|
> | J. C. Davis | 10 |
> | John R. Eakin | 6 Hempstead |
> | William M. Harrison | 50¼ Jefferson |
> | John T. Bearden | 24¾ Ouachita |

29. Letter from A. H. Garland to David Walker, Fayetteville, Ark.; Little Rock, September 12, 1874. University of Arkansas, Walker Letters, fol. 3.

30. *Gazette*, September 11, 1874, p. 1, cc. 2–3.

31. *Ibid.*, p. 1, c. 5.

32. *Gazette*, October 27, 1874, p. 1, cc. 5–6. Madison County not included in these returns. Staples, *op. cit.*, p. 431.

33. See Table 5, p. 165.

34. *Gazette, loc. cit.*

35. *Ibid.*, p. 1, c. 2.

36. Letter from Jesse Turner to his wife, Rebecca, Van Buren, Ark.; Little Rock, November 12, 1874. Duke University, Turner Papers.

37. Staples, *op. cit.*, pp. 432–33; Ross, *op. cit.*, p. 2F, c. 5.

38. Staples, *op. cit.*, p. 433; Atkinson, "The Adoption of the Constitution of 1874 . . .," *op. cit.*, p. 294.

39. *Ibid.*, p. 295. The Poland Committee conducted hearings in Little Rock from July 18–28 and from November 12–21.

40. Letter from Jesse Turner to his wife, Rebecca, Van Buren, Ark.; Little Rock, January 10, 1875. Duke University, Turner Papers.

41.  Letter from Jesse Turner to his son, Jesse, [Amherst Court House, Va.] ; Little Rock, February 1, 1875. Duke University, Turner Papers.
42.  *Ibid*.; Staples, *op. cit*., p. 439. During the Brooks-Baxter War President Grant had personally sympathized with Brooks' claim and believed that Brooks had been elected. But when Attorney General Williams' opinion took the position that "the people, through the expression of their last legislature, had endorsed Baxter," President Grant felt he had to acquiesce. Mifflin Wistar Gibbs, *Shadow and Light: An Autobiography* (Washington, D. C.: n.p., 1902), p. 156.
43.  Staples, *loc. cit*.
44.  *Ibid*., p. 438.
45.  *Ibid*., pp. 438–39.
46.  Letter from A. H. Garland to Alexander H. Stephens, [Washington, D. C.] ; Little Rock, February 11, 1875. Library of Congress, Alexander H. Stephens Papers.
47.  Letter from A. H. Garland to Alexander H. Stephens, [Washington, D. C.] ; Little Rock, February 27, 1875. Library of Congress, Alexander H. Stephens Papers.
48.  Staples, *op. cit*., p. 440; Atkinson, "The Adoption of the Constitution of 1874 . . .," *op. cit*., p. 296.
49.  Staples, *loc cit*., quoting the *Republican*.
50.  Letter from E. H. English to David Walker, Fayetteville, Ark.; Little Rock, March 5, 1875. University of Arkansas, Walker Letters, fol. 4.
51.  Letter from A. H. Garland to Alexander H. Stephens, [Washington, D. C.] ; Little Rock, March 7, 1875. Library of Congress, Alexander H. Stephens Papers.

## CHAPTER 11: BANKS: THE FIRST ATTEMPT TO USE STATE CREDIT

1.  Quoted in W. D. Blocher, *Arkansas Finances* (Little Rock: *The Evening Star*, 1876), p. 34.
2.  W. C. Evans, "The Public Debt," *Arkansas and Its People: A History, 1541-1930,* ed. David Y. Thomas (New York: The American Historical Society, Inc., 1930), I, p. 355.
3.  Blocher, *op. cit*., pp. 36–37.
4.  Ted R. Worley, *op. cit*., pp. 403 –405. A branch bank at Van Buren was authorized February 24, 1838. Blocher, *op. cit*., p. 6.
5.  A branch was established later at Arkansas Post in eastern Arkansas, *Ibid*., p. 14.
6.  Evans, *loc. cit*.
7.  Carmichael, *op. cit*., p. 190.
8.  Herndon, *op. cit*., p. 1008.
9.  Blocher, *loc. cit*.
10.  *Ibid*., p. 15. From a report of William M. Gouge and A. H. Rutherford to Governor Conway, 1855, quoted by Blocher.
11.  Evans, *op. cit*., p. 357.
12.  Blocher, *loc. cit*. From a report by Major Jacob Brown, President of the State Bank, to the Arkansas Senate, November 7, 1837, quoted by Blocher.
13.  Evans, *op. cit*., p. 358.
14.  *Ibid*., p. 359. Part of the appearance of affluence was due to the buildings constructed to house their operations. These were sold in 1845 to satisfy claims of creditors and resulted in the following losses:

| Bank | Cost | Sold for | Loss |
|---|---|---|---|
| Arkansas Post | $16,000 | $100 | $15,900 |
| Batesville | 15,000 | 100 | 14,900 |
| Fayetteville | 7,500 | 800 | 6,700 |
| Little Rock | 28,000 | 200 | 27,800 |
| | $66,500 | $1,200 | $65,300 |

Herndon, *op. cit*., p. 493.

15.  Carmichael, *op. cit.*, p. 191.

16.  Evans, *loc. cit.*

17.  Blocher, *op. cit.*, p. 35.

18.  Evans, *op. cit.*, p. 359.

19.  David Walker settled in Fayetteville in 1830, migrating from Kentucky *via* Little Rock.  Archibald Yell came to Fayetteville in 1832 as District Judge of Arkansas Territory, receiving his appointment from Andrew Jackson, under whom he had served at New Orleans and in the Seminole War. Yell was the first U. S. Congressman from Arkansas, 1836–1839; governor, 1840 – 1844; and elected to Congress in 1844 as the Democratic candidate over David Walker for the Whig party. Hallum, *Biographical . . . History of Arkansas, op. cit.,* pp. 111-12.

20.  Blocher, *op. cit.*, p. 25.

21.  *Ibid.*, p. 26. Quoted from the report of the commissioners, June 20, 1841.

22.  Hall, *op. cit.*, p. 252.

23.  Blocher, *op. cit.*, p. 29.  One possible reason for resenting David Walker as a commissioner was the fact that his father, Jacob W. Walker, had served as president of the bank from February 7, 1837 to December 15, 1838. *Ibid.*, p. 38.

24.  *Ibid.*, pp. 29, 31.

25.  *Ibid.*, p. 33. Blank impressions of notes missing totaled $12,290, while other funds missing amounted to $33,279.60 .

26.  *Ibid.*, pp. 32–33.

27.  *Ibid.*, p. 35.  State Bank and branches to the receivers: Little Rock, June 9, 1843; Post of Arkansas, June 15, 1843; Batesville, July 1, 1843; and Fayetteville, July 21, 1843.

28.  Worley, *op. cit.*, p. 403.

29.  Carmichael, *op. cit.*, pp. 191–92.

30.  *Ibid.*, p. 192.

31.  Worley, *loc. cit.*

32.  *Ibid.*, p. 407.  Worley says of the original distribution of stock in 1837: "They awarded 22,500 shares of stock, each of $100 par value, to 184 individuals, in fourteen of the state's thirty-odd counties.   To two of its members the board awarded the limit of 300 shares of stock; a third member received 130 shares, and a fourth, 50 shares. Of the 22,500 shares of stock awarded, 6,286 went to twenty-eight residents of Chicot County.  Six counties were awarded more than 1,500 shares; with the exception of Pulaski, in which the capitol was located, all these counties touched the Mississippi or the Red River and were in the best cotton producing sections."

33.  *Ibid.*, p. 405.

34.  *Ibid.*, p. 406.

35.  *Ibid.*, pp. 405–406.

36.  Evans, *op. cit.*, p. 358.

37.  Blocher, *op. cit.*, p. 6.  Dates of openings: Little Rock, December 12, 1838; Helena, February 15, 1839; Columbia, March 5, 1839; and Washington, April 1, 1839.

38.  Evans, *loc. cit.* By the end of November, 1838, all of the banks had suspended specie payments.

39.  Blocher, *op. cit.*, p. 7.

40.  Worley, *op. cit.*, p. 423. Worley quoting the *Gazette*, February 17, 1841.

41.  Copy of letter from Governor Archibald Yell to C. A. Harris, [President of the Real Estate Bank], [Prescott?], Ark.; Little Rock, July 20, 1841. Arkansas History Commission, Governor Archibald Yell's Letterbook. Hereafter this will be referred to as the Yell Letterbook.

42.  Copy of letter from C. A. Harris to Governor Archibald Yell, Little Rock, Ark.; Little Rock, October 25, 1841. Yell Letterbook.

43.  Letter from Archibald Yell to the President and Directors of the Real Estate Bank, [Little Rock, Ark.] ; Little Rock, October 29, 1841. Yell Letterbook.

44.  Letter from Archibald Yell to Messrs. Talmage, Holford & Co., New York, N. Y.; Little Rock, November 10, 1841. Yell Letterbook.

45.  Blocher, *op. cit.,* p. 8.

46.  Copy of letter from David Walker to Governor Archibald Yell, n.p.; n.d. University of Arkansas, Walker Letters, fol. 5. This letter is believed to have been written in 1842.

47.  Evans, *op. cit.*, p. 358.

48.  *Ibid.*, p. 359.

49.  *Ibid.*, p. 360.

50.  Blocher, *op. cit.*, p. 34.

51.  *Ibid.*, p. 9.

52.  *Report of the Senate Bank Committee, in Relation to the Real Estate Bank,* 1852. George W. Lemoyne, Chairman. p.3. University of Arkansas, Microfilm, 27. Original in the University of Texas Library.

53.  *Ibid.*, p. 7.

54.  *Ibid.*, pp. 8–9.

55.  *Ibid.*, p. 10.

56.  Blocher, *loc. cit.*

57.  *Ibid.*, p. 10.

58.  Richard H. Johnson, *Address to the People of Arkansas*, (Little Rock, n.p., May 31, 1860), p. 11. University of Arkansas, Microfilm, 27. Original in the University of Texas Library.

59.  Letter from John Quindley [State Treasurer] to Richard H. Johnson, Little Rock, Ark.; Little Rock, May 14, 1870. Quoted by Johnson. *Ibid.*, p. 12.

60.  *Ibid.*, pp. 12–13.

61.  Evans, *op. cit.*, p. 363. Three weeks after a suit had been filed in behalf of the Holford claim, the Arkansas legislature passed an act requiring the original bonds to be filed as a prelude to any suit for the collection of principal or interest. Since the Holford lawyers had only photostatic copies, the court dismissed the suit lacking jurisdiction. The state Supreme Court affirmed the lower court's decision. Carried to the United States Supreme Court, Chief Justice Taney argued that his court had no jurisdiction to override a legislative decree of a state. *Ibid.*, pp. 362–63.

62.  Carmichael, *op. cit.*, pp. 199–200.

63.  *Ibid.*, p. 200.

64.  *Ibid.*, p. 196.

65.  *Ibid.*, p. 197.

66.  Evans, *op. cit.*, p. 364.

## CHAPTER 12: JESSE TURNER

1.  Johnson, Richard H., *op. cit.*, p. 15.

2.  *Gazette*, August 15, 1960, p. 1, c. 7.

3.  Carmichael, *op. cit.*, p. 184.

4.  Thomas, I, *op. cit.*, p. 98.

5.  *Ibid.*, p. 99.

6.  *Ibid.*, p. 101.

7.  *Ibid.* An internal improvement board was created to supervise the sale of lands.

8.  Carmichael, *op. cit.*, p. 167.

9.  *Ibid.*, p. 165.

10.  John L. Ferguson and J. H. Atkinson, *Historic Arkansas* (Little Rock, Ark.: Arkansas History Commission, 1966), p. 101. This vast acreage represented over one-fourth of all the land in the state.

11.  Herndon, *op. cit.*, p. 446.

12.  Ferguson and Atkinson, *op. cit.*, p. 103.

13.  Carmichael, *op. cit.*, pp. 178–79.

14.  *Ibid.*, p. 153.

15.  Walker to "Dear Sir," April 3, 1860, *op. cit.* River planters in the delta were favored in the use of these funds. Carmichael, *op. cit.*, p. 179.

16.  See above p. 11.

17. Carmichael, *op. cit.*, pp. 175-76.
18. *Ibid.*, p. 175.
19. *Ibid.*, p. 169.
20. Roswell Beebe, *et al. Memorial to the Legislature* (Little Rock, Ark.: *True Democrat*, 1852), pp. 3-4. University of Arkansas, Microfilm 27. Original in the University of Texas Library.
21. Carmichael, *op. cit.*, p. 166; Stephen E. Wood, "The Development of Arkansas Railroads, Part I: Early Interest and Activities," *Arkansas Historical Quarterly*, VII, No. 2 (Summer, 1948), p. 107. Napoleon was also considered as a possible eastern terminal. *Ibid.*, p. 104.
22. *Ibid.*, p. 106.
23. *Ibid.*, p. 107.
24. Carmichael, *op. cit.*, p. 175; Ferguson and Atkinson, *op. cit.*, p. 129.
25. Samuel W. Moore, "State Supervision of Railroad Transportation in Arkansas," *Publications of the Arkansas Historical Association, op cit.*, III, p. 271.
26. Carmichael, *op. cit.*, pp. 172-73. The first survey for this line made use of the geological line which crossed the state from northeast to southwest. Wood, *op. cit.*, pp. 103-104.
27. Cairo and Fulton Railroad Company, *Proceedings . . . Meeting of Stockholders*, May 7, 1855, *op. cit.*, p. 16.
28. Carmichael, *op. cit.*, p. 172.
29. Carter Goodrich, "American Development Policy: The Case of Internal Improvements," *The Journal of Economic History*, XVI (December, 1956), pp. 449-60.
30. *Ibid.*, p. 451.
31. Hallum, *op. cit.*, p. 247.
32. Letter from J. H. Haney to Jesse Turner, Van Buren, Ark.; Van Buren, July 31, 1860. Duke University, Turner Papers.
33. Financial statement of the Little Rock and Fort Smith Railroad Company, August 1, 1860. Duke University, Turner Papers.
34. Letter from Robert J. T. White to the President and Directors of the Little Rock and Fort Smith Railroad Company, Van Buren, Ark.; Van Buren, August 15, 1860. Duke University, Turner Papers.
35. Gunnar Myrdal, *Rich Lands and Poor: The Road to World Prosperity*, Vol. XVI of *World Perspectives* ed. Ruth Nanda Anshen (In process; New York: Harper & Brothers, 1957), pp. 11-12.
36. Letter from James M. Brown to Jesse Turner, Van Buren, Ark.; Little Rock, November 7, 1860. Duke University, Turner Papers.
37. Letter from Andrew Morton to Jesse Turner, Van Buren, Ark.; Little Rock, November 9, 1860; letter from Grace J. Clark to Jesse Turner, Van Buren, Ark.; Little Rock, November 17, 1860; Clark to Turner, November 29, 1860, *op. cit.*; letter from J. H. Haney to Jesse Turner, Van Buren, Ark.; Little Rock, December 13, 1860; letter from J. H. Haney to Jesse Turner, Van Buren, Ark.; Little Rock, December 29, 1860. Duke University, Turner Papers.
38. Brown to Turner, November 7, 1860, *op. cit.*
39. Haney to Turner, December 13, 1860, *op. cit.*
40. Letter from J. H. Haney to Jesse Turner, Van Buren, Ark.; Little Rock, January 12, 1861. Duke University, Turner Papers; Clark to Turner, November 29, 1860, *op. cit.*
41. Clark to Turner, November 17, 1860, *op. cit.*
42. *Acts of Arkansas* (1860-61), No. 63, 136-37.
43. *Ibid.*, No. 116, 243; *ibid.*, No. 108, 226.
44. Letter from State Auditor W. R. Miller to Jesse Turner, President of the Little Rock and Fort Smith Railroad Company, Van Buren, Ark.; Little Rock, February 4, 1861. Duke University, Turner Papers.
45. Haney to Turner, July 31, 1860, *op. cit.*
46. Turner to Editor of the *New York Express,* December 10, 1861, *op. cit.*; petition from Mathew Ham, *et al.* to Jesse Turner, Van Buren, Ark.; Crawford County, January 29, 1861. Duke University, Turner Papers; *Gazette*, February 23, 1861, p. 2, c. 4.

47.   James P. Henry, *Resources of the State of Arkansas* (3rd ed,; Little Rock, Ark.: Price & McClure, State Printers, 1873), pp. 87–132, *passim.*

48.   Letter from J. H. Haney to Jesse Turner, Van Buren, Ark.; Memphis, [Tenn.], January 12, 1866. Duke University, Turner Papers.

49.   Letter from Governor Isaac Murphy to Jesse Turner, Van Buren, Ark.; Little Rock, March 2, 1866. Duke University, Turner Papers; see above p. 194.

50.   Hall, *op. cit.*, p. 184; letter from W. Byers to Jesse Turner, Van Buren, Ark.; Washington, D. C., February 5, 1866. University of Arkansas, Turner Papers, fol. 2.

51.   Letter from J. H. Haney to Jesse Turner, Van Buren, Ark.; Russellville, April 26, 1866. University of Arkansas, Turner Papers, fol. 2.

52.   Letter from W. Byers to Jesse Turner, Van Buren, Ark.; Washington, D. C., July 20, 1866. Duke University, Turner Papers,

53.   Morris, *op. cit.*, p. 247.

54.   U. S. *Congressional Globe,* 39th Cong., 1st Sess., 1866, Part 5, Appendix, 422.

55.   Paige E. Mulhollen, "The Public Career of James H. Berry" (unpublished Master's thesis, Dept. of History, University of Arkansas, 1962), pp. 19 - 20. Jesse Turner was a Senator in this legislature.

56.   *Acts of Arkansas* (1866–1867), No. 166, 432.

57.   *Ibid.,* p. 429.

58.   *Ibid.,* p. 430.

59.   Message from Governor Isaac Murphy to the Speaker of the House of Representatives [Bradley Bunch], Little Rock, Ark.; Executive Office, March 19, 1867. *Arkansas House Journal* (1866–1867), pp. 946-49.

60.   *Ibid.,* p. 947.

61.   *Ibid.,* p. 948.

62.   *Ibid.,* p. 949.

63.   *Arkansas House Journal* (1866–1867), p. 953.

64.   *Ibid.,* p. 962.

65.   Letter from J. H. Haney to Jesse Turner, Van Buren, Ark.; Little Rock, May 26, 1867. Duke University, Turner Papers. Haney revealed that in the absence of Congressional representation other channels had been utilized to obtain the certificate. He wrote: "You will remember that at the last meeting of the Board it was resolved that as soon as the above-mentioned certificate was made the Secy of the Company should draw a check for $1000. in favor of John Edwards & if you now think all the conditions are fully complied with & that it may safely be done I will send Gen. Edwards a check for that amount."

66.   Letter  from J. H. Haney to Jesse Turner, Van Buren, Ark.; New York, September 27, 1867. Duke University, Turner Papers.

67.   *Ibid.;* letter from J. H. Haney to Jesse Turner, Van Buren, Ark.; Little Rock, October 18, 1867. Duke University, Turner Papers.

68.   *Ibid.;* Haney to Turner, September 27, 1867, *op. cit.*

69.   Haney to Turner, October 18, 1867, *op. cit.*

70.   Haney to Turner, September 27, 1867, *op. cit.*

71.   Haney to Turner, October 18, 1867, *op. cit.;* letter from J. H. Haney to Jesse Turner, Van Buren, Ark.; Little Rock, January 17, 1868. Duke University, Turner Papers.

72.   *Debates and Proceedings, op. cit.*, p. 159.

73.   *Ibid.,* p. 165.

74.   Letter from J. H. Haney to R. S. Gantt, Member of the Convention, Little Rock, Ark.; Little Rock, January 20, 1868. *Ibid.,* pp. 227-28.

75.   *Debates and Proceedings, op cit.*, pp. 229-30.

76.   Letter from A. H. Garland to the President and Directors of the Little Rock and Fort Smith Railroad Company, n.p.; Little Rock, January 20, 1868. Arkansas History Commission, Jesse Turner Papers.

77.   Copy of the Report on Treasurer Pennywit's Railroad Account to the President and Directors of the Little Rock and Fort Smith Railroad Company, February, 1868. Duke University, Turner Papers.

78. Garland to the President. . . , January 20, 1868, *op. cit.*
79. Copy of the Report on Treasurer . . . , February, 1868, *op. cit.*
80. Letter from J. H. Haney to Jesse Turner, Van Buren, Ark.; Little Rock, February 21, 1868. Duke University, Turner Papers.
81. Letter from J. H. Haney to Jesse Turner, Van Buren, Ark.; Little Rock, July 15, 1868. Duke University, Turner Papers.
82. *Ibid.*
83. Blocher, *op. cit.*, pp. 42-45.
84. *Ibid.*, p. 44.
85. Letter from J. H. Haney to Jesse Turner, Van Buren, Ark.; Little Rock, August 29, 1868. Duke University, Turner Papers.
86. Letter from Jesse Turner to John J. Walker, n.p.; Van Buren, Ark., January 6, 1869. Duke University, Turner Papers.
87. Letter from J. H. Haney to Jesse Turner, Van Buren, Ark.; Little Rock, February 16, 1869. Duke University, Turner Papers.
88. Letter from J. H. Haney to Jesse Turner, Van Buren, Ark.; Little Rock, February 5, 1869. Duke University, Turner Papers.
89. Haney to Turner, February 16, 1869, *op. cit.*
90. See above p. 195.
91. Letter from James G. Blaine to [Warren Fisher, Jr.], [Boston, Mass.]; Augusta, Maine, October 4, 1869. Quoted in Charles Edward Russell, *Blaine of Maine: His Life and Times* (New York: Cosmopolitan Book Corporation, 1931), p. 297.
92. U. S., *Congressional Globe,* 40th Cong., 3d Sess., 1869, Part 3, 1897. Blaine's action was later recorded in his correspondence with Warren Fisher, Jr. and became part of the "Mulligan letters," which were a factor in preventing Blaine from receiving the Republican nomination for the Presidency in 1876. These letters were again exploited, this time by the Democrats, in Blaine's campaign against Grover Cleveland in 1884. The chant "Burn this letter, Burn this letter, Kind regards to Mrs. Fisher" was used in a New York City parade up Fifth Avenue late in the campaign in order to discredit Blaine in that state. During the parade men carrying sticks to which were attached sheets of writing paper monotonously repeated the chant. David Saville Muzzey, *James G. Blaine: A Political Idol of Other Days* (New York: Dodd, Mead & Company, 1935), p. 304. For the nature and for the significance of the Mulligan letters consult: Russell, *Blaine of Maine: His Life and Times, op. cit.*; and Muzzey, *James G. Blaine.*
93. U. S., *Congressional Globe*, 40th Cong., 3d Sess., 1869, Part 3, Appendix, 329.
94. Blocher, *op. cit.*, pp. 51-53.
95. *Acts of Arkansas* (1868-1869), No. 81, 159-60.
96. Blocher, *op. cit.*, p. 46.

## CHAPTER 13: ASA P. ROBINSON

1. Letter from Asa P. Robinson to Josiah Caldwell, Boston, Mass.; Little Rock, April 26, 1870. Arkansas History Commission, Clara Bertha Eno Collection, Asa P. Robinson Papers, Asa P. Robinson Letterbook 2, p. 415. So much of the documentation concerning the Little Rock and Fort Smith Railroad has come from Asa P. Robinson's five letterbooks that only sources other than those letterbooks will be noted in this chapter. Hereafter, an abbreviated system of reference will be used. Most of the correspondence is from Asa P. Robinson in Little Rock to Josiah Caldwell in Boston; therefore, unless noted otherwise, these places and these Christian names will be understood. The correspondence comprises both letters and telegrams. Notice will be given for a telegram, but without such notice the reader will understand that the communication is a letter. An "L" will be used as an abbreviation for letterbook, and the number of that book will follow, e.g., L 2, p. 300.
2. *Biographical and Historical Memoirs of Central Arkansas* (Chicago, Ill.: Goodspeed Publishing Co., 1889), pp. 735-36.
3. Robinson wrote Caldwell proposing the purchase of a steamer to help reduce their

freight costs. This solution, however, was not without its problems. A boat which could navigate the river could only bring 500 tons of rails per load, and a round trip required twenty-one days. For twenty miles of track 1500 tons of rails were required; therefore, more than one boat would have to be used to keep the work from being interrupted.

4.  The engine *Pope* was upset into the Ohio River while being loaded at New Albany late in 1870 and sustained considerable injury. Robinson spent $250 for repairs after she arrived including $85 for a new headlight. The cab was also destroyed and another ordered from the factory, but it had not yet arrived at the time Robinson was writing.

5.  Robinson estimated the distance from Little Rock to Van Buren as being 159½ miles. Arkansas History Commission, Asa P. Robinson Papers.

6.  *Gazette*, November 20, 1870, p. 4, c. 2.

7.  *Gazette*, November 23, 1870, p. 1, c. 3.

8.  *Steacy* v. *Little Rock & Ft. S. R. Co., et al.*, 22 Fed. Cas. 1142, No. 13,329, (1879-1880), 1150.

9.  The estimate of interest due on bonds delivered to Warren Fisher, Jr. is based on the following source: Report of Secretary Gordon N. Peay to C. G. Scott, Director of the Little Rock and Fort Smith Railroad Company, Little Rock, Ark.; Little Rock, August 13, 1871. *Gazette*, August 26, 1871, p. 1, cc. 2-3.

| Date | Type Bond | | Amount | Interest Due |
|------|-----------|---|--------|--------------|
| 2/15/70 | First Mort., | 6% | $   700,000 | $  21,000 |
| 3/3/70 | First Mort., | 6% | 1,000,000 | 30,000 |
| 7/28/70 | First Mort., | 6% | 450,000 | 11,745 |
| 8/8/70 | First Mort., | 6% | 350,000 | 6,930 |
| 7/28/70 | Land Mort., | 7% | 300,000 | 39,585 |
| 8/8/70 | Land Mort., | 7% | 1,500,000 | 35,970 |
| | Total | | $4,300,000 | $145,230 |

10.  *Shaw et al.* v. *Little Rock & Ft. S. Ry.*, 100 U. S. 605 (1880); 25 LEd., 757.

11.  Letter from "Stockholder" to Editor of the *Gazette*, [Little Rock, Ark.]; Clarksville, August 8, 1871. *Gazette*, August 11, 1871, p. 1, c. 1.

12.  Letter from Peirce, Steacy, and Yorston to the Editor of the *Gazette*, Little Rock, Ark.; Little Rock, August 5, 1871. *Gazette*, August 6, 1871, p. 1, cc. 1-2.

13.  Letter from John C. Pratt to Editor of the *Gazette*, Little Rock, Ark.; [Boston Mass.]. July 25, 1871. *Gazette*, August 4, 1871, p. 1, c. 4.

14.  *Gazette*, August 26, 1871, p. 1, cc. 1-3.

15.  Letter from unknown author from Conway County to Editor of *Gazette*, Little Rock, Ark.; Conway County, n.d. *Gazette*, October 3, 1871, p.4, c. 4.

16.  Letter from "Brooklyn Waterworks" to the Editor of the *Gazette*, Little Rock, Ark.; n.p., n.d. *Gazette*, September 29, 1871, p.1, cc. 2-3.

17.  Telegram from Robinson to Caldwell, New York, N. Y., October 19, 1871. L5, p. 159; *Gazette*, October 24, 1871, p. 4, c. 2.

18.  *Ibid.*

19.  *Gazette*, November 23, 1871, p. 2, c. 3.

20.  Letter from Josiah Caldwell to J. H. Haney, [Little Rock, Ark.]; Little Rock, December 21, 1871. *Haney* v. *Caldwell*, 35 Ark., 156 (1879).

21.  Robert L. Gatewood, *Faulkner County, Arkansas: 1778-1964* (rev. & enl.; Conway, Ark.: published by the author, 1964), p. 37.

22.  Gatewood, *op. cit.*, p. 46.

23.  *Biographical and Historical Memoirs of Central Arkansas, op. cit.*, p. 736; Gatewood, *op. cit.*, pp. 37-43.

CHAPTER 14: FINANCING A "STUMPTAIL" RAILROAD

1.    Letter from J. H. Haney to Jesse Turner, Van Buren, Ark.; Hot Springs, August 26, 1873. Duke University, Turner Papers.
2.    Robinson to Caldwell, October 20, 1869. L 1, p. 67.
3.    Robinson to Caldwell, November 16, 1869. L 1, p. 171.
4.    *Steacy* v. *Little Rock & Ft. S. R. Co. et al., loc cit.*
5.    Report on Estimate of Warren Fisher, Jr. from Asa P. Robinson to J. H. Haney, July, 1870. Arkansas History Commission, Asa P. Robinson Papers.
6.    *Ibid.*
7.    *Ibid.*
8.    Robinson had increased his estimate from $9,000 on the first eighty miles, mentioned earlier, to $10,000 over the entire road. He allowed $415 per mile for contingencies, which amounted to $2,133.92 per mile when multiplied by the 5.142 factor. *Ibid.*
9.    Report from J. H. Haney to C[harles] G. Scott, n.p.; Little Rock, August 17, [1871]. *Gazette*, August 26, 1871, p.1, c. 2; Rail Road Convention, *Proceedings* (Fayetteville, Ark., August 15, 1870), p. 3. University of Arkansas, Sue Walker Papers.
10.   Matthew Josephson. *The Robber Barons: The Great American Capitalists, 1861-1901* (New York: Harcourt, Brace & World, 1934), p. 92.
11.   Haney to Turner, August 26, 1873, *op. cit.*
12.   Report on Estimate of Warren Fisher, Jr., *op. cit.*
13.   *Ibid.*
14    *Steacy* v. *Little Rock & Ft. S. R. Co. et al.,loc. cit.*
15.   Report from Gordon N. Peay to Charles G. Scott, August 13, 1871, *loc. cit.*
16.   *Steacy* v. *Little Rock & Ft. S. R. Co. et al., loc. cit.*
17.   *Ibid.*
18.   Report from Peay to Scott, August 13, 1871, *loc. cit.*

|  | To Fisher by September 28, 1870 |
|---|---|
| First Mortgage Bonds | $2,500,000 |
| State Aid Bonds | 800,000 |
| Land Mortgage Bonds | 2,800,000 |
| Common Stock | 1,650,000 |
| Preferred Stock | 1,650,000 |
|  | $9,400,000 |

19.   Robinson to Caldwell, September 14, 1870. L 2, p. 755.
20.   *Steacy* v. *Little Rock & Ft. S. R. Co. et al., loc. cit.*
21.   See above p. 209.
22.   Calculated from: *Steacy* v. *Little Rock & Ft. S. R. Co. et al., loc cit.*

|  | To Fisher by June 9, 1871 |
|---|---|
| First Mortgage Bonds | $3,285,000 |
| State Aid Bonds | 900,000 |
| Land Mortgage Bonds | 4,386,000 |
| Common Stock | 1,650,000 |
| Preferred Stock | 1,650,000 |
|  | $11,871,000 |

23.   Telegram from Robinson to John C. Pratt, Boston, [Mass], January 5, 1871. L 5, p. 1.
24.   Sanford to C. T. Melby, n.p., April 27, 1871, *loc cit.*

25. Telegram from J. W. Lemon to Caldwell in care of Robinson, New York, N. Y., March 14, 1871. L 5, p. 37.

26. Report from Haney to Scott, August 26, 1871, *loc. cit.*

27. Some modifications have had to be made in order to compare the two estimates. These modifications can be seen from an examination of the table.

28. The basis for this estimate is shown below. I am indebted to Samuel Sizer of the Arkansas History Commission who secured information about the bond prices from the *New York Times* when he was at the University of Arkansas.

|  |  |  |  |
|---|---|---|---|
| $500,000 | state bonds | @ 70 | $350,000 |
| 300,000 | state bonds | @ 58½ | 175,000 |
| 100,000 | state bonds | @ 64 | 64,000 |
|  |  |  | $589,000 |

This is only a rough estimate and is based on a random sampling of prices bid during the time period under consideration. *New York Times*, September 21, 1870, p. 3, c. 4; *ibid.*, October 2, 1870, p. 6, c. 5; *ibid.*, November 2, 1870, p. 3, c. 3; *ibid.*, December 2, 1870, p. 3, c. 3.

29. *Steacy* v. *Little Rock & Ft. S. R. Co. et al., loc. cit.* Members present at this directors' meeting included John C. Pratt, Charles G. Scott, U. M. Rose, E. Wheeler, [?] Lawson, and James A. Martin. *Ibid.*

30. Robinson to Caldwell, March 29, 1870. L 2, pp. 296–300.

31. *Ibid.*, p. 296.

32. *Ibid.*, p. 298.

33. *Ibid.*, pp. 299–300. Robinson's calculations are given below. His figures in the right-hand column ran off his blotter, and part of them have had to be supplied. In another part of his letter, however, he mentioned the expenditure figure of $16,153.99, and from that evidence, the missing figures have been supplied.

*Balance on Hand*
*October 6, 1866*

| Debit | | Credit | |
|---|---|---|---|
| Gold | $27,789.21 | (Gold) allowance of salary | $ 2,010.00 |
| Confederate | | Expenditures | |
| Currency | 3,515.00 | currency to Dec. 21, 1867 | ( 16,153.99) |
| | $31,304.21 | Reduced to gold at 133 1/3 | 12,115.79 |
| | | Balance gold | 13,663.42 |
| | | Confederate Currency | 3,515.00 |
| | | | $31,304.21 |

There is a forty-nine cent discrepancy between Robinson's total of $13,663.91 and the $13,663.42 necessary to achieve a balance, which is unexplained.

34. *Ibid.*, p. 300.

35. *Ibid.*

36. Letter from J. H. Haney to Jesse Turner, Van Buren, Ark.; Little Rock, February 18, 1874. Duke University, Turner Papers.

37. Robinson to Charles G. Scott, [Little Rock, Ark.], May 16, 1870. L 2, p. 463; Robinson to C. C. Reid, [Little Rock, Ark.], January 2, 1870. L 4, p. 1.

38. Robinson to Scott, May 16, 1870, *loc. cit.*

39. *Ibid.*

40. Robinson to "My Dear Sir," August 13, 1870. L 2, p. 662.

41. *Ibid.*; Robinson to Caldwell, May 20, 1870. L 2, p. 494. Robinson's opinion of Republican John N. Sarber was very low. He wrote Caldwell: "Mr. Scott's disbursements commence by a payment of $450 to Mr. Sarber a little whipper snapper member of the Legislature whom you know and whose meddling in the matter will do us no good whatever. He is a d— — —d skunk but has just cheek enough to be importunate and to estimate his agency in any such matter at an exhorbitant [*sic*] value." *Ibid.*

42. See above p. 224.

43. James Ford Rhodes, *History of the United States from the Compromise of 1850* (New York: The Macmillan Company, 1906), VII, p. 195.

44. *New York Times*, July 2, 1870, p. 3, c. 4; *ibid.*, October 2, 1870, p. 6, c. 5; *ibid.*, November 2, 1870, p.3, c. 2; *ibid.*, p. 3, c. 3; *ibid.*, December 2, 1870, p. 3, c. 3; *ibid.*, June 2, 1871, p. 3, c. 2; *ibid.*, November 12, 1871, p. 6, c. 1.

45. *Haney* v. *Caldwell, op. cit.*, 158.

46. *Ibid.*, 159.

47. Haney to Turner, February 18, 1874, *op. cit.*

48. *Ibid.*

49. *Ibid.*

50. Auditor, *Biennial Report, 1872–1874, op. cit.*, p. 35; Robinson to A. P. Curry & Co., n.p., June 12, 1873. L 4, p. 348.

51. On May 12, 1874, Henry W. Paine, William B. Stevens, and Charles W. Huntington began suits as trustees for the bondholders to foreclose their respective mortgages. *Shaw et al.* v. *Little Rock & Ft. S. Ry., loc. cit.*

52. *Ibid.*, 758.

53. *Ibid.*

54. *Ibid.*

55. *Huntington et al. Trustees* v. *Little Rock & Ft. S. R. Co. et al.*, 100 U. S. 605; 16 F 906 (1882). The court records in Little Rock for the U. S. Circuit Court Eastern District of Arkansas contain the exhibit which can be found in Chancery B (1874), pp. 558–60.

56. *Ibid.*

57. It should be remembered that Elisha Atkins was a director of the Union Pacific. Instead of the Caldwell interests, Atkins might well have been representing the Union Pacific as bondholders. Josephson, *The Politicos, op. cit.*, p. 210.

58. Letter from Jesse Turner to his son, Jesse, [Amherst Court House, Va.] ; Little Rock, February 1, 1875. Duke University, Turner Papers.

59. Letter from Jesse Turner to his son, Jesse, [Amherst Court House, Va.] ; Little Rock, February 28, 1875. Duke University, Turner Papers.

60. Letter from Jesse Turner to his son, Jesse, [Amherst Court House, Va.] ; Van Buren, October 24, 1875. Duke University, Turner Papers.

61. Ellis Paxon Oberholtzer, *A History of the United States since the Civil War* (New York: The Macmillan Company, 1922), II, p. 614.

62. Letter from Jesse Turner to his son, Jesse, [Amherst Court House, Va.] ; Van Buren, June 6, 1876. Duke University, Turner Papers.

NOTE: The incomplete nature of the evidence relating to the Little Rock and Fort Smith Railroad Company makes it possible to misinterpret the available evidence. The relationship existing between the railroad company and the construction company may be such a case. It is possible to interpret this episode as an example of a handful of corrupt railroad company managers enriching themselves through overpayments to the construction company, which was under their control. Essentially, excess payments made by the railroad company might have gone to "insiders" who controlled, or were allied with, the contractor. The involvement of the Union Pacific calls to mind the *Crédit Mobilier* scandal in which the railroad company "insiders" used the construction company in this way to make their profits. To interpret the available evidence pertaining to the Little Rock and Fort Smith Railroad in this manner, however, does not satisfactorily explain why Caldwell and Robinson were driven to the point of being personally discredited in their efforts to construct the road.

## CHAPTER 15: THE LOSS OF STATE CREDIT

1. Evans, *op. cit.*, p. 365.
2. See Chapter XI, p. 173
3. Evans, *loc. cit.*
4. *Fayetteville Democrat,* April 24, 1869, p. 2, c. 2.
5. Powell Clayton, *Aftermath of the Civil War in Arkansas* (New York: Neale Publishing Co., 1915), pp. 258–60.
6. Harrell, *op. cit.*, p. 59. Harrell comments: "One of the most shameless acts for depleting the treasury and creating a vast debt for posterity, without any earthly reason in morals or propriety, was the funding of the Holford claim for $1,370,000."
7. Evans, *loc. cit.*
8. Letter from Powell Clayton to George Cox, American Exchange National Bank, New York, N. Y.; Little Rock, January 10, 1870. Arkansas History Commission, Clayton Letterbook, p. 323.
9. Letter from Powell Clayton to George Cox, American Exchange National Bank, New York, N. Y.; Little Rock, May 14, 1870. *Ibid.*, pp. 170–71.
10. Carmichael, *op. cit.*, p. 395.
11. Evans, *op. cit.*, p. 366.
12. Constitution of the State of Arkansas, 1868, Article X, Sect. 6, *Debates and Proceedings, op. cit.*, p. 883.
13. Blocher, *op. cit.*, p. 45. This act authorized $10,000 per mile in state aid to roads without land grants and authorized $15,000 per mile to roads with land grants. *Ibid.*, p. 42.
14. *Ibid.*, p. 45.
15. *Ibid.*, p. 46.
16. Letter from Powell Clayton to Josiah Caldwell, New York, N. Y.; Little Rock, April 22, 1870; letter from Powell Clayton to [P. H.] Young, n.p.; Little Rock, June 29, 1870; letter from Powell Clayton to R. C. Brinkley, President of the Memphis and Little Rock Rail Road, n.p.; Little Rock, September 5, 1870. Arkansas History Commission, Clayton Letterbook, pp. 131, 369, 883–84.
17. Clayton, *Aftermath of the Civil War in Arkansas, op. cit.,* pp. 238–39; *Fayetteville Democrat,* March 27, 1869, p. 3, c. 3.
18. Letter from Asa P. Robinson to W. P. Denkla, n.p.; Little Rock, May 20, 1870; Arkansas History Commission, Asa P. Robinson, L 2, p. 490; Carter Goodrich, "Public Aid to Railroads in the Reconstruction South," *Political Science Quarterly,* LXXI, No. 3 (September, 1956), p. 425.
19. *Gazette,* April 18, 1869, p. 2, c. 2; Driggs, *op. cit.*, pp. 32, 32n.
20. Goodrich, "Public Aid . . .," *op. cit.*, p. 426.
21. *Ibid.*, p. 426n.
22. Clayton, *Aftermath of the Civil War in Arkansas, op. cit.*, p. 238; Blocher, *op. cit.*, p. 47. The Cairo and Fulton relinquished its grant and the Arkansas Central received part of that grant plus the Little Rock and Helena grant.
23. Goodrich, "Public Aid . . . ," *op. cit.*, pp. 426, 436. Powell Clayton claimed that 445 miles of railroad had been constructed with the bonded aid before the Democrats discontinued the practice in May, 1874. Clayton, *Aftermath of the Civil War in Arkansas, op. cit.*, p. 239.
24. William A. Scott, *The Repudiation of State Debts,* Vol. II of the *Library of Economics and Politics,* University of Wisconsin, ed. Richard. T. Ely (New York: Thomas Y. Crowell, 1893), p. 121.
25. Blocher, *op. cit.*, p. 54. This act was amended on March 23, 1871, and the bonds were issued under the authority of this latter act. *Ibid.*, p. 55.
26. *Ibid.*, p. 57.
27. Arkansas, Commissioner of State Lands, *Biennial Report, 1872–1874,* pp. 17–18. University of Arkansas, Microfilm 27. On August 13, 1874, the Constitutional Convention passed William Fishback's ordinance to refuse the levee bonds as payment for the land. On December fourteenth the legislature passed an act preventing the use of these bonds for the purchase of internal improvement lands. Blocher, *op. cit.,* pp. 59-60.

28.  Carmichael, *op. cit.*, p. 393.
29.  Abstract of State Indebtedness, July 1, 1874. Arkansas History Commission, Calvin C. Bliss Papers.
30.  *Ibid.*
31.  Testimony of State Auditor James R. Berry before the Poland Committee, quoted in Harrell, *op. cit.*, p. 56.
32.  Blocher, *op. cit.*, p. 80.
33.  *State of Arkansas* v. *Little Rock, Mississippi River and Texas Railway Company,* 31 Ark., 701 (1877).
34.  Clayton, *Aftermath of the Civil War in Arkansas, op. cit.*, pp. 247–49.
35.  *State of Arkansas* v. *Little Rock, Mississippi River and Texas Railway Company, op. cit.*, 722.
36.  *Gazette,* June 16, 1877, p. 2, cc. 1–2.
37.  *Gazette,* June 28, 1877, p. 2, cc. 1–2, quoting the *New York Times.* By September, 1878, the Supreme Court had also declared the levee bonds null and void. In these two decisions the Supreme Court had eliminated in principal and interest $9,990,787.74 from the state debt. Evans, *op. cit.*, p. 369.
38.  Letter from John D. Adams to David Walker, Fayetteville, Ark.; New York, N. Y., August 6, 1877. University of Arkansas, Walker Letters, fol. 4.
39.  In February, 1877, Governor Miller presented a plan of debt settlement to the legislature the provisions of which almost met the terms on which the bondholders were willing to settle the debt:

|  | Committee of Arkansas Bond-holders Offer | Governor Miller's Offer |
|---|---|---|
| Six percent bonds | 50¢ | 50¢ |
| Railroad-aid bonds | 35¢ | 25¢ |
| Levee bonds | 15¢ | 10¢ |

Governor William R. Miller, *Special Message to the Senate and House of Representatives, Respecting the Bonded and the Floating Indebtedness of the State,* February 13, 1877 (Little Rock: *Gazette* Book and Job Printing House, 1877), p. 8. The Adams-Redfield plan called for a refunding of the debt in which for each new $1,000 bond issued $3,800.58 of the old debt would be surrendered. Consult the following sources on Adams' proposals: *Gazette,* August 25, 1877, p. 2, cc. 2 – 3; August 26, 1877, p. 1, cc. 3 – 4; September 16, 1877, p. 2, cc. 2 – 3; September 22, 1877, p. 2, c. 2. Information on both the Adams-Redfield plan and the proposal of the state board of finance can be found in the following source: letter from the State Board of Finance to the People of Arkansas, Little Rock, October 8, 1877. University of Arkansas, Sue Walker Papers.
40.  Letter from James Mitchell to David Walker, Fayetteville, Ark.; Little Rock, December 28, 1877. Arkansas History Commission, A. Howard Stebbins, Jr. Collection, lot D.
41.  Evans, *op. cit.*, pp. 369 – 70.
42.  *Ibid.*, p. 370.
43.  *Ibid.*, pp. 370 – 71.
44.  Hall, *op. cit.*, p. 193.
45.  Evans, *op. cit.*, p. 374.


## CHAPTER 16: CONCLUSION

1.  Watkins to Walker, August 22, 1868, *op. cit.*
2.  Williams, "To the People . . . ," *op. cit.*
3.  Theodore B. Mills, *Financial Resources of the State of Arkansas, with the State and Municipal Debt of Each State in the Union* (Little Rock, Ark.; Little Rock Printing and Publishing Co., 1873), p. 18.
4.  Scott, *op. cit.*, p. 214.
5.  *Ibid.*

# INDEX

Adams, John D., 208; concerned about state credit, 237
Apportionment in state legislature, 1838, 64; 1860, 64; 1867, 64-65; 1868, 66; Constitution of 1868, 68
Askew, B. F., constitutional convention bill, 157-58

Banks, ante-bellum legacy, 185-86; State Bank, 174; early experience, 175-78; Fayetteville branch investigated, 177-78; liquidation, 182; Real Estate Bank, 174; early experiences, 178-82; 1843-1861, 183-84; liquidation resisted, 1843, 182-83
Blaine, James G., aid to Roots for extension of time, 202; bondholder, 230
Baxter, Elisha, 82; actions thwart removal, 124-25; Brooks' *coup d' etat,* April 15, 1874, 149; *Brooks* v. *Baxter,* 127; calls legislature, 153; declares martial law, 152; declines nomination, 163; Grant recognizes as governor, 156-57; growing Democratic influence, 115-16; heads "minstrel" ticket, 1872, 96; importance of early months as governor, 109-10; legislature recognizes as governor, 156; northwest opposes him, 1874, 161; personal background, 108; popularity grows, 127-28; public printing and popularity, 127; recommends constitutional convention, 156; refuses to issue railroad-aid bonds, 147; Republicans break with, 148; Republicans lose,

Democrats gain influence, 147; retires to St. John's College, 152; support from Washington, 129-130
Bowen, Thomas M., 110
Brooks–Baxter War, 116; 149-150; state press position, 155
Brooks, Joseph, 144; appeals to Grant, 152-53; "brindletail" leader, 90; *Brooks* v. *Baxter,* 127; calls legislature, 156; conservative support continues, 130; *coup d'etat,* 149; Garland's view of Brooks, 93-95; northwest continues support, 128; petition, 117, 124; strategy of candidacy, 98
*Brooks* v. *Baxter,* 149

Caldwell, Henry C., 49
Caldwell, Josiah P., 200, 208
Carmichael, Maude, geographical division of state, 13n; 190
Clark, Sol F., 143
Clayton, Powell, 144; message of surrender, 169; railroad president, 236; refunds Holford debt, 231; refuses issuance of bonds, 209; supports Baxter, 126; use of powers, 79-82; use of state aid to railroads, 232-33
Clendenin, J. J., concern over removal, 61-63
Compton, F. W., 61; view on *de facto* government, 76, 126, 152
Constitution of 1868, apportionment, 68-69; apportionment, registration and population, 69-71; as party instrument,

68-69; civil equality for Negroes, 66; constitutional convention, 1868, 66-71; features, 66; first legislature, 1868, 83; powers of governor, 79-83
Constitution of 1874, constitutional convention, 160; features, 160-61
Continuing influences in Arkansas history, 243

Danley, C. C., 33-34
*De jure* v. *de facto* government, David Walker's view, 60
Denkla, W. P., 198, 200, 201
Dorsey, Stephen W., candidate for U. S. Senator, 110; Democrats shift support to him, 110; supports Baxter, 126

Eakin, John R., concern over Supreme Court decisions, 61; despair, 77; modifies position, 87-88; opposes registration, 63; view of candidates, 1874, 162
Elections, 1860, 22, 25; 1867, 63-66; 1868, 71-75; 1868, 86-87; 1870, 88-89; 1872, 95-105, 117; 1874, 164
English, E. H., 115, 126, 143; writes Walker in jubilation, 169
*Ex parte* Garland, 138-39

Fishback Amendment, 237-38
Fishback, William M., 28; associates unjust debt with *de facto* government resentment, 237; elected governor, 1892, 239; sponsors amendment, 237-38
Fisher, Warren, Jr., 200, 208
Flanagin, Harris, influence in southwestern Arkansas, 91; objects to Woodruff's editorials, 130-31; potential Reconstruction leader, 136; significance in Reconstruction, 244; suggested as candidate for governor, 161
Franchise Amendment, 110, 148; enthusiasm for constitutional convention, 128-29; passes March 3, 1873, 113; political significance, 113-14; threat to Republican system, 114; vacancies filled by Democrats, 128-29

Garland, Augustus H., 152; amnesty, 47-51; as Reconstruction leader, 145-46; asks Walker to join opposition to Republicans, 1868, 144; associated with *Mississippi* v. *Johnson,* 140; biographical sketch, 4-5; candidate for U. S. Senator, 110; chief objective the legislature, 92; *Ex parte Garland,* 138-39; grateful to

Stephens, 169; family background and career, 136-38; Garland-Baxter collaboration, 152; gratitude for his leadership, 158; lawyer for Pennywit, 199; nominated candidate for governor; 163; on Brooks-Baxter situation, 153-54; on *de jure* v. *de facto* government, 60; on *de facto* government, 82-83; on political situation, 1872, 92-94; opposes Democratic Conservative party's plans, 1872, 94-95; opposes Fishback Amendment, 237; optimistic over 1872 election, 97; plan to moderate Grant's position as President, 144-45; potential Reconstruction leader, 136; quietly inaugurated as governor, 164; qualities as leader, 142-43; reads Grant's proclamation recognizing Baxter, 157; significance in Reconstruction, 244; slave contract argument in *Osborn* v. *Nicholson,* 140-42; strategy in Brooks-Baxter War, 156-57; suggested as candidate for governor, 1872, 145-46
Goodrich, Carter, 191, 233

Hadley, O. A., 92, 97
Haney, J. H., chief engineer of Little Rock and Fort Smith Railroad, 191; railroad efforts revived, 194; seeks capital in East, 197-98
Hanly, Thomas B., motion to secede, 28
*Hawkins* v. *Filkins,* 59-60; authority rejected in Reconstruction, 63
Hindman, Thomas C., 143
Hinds, James, 144
Hodges, Asa, 144
Holford bonds, 180-81; 184-85; 192, 234; payment prohibited by Fishback Amendment, 237-38; refunded by Republicans, 231
Hunter, Andrew, Hunter movement, 95, 99-100; supported by Garland, 93

Jackson, Andrew, 20
Johnson, Richard H., 20; "Address . . .", 187
Johnson, Robert W., 28, 30, 154, 155; amnesty, 45-47; view of secession, 23
Julian, George W., 202

Land used to promote economic development, 188-89
Leadership, Flanagin, Walker, Garland as potential leaders, 136-38; Garland's advantages, 143; Garland and Reconstruction, 1867-1874, 143-46; Garland as Reconstruction leader, 145-46;